Subjects, Themes and Images

of the Bible

A DREAMSTAIRWAY BOOK

Subjects, Themes and Images

of the

Bible

———

Edited by Dominic Breeze

British Library Cataloguing in Publication Data
A catalogue record for this book is available from the British Library

ISBN 978-1-907091-18-6

This edition published in the UK by Dreamstairway
copyright © 2010 Dreamstairway

www.dreamstairway.co.uk

Printed and bound in the UK by the MPG Books Group,
Bodmin and King's Lynn

Introduction

Subjects, Themes and Images of the Bible covers both the Old and New Testaments in more than one translation, and is intended chiefly for the interested lay-person, and also perhaps for the writer and speech-maker looking for a useful quotation. It is neither a commentary nor a criticism of the Bible itself, which is certainly the most important set of ancient books ever assembled.

To be fully understood, the Bible should be treated as one book with many styles and read as a whole like any other book, progressing smoothly from the Creation to the Apocalypse, and we would not wish to compromise its wholeness by analysing, let alone fragmenting its spiritual message. But reading the entire Bible in this way may seem a formidable (not to say boring) task, and it is our hope that this totally new approach, by way of subjects and themes, may offer the reader an easy "way in" via some special interest or intriguing reference.

Many of the references will be found to refer to imagery rather than hard fact. Over-literal interpretation in the past has frequently caused misunderstandings when devotion shades into credulity. No-one would claim, for instance, to be descended from the "Good Samaritan" whom everybody knows to be a fictitious character in one of the parables related by Jesus; but in the books of the Old Testament ancient parables have become entangled with historical record, and occasionally folk tales with a moral have become incorporated and thereby gained a measure of divine authority. The gruesome story of a gang of little boys mauled by bears for teasing Elisha (in the Second Book of Kings) could have come straight out of some 800BC precursor of Grimm's Household Tales.

At the risk of over-stating the obvious, it may be pointed out that the Bible is well packed with ancient history interspersed with parables and moral stories, and rich in symbols, allegories, analogies, metaphors and similes. This is inevitable, for it represents mankind's relationship with the divine, and spirituality, being non-material, cannot be expressed in material terms. For example, no-one would suppose the Bible to be a farming textbook, and yet our "Farming" section is substantial. Even prophets such as Isaiah, Jeremiah and Ezekiel were close enough to the land for farming metaphors to come readily to their lips. Such references are all included here, and given equal weight to practical observations. As such they form a valid and valuable picture of the rural and industrial scene, and thence the everyday concerns of those ancient people.

The case is similar, for instance, with the category "Buildings", in which Ezekiel's purely visionary but extraordinarily detailed description of the temple of the New Jerusalem is given equal status to the historically real temple of Solomon. But this is how the Bible as a whole works: because its individual descriptions originate some from outward and others from inward perception, the general structure can be seen as a fine balance of inner and outer. Inspired writing and all religious inspiration use the outward, material imagery to portray that which is inward and non-material. Kings of the earth may always have ruled the land and the physical body, but the kingdom of heaven is within.

This index deliberately makes no attempt to interpret, or explain, or excuse, or gloss over the more hair-raising incidents that are normally excused or glossed over. It is completely non-partisan in that it merely indexes exactly what was written by those ancient sages, and equal weight is thereby given to all the participants in this great historical saga.

D.B.

Categories: Special Interests

Categories (continued)

Abbreviations: Old Testament

Am	Amos
CF	First Book of Chronicles
CS	Second Book of Chronicles
D	Daniel
De	Deuteronomy
E	Ezekiel
Ec	Ecclesiastes
Est	Esther
Ex	Exodus
Ez	Ezra
Gen	Genesis
H	Habakkuk
Hg	Haggai
Ho	Hosea
Is	Isaiah
Je	Jeremiah
Job	Job
Joe	Joel
Jon	Jonah
Jos	Joshua
Ju	Judges
KF	First Book of Kings
KS	Second Book of Kings
La	Lamentations
Le	Leviticus
Ma	Malachi
Mi	Micah
Na	Nahum
Ne	Nehemiah
Nu	Numbers
Ob	Obadiah
Pro	Proverbs
Ps	Psalms
Ru	Ruth
SF	First Book of Samuel
So	Song of Solomon
SS	Second Book of Samuel
Z	Zechariah
Zp	Zephaniah

Abbreviations: New Testament

A	Acts of the Apostles
J	Gospel According to John
L	Gospel According to Luke
LH	Letter to the Hebrews
LJ	Letter of James
LJF	First Letter of John
LJS	Second Letter of John
LJT	Third Letter of John
LJu	Letter of Jude
LPF	First Letter of Peter
LPS	Second Letter of Peter
Mk	Gospel According to Mark
Mw	Gospel According to Matthew
PCF	First Letter of Paul to the Corinthians
PCo	Letter of Paul to the Colossians
PCS	Second Letter of Paul to the Corinthians
PE	Letter of Paul to the Ephesians
PG	Letter of Paul to the Galatians
Ph	Letter of Paul to Philemon
PPs	Letter of Paul to the Philippians
PR	Letter of Paul to the Romans
PTF	First Letter of Paul to Timothy
PTS	Second Letter of Paul to Timothy
Rev	Revelation of John
ThF	First Letter of Paul to the Thessalonians
ThS	Second Letter of Paul to the Thessalonians
Tt	Letter of Paul to Titus

1 *Accessories and grooming*

OLD TESTAMENT

aloes Pro7; So4
 powder of Ps45
amulet, phylactery Ex13; De6, 11
anklet Is3
antimony, make your eyes big with Je4
armlet Nu31; SS1;Is3
 gold Nu31
balm Je8, 51; E27
balsam E27
bandage Is1; E30. 34
bangle Is3
beads, gold E28
bell, golden, sown to clothes Ex28ff
belt SF18
 of honour SS21
bracelet Gen24; Nu37; SS1; Is3; E16, 23
 gold Gen24; Nu37
braided plaits So1
buckle SF25
buckler KF10; CS29, 23; Ps35; So4; Je46; E23, 26, 38ff
 gold CS9; Ec9
canopy, wedding Ps19
cassia Pro7; E27
cauls, ornamental Is3
chain, ornamental Ex28ff; KF6; Pro1; Is3, 40; D5; E16
 gold Ex28ff; D5
 of honour Pro1
 silver Is40
charm, hung about your neck Pro3
 ornamental Is3
 phylactery Ex13; De6, 11
cinnamon Pro7
coronet Is3
cosmetics for virgins Est2
crescent, ornamental Ju8; Is3

11

1 ACCESSORIES AND GROOMING

crisping pin, curling iron   Is3
decked in finery   E23
discs, ornamental   I
dressed her hair, Jezebel   KS9
dressing, wound   E30
earrings   Gen35; Ex32; Nu31; Ju8; Pro25; Is3; E16; Ho2
  gold   Ex32; Nu31; Ju8; Job24; Pro25
  Ishmaelite   Ju8
finger-ring   Nu31; Est3ff, 7; Pro7, 11; So5; Is3; Je22
fragrant oil   KS20
frankincense   Is60
garland   Pro1, 4; Is28, 61
  on their heads   E23
glass, ornaments of   Is3
golden ornaments   Ju8
gum resin   Ex30ff
hair, elegantly coiled   Is3
  grew like eagle's feathers   D4
  long as goat's hair   D4
henna   So4, 7
jewels, collar of   Ps73
  decked herself with   Ho2
  nose   Is3
  wear them proudly as   Is49
jingles, adorn yourself with   Je31
liniment   Pro3
locket   Is3
lye, cleansing   Job9
medicine   Pro3, 17
  the leaf of the trees shall be for   E47
mirror   Job37
myrrh   Ps45; Pro7
  oil of   Est2
nails grew long like eagle's talons   E4
necklace   Pro25; Is3; Ho2
  jewelled chain   So1
  of jewels   So4
nose-ring   Gen24; Is3; E16
oil, anointing   Ps23, 45, 89, 92, 104, 133, 141; E16, 23
  drenched your tresses in   Is57

1 ACCESSORIES AND GROOMING

oil, fragrant   Is39
  of gladness   Is61
  skin care   Est2
ointment   Pro27; Ec9ff; So1, 4; E24
  precious   KS20
ornaments, can a maid forget her   Je2
  deck yourself out with golden   Je4
  gold   Nu31
  gold and silver   E16
  leg   Is3
  stripped of   Ex33
painting the eyes   KS9; E23
  Jezebel   KS9
pendant   Is3
  ear   E16
  gold   Nu31
  of Midianite kings   Ju8
perfume   KF10; Est2; Pro27; So1, 4ff; Is3, 28; Ho2
  blended with oil   Is57
phylactery   Ex13; De6, 11
  on the forehead   De6, 11
piping, ornamental   E28
plaited tresses   So1
pouch   SF17
privy, toilet   De23; KS10
purple, nurtured in   La4
purse   Hg1
ring   Pro7; Is3
  ear   Gen35; Ex32; Nu31; Ju8; Pro25; Is3; E16; Ho2
  finger   Nu31; Est3ff, 7; Pro7, 11; So5; Is3; Je22
  gold   Ex32; Nu31; Ju8; Pro11, 25; So5
  nose   Is37; E16
  signet   Est3ff, 7; Is3; Je22
roller bandage   E30
rosette, gold   Ex28ff; Le8
scarlet, brought up in   La4
shell, aromatic   Ex39ff
shepherd's bag   SF17
signet ring   Est3ff, 7; Is3; Je22
soap   Job9; Je2; Ma3
  do not stint the   Je2

13

1 ACCESSORIES AND GROOMING

Soda, washing   Je2
spangles made for you at birth   E28
spices, fragrant, cosmetic   Je6
tablet, ornamental   Is3
tabret, ornamental   Je31; E28
target between shoulders   SF17
tassel at each corner of cloak   De22
  made like flowers   Nu15
toilet   De23; KS10
  trowel   De23
vanity, all is   Ec1
vermilion, painted with   Je22
wardrobe   Je38
wax   Ps22, 68, 97; Mi1
wormwood   Pro5

NEW TESTAMENT

adornment, outer   LPF3
aloes, myrrh and   J19
anoint with oil   Mk6; L10; LH1; LJ5
anointed his feet with ointment   L7
  with the oil of gladness   LH1
apron   A19
aromatic oils   Mk16
bandage   L10
beauty, inner   LPF3
  should reside not in outward adornment   LPF3
bedizened, the woman   Rev17
belt   Mw3; Mk1, 6; L12, 17; J21; A12, 21; PE6
  fasten your   L17
  leather   Mw3; Mk1
  money   Mk6
braiding hair   PTF2; LPF3
covering, head   PCF11
decked out in gold and pearls   PTF2
eyes, ointment for   Rev3
fragrant oil   Mw26; Mk16
frankincense, cargoes of   Rev18

1 ACCESSORIES AND GROOMING

garland of glory   LPF5
  of righteousness   PTS4
garlands to Jupiter   A14
girdle, golden   Rev1, 15
  leather   Mw3; Mk1
  Paul's   A21
  skin   Mk1
glass darkly, we see through a   PCF13
  looking   PCS3; LJ1
hair, braiding   PTF2; LPF3
  if a man have long   PCF11
  styles, elaborate   PTF2
  woman's glory   PCF11
handkerchief   L19; A14
incense, great quantity of   Rev8
  perfumes and frankincense   Rev18
jewellery, jewelry   LPF3
latchet, shoe   J1
leather belt   Mw3; Mk1
looking glass   PCF13; PCS3; LJ1
mirror   PCF13; PCS3; LJ1
money-belt   Mk6
myrrh and aloes   J19
  anointed his feet with   L7
napkin   L19; J11, 20
nard, oil of   Mk14
oil, anoint with   LJ5
  anointed sick people with   Mk6
  aromatic   Mk16
  bathed his wounds with   L10
  of exultation   LH1
  fragrant   Mw26
  of myrrh   L7
  of nard   Mk14; J12
ointment, alabaster box of   L7
  for your eyes   Rev3
  of spikenard   Mk14; J12
  very precious   Mw26
  who anointed the Lord with   J11
ointments, odours and   Rev18
  prepared   L23

1 ACCESSORIES AND GROOMING

pack for the road   Mw10
  purse or   L10, 22
  take neither stick nor   L9
  take no   Mk6
patch of unshrunk cloth   Mk2
perfume bottle   Mk14
  cargoes of   Rev18
  might have been sold   Mk14
  oil of nard   J12
  small bottle of   Mk14
  very costly   Mk14
purse   Mw10; L10, 12, 22; J13
ring, gold   LJ2
  on his finger, put a   L15
sandals, put on your   A12
  they might wear   Mk6
scarf   A19
scrip, purse nor   Mw10; L10, 22
  take no   Mk6
shoes   Mk1; L10, 15; J1; A7, 13; PE6
  not fit to unfasten   Mk1
  on his feet, put   L15
spices, funeral   L24
tassels on their robes   Mw23
veil   PCF11; PCS3f
vials full of odours   Rev5
woman's glory, flowing locks are a   PCF11
wrapping, linen   L24

2 *Affliction and Suffering*

abominable thing that causes desolation   D11, 12
affliction, bound in   Ps107
  bread of   De16
  choice of by David   CF21
  in the furnace of   Is48
  the discipline of   Job36
  water of   CS18; Is30
ague, curse of the burning   Le26; De28
alas, my mother, that you ever gave me birth!   Je15
anguish and affliction, day of   Zp1
  my bowels writhe in   La1
ashes of repentance   Ex9; SS13; Est4; Job42; Je6, 25; E27
  sat down among the   Job2
baldness, examination of   Le13
beard plucked from my chin   Is50
beggary, reduced to   Zp2
blast, pestilence of   Ps195
blasting (blight)   KF8; CS6
blight, black or red   KF8; Am4; Hg2
  curse of   De28
blind and lame   Je31
  none shall come in   SS5
  the prophet Ahijah   KF14
blindness, curse of   De28
  strike this host with   KS6
blood, Nile turned to   Ex4, 7
  waters turned to   Ps105
blows, cower beneath   Ps88
  exhausted by thy   Ps39
boil, poulticed   KS20; Is38
boils, covered with   Job2
  malignant Egyptian curse of   De28
  plague of   Ex9
botch, curse of   De28

dung, reduced to eating their own   KS18; Is36
dust, wouldst thou turn me into   Job10
dysentery, curse of   De28
earth swallowed them   Nu16
earthquake   Ps18, 46, 60, 68, 77, 104; Is29
end is coming   E7
eruptions, curse of   De28
evils, choose one of three   SS24
eyes failing   Ps88
  grow dim   Ps69
  person with blemished   Le21
famine   Gen12, 26; Ps33, 105; Is51; Je5, 16, 18, 21, 24, 27, 29, 32, 34, 38, 42, 44, 52; La2;
      E5ff, 12, 14; Am8
  at Gilgal   Ks4
  decreed seven years   KS8
  I will increase   E5
  in David's reign   SS21, 24
  in Judah   Ru1
  in Samaria   KF18
  make an end of them with   Je14
  on all your settlements   Am4
  ruin and havoc   Is51
  severe during siege   Ks25
  their sons and daughters shall die by   Je11
  three years   CF21
  under siege   KS7
fasting,   Ps35, 69, 109
  for the sick   Ps35
  knees weak with   Ps109
feet crippled by disease   KF15
fever   Is10; Je51
  like fire shall burn   Is10
  loins burn with   Ps38
  my mind wandered in   Ps37
  recurrent   Le26; De28
fig-plaster poultice   KS20; Is38
fire and brimstone, pour down   E38
  struck the shepherds   Job1
fit, man falls in a   Is10
flight, whole country in   Je4

flood Gen2, 6ff; Ps29, 69, 88, 104; Is28, 54
  the great Gen6ff; Ps104
fracture for fracture Le24
fungus infection Le14
gall, judgement turned to Am4
  to drink Je8ff
  wormwood and La3
gangrene of the foot CS16
gloom with no dawn Am5
grief, eyes dim with Job17
  full of drunkenness and E23
  head bowed in Ps35
  mine eye is consumed with Ps31
haemorrhoids SF5ff
  curse of De28
harried by enemies CF21
head, sore on Le13
  strike at Gen3
heel, strike at Gen3
helplessness, curse of De28
homelessness Ps52
horror written on their faces E27
hungry Ps107
ill, Elisha fell KS13
illness of Hezekiah Is38
ill-omened country Je2
infection, fungal Le14
inflammation, curse of De28
  of the skin Le13
issue, one that hath an SS3
itch, curse of the De28
Job's comforters Job2ff
lame debarred from altar Le21
  in both feet SS4
lament, hear my loud Ps88
  lies open before thee, my Ps38
  mark the foreheads of those who E9
lamentation is heard in Ramah Je31
leper SS3; KS5; CS26
lepers at the city gate KS7

2 AFFLICTION AND SUFFERING

leprosy, dull white   Le13
  Gahazi caught   KS5
  the king struck with   KS15
leprous, Miriam became   Nu12
  Moses's hand   Ex4
massacre by invaders   Nu21, 31; De2, 3; Jos6, 8, 10f; Ju9, 11, 18, 20f; SF7, 15, 22; CS14
medicine, in vain shalt thou use   Je46
  thou hast no   Je30
mildew   KF8; CS6
  curse of   De28
miscarriage, country troubled with   KS2
mortified with fasting   Ps35
mould, rotting   Le13
mourning   Gen23, 37f, 50; Le21; SS13, 18; KF13; Ez10; Job30; Ps35, 42; Ec3; Je9, 16, 34;
          La5; E7, 24; D10; Am8; Mi1; Z12
  every head shorn in   Je48
muzzle on my mouth   Ps39
natural order upset   Je5
oblivion, land of   Ps88
oil for soothing wounds   Is1
ointment, wounds mollified with   Is1
pain, day of incurable   Is17
  pierces my very bones   Job30
panic shall fall on them   Z14
paralysed, Jeroboam's hand   KF13
pestilence   Ps91; Je24, 27, 29, 32, 34, 38, 42, 44; E5ff, 12, 14; Am4
  70,000 people died in one day of   SS24; CF21
  and famine   Je14; E5
  beasts killed by   Ex9; Ps78
  curse of   De28
  for three days   SS24; CF21
  in dens and caves they shall die by   E33
  in Egypt   Ex9
  judgement with   E38
  make an end of them with   Je14
  men and cattle shall die of a great   Je21
  of fish   Ps105
  the noisome   Ps91
  threat of   Le26
piss, they shall drink their own   KS18; Is36

21

2 AFFLICTION AND SUFFERING

plague   Ps78, 91
 brake in upon them   Ps106
 curse of   De28
 for the offence of Korah   Nu16
 killed 70,000 in one day   SS24; CF21
 makes orphans   La1
 of a house   Le14
 of caterpillars   KF8; CS6; Je51; Joe1ff
 of Egypt   Ps78; Am4
 of flies   Ex8; Ps105
 of frogs   Ex8; Ps78, 105
 of grasshoppers   Job39
 of grubs   Ps78; Joe2
 of hoppers   Je51; Joe1ff
 of Israelites ceased   Nu25
 of Kibroth-Hattaavah   Nu11
 of locusts   Ex8, 10; De28; KF8; CS6; Job39; Ps78, 105; Joe1ff
 of maggots   Ps105
 of moths   Job14; Ho5
 of worms, canker   Joe1ff
 tests for   Le13
 threat of   Le26
plagues upon you, all my   Ex9
poison in my food   Ps69
polluted, the water is   KS2
prison, set me free from my   Ps142
prolapse of the bowels   CS21
racked with sickness   La1
raw wounds, nothing but   Is1
rending clothes   SF4; SS1, 3, 13; KF21; KS2, 5, 19, 22; Est4; Job1; Is37
rot, her thigh shall   Nu5
rotten to the core   Ps53
ruin, a cup of   E23
 as never before   E21
 famine and havoc   Is51
ruins, Damascus a heap of   Is17
 homesteads lie in   Je25
running sores   Job2
sackcloth and ashes   Gen37; SS3, 21; KF20ff; KS6, 19; CF21; Ne9; Est4; Job16;
   Ps30. 35. 69; Is3, 15, 20, 22, 32, 37, 50;Je4, 6, 49; La2; E7, 27; D9;

sackcloth and ashes   Joe1; Am8; Jon3
  beat your breast and put on   Je49
  every waist girded with   Je48
salt land where no man can live   Je17
scab on the head   Is3
scabs, curse of   De28
scorpions, chastise you with   KF12
scourge   Ps129
scurf in skin disease   Le13ff
seizure, Nabal had a   SF25
shadow of death   Job16; Ps23, 107; Je2
shame, end my days in   Je20
shaved every head   Je16, 48
sick-bed   Ps41
sickness, curse of   De28
  racked with   La1
sign upon hand and forehead   Ex13
skin disease, examination of   Le13
  of Miriam   Nu12
  sufferers from, expelled   Nu5
snuffed out like a wick   Is43
soot to cause festering boils   Ex9
sores of the head   Is1
sorrow, come forth to know only   Je20
  of heart   Le26
  their daily bread   Ps80
stink, the River Nile will   Ex7
stone for a pillow   Gen28
streams turned to blood   Ps78
stricken in age, Joshua   Jos23
sweating, I lay   Ps77
sword makes orphans   La1
tears, the bread of   Ps80
  water my couch with   Ps6
teeth idle with famine   Am4
terror and rapine, abandon them to   E23
terrors, the king of   Job18
thirst, infant's   La4
thirsty   Ps107
throat is sore   Ps69

trouble and sorrow, I found   Ps116
  man is born to   Job5
tumours, curse of   De28
  plagued with   SF5ff
ulcerated bowels   CS21
ulcers, curse of   De28
  struck down by deadly   Je16
unburied bones as dung   Je16
unclean, away!   La4
urine, constrained to drink their own   KS18; Is36
wandering in a pathless wilderness   Job12
waste away, the fat on his limbs shall   Is17
wasting disease in the day of incurable pain   Is17
  sickness   Ps196
weals, nothing but   Is1
weep, a time to   Ec3
weeping and wailing   SS15; Est4
  cheeks flushed with   Job16
  in the public squares   Is15
  is heard in Ramah   Je31
  mingled my drink with   Ps102
  Rachel for her sons   Je31
weeps in the night, she   La1
wept all night   Nu14
  I sat down and   Ne1
whirlwind, reap the   Ho8
wormwood and gall   La3
wound, grievous   Je30
wounds fester   Ps38
wrath, day of   Zp1

NEW TESTAMENT

abomination of desolation   Mw24; Mk13
affliction of hardship cannot separate us   PR8
agitation of spirit, Jesus in deep   J13
agony, men gnawed their tongues in   Rev16
beasts at Ephesus, I fought wild   PCF15
beating their breasts, they went home   L23
bed of pain, throw her on to a   Rev2

beggar, a blind   Mk10
bent double, she was   L13
blind and dumb   Mw12
  for a time, you shall be   A13
  from birth   J9
  man sat at the roadside   L18
  men, at the roadside sat two   Mw20
  men, Jesus followed by two   Mw9
  why was he born   J9
blood, an issue of   L8
bloody flux   A28
bodies burnt outside the camp   LH13
branded, marks of Jesus   PG6
broken-hearted, sent to heal the   L4
burden, every man shall bear his own   PG6
burn men, the sun allowed to   Rev16
calamity is upon them   ThF5
calumny for my sake, when you suffer   Mw5
cankered, gold and silver is   LJ5
convulsions, threw the boy into   Mk9
  throws him into   L9
cripple, better to enter life a   Mk9
  from birth, at the gate of the temple   A3
crippled for eighteen years   L13
  man, lame from birth   A14
cross, a stumbling-block   PCF1
  carrying his own   J19
  come down from the   Mw27
  discarded cosmic powers on the   PCo2
  endured the   LH12
  fastened him to the   Mk15
  in weakness, died on the   PCS13
  must take up the   Mk8
  obedient unto death of the   PPs2
  of Christ, enemies of the   PPs3
  on his back, put the   L23
  on which he killed the enmity   PE2
  openly displayed upon his   PG3
  peace through the shedding of blood on the   PCo1
  pressed him to carry the   Mk15
  take up his   Mw16

grinds his teeth and goes rigid   Mk9

haemorrhages, suffered from   Mw9; Mk5; L8

hardship in service of the gospel   PTS2

  like a good soldier   PTS2

hardships, stand firm under   ThF3

  we must pass through many   A14

hated of all men   Mk13

humiliation, sown in, raised in glory   PCF15

hungry and thirsty and in rags   PCF4

impediment of speech   Mk7

imprisonment in Christ's cause   PPs1

infirmities, I glory in my   PCS12

issue of blood   L8

Jesus wept   L19; J11

lament in remorse, all the people shall   Rev1

leper approached him   Mw8; Mk1

lepers, cleanse   Mw10

  in Israel, many   L4

  ten men that were   L17

leprosy, a man covered with   L5

Lot's wife, remember   L17

lunatic, sore vexed   Mw17

  those which were   Mw4

mad, he hath a devil and is   J10

madman possessed by the legion of devils   Mk5

millstone hung round his neck   Mw18; Mk9; L17

mist and darkness came over him   A13

moth-eaten, your fine clothes are   LJ5

myrrh, wine mingled with   Mk15

numbness of spirit, brought upon them a   PR11

ordeal to fall on the world   Rev3

  who have passed through the great   Rev7

orphans and widows, go to the help of   LJ1

overworked, sleepless, starving   PCS6, 11

pain and grief, those who marry will have   PCF7

  racked with   Mw4

palsy, one sick of the   Mk2

  those which had the   Mw4

paralysed   Mw4, 8f; Mk2; L5

persecution for my sake, when you suffer   Mw5

  for the cause of right   Mw5

speechless, possessed by a spirit which makes him   Mk9
spiked themselves on many thorny griefs   PTF6
struck down, we are not left to die   PCS4
suffer and rise from the dead, the Messiah had to
  cruelly for ten days, you will   Rev2
  for you, my happiness to   PCo1
  Messiah must   A26
suffering, Christ's cup of   PCS1
  endure the pain of undeserved   LPF2
  learned obedience in the school of   LH5
  passed through the test of   LH2
  plunge her lovers into terrible   Rev2
  take your share of   PTS1
  to come, do not fear   Rev2
  train us to endure   PR5
sufferings, a share in Christ's   LPF4
  Son of Man has to undergo great   Mk8f; L9
suicide, the jailer intended   A16
terrified, he did not know what to say, they were so   Mk9
thorn in the flesh, given me a   PCS12
torment, Hades a place of   L16
  like a scorpion's sting   Rev9
trial, stood firmly by me in my time of   L22
troubles are slight and short-lived, our   PCS4
wailing and grinding of teeth, place of   Mw8, 13
weep for yourselves and your children   L23
  no more   L7
  with them that weep   PR12
weeping and gnashing of teeth   Mw8, 24
  and lamenting for the child   L8
wept, Jesus   L19; J11
widow alone in the world   PTF5
  parable of the persistent   L18
widows, I say to   PCF7
  men who eat up the property of   L20
withered arm, man with a   Mk3; L6
wormwood, name of the star is   Rev8
wrath, God has not appointed us to   ThF5

3 *Altars, Monuments and Holy Places*

altar, acacia wood   Ex27ff
  acceptable offerings on my   Is60
  at Beersheba   Gen26
  at Bethel   Gen35
  at El-bethel   Gen35
  bread on the   SF21; KF7; CF9. 23ff, 28; CS4ff, 13, 29; Ne10
  bowl   KF7
  bronze   KF7; KS16; CS1, 4; E9
  build of the proper pattern   Ju6
  built at Bethel   Ju21; De27
  buy the threshing floor to build an   SS24
  by the River Jordan   Jos22
  cedar   KF6
  censers   KF7; E8
  chest beside the   KS12
  cup, golden   CF28
  dishes, gold and silver   CF28
  drenched like the corners of the   Z9
  El-Elohy-Israel   Gen33
  Ezekiel's vision of the temple   E40ff
  facing the land of Canaan   Jos22
  fire from the Lord   KF18
  firepans   Ex27ff; Le10; KF7
  flame went towards heaven   CS7
  flowers, golden   KF7
  forks, golden   Ex27ff; CF28
  frankincense   CF9; Ne13
  gate, Jerusalem   E8
  golden   KF7; CS4
  great, at Geliloth   Jos22
  horns of the   KF1ff; Ps118; E43; Am3
  in the house of the Lord   Z14
  incense   Ex30ff; Le10, 16; KF13, 22; CF6, 9, 28; CS2, 13, 26;
  lamp-stands   KF7
  light falls in vain on my   Mal
  Lord spurned his own   La2

3 ALTARS, MONUMENTS AND HOLY PLACES

altar, Lord's house   E8
  men lie down beside every   Am2
  mount the steps of my   SF2
  named "Witness"   Jos22
  of Abram   Gen12
  of Ahaz   KS16
  of David   SS24
  of El-Elohey-Israel   Gen33
  of Gideon   Ju6
  of God, come to the   Ps43
  of Isaac   Gen26
  of Jacob   Gen33
  of Jehovah-Nissi   Ex17
  of Jehovah-shalom   Ju6
  of Jeroboam   KF12
  of Moses at Sinai   Ex24ff
  of Noah   Gen8
  of Samuel   SF7
  of Saul   SF14
  of Solomon   KF7
  ointment   CF9
  miraculous fire on the   CS7
  on Mount Ebal   Jos8
  pattern for building the   Ju6, 21
  plan and design of the   KS16
  pot   KF7
  procession round the   Ps26
  rebuilding of the   Ez3
  rent in pieces   KF13
  saucer, golden   KF7
  saw the Lord standing by the   Am9
  set up on the threshing floor   SS24
  shovel   KF7
  snuffers, golden   KF7
  Solomon's golden   KF7
  spice   CF9
  spoons, golden   KF7
  sword swung over their blood-spattered   Ho11
  table, golden   KF7
  thorns and thistles shall grow over their   Ho10
  threshing floor   CF21; CS23

altar to the Lord in the heart of Egypt   Is19

   tongs, golden   KF7

   tossing bowl   KF7

   trolley   KF7; KS16, 25

   undressed stone   De27

   unhewn stone   Ex20; Jos8

   utensils   CS4, 13, 24, 35; Ez1, 8

   wafers   CF9, 23

   weeping between the porch and the   Joe2

   ye offer polluted bread on my   Mal

altars, blood-spattered   E6; Ho11

   common as heaps of stones beside a ploughed field   Ho12

   Ephraim in his sin has multiplied   Ho8

   have become his sin   Ho8

   made desolate   E6

   of Bethel   Am3

   pull down their   De7, 12

   rears her brood beside thy   Ps84

   seven, of Balaam   Nu23

   thorns grow over their   Ho10

arcades of the temple in Ezekiel's vision   E41ff

arches of the temple in Ezekiel's vision   E40

Ark of God   SS6; CF13ff; CS1ff

   send it back   SF6

   taken by Philistines   SF4ff

   of the Covenant   Ex25ff; Le16; Nu10; SF4; SS15; KF2ff, 6ff;   CF6, 22, 28; CS5, 35; Je3

   of the Lord   KF2ff, 6ff

   of the Tokens   Nu4ff

   of thy power   Ps132

Baal-berith, temple of   Ju9

Bohan, stone of   Jos18

cairn of Gal-ed   Gen31

   of Jegar-sahadutka   Gen31

   of Mizpah   Gen31

censer, King Uzziah's   CS26

censers in Ezekiel's vision   E8

   in Solomon's house of the Lord   KF7

   in the tent of the Presence   Nu4

   make beaten plates of the   Nu16

3 ALTARS, MONUMENTS AND HOLY PLACES

cherubim of gold, enthroned on   Ex25ff; SF4; SS6; KF6; KS19; CF13
corridors of the temple in Ezekiel's vision   E42
court, inner   E8, 10
door-keepers, temple   Ne7, 10, 13
doors of the temple broken up   KS18
El-berith, temple of   Ju9
gallery in Ezekiel's vision of the temple   E43
Gibeon, great stone in   SS21
hill-shrine in Gibeon   KF3; CF16
  of the Hill of God   SF10
  of the Tabernacle   CF21
  what is this   E20
hill-shrines allowed to remain   KF22
  for Kemosh and Moloch   KF11ff
  I will destroy your   E6
  of Isaac   Am7
  sacrifice at the   KF3
holy of holies   Ex26ff
  offerings   CS35
  place   Ex26ff; CS35; Ec8
house of God   Ne6; Ec5; Di
    officer in charge of the   CF9
    repairs to the   CS34
    security of the   CF
    Solomon's   KF5ff; CF6
  of prayer   Is56
  of the Lord   KS16, 18, 22; CS23; Je20, 36, 38, 41
    burnt down   Je39, 52
    in Babylon   Je27
    purified   CS29
    repairs to the   Ks22
    sacred contents of the   Je51
    Solomon's   KF5ff; CF6
    time for rebuilding the   Hg1ff
    treasury in the   Z11
    vessels and trolleys in the   Je27
Jerusalem, thy holy hill   D9
memorial in the temple of the Lord   Z6
mercy seat, the Lord's   Ex26
monument of Absalom   SS18
  of Eben-ezer   SF7

monument of Hadadezer   SS8
  of victory   SS8; CF18
  Samuel set up a   SF7
most holy place   KF6ff; CS2ff; D9
mount of Jerusalem   Is27
mountain of God   Ex3, 19
    no man may touch the   Ex19
palaces of Zion   Ps48
pillar at Bethel   Gen35
  at Bethlehem   Gen35
  at Rachel's grave   Gen35
  in the king's vale   SS18
  of Jacob   Gen28, 31
  of salt   Gen19
  of the Lord's house   Je27
  of the temple   Je52
pillars, sacred   KF14
    break their   De7, 12
    twelve   Ex24
ramparts of Zion   Ps48
rocks called Bozez and Seneh   SF14
sacred pillars   KF14
  vessels   KF15
sanctuary, Gentiles entering her   La1
  her priests profaned the   Zp3
  horns of the altar   KF2
  in the midst of them, set my   E37
  Judah was his   Ps114
  land set aside for   E45, 48
  measurements of the   E45
  my holy   Is60
  of Moab   Is16
  of Shechem   Gen12
  of the tabernacle   Ex25ff
  of the Lord   Je24; E8
  princes profaned my   Is43
  shall be profaned, their   E7
  temple   KF6
    in Ezekiel's vision   E41ff
    thou hast defiled my   E5

sanctuary, vessels of the   D5
  within the veil of the tabernacle   Le16
sanctuaries of the Lord's house   Je51
sarcophagus of Og   De3
sea, molten   Je27
  of bronze   CF18; Je52
    broken up   KS25
  of cast metal   CS4
shrine at Shiloh   Je7
  inner   KF6; CS4
  Micah had a   Ju17ff
  of expiation   CF28
  Solomon's inner   CS4
  thy holy   Ps28, 74
stone at Shechem, set up a great   Jos24
  blocks of, copy of the law of Moses   Jos8
  great, at Beth-shemesh   SF6
  Joshua set up a great   Jos24
  of Bohan   Jos15, 18
  of Ezel   SF20
  of Help   SF7
  of Zoheleth   KF1
  roll a great   SF14
  Samuel set up a   SF7
  set up a great   De26
stones at Gilgal, carved   Ju3
  great pile of, at Achor   Jos7
    at Ai   Jos8
  over Absalom's body, a huge pile of   SS18
  piled against the cave at Makkedah   Jos10
  twelve, set up   Jos4
tabernacle at Gibeon   CF16
  at the hill-shrine   CF21
  bring me to thy   Ps43
  brought to Solomon   KF8
  design for the   Ex26ff
  dwelling place of the   CF6
  from one to another   CF17
  guards   CF9
  Jerusalem   Is33
  Levites placed in charge of the   Nu14

3 ALTARS, MONUMENTS AND HOLY PLACES

tabernacle Moses made in the wilderness   CF21
  of David   Is16
  of Ham   Ps78
  of the Covenant   Ex26ff
  of the Lord   Jos22; CF16; CS1
  place of refuge   Is4
  porter at the door of the   CF9
  spoiled   Je10
  violently taken away his   La2
  who shall abide in thy   Ps15
  Zadoc took a horn of oil out of the   KF1
table of the Lord   Ma1
tables, altar   CF28
temple, all cry "Glory" in his   Ps29
  avenging of his   Je51
  bitter enemies of thy   Ps69
  bow down towards thy holy   Ps138
  bow low in thy holy   Ps5
  bring sacrifices into thy   Ps66
  courts of the Lord's   Ps84
  defiled thy holy   Ps79
  fittings   Je52
  foundation may be laid   Is44
  gallery, in Ezekiel's vision   E43
  glory added to glory in my   Is60
  great hall of the   Ju9
  he heard me from his   Ps18
  holiness is the beauty of thy   Ps93
  implements removed   Je52
  in Ezekiel's vision   E8, 40ff
  Lord is in his holy   Ps11
  of Ashtoreth   SF31
  of Baal-berith   Ju9
  of the Lord   CS25ff; Z6
  prostitute   De2
  servitors   CF9; Ne3, 7, 10ff
  Samuel slept in the   SF3
  seek him in his   Ps27
  Solomon's   KF6ff
  terrace, those who dance on the   Zp1

temple, that uproar in the   Is66
  the Lord's   Is6
  thy holy   Ps65
  time to rebuild the   Hg1ff
  trolleys   KF7; CS4; Je27, 52
  vault of the   Ju9
  vengeance of his   Je50
  vessels   Ne13
temples, carried off my treasures into your   Joe3
  drank wine in their   Ju9
tent, David's   Is16
  for the Ark of God   CF9
  of the Covenant   Ex26ff
  of the Lord   KF1ff, 6ff
  of the Presence   Ex26, 29ff, 33ff; Le1ff; Nu1ff, 6ff, 18; De31; Jos18; SF2; KF8;
          CF6, 9, 23; CS1ff
  of the Tokens   Nu18; CS24
  pitched for the Ark of God   SS6
threshing floor redesigned as an altar   CS3
tomb of Abner at Hebron   SS4
  of Abraham, cave of the   Gen23
  of Rachel   SF10
  of Sarah, cave of the   Gen25
tossing-bowls, gold   CF28
  silver   Ne7
towers of Zion   Ps48
treasury, Lord's house   Ma3
vessels of the house of God   D1
  of the sanctuary   Ne10
  of the temple   D5
  sacred   KF15

NEW TESTAMENT

altar and sanctuary, between   L11
  cry, I heard the   Rev16
  golden   LH9; Rev8f
  horns of the   Rev9
  in Athens   A17
  leave thy gift before the   Mw5
  life poured out on the   PTS4

3 ALTARS, MONUMENTS AND HOLY PLACES

altar, measure the   Rev11
  of incense   L1
  our, from which priests have no right to eat   LH13
  shares in the   PCF10
  swears by the   Mw23
  to an unknown god   A17
  tribe which had nothing to do with the   LH7
  underneath the   Rev6
altars, they have torn down thine   PR11
ark of his covenant in heaven   Rev11
censer, golden altar   LH9; Rev8
church at Ephesus   Rev2
  at Laodicea   Rev3
  at Pergamum   Rev2
  at Philadelphia   Rev3
  at Sardis   Rev3
  at Smyrna   Rev2
  at Thyatira   Rev2
  his body which is the   PCol
  in Jerusalem, persecution for the   A8
  of God, tried to destroy the   PG1
  on this rock will I build my   Mw16
  supreme head to the   PE1
  was left in peace to build up its strength   A9
churches, seven   Rev1
court of Areopagus   A17
  of Mars Hill   A17
Diana, temple of   A19
God's temple, where the spirit of God dwells   PCF3
heavenly temple, angel came out of the   Rev14
holy city, entered the   Mw27
   new Jerusalm   Rev21
   the devil took him to the   Mw4
   the Gentiles will trample underfoot   Rev11
  place, called the   LH9
   Paul has profaned this   A21
house of God   Mw12; PTF3
  of prayer for all the nations   Mk11
incense altar   L1; LH9; Rev8
living God, city of the   LH12

3 ALTARS, MONUMENTS AND HOLY PLACES

mercy seat LH9

monuments of the saints Mw23

most holy place, called the LH9

parapet of the temple, set him on a L4

pinnacle of the temple Mw4

sacred mountain, with him on the LPS1

sanctuary, a material LH9

  between altar and L11

  curtain of the LH9f

  gold in the Mw23

  minister of the LH8

  of the heavenly tent Rev15

  this fellow is attacking our A21

  veil of the LH9

seats in the synagogue Mk12

shrine of Moloch A7

shrines, god does not live in A17

  of Diana, silver A19

Sion Mw21; PR9, 11; LH12; LPF2; Rev14

Solomon's portico J10

synagogue at Thessalonica A17

  banned from the J9

  began to teach in the Mk6

  chief ruler of the A18

  for fear of being banned from the J12

  he taught in their L4

  he was teaching in the A18

  healing in the Mw12; Mk2f

  held office in the A18

  I have always taught in the J18

  Jesus taught in the Mw13

  of the Libertines A6

  officials of the A13

  prayers standing up in the Mw6

  president of the Mw9; Mk5; L8

  punished them in every A26

  ruler of the Mk5

  Sabbath they went to the A13

  seats of honour in the L11

  spoken in the J6

  teach in the Mk1

synagogue, they will ban you from the   J16
   they will flog you in the   Mw10
synagogues, chief seats in the   Mw23; Mk12; L20
   Saul proclaiming Jesus in the   A9
   teaching in the   Mw4
tabernacle a worldly sanctuary   LH9
   called the holiest   LH9
   of David   A15
   of the testimony   Rev15
   of witness   A7
   put off   LPS1
   true, which the Lord pitched   LH8
tabernacles, let us make here three   Mw17
temple, accused of profaning the   A24
   Anna never left the   L2
   appeared again in the   J8
   at Jerusalem   Mk11
   between the altar and the   L11
   brought Greeks into the   A21
   buildings   Mw24
   captain of the   L22; A4f
   controller of the   A4f
   court   Mk11
   curtain of the   Mw27; Mk15; L23
   daily attendance at the   A2
   dealers in the   Mw21; Mk11; L19; J2
   forsaken by God   Mw23; L13
   forty six years to build the   J2
   found him sitting in the   L2
   fund   Mw27
   gate called Beautiful   A3
   go and take your place in the   A5
   grows into a holy   PE2
   he came again into the   J8
   he came by the Spirit into the   L2
   he taught in the   Mk12
   I have always taught in the   Mw26
   I sat teaching in the   Mw26
   I was praying in the   A22
   I will pull down the   Mk14

3 ALTARS, MONUMENTS AND HOLY PLACES

temple in heaven was laid open, God's   Rev11
  Jesus drove out all who were trading in the   Mw21
  made a robbers' cave of the   Mk11
  of Diana   A19
  of God   PCS6
    even takes his seat in the   ThS2
    is holy   PCF3
    measures the   Rev11
  of Jupiter   A14
  of our living God   PCS6
  officers   L22
  parapet of the   Mw4; L4
  people flocked to listen to him in the   L21
  pinnacle of the   L4
  police   L22; J7
  praising and blessing God in the   L24
  Romans will sweep away our   J11
  seized me in the   A26
  seized Paul and dragged him out of the   A21
  service, those who perform the   PCF9
  something greater than the   Mw12
  stones of the   Mk13
  swear by the   Mw23
  tax, collectors of   Mw17
  teaching in the   Mw26; Mk12; L20f
  traders in the   Mw21; Mk11; L19; J2
  treasury   Mk12; L21
  to pray, two men went to the   L18
  veil of the   Mk15; L23
  was filled with smoke from the glory of God   Rev15
  worship, theirs the   PR9
  you know that you are in God's   PCF3
temples, God dwelleth not in   A17
tent of testimony   A7; Rev15
  pitched by the Lord   LH8
  priests of the sacred   LH13
  sacred   LH13
  sanctuary   LH9
unknown God, altar to the   A17
Zion   Mw21; PR9, 11; LH12; LPF2; Rev14
  I lay in, a corner-stone   LPF2

4 *Animals, Birds and Insects*

OLD TESTAMENT

adder   Ps91; Pro23
animals given as food   Gen9
  to be eaten   De14
ant   Pro6, 30
antelope   Is51
  long-horned   De14
ape   KF10; CS9
asp   De32; Job20; ps58, 91; Is11
ass   Ju10, 12; SF9, 16, 25, 27; SS16ff; KF2, 13; KS4, 7; CF5, 12; CS28; Ez2; Ne7; Job1, 24, 42; Pro26; Is1, 21, 30; E23; Z9, 14
  Balaam's   Nu22
  gelded   Gen49
  levied   Nu31
  made to speak   Nu22
  of Achsah   Jos15
  tethered to the vine   Gen49
  wild   Job6, 11, 24, 39, 41; Ps58, 104; Is32; Je2, 14; D5; Ho8
    snuffing the wind   Je14
asses, laden   Ju19
  of Jericho slaughtered   Jos9
  straw and provender for   Ju19
baboon   SS3
badger   E16
  skin   Ex25ff; Nu4
bat   Le11; De14; Is2
bear   SF17; SS17; KS2; Pro17, 28; Is11, 59; La3; D7; Ho13; Am5
beasts of burden   Is46
bees   Ps118
  from Assyria   Is7
  swarming   Ju14
behemoth   Job40
beetle   Le11
bird   Ps8, 11
  on those hills, I know every   Ps50

bird, speckled   Je12
birds, caught in a snare   Ec9
  dietary laws of Moses concerning   Le11
  made to settle all over the camp   Ps78
  migration of   Je8
  of prey   Gen15; Is18; Je12, 15
  sacrifice of small   Le14
bird's nest, take only the young   De22
bison   Is34
bittern   Is14, 34; Zp2
boar, wild   Ps80
buck   De12, 14
buffalo   SS6; KF1; Is1, 34; E39; Am5
bull   Nu7; SF1; CS29; Ez6ff; Job21, 42; Ps50ff, 69, 106; Is1, 34; Je50; E39, 43, 45
  image   Ps106
  offering of a   Le1ff
  without blemish   Nu28ff
  yearling   Ju6
bull-calf, image of   De9
bullock   Ju6; SF14; KF18; Ez6ff; Job42; Is1, 5, 10, 34, 65; Je31, 46, 50; E39, 43
bulls, herd of   Ps22
  sacrifice of   Ex29ff
bustard   Is14, 34; Zp2
  ruffed   Zp2
calf   SF6, 14, 28; Ps29, 68; Is11, 27; Je31, 46; E1; Am6; Mi6
  bull   Ps68
  image   De9
  Passover victim   De16
camel   Gen24, 31; Ex9; Le11; De14; Ju8ff; SF27, 30; KF4, 10; KS8; CF5, 12; CS9; Ez2;
          Ne7; Est8; Job1, 42; Is21, 30, 60; Je2, 49; E25; Z14
  caravan   Gen37
  neck crescents for   Ju8
camels, pestilence of   Ex9
  without number   Ju9
cankerworm   Joe1ff; Na3
caterpillar   KF8; CS6; Ps78, 105; Is33; Je51; Joe1ff
cattle   Ex9; Le3ff; SF14; CF5; Ez1; Is5, 11, 22, 46, 63; E14, 32, 34, 38; Ho5, 14; Joe1ff;
          Jon4; H3; Hg1; Z2, 13
  offering of   Le3ff

cattle, pestilence of Ex9

chameleon Le11

cheetah H1

cobra Ps91; Pro23; Is11

cobweb Is59

cock Pro30

cockatrice Is11, 14, 59; Je8

  eggs of a Is59

colt Z9

coney Le11; De14; Ps104; Pro30

cormorant Le11; De14; Is34; Zp2

cow Nu14; SF6; Job21; Is7, 11; Am4

  milch, harnessed to a wagon SF6

  red, without blemish Nu19

crane Je8

creatures, all living Gen1

  of the sea Ps98

crocodile Job40

crow Le11; De14

cuckoo Le11; De14

cud-chewing animals Le11

dangerous beasts, rid your land of Le26

deer, Job39; Is35; La1

  white-rumped De14

doe Pro5

  wild Job39

dog SF17, 24; KS9; Ps68; Pro26; Ec9; Is56, 66; Je15

dogs, run wild like Ps59

dove So1ff, 5; Is38, 59, 60; Je8, 48; E7; Ho7, 11; Na2

  image of Ps68

  oh that I had the wings of a Ps55

  released from the ark Gen8

dragon Job30; Ps91; Is13, 34ff, 43, 51; Je9, 14, 49, 51; E29; Mi1; Ma1

  return from the Ps68

dromedary KF4; Est8; Is60, 66; Je2

dung-beetle Is2

eagle Le11; De14; Job9, 39; Ps103; Pro30; La4; E1, 10, 17; D4, 7; Ho8; Ob1; Is40; Je4, 48ff; Mi1; H1

  gier De14

ewe   Ps78; Is7, 40, 53
  without blemish   Le4; Nu6
falcon   Le11; De14; Job28
fallow deer   KF4
fatling   SS6; KF1; Is11; E39;
fawn   Job39; So4, 7
ferret   Le11
fins and scales, creatures with   De14
flat paws, creatures with   Le11
fish   Ps8, 105; Ec9; Is19
  a great   Jon1
  dietary laws concerning   Le11
  for the asking in Egypt   Nu11
  in shoals   E47
  pestilence of   Ps105
  taken in a net   Ec9
flea   SF24, 26
flies   Ps78, 105; Ec10
  from Egypt   Is7
  plague of   Ex8; Ps105
  swarms of   Ps78
foal   Z9
food, animals given for   Le11
fox   Ne4; So2; La5; E13
frogs, plague of   Ex8; Ps78, 105
fruit bat   So2
gadfly   Je46
gazelle   De12, 14; SS2; Pro6; So2, 4, 7ff; Is13
gecko   Le11
gier   Le11; De14
glede   De14
goat   Gen27, 30ff; Le16; Nu7; De14; SF25; CS17, 29; Ez6ff; Ps50, 66; Pro27, 30; So4, 6;
      Is1, 13, 34; Je50ff; E27, 34, 39, 43; D4
  as scapegoat   Le16
  as sin-offering   Nu28ff
  brindled   Gen30ff
  driven into the wilderness   Le16
  mountain   Job39; Ps104
  offering of   Le3
  rock   De14

goat, wild   De14; So2, 8

goats, gift of 7,700   CS17

grasshopper   Le11; Job39; Ec12; Is40; Je46; Am7; Na3

 great   Na3

greyhound   Pro30

grouse, sand   Je48

grub   Ps78; Is51; Joe2

grubs, plague of   Ps78

hare   Le11; De14

hart   KF4; So2; La1

hawk   Le11; De14; Job39

heifer   Nu17; De21; Ju14; SF16; Je46, 48, 50; Ho4, 10

 broken neck in the ravine   De21

 ploughed with   Ju14

 red, without spot   Nu17

 roped   Is5

heron   Le11; De14

hoopoe   Le11; De14

hoppers   Ps105; Je51; Joe1ff; Na3

hornet   Jos24

horse   Ex9; Jos11; SS15; KF4, 9ff, 20; KS5ff; Ez2; Ne2; Est6, 8; Job39; Ps20, 32ff, 76,
        147; Pro21, 26; Is2, 5, 21, 30ff, 43, 63, 66; Je4, 6, 8, 11ff, 17, 22, 46, 50ff; E23,
        26ff, 38ff; Ho1,14; Joe2; Am6; Mi5; Na2ff; H1, 3; Hg2; Z1, 6, 9, 12, 14

horses, pestilence of   Ex9

hunting leopard   H1

hyena   Je12

insects, swarming   Ps80

jackal   Ju15; Ps63; So2; Is13, 34; Je50; La5; E13

jerboa   Le11; Is66

kid   Ex12; De16; Ju6, 13; SF10, 16; Ps29; So1; Is5, 11; E43

 Passover victim   De16

 without blemish   Ex12

kite   Le11; De14; Is34

lamb   Gen30; Ex12; Nu28ff; De16; SF7; KS3; CF29; CS29; Ez6ff; Ps144; Pro27; So4, 6;
       Is1, 11, 16, 34, 40, 65; Je11, 51; E27, 39, 45; Ho4; Am6

 black   Gen30

 Passover victim   De16

 without blemish   Ex12; Nu28ff

lammergeier   Le11; De14

lapwing   Le11; De14

leopard   So4; Is11; Je5, 13; D7; Ho13; Hi

  hunting   H1

leviathan   Job3; Ps74, 104

lion, lioness   Nu24; Ju14; SF17; SS23; KF13, 20; KS17; CS9;Job4, 10, 28, 38; Ps7, 10,

        17,22, 57, 91,104; So4;Pro19ff, 22, 26, 28; Ec9; Is5, 11, 15, 21, 30ff, 35, 38, 65;

        Je2, 4ff, 12, 25, 49ff; La3; E1, 10, 19, 22, 32; D6ff; Ho5, 11, 13; Joe1; Am3, 5;

        Mi5; Na2; Zp3; Z11

  cub   De33; Job28; Ho9; Na2

lizard   Pro30

  chameleon   Le11

  gecko   Le11

  great   Le11

  sand-gecko   Le11

  thorn-tailed   Le11

  wall-gecko   Le11

locust   Ex10; Le11; KF8; CS6; Job39; Ps78, 105, 109; Pro30; Ec12; Is33, 40; Je46, 51;

        Joe1ff; Am4, 7; Na3

  desert   Le11

  bald   Le11

  great   Le11

  green   Le11

  long-headed   Le11

locusts, plague of   Ex10; Ps78, 105

louse, lice   Ex8; So1; Is22, 41;

  plague of   Ex8

maggots   Ex8; Ps105; Is41, 51

  plague of   Ex8; Ps105

magpie   Pro30

marmot   Is13, 34; Je50

mare   E27

mole   Le11; Is2

mole-rat   Le11

monkey   KF10; CS9

moth   Job14; Is50ff; Ho5

mouse, mice   Le11; SF5, 6; Is66

mule   SS13, 18; KF1, 10; CF12; Ez2; Ne7; Est8; Ps32; Is66; E27; Z14

night hawk   Le11; De14

4 ANIMALS, BIRDS AND INSECTS

nightjar Is34

osprey Le11; De14

ossifrage Le11; De14

ostrich Job39; Is43; La4

owl Job30; Is34, 43

  desert Le11; De14; Ps102; Is13, 34; Je50; Mi1

  fisher Le11; De14

  great Le11; De14

  horned Le11; De14; Is34; Zp2

  little Le11; De14

  long-eared Le11; De14

  screech Le11; De14

  short-eared Le11; De14

  tawny Le11; De14; Zp2

ox Nu7; De14; SF11, 14; SS6, 24; KF1, 4, 8, 19; KS5; CF12; Ne4; Job1, 24; Ps8, 49, 66, 144;Je11; E1; D4ff; Am6

  wild Nu23ff; Job39; Ps22, 29, 92; Is34

    with horns to gore nations De33

pack animals Ks3

palmer worm Joe1ff; Am4

panther Ho5, 13

partridge SF26; Je17

  sand Is34

peacock KF10; CS9; Job39

pelican Le11; De14; Ps102

pig Le11; De14; Pro11; Is66

  prohibited as food Le11

pigeon Ho7, 11

  young, sacrifice of Le1ff

porcupine Is13

porpoise hide Nu4

quail Ex16; Nu11; Ps105

ram Gen30; Ex25ff, 29ff; Le3; Nu5ff, 28ff; KS3; CS17, 29; Ez6ff, 10; Job42; Is1, 5, 34, 60; Je49ff; E27, 34, 39, 43, 45; D8; Mi6

  of the Atonement Nu5

  offering of Le3

  sacrifice of Ex29ff

  skins Ex25ff

  without blemish Nu6, 28ff

ram, wool of   Ks3
rams, black   Gen30
  gift of 7,700   CS17
  of Nabaioth   Is60
rat   SF5, 6; Is66
raven   Le11; De14; KF17; Job38; Ps147; Pro30; So5; Is34
  released from the ark   Gen8
reptiles, carvings of   E8
rock badger   Le11; De14; Ps104; Pro30
  goat   De14
  rabbit   De14
roe, roebuck   De14; SS2; KF4; Pro5ff; So2, 3, 4; Is13
sand grouse   Je48
  partridge   Is34
  viper   Is30
scapegoat   Le16
scorpion   De18; KF12; CS10; E2
sea monster   Ps74
  serpent   Ps44, 74; Job7; Am9
serpent   Gen3; Ex4, 7; Ps58, 91, 140; Pro23, 30; Ec10; Is14, 65; Je8, 46; Am5, 9; Mi7
  Aaron's rod became a   Ex4, 7
  fiery flying   Is14, 30
  flying   Is14
  more crafty than other beasts   Gen3
  of bronze   Nu21
  venom of   Ps58
  venomous flying   Is30
shark   Ps74
sheep   Gen37ff; Ex9, 12; Le4; Nu31; De14; SF14, 16, 25; KF1, 4, 8; KS5; CF5, 12; Job1,
       42; Ps44, 49, 65, Ps77ff, 80, 107, 144; So1; Is1, 5, 7, 11, 13, 22, 43, 53, 66; Je12,
       23, 50; E25, 34, 36, 39, 45ff; Ho5, 12; Joe1; Am1; Mi2, 5; Z9
  levied   Nu31
  offering of   Le4
  pestilence of   Ex9
  slaughter for the Passover   Ex12
snail   Le11; Ps58
snake   Gen3, 49; Ex4, 7; Nu21; De8; Ps58, 59, 140; Pro23, 30; Ec10; Is14, 59, 65; Je8, 46;
       Am5, 9; Mi7
  bite, Moses's remedy for   Nu21

snake eggs   Is59
  horned, on the path   Gen49
  poisonous   Nu21; De8
  staff became a   Ex4, 7
song-birds   Ec12
sparrow   Ps84, 102; Pro26; Ec12
spider   Ps140; Pro30; Is59
stag   KF4
stallion   Je8, 50
stork   Le11; De14; Ps104; J8; Z5
swallow   Ps84; Pro26; Is38; Je8
swan   Le11; De14
swift   Je8
swine   De14; Is66
tortoise   Le11
turtle-dove   Ps74; So2; Je8
  sacrifice of   Le1ff
unclean, animals classified as   Le11
unicorn   Nu23ff; De33; Job39; Ps29, 92; Is34
viper   Gen49; Job20; Is11, 14, 30, 59; Je8
  on the road   Gen49
  sand   Is30
vulture   Job9, 15, 28, 39; Pro30; Is34; Je49; La4; Ho8; Ob1; Mi1; H1
  bearded   Le11; De14
  black   Le11; De14
  gier   Le11
  griffon   Le11; De14
water creatures, dietary laws concerning   Le11
weasel   Le11
whale   Job41; La4; E32
wild beasts, I will rid your land of   Le26
wolf   Gen49; Job30; Is11, 13, 34ff, 43, 65; Je5, 9ff, 14, 49, 51; E22; Mi1; H1; Zp3
  ravening   Gen49
worms   De28; Ps22; Is14, 41, 51, 66; Es2; Jon4; Mi7
  canker   Joe1ff; Na3
  curse of   De28
  palmer   Joe1ff; Am4
wryneck   Je8
adder   PR3
ass   Mw21; L13f; J12; LPS2

NEW TESTAMENT

beast   Rev13ff

birds came and ate the seeds   Mw13; Mk4; L8
   came to roost among its branches   L13
   can settle in its shade   Mk4
   gathered to eat the flesh   Rev19
   haunt for vile and loathsome   Rev18
   have their nests   Mw8
   have their roosts   L9
   lodge in the branches   Mw13
   of the air do not sow   Mw6
   unclean and hateful   Rev18
   you are worth more than the   Mw6

bear, feet like a   Rev13

bull   LH9f
   calf idol   A7

bullocks   Mw22

calf   L15; LH9
   beast like a   Rev4
   bring the fatted   L15

camel   Mw23; Mk1, 10; L18

cattle   L17; J2; LJ5

cock   Mw26; Mk13f; L22; J13, 18

colt, ass's   Mw21; J12
   which no one has yet ridden   Mk11; L19

creatures lowered in a sheet   A10f

dog returns to its own vomit   LPS2

dogs, beware of those   PPs3
   came and licked his sores   L16
   eat the scraps   Mw15
   outside are   Rev22
   throw children's bread to the   Mk7
   under the table   Mk7
   what is holy, do not give   Mw7

donkey   Mw21; L13f; J12

dove   Mw3, 10; Mk11; L3; J1f
   descending like a   Mw3
   spirit like a   Mk1

dragon in John's vision   Rev12f
  out of the mouth of the   Rev16
  spoke like a   Rev13
  that serpent of old,   Rev20
eagle   Mw24; L17; Rev4, 8
fish   Mw7, 13ff, 17; Mk6, 8; L5, 9, 11; J6, 21
  with a silver coin in its mouth   Mw17
foal, ass's   Mw21
fowls of the air, behold the   Mw6
    came and devoured the seed   Mw13; Mk4; L8
    may lodge under the shadow of it   Mk4
  were filled with their flesh   Rev19
fox, foxes   Mw8; L9, 13
  have their holes   L9
frogs, unclean spirits like   Rev16
gazelle   A9
gnat   Mw23
goat   Mw25; LH9ff
heifer   LH9
hen chicken   Mw23
    gathers her brood   L13
horse, black   Rev6
  red   Rev6
  sickly pale   Rev6
  white   Rev6, 19
horses and chariots, cargoes of   Rev18
  bridle, the height of a   Rev14
  in John's vision   Rev6, 9
  locusts like   Rev9
  mouth, put a bit in a   LJ3
kid, never gave me so much as a   L15
lamb among wolves   L10
  before the shearer   A8
  of God   Rev19ff
  Passover   Mk14
  with the marks of slaughter   Rev5
  without blemish   LPF1
lambs, feed my   J21
leopard, beast like a   Rev13
lion   PTS4; LH11; LPF5; Rev4f, 9f, 13

4 ANIMALS, BIRDS AND INSECTS

locusts   Mw3; Mk1
  in John's vision   Rev9
midge   Mw23
moth   Mw6; L12; LJ5
ox   M22; L13f; J2; A14; PCF9; PTF5 Rev4
pig   Mw7f; Mk5; L8, 15
pigeon, pigeons, offering of   L2
  dealers in   Mw21; Mk11; J2
raven   L12
scorpion   L10f; Rev9
sea-monster   Mw12
serpent, serpents   Mw7, 10, 23; Mk16; L10f; J3; PCF10; PCS11; LJ3; Rev20
  of old, the dragon   Rev20
  they shall take up   Mk16
sheep   Mw7, 9f, 12, 15, 18, 25f; Mk6, 14; L15, 17; J2, 5, 10, 21; A8; PR8; LH11, 13;
        LPF21; Rev18
  feed my   J2, 5, 10, 21
  for slaughter   PR8
  suppose a man has a hundred   Mw18
  will be scattered   Mk14
  without a shepherd   Mk6
  wolves dressed as   Mw7
snake, snakes   Mw7, 23; Mk16; L10f; A28; Rev9
  in John's vision   Rev9
  Paul shook off the   A28
  if they handle   Mk16
sow rolls in the mud   LPS2
sparrow   Mw10, L12
swine, a great herd of   Mw8; Mk5; L8
  casting pearls before   Mw7
  did eat, husks   L15
turtle dove   L2
viper   Mw3, 12, 23; L3; A28
vulture   Mw24; L17
whale, in the belly of the   Mw12
wild beasts   Mk1; Rev6
wolf   Mw7, 10; L10; A20
  dressed as a sheep   Mw7
  hireling sees the   J10
worm, worms, devouring   Mk9
  eaten up with   A12

5 *Blessings and Curses*

accursed serpent   Gen3
  thing, take from you   Jos7
bless the Lord   Job1; Ps34, 72, 103, 115, 134
blessed, all nations shall call him   Ps72
  be they that bless you   Nu24
  the people, David   CF16
blessing be on the fruit of your body   De28
  be on you in the city   De28
  be on you in the country   De28
  be on your basket and kneading trough   De28
  be on your basket and store   De28
  be on your coming in and going out   De28
  be on your fruit and cattle   De28
  be on your granaries and labours   De28
  be on your lands and herds   De28
  for considering the poor   Ps41
  for fearing the Lord   Ps111, 128
  of Ezra   Ne8
  of Naomi   Ru2
  of Solomon   KF8
  of the Levites   Ne9
  of the people   De27
  on the man who took notice   Ru2
  recited word by word   Jos8
blindness, strike this host with   KS6
children cursed in the name of the Lord   KS2
curse against the house of Joab   SS3
  Balaam sent to lay a   Jos24
  be on he who carves an idol   De27
  be on he who fulfils not the law   De27
  be on he who lies with an animal   De27
  be on he who lies with his father's wife   De27
  be on he who lies with his mother in law   De27
  be on he who lies with his sister   De27
  be on he who lies with his wife's mother   De27

curse be on he who makes a graven image   De27

  be on he who makes a molten image   De27

  be on he who misdirects the blind   De27

  be on he who removes landmarks   De27

  be on he who sacrifices a damaged victim   Ma1

  be on he who slights his parents   De27

  be on he who smiteth his neighbour secretly   De27

  be on he who strikes a man in secret   De27

  be on he who takes reward for killing   De27

  be on he who withholds justice   De27

  be on the cheat   Ma1

  be on the fruit of your body   De28

  be on you as you come out and go in   De28

  be on you in the city   De28

  be on you in the country   De28

  be on your basket and kneading trough   De28

  be on your land and flocks   De28

  David, let him   SS16

  for defrauding tithes   Ma3

  for non-observance of the covenant   Je11

  for rebuilding Jericho   Jos6

  for trusting in man   Je17

  for withholding contributions   Ma3

  in Zechariah's vision   Z5

  lay on Jacob   Nu23

  lay on the Israelites   Nu22

  of Cain   Gen4

  of children's death   Jos6

  of darkness   Job3; Ps35, 69

  of disease   SS3; Ps69

  of early death   SF2

  of fire   Ps140

  of flight with the enemy at your heels   SS24

  of Joshua on Jericho   Jos6

  of Jotham   Ju9

  of the people   De27

  of thistles   Job31

  of weeds   Job31

  on the thief   Ju17

  on the worthless shepherd   Z11

  Lord laid upon his sanctuary a   La2

5 BLESSINGS AND CURSES

curse recited word by word   Jos8
  sevenfold   Ps79
  the day   Job3; Je20
  the proud   Ps119
  them, hired Balaam to   Ne13
  turn your blessings into a   Ma2
  you to your face, he will   Job1
cursed be Canaan   Gen9
  be they that curse you   Nu24
  by Elisha, little boys mauled by bears   KS2
  in the name of the Lord   KS2
  to crawl on your belly   Gen3
curses, he loved   Ps109
  oath of   Nu5
  set out in the law of Moses   D9
distaff, sons fit only to ply the   SS3
evil eye, man with the   Pro28
old age, no man in your house shall come to   SF2
plague on nations who warred against Jerusalem   Z14
serpent accursed   Gen3
unblessed, be it for ever   Je20

NEW TESTAMENT

accursed thing, Christ became for our sake an   PG3
beatitudes   Mw5
bless, and curse not   PR12
  the cup of blessing   PCF10
  them which persecute you   PR12
  those who persecute you   Mw5; 16
blessed, all generations shall call me   L1
  and brake the loaves   Mw14
  are they that have not seen and yet believed   J20
  are they whose iniquities are forgiven   PR4
  are ye that hunger   L6
  are ye that weep   L6
  are ye, when men shall hate you   L6
  are you, how   L6
  art thou among women   L1

5 BLESSINGS AND CURSES

blessed be ye poor   L6
  is the man to whom the Lord will not impute sin   PR4
  them, he lifted his hands and   L24
blessing and cursing out of the same mouth   LJ3
  earth receiving its share of   LH6
  he looked up to heaven and said the   Mw14
  of Abraham   PG3
  on the fruit of your womb   L1
  over the food, said   L9
  retaliate with   LPF3
  said the   Mk6
  that ye should inherit a   LPF3
  the cup of   PCF10
blessings not curses, call down   OR12
  on him who comes in the name of the Lord   L13, 19
  on your persecutors, call down   PR12
cleverness of the clever, bring to nothing   PCF1
consecrate them by the truth   J17
cured, all of them were   A5
curse, bound themselves under a great   A23
  God's, hangs over the earth   LH6
  is on everyone who is hanged from a gibbet   PG3
  is on them, God's   LPS2
  is on this rabble   J7
  of the law   PG3
  on Jesus, no one who says   PCF12
  those who rely on the law are under a   PG3
  you, bless those who   L6
cursed God for the plague of hail   Rev16
  is everyone that hangeth on a tree   PG3
  the fig tree   Mk11
curses, Peter broke into   Mk14
  their mouth is full of bitter   PR3
cursing and angry shouting, have done with   PE4
  and bitterness, whose mouth is full of   PR3
  lay aside all   PCo3
damned who believe not the truth   ThS2
delusion, God puts them under a   ThS2
God bless the king of Israel!   J12
good to those who hate you, do   Mw5

gospel to proclaim, an eternal   Rev14
grace abounding   PCS4
  called me through his   PG1
  mercy and peace shall be with us   LJS1
  of God dawned upon the world   Tt2
  the gift of   LPF1
hosanna, blessings on him who comes in the name of the Lord   J12
  in the heavens   Mk1
  in the highest   Mk11
hungry, blest are you who now go   L6
kindness and generosity dawned in the world   Tt3
law, curse of the   PG3
Lord God of Israel, blessed be the   L1
love banishes fear, perfect   LJF4
  of Christ, what can separate us from the   PR8
mercy, peace and love be yours   LJu1
money go with your damnation, your   A8
peace of God beyond our understanding   PPS4
praises and curses, out of the same mouth came   LJ3
prayers of the saints   Rev5, 8
rejoice in the Lord alway: and again I say, Rejoice   PPS4
sin no more, lest a worse thing befall thee   J5
spirit, the grace of our Lord Jesus Christ be with your   PPS4
vital fragrance that brings life   PCS2
wealth to many we bring   PCS6
weep, blest are you who   L6
wisdom of the wise, I will destroy the   PCF1
woe unto you that are rich! for ye have received your consolation   L6

6 *Buildings and Shelters*

OLD TESTAMENT

build houses, but not live in them   Zp1
builder   E27
building, decaying through sloth   Ec10
  of houses, none yet awhile   E11
cabin   Je37
canopy, wedding   Ps19
capital   Am9; Zp2
  bronze   Je52
  copper KF7
  pillar   KS25; CS4
castle, I will pull down your   Ju8
  of Shechem   Ju9
  of Thebez   Ju9
causeway   KS18; CF26
cedar, beams of   KF7; So1
  boards, lining of   KF6
  panelling   Je22
  wood, a house of   SS5, 7
    building   CS2
  work, ruined   Zp2
ceiling, wooden   So1
cell, measurement of   E40ff
cement, stones set in   Je43
chamber, house   SS13
  temple   KF6
chapiter, pillar   KS25; CS4; Je52
  brass   KF7
cistern, rock-hewn   Ne9
citadel   KF20; Ne2; Is32
cities in the east, Moses set apart three   De4
city, Samson pulled out the gateposts of the   Ju16
  great towering   De9
  of Jerusalem pulled down   KS25
  of refuge   De19
  wall   KS6
    damaged   CS25
  which you had never built   Jos24
  without walls, Jerusalem to be a   Z2
clamps, iron   CF22
closet in Eglon's palace   Ju3

coffering in Solomon's house   KF6

colonnade   KS23; CF26

  in Solomon's house   KF7

columns, cedar   KF7

conduits, city to be rebuilt with   D9

coping   KF7

corner-stone   Ps118; Je51; Z10

  a block of granite   Is28

cornice, Solomon's house   KF7

  wooden   E41

corridors of the temple in Ezekiel's vision   E42

cottage   Is1, 24; Zp2

  shall be matchwood   Am6

court   KF7

  garden   Est1

  inner   CF28; Est4

    of stone and cedar   KF6

  of the guard, Jerusalem   Ne3

  temple, inner   E10

    in Ezekiel's vision   E40ff

  upper   Je36

courts of the house of the Lord   KS23

crib, farm   Is1

cushion, bronze pillar   KF7

elevation and plan of the temple   E43

embrasures, furnished with   KF6

dais   KS11, 22

dam   E31

demolish the house   Z5

dining-hall   SF9

door   CS3; Ps24, 107; Pro26; Is57

  bronze   Ps107

  double   KF6; E41

  frames broken up   KS18

  golden altar   KF7

  great   Ma1

  pinewood   KF6

  post   Is57

    pentagonal   KF6

    write commandments on the   De6, 11

  wild olive wood   KF6

doors of the temple broken up   KS18
dovecote   Is60
draught house   De23; Ju3; KS10
drawing of Jerusalem, Ezekiel's   E4
dungeon   La3; Z9
dwelling house, sale and redemption   Le25
fillets, hammered bronze   KF7
  pillar   Je52
floor boards, pine   KF6
forecourt   Ez10
fortified city   KS18; Ne9; Je1, 34; D11
fortresses built   CS17
forts and towers on the wooded hills   CS27
foundations   KF5, 7; Ps11, 87; Is54; Je51
  blocks of hewn stone   KF5
  laid bare   E13; Mi1
  of the new temple   Ez3; Hg2
  of the old temple   Z8
  stones, size of   KF7
  uncovered to the bare rock   H3
  Zerubbabel laid bare the   Z14
foundry   CS4
frames, gold-covered   CS3
furnace, furnaces   Ps21, 37; D3
  tower of the   Ne12
gallery, temple in Ezekiel's vision   E43
garden court, Persian   Est1
  house, fled by way of   KS9
gate   Ps24, 87; E26
  altar   E8
  bars   Na3
  Benjamin   Je17, 37; Z14
    upper   Je20
  between the two walls   KS25; Je39, 52
  corner   KS14; CS25ff; Je31; Z14
  dung   Ne2ff, 12
  east   CS31; Ne3; Je19
  eastern, Lord's house   E10ff
  Ephraim   KS14; CS25; Ne8, 12

gate, fish   CS33; Ne3, 12; Zp1
  foundation   CS23
  fountain   Ne2ff, 12
  guards   KS11
  hope   Ho2
  horse   CS23; Ne3; Je31
  inner   E8
  Jeshanah   Ne3, 12
  king's   CF9
  Lord's house   E8
  middle   Je39
  Miphkad   Ne3
  mustering   Ne3
  of Asher   E48
  of Benjamin   E48
  of Dan   E48
  of Gad   E48
  of Issachar   E48
  of Joseph   E48
  of Judah   E48
  of Levi   E48
  of Naphtali   E48
  of Reuben   E48
  of Samaria   KF22
  of Simeon   E48
  of the guardhouse   Ne12
  of the Lord's house   Je7
  of the potsherds   Je19
  of Zebulun   E48
  outrunners   KS11
  Shallecheth   CF26
  sheep   Ne3, 12
  Sur   KS11
  threshold   CS23
  upper, house of the Lord   KS15; CS23
  valley   CS26; Ne2ff
  water   Ne3, 8, 12
gates, city   Ps9, 122; E48
  of bronze   Is45
  of Jerusalem   KS11, 14, 25; CS23, 25ff, 31, 33; Ne2ff, 8, 12; Is60; Je1, 13, 17, 19ff, 31, 39, 52; Zp1; Z14

house, uninhabited, a fine large   Is5
   unless the Lord builds the   Ps127
houses bought and sold   Je32
   build, but not to live in   Zp1
      on their native soil   E28
      while in exile   Je29
   I builded   Ec2
   laid waste   Zp1
   mortgaged   Ne5
hut   So1; Zp2
inner court, royal   Est4
kerb, measurements of   E40ff
king's house   Ne3
latch-hole   So5
lattice   Pro7; So2
lavatory, sign for a   De23
ledges of the temple in Ezekiel's vision   E40ff
lime   Am2
lintel   Am9; Zp2
lining, cedar board   KF6
lock, handles of the   So5
lodge   Is1
loft   Kf17
loopholes, cell and pilaster   E40ff
mansion   KS25
   never to be rebuilt   Is25
   of Gedaliah burnt   Je52
   towering   La2
marble   CF29
   red, blue, white and black, pavement   Est1
   pillars of   Est1
measurements, inner shrine,   KF6
   Solomon's temple   KF6
measuring line   Am7
mill   Ec12
Millo, Solomon's tower   KF6, 9, 11; KS12; CF11; CS32
mortar   Is54; E13; Na3
mosaic pavement   Est1
oil-store   CF27
overlay, gold   KF6

undersetters, base   KF7
upper chamber of Ahaz   KS23
   of Solomon's temple   CS3
   tower of the court of the guard   Ne3
vault   Is45
   of the temple   Ju9
vaulted pit   Je37
vestibule   KF6ff; CS3
   of the gate   E40ff
wall   Ps18, 62, 89; Ho2
   bowing   Ps62
   breached   Ps89
   break a hole in the   E12
   broad, of Jerusalem   Ne3, 12
   bronze   Je1, 15
   building a   E13
   dig into the   E8
   farm   Pro24; Is5
   found a hole in the   E8
   plumbed   Am7
   repair, gone up into the breach to   E13
   stone   Pro24
   stones will cry out from the   H2
walled cities, sixty large   KF4
   city   Mi5
      of Tyre   SS24; E26ff; Am1
walls, breaches in the   Am4
   cracked and bulging   Is30
   day has come for rebuilding the   Mi7
   of Gaza   Am1
   of Jericho fell down   Jos6
   of Jerusalem destroyed   Je39
      time to rebuild the   Ne6
   of Rabbah   Am1
   of the temple in Ezekiel's vision   E43
   of Tyre, they will destroy the   E26
   of Zion   SS5
   repair Israel's gaping   Am9
watch tower   CS20
whitewash   E13

window   Pro7; Je22; D6; Joe2; Zp2; Ma3
window frames   KF7
  latticed   KS1
  vestibule   E40ff
wine cellars   CF27
winter-house   Am3
women's quarters, royal   Est2

NEW TESTAMENT

architect   LH11
audience chamber   A25
barn, barns   Mw13; L12
  pull down and build greater   L12
  store in   Mw6
barracks   A21, 23
beam   L6
Beautiful Gate   A3
build with hay and straw   PCF3
builder   A4; LH11; LPF2
building a tower without calculating the cost   L14
  bonded together   PE2
  rocked, when they had ended their prayer   A4
  up, not for pulling down   PCS13
  which God has provided   PCS5
  you are God's   PCF3
buildings, you see these great   Mk13
camp, bodies burnt outside the   LH13
castle, captain's   A21f
  on guard over his   L11
city built as a square   Rev21
  gate, they kept watch on the   A9
  square, Athens   A17
closets, that ye have spoken in   L12
colonnades, a place with five   J5
corner stone   Mk12; L20; A4
   Jesus Christ the chief   PE2
   of great worth   LPF2
courtyard, governor's   Mk15
  high priest's   Mw26; Mk14; J18

courtyard, lit a fire in the   L2

custom house   L5

door, knocking at the   Rev3

  Peter knocked at the   A12

  prison   A5

  struggle to get through the narrow   L13

  will be opened   Mw7; L11

doors, burst open all the   A16

dungeon, Satan let loose from his   Rev20

dwelling, built into a spiritual   PE2

  places, in my father's house are many   J14

foundation, God has laid a   PE2

  laid by the apostles and prophets   PE2

  laid the   L14; PCF3

  stone   PE2

    of the holy city   Rev21

  to build on another man's   PR15

foundations of the jail were shaken   A16

  on rock   Mw7; L6

gate, beautiful   A3

  city   A16

  enter in at the strait   L13

  iron   A12

  Jesus suffered outside the   LH13

  Lazarus laid at his   LH13

  narrow   Mw7

  of the town   L7

  temple   A3

  wide   Mw7

gates of faith, thrown open the   A14

  of hell   Mw16

  twelve   Rev21

hall, Herod's judgement   A23

  of judgement   J18

headquarters, governors   J18; A23; PPs1

homestead fall desolate, let his   A1

house built on sand   Mw7

  built upon rock   Mw7; L6

  flood could not shift the   L6

  he who hath builded the   LH3

house, high priest's   Mk14
  many dwelling places in my father's   J14
  not made by human hands   PCS5
  peace to this   L10
  Solomon built God a   A7
  to house, wandering about from   PTF5
  without foundations   L6
houses and lands sold   A4
inn   L10
jail   Mw5; A5
  foundations were shaken   A16
keystone   Mk12; L20; A4; PE2; LPF2
lecture hall   A19
main square of Philippi   A16
mansions, in my Father's house are many   J14
market place   Mw20; J2
palace, governor's   PPs1
  of the high priest   Mw26; Mk14; J18
  strong man keepeth his   L11
parapet of the temple   Mw4
pillar in the temple   Rev3
pinnacle of the temple   M4; L4
plank, great   L6
porch at the high priest's house   Mk14
  Solomon's   A3, 5
portico, Solomon's   J10; A3, 5
praetorium   Mk15
prison   Mw5, 11, 25; Mk1, 6; L21, 23; J3; A4, 12, 26; PPs1; Ph1
  doors during the night, an angel opened the   A5
  Herod had thrown John in   Mw14
  remember those in   LH13
  why I am now in   PCo4
private houses, breaking bread in   A2
  the sort that insinuate themselves into   PTS3
residency, the governor's   PPs1
roof, if a man is on the   Mw24; Mk13; L17
  let him down through the   Mk2; L5
room, a large upper   Mk14
  dining   Mk14
  for the Passover supper   L22

7 *Childhood, Birth and Infancy*

babes at the breast   Joe2
   in arms of the priests killed   SF22
   newly weaned, just taken from the breast   Is28
baby, Solomon's judgement for the disputed   KF3
   substituted another for a dead   KF3
bastard offspring debarred to the tenth generation   De23
birth of Ichabod   SF4
   of Jerusalem   E16
   of Obed   Ru4
   of Samson   Ju13
   of Samuel   SF1
   of Solomon   SF1
   untimely, the curse of   Nu5
birthright of Esau   Gen25
born a time to be   Ec3
   in the wilderness   Jos5
boy, every Midianite, killed by Moses   Nu31
   every newborn Israelite, to be killed   Ex1
   every newborn, to be thrown into the Nile   Ex1
boys mauled by bears for mocking Elisha   KS2
breast, mother's   Ps8, 22
child, I will give to the Lord my   SF1
   king, Amon   KS21
      Azariah   KS15
      Joash   KS12
      Josiah   KS22
   Samuel, surely you call me   SF3
   sneezed seven times, the revived   KS4
   the living, cut in two   KF3
childbirth, Hebrew women in   Ex1
children, beheaded seventy royal   KS10
   burnt as sacrifice   Le20; KS17; CS28; Is57; E16, 23
   come back to me, apostate   Je3
   dash to the ground their   KS8; Is13; Ho13; Na3
   eaten during siege   KS6
   given in pledge   Ne5

7 CHILDHOOD, BIRTH AND INFANCY

reins, children's   Ho11
sacrifice of children   Le20; KS3, 17; CS28; Is57; E16, 23
  of the Moabite king's son   KS3
salted, newborn baby   E16
shepherd boys, turn my hand against the   Z13
son, eldest, curse of Jericho   Jos6
  of a crooked and unfaithful mother   SF20
  punished for the iniquity of the father   Nu14
  youngest, curse of Jericho   Jos6
sons, disobedient, stoned to death   De21
  of Ahab beheaded   KS10
  of Saul hanged   SS21
  shall be punished to the third and fourth generation   Nu31
still-born child better than a dissatisfied man   Ec6
    may they wither like a   Ps58
substitute Levites for eldest sons   Nu3
suckled, Moses   Ex2
swaddling clothes   E16
twins of Judah   Gen38
  of Rebecca   Gen25
  of Tamar   Gen38
virgin, apparel of a   SS13
  Midianite girls spared for Israeli men   Nu31
  mourn that I must die a   Ju11
  rejoice in the dance, then shall the   Je31
  to keep King David warm   KF1
virgins be sought for your majesty, let beautiful young   Est2
  follow the king's daughters   Ps45
  for the king, commissioners appointed to bring young   Est2
weaned child   Ps131
womb, before thou camest forth from the   Je1
  formed thee from the   Is44
  he drew me from the   Ps22
  how the bones do grow in the   Ec11
  in my mother's   Ps139
  left in my mother's   Ps71
  named me from my mother's   Is49

7 CHILDHOOD, BIRTH AND INFANCY

NEW TESTAMENT

adoption, spirit of, whereby we say 'Father'   PR8
babe unskilful in the world as a   LH5
babes and sucklings, out of the mouths of   Mw21
  at breast, children and   Mw21
  be as innocent as   LPF14
  hast revealed these things unto   Mw11
babies for him to touch, they brought   L18
baby wrapped in swaddling clothes   L2
baptism, brought into the body by   PCF12
bearing children into slavery   PG4
birth, it was like an abnormal   PCF15
  of Jesus   L2
  of John the Baptist   L1
  of the child, woman shall be saved through the   PTF2
  pangs of the new age   Mw24; Mk13
  story of the Messiah's   Mw1
  to the son, she gave   L2
born again   J3
  of a woman, God sent his own son   PG4
  this day, unto you is   L2
boys in the temple shouting   Mw21
breasts that suckled you, happy the   L11
bride-chamber, children of the   Mk2
child, accept the kingdom of God like a   Mk10; L18
  also for women who are with   Mk13; L21
  birth, the universe groans as if in the pangs of   PR8
  by the Holy Ghost   Mw1
  every man who does right is his   LJF2
  grew and waxed strong in spirit   L2
  he called a   Mw18
  he took by the hand   L9
  Herod is going to search for the   Mw2
  in my name, who receives this   Mw18
  Jesus, thy holy   A4
  make careful inquiry for the   Mw2
  of God   LJF3ff

child, rise up, take the   Mw2
  of the devil   LJF3
  receive the kingdom of God like a little   L18
  saved through the birth of the   PTF2
  when I was a   PCF13
  who was born, where is the   Mw2
  whoever receives this   L9
  with Mary his mother, saw the young   Mw2
  woe unto them that are with   Mk13
  woman saved through the birth of the   PTF2
childish things, I put away   PCF13
children and babes at breast sang aloud thy praise   Mw21
  are with me in bed   L11
  at the breast, alas for those who have   Mw24; Mk13; L21
  bread of the   MW15
  dead, I will strike her   Rev2
  fathers must not goad their   PE6
  for Abraham out of these stones   Mw3
  he laid his hands on the   Mw19
  if she have brought up   PTF5
  into slavery, bearing   PG4
  leader wins obedience from his   PTF3
  massacred by Herod   Mw2
  nurse caring fondly for her   ThF2
  obey your parents   PE6; PCo3
  of a family share the same flesh and blood   LH2
  of light, children of day   ThF5
  of light, walk as   PE5
  of the bride-chamber   Mk2
  of the highest, ye shall be the   L6
  of the kingdom, the good seed stands for the   Mw13
  of the wicked one   Mw13

  of your heavenly Father   Mw5
  parents should make provision for their   PCS12
  provoke not your   PE6
  Rachel weeping for her   Mw2
  receive in my name   Mk9
  should repay what they owe to their parents   PTF5
  sitting in the market place, they are like   L7
  suffer little   Mw9; Mk10; L18

children, unless you become like little   Mw18
   we are called God's   LJF3
   we are no longer to be   Pe4
   who are not our of control   TF1
   you are my dear   PCF4
circumcise him, the time came to   L2
   the child, on the eighth day   L1
circumcised on my eighth day   PPS3
circumcising their children, telling them to give up   A21
circumcision makes no difference at all   PG5
   mutilation, those who insist on   PPs3
   of Jesus Christ   L2
   of John the Baptist   L1
daughter of Herodias danced   Mk6
father and mother, honour thy   Mw15, 19; PE6
   in the secret place   Mw6
fathers, do not exasperate your children   PCo3
   must not goad their children to resentment   PE6
first-born from the dead   Rev1
   male belongs to the Lord   L2
   presents to the world   LH1
honour your father and mother   Mw15, 19; PE6
infants in Christ, deal with you as   PCF3
   they brought him   L18
little children, keep yourselves from idols   LJF5
    yet a while I am with you   J13
   ones have their guardian angels in heaven   Mw18
    who shall offend one of these   Mk9
manger, laid him in a manger   L2
massacre of all children in Bethlehem   Mw2
mother, who is my   Mk3
naughtiness, lay apart all   LJ1
new-born infants crave for pure milk   LPF2
nurse, children's   THf2
parents, children should repay their   PTF5
   honour your   L18
   they show no loyalty to their   PR1
purification after birth   L2
scion and offspring of David   Rev22
son disciplined by his father   LH12

son, my beloved   Mk1; L3

   of a Christian mother and a Gentile father   A16

   of David, can this be the   Mw12

   only begotten   LJF4

   working under his father, like a   PPs2

sons of God, that we should be called the   LJF3

suck, them that give   Mk13

suckled you, happy the breasts that   L11

sucklings, babes and   Mw21

suffer little children to come unto me   Mw9; Mk10; L18

swaddling clothes, wrapped him in   L2

tolerant and gentle when discipline is needed   PTS2

twin, Thomas the   J20f

womb, a cripple from his mother's   A14

   a second time, enter his mother's   J3

   his blessing is on the fruit of your   L1

   that carried you, happy the   L11

   the baby stirred in her   L1

young, let no one slight you because you are   PTF4

youth, let no man despise thy   PTF4

   turn from the wayward impulse of   PTS2

8   *Cloth and Clothes*

apparel of blue and white   Est8
apron, fig leaf   Gen3
  leather   KS1
armour   SF14, 17, 31; KF10, 22; CS18; Ps45; E38
awning, violet and purple   E27
badger skin, shod with   E16
belt,   KF2; Ps109; Is5; E23, 44
  gold   D10
blue and gold is their clothing   Je10
  officers dressed in   E23
bonnet   Is3; E44
  linen   E44
breastplate   KF22; CS18; Is59
breeches, linen   Ex28ff; E44
brocade   E27
  dress of   E16
  robes of   E16, 26
broidered work   E6, 26ff
    purple   E27
buckler   KF10; CS23; Ps35; So4; Je46; E23, 26, 38ff
canvas, patterned   E27
  sail   E27
cloak   SF2, 15, 18, 21, 24; SS20; KS2; Job29; Ps102, 109; Pro31; So5; Is3, 61; E26; Mi2
  Ahijah's new   KF11
  Elijah's   KF19
  fold of Moses'   Ex4
  of fine linen and purple   Est7
  purple, of the Midian kings   Ju8
cloth, blue   Nu4
  chariot lining   E27
  cobwebs will never make   Is59
  round your waist   Is32
  scarlet   Nu4
  violet   Nu4; E27
cloth-of-gold   Ps45

clothed but never warm   Hg1
  in scarlet   D5
clothes   Ps109
  blue   E23
  cast lots for   Ps22
  David took from his victims   SF27
  Joshua was wearing filthy   Z3
  large stores of   Jos22
  Saul stripped off his   SF19
  symbolizing guilt   Z3
  tattered cast-off   Je38
  ten changes of   Ju15
  the elders rent their   Jos7
  thirty changes of   Ju15
  torn   Le13
clouts, old cast off   Je38
coat   So5
  long-sleeved   Gen37
  of many colours   Gen37
  of mail   CS26; Ne4; Is59; Je46, 51
collar   Ps133; Is52
  of jewels   Ps73
cord   Na1
  let us wind round our heads   KF20
  linen   E27, 40
  scarlet   Jos2
  silver   Ec12
  white and purple   Est1
coverlet   Is14
cross-dressing, prohibition of   De22
crown. SS1, 12; KS11
  golden   Est7; Ps21
  jewelled   Z9
  Queen Vashti's   Est1
  royal   Est6
curtain   So1; Is40
  rings, silver   Est1
  tabernacle   Ex26
  tent   Je4, 10, 49; H3
  white, green and blue   Est1
diadem   Job29

8 CLOTH AND CLOTHES

mantle, priestly   Ex28ff; Le8
mend, a time to tear and a time to   Ec3
mitre   Z3
muffler   Is3
needlework of divers colours   Ju5
net   E12
plate-armour   SF15
porpoise-hide   Ex25ff
purple and fine linen   Pro31
  stuff, seat of   So3
rags, old rotten   Je38
robe, a fold of his   Hg2
  brocade   E16, 26
  Esther's royal   Est5
  for the ministers of Baal   Ks10
  fragrant   Ps45
  he tucked up, and ran   KF18
  invest him with your   Is22
  Joseph's   Gen37
  long-sleeved   Gen37; SS13
  of coarse hair   Z13
  of Job's judgement   Job29
  of violet and white   Est7
  priestly   Ne7
  pull off the   Mi2
  rent my   Ez9
  royal   KF22; CS18; Est6
  shook out a fold of my   Ne5
  tie it in a fold of your   E5
robed in purple   D5
sackcloth   Ps30, 35, 69; Is15, 20, 22, 32, 37, 50; Je6, 49; La2; E7, 27; D9; Joel; Am8; Jon3
  David wore   CF21
  for Jacob   Gen37
  gird themselves with   Is15
  gird up your loins with   Is32
  is my clothing   Ps69
  let us wear   KF20
  put on   SS3
  stitched together   Job16
  worn for fasting   Ne9
  worn for mourning   Est4

sacking, loin cloth of   Is3
saddle cloth   Ju5
  woollen   E27
sandals   KF2; So7; Is5, 20; E16, 24
  as symbol of property exchange   Ru4
  of stout hide   E16
sash   Pro31; Is22
  priestly   Ex28ff
scarf of gauze   Is3
scarlet and rich embroideries   SS1
  clothed in   Pro31
  dress yourself in   Je4
sew, a time to rend and a time to   Ec3
shirt   D3
shoes   KF2; Ps108; So7; Is5; E16, 24; Am2, 8
  badger-skin   E16
silk   E16
  and purple clothing   Pro31
skins, tunics of   Gen3
skirt   Is47; Je13; La1; Na2
  flounced   Is3
stomacher   Is
stuff, gorgeous   E27
surplice, ephod   Ex25, 28ff
swaddling clothes   E16
tapestry   Pro7, 31
tent covering   Je4
  curtain   So1; Is54; H3
thong, sandal   Is5
thread   Job7
  linen   E40
  scarlet   Le14; Nu19
  violet, for tassels   Nu15
tire (headdress)   E24
tow   Is1
trousers   D3
tunic   SS20
  chequered   Ex28ff
  priestly   Le8
  skin   Gen3
turban   Job29; Is3; E23; Z3

NEW TESTAMENT

cloak, hole in a new   L5
  let him have your   Mw5
  purple   J19
  sell to buy a sword   L22
  shook out the skirts of his   A18
  threw off his   Mk10
  touched the hem of his cloak   Mw9; Mk5f
  wrap around you   A12
cloaks, carpeted the road with their   M21; L19
  spread their   Mk11
  threw on the colt   L19
  yelling and waving their   A22
coat, he must not turn back for his   M24; Mk13
  let him have your   Mw5
  not to take a second   Mw10; Mk6; L7
  of camel's hair   Mw3; Mk1
  of mail   PE6
  patch an old   Mw9
  when a man takes your   L6
  without seam   J19
  wrapped about him   J21
coats that Dorcas used to make   A9
cloth, funeral   J11
  linen   Mk14
  patch of unshrunk   Mw9; Mk2
clothe you, he will not   Mw6
clothed in purple and scarlet   Rev17
clothes became dazzling white   Mw17; Mk9; L9
  decked out in expensive   PTF2
  divided by lots   Mw27; J19
  happy the man who keeps on his   Rev16
  he wore no   L8
  in the way, spread their   L19
  put away anxious thoughts about   Mw6; L12
  put on the ass   Mw21
  soldiers took possession of his   J19
  they divided among them his   Mk15; L23
  tore off the prisoners'   A16
  when they heard of it they tore their   A14
  who touched my   Mk5

clothing, cast lots for my   J19
  contaminated with sensuality   Lju1
  gay   LJ2
  of camel's hair   Mw3
  of John the Baptist   Mw3
  white   Rev3
cloths of purple and scarlet, cargoes of   Rev18
curtain of the temple   Mw27; Mk15; L23
  sanctuary   LH9
dress, fine linen   Rev19
  in becoming manner, women must   PTF2
dressed in purple   L16
fine clothes are moth-eaten, your   LJ5
garment drenched in blood   Rev19
  you have put on Christ as a   PG3
  young man clothed in a long white   Mk16
garments, Jesus laid aside his   J13
  moth-eaten   LJ5
  that suit God's chosen people   PCO3
  they parted his   Mk15
  two men in dazzling   L24
girdle, leathern   Mw3
  of skin   Mk1
goatskins   LH11
leather belt   Mw3
  girdle   Mw3
linen cloth   Mk14; J19f
  clothed in fine   Rev19
  dressed in the finest   L16
  dress, fine   Rev15, 19
  pure white   Rev15
  sheet   Mw27; Mk15
  silk and fine   Rev18
  wrapped his body in   L23
  wrapping   L23f
mantle, they dressed Jesus in a scarlet   Mw27
moth-eaten clothes   LJ5
   treasure   Mw6
napkin   L19
purple, a rich man dressed in   L16

8 CLOTH AND CLOTHES

purple and scarlet, clothed in   Rev17
 dressed him in   Mk15
 fabric   A16
 raiment, a man clothed in soft   L7
  became shining   Mk9
  parted among them   J19
  was white and glistening, his   L9
  white as the light   Mw17
 robe, fetch a   L15
  scarlet   Mw27
  sent him back to Pilate dressed in a gorgeous   L23
  the high priest tore his   Mw26; Mk14
  wearing a white   Mk16; Rev6
 robed all in white   Rev3f, 7
  down to his feet   Rev1
  in fine linen   Rev15
 robes, a man in shining   A10
  love to walk up and down in long   Mk12; L20
  royal   A12
  tasselled   Mw23
  washed their   Rev7
 sackcloth of hair   Rev6
  witnesses dressed in   Rev11
 sail-cloth, sheet of   Mw27; Mk15; A10f
 satin, a man dressed in silk and   Mw11; L7
 shabby clothes, a poor man in   LJ2
 sheepskins   LH11
 sheet, linen   Mw27; Mk15
  of sail-cloth   Mw27; Mk15; A10f
 shirt, let him have your   L6
  sues you for your   Mw5
  that Dorcas used to make   A9
  the man with two   L3
 shoes   Mw10
  not fit to take off his   Mw3
 silk and fine linen, cargoes of   Rev18
  and satin, a man dressed in   M11; L7
 skins, dressed in   LH11
 tunic, seamless   J19
 veil of the sanctuary   LH9

8 CLOTH AND CLOTHES

veil of the temple   Mw27; Mk15; L23
wearing of gold   LPF3
well-dressed man   LJ2
women must dress in becoming manner   PTF2
wool, scarlet   LH9
  snow-white   Rev1

9   *Culture and Custom*

OLD TESTAMENT

bruised reed, Egypt   KS18
calendar   KF4; Z1, 7
census of David   SS24; CF21
  of Israel   CF9
    and Judah   SS24
  of Israelites   Ex30; Nu26
  of Levites not recorded   Nu1
  of male first-born   Nu3
  of young Israeli men   Niff
chain of honour   Pro1
champions there were none   Ju5
chemarims, heathen priests so-called   Zp1
chronicle of daily events   Est6
  royal Persian   Est2
college at Jerusalem   KS22
commission for Joshua   Nu27
confession, make your   Jos7
  of Acham   Jos7
  of Ezra   Ex9ff
  of Nehemiah   Ne1
Gentiles, bring judgement to the   Is42
  eat defiled bread among the   E4
  forbidden to enter   La1
  glory of the   Is66
  horns of, in Zechariah's vision   Z1
  Israel among the   Ho8
  light to the   Is49
  my name shall be great among the   Mal
  proclaim among the   Joe3
  remnant of Jacob shall be among the   Mi5
  their seed known among the   Is61
  thy seed shall inherit   Is54
  word came against the   Je46
  Zion among the   La2
gifts to the poor, days for giving   Est9
grudge of Esau   Gen27
guilt for unfaithfulness   Nu5
heart, harden not your   De15
  prompted not by my own   Nu16
heathen, all the isles of the   Zp2

heathen, ambassador sent among the   Ob1
   day of the Lord is near upon all the   Ob1
   dwell among the   E31
   gathered together, the wealth of all the   Z9
   it shall be a time of the   E30
   possession of the   E36
   priests, wipe out the name of   Zp1
   realms, break the power of   Hg2
   reproach among the   Joe2
   scattered them among the   E36
   set my glory among the   E39
   should not rule over them   Joe2
   thresh in anger   H3
Hebrew, Jonah answered, I am a   Jon1
   language   Is36
history, to brood over past   Is43
ink   E9
inkhorn   E9
interest, not to charge   De23
investment of Eleazar   Nu20
Jashar, book of   Jos10; SS1
knowledge of good and evil   Gen2
lament of Jeremiah   CS35
language, Aramaic   KS18; Ez4; Is36; D2
   Hebrew   KS18; Is36
     shouted in   CS32
   of Canaan, cities of Egypt speaking the   Is19
   of the Chaldeans   D1
   of the Jews   Is36
   turn to the people a pure   Zp3
lender and borrower   Is24
letter of Artaxerxes to Ezra   Ez7
   of Jeremiah to Babylon   Je29
   to Artaxerxes   Ex4ff
   to Asaph   Ne2
levy, enforced   KF4
literature of the Chaldeans   D1
living and the dead, Aaron between the   Nu16
lot fell to Jonah   Jon1
lots cast   Est3
   by the sailors   Jon1

lots cast to decide who should live in Jerusalem   Ne11
memorial in the temple of the Lord   Z6
money-lenders strip my people bare   Is3
month, Abib   Ex13; De16
  Adar   Ez6; Est3
  Bul   KF6
  Chisleu   Ne1; Z7
  Elul   Ne6
  Ethanim   KF8
  Kislev   Ne1; Z7
  Nisan   Ne1; Est3
  Sebat, Shebat   Z1
  Sivan   Est7
  Tebeth   Est2
  Ziv   KF6
name of the Lord, misuse of the   De5
night watch   Ps59, 90
orator, eloquent   Is3
peculiar people, to be his   De26
pedigree declared   Nu1ff
pen   Is8; E9
  and ink at his waist   E9
petition, present to the Lord   Je36
pledge, persons held in, to be released   Ne10
  for food, sons and daughters given as   Ne5
poem about you, they shall take up a   Mi2
  of Solomon   KF8
poet, the skill of a   Ps71
pottage, birthright sold for   Gen25
prayer of David   SS7
  of Ezra   Ez9ff
  of Habbakuk   H3
  of Hannah   SF2
  of Solomon   CS6ff; KF8
presents sent to one another   Est9
procession into the sanctuary   Ps68
  round the altar   Ps26
proverb, shall become a   De28
proverbs current in Israel   E12

proverbs, Solomon uttered 3000   KF4

provinces ruled by Ahasuerus   Est1

public duty, newly married exempt from   De24

publish in the palaces of Ashdod   Am3

purifying the women   Est2

Rahab as personification of excessive pride   Job9, 26

  hacked in pieces   Is51

  quelled, as Egypt   Is30

refuge, cities of   Nu35; De19

register of first-born males   Nu3

  of genealogy   Ne7

registration of Israel   CF9

  of the Israelites   Ex30

remission of debts   De15

  year of   De15

restitution for wronging another   Nu5

riddle, how I read the   Ps49

  of Samson   Ju14

  of things past   Ps77

riddles, gift of explaining   D5

rod, Aaron's   Ex7

   produced almonds   Nu17

  for each tribe   Nu17

  lift up your   Ex14

  Moses'   Ex4; Nu20

  of the chosen man   Nu17

  struck the rock   Nu20

roll of a book   Je36; E2ff

  of exiled captives   Ne7

  of Israel   E13

  of nations   Ps87

  writing   Is8

rule of life   De31

rules in writing   Ho8

sandal, pull off his foot   De25

scapegoat presented by Aaron   Le16

science, understanding   D1

scribe, position of   Ne8, 12

scroll, an allegorical flying   Z5

  I swallowed the   E3

scroll, king Jehoiakim cut and burnt the   Je36
  register the country on   Jos18
  rolled up in a   Is34
  tied up in a   Ho13
  writing   Je36
  written on both sides   E2ff
seal, shaping clay with a   Job38
seamanship in vain   Ps107
seven pillars of wisdom   Pro9
shadow moved backwards   Is38
  of the hills, looking like men   Ju9
Shamgar, in the days of   Ju5
share and share alike   SF30
  the spoils with your kinsmen   Jos22
shibboleth, if he could not pronounce   Ju12
shoe loose, house of him who has his   De25
sign put up by the door   Is57
signet   Is3
  make thee as a   Hg2
  of Darius over the mouth of the lions' den   D6
signet-ring   Je22
  the royal   Est3f, 7
similitudes, I have used   Ho12
Solomon, sayings of   Pro1ff
song at the house of the Lord   KS11
  of David   SS22
songs of Solomon number 1005   KF4
speech, a time for silence and a time for   Ec3
  recover the power of   E24
  thick and difficult   E3
splintered cane, Egypt   Is36
staff, Aaron's   Rx7
  for each tribe   Nu17
  Moses'   Ex4; Nu20
  of Judah   Gen38
  of the chosen man shall sprout   Nu17
  produced ripe almonds   Nu17
  raise high   Ex14
  struck the rock   Nu20
  the stay and the   Is3

statute, Joshua drew up   Jos24
stone, tablets of   Ex24, 31
strength of Israel   SF15
sun dial of Ahaz   Is38
supplication of Ezra   Ex9ff
  of Solomon   CS6
swimmer spreads his hands to swim   Is25
Syrian language, Aramaic   Is36
tablet, folding   E37
  inscribe the vision on   H2
  of stone   Ex24, 31; De9f
  separate leaves of   E37
  wooden   E37
  writing   Is8, 30; E37
thorn in your side   Nu33
token, Ark of the   Jos3ff
  of good faith   Jos2
true, everything he says comes   SF9
truth, water of contention brings out the   Nu5
uncircumcised, die the deaths of the   E28
  in the midst of the   E31
  into the nether parts of the earth, gone down   E32
  laid with the   E32
  never enter you again   Is52
  rascals, these   SF14
understanding, display your   De4
undertaking, to bring first-born of sons and cattle   Ne10
  to bring first kneading of dough   Ne10
  to bring first-fruits   Ne10
unsandalled man, house of the   De25
upright, book of the   Jos10; SS1
usurers lord it over them   Is3
usury, not put his money to   Ps15
  taker and giver of   Is24
wage to be paid the same day   De24
watches of the night   Ps63
wheel of fortune   Pro20
wisdom and wealth promised to Solomon   CS1
  choose men of   De1
  display your   De4
  seven pillars of   Pro9

wisdom, spirit of   De34
  who gave him lessons in   Is40
wise men, Pharaoh's   Ex7
  women   SS14, 20
witness against yourselves   Jos24
  altar of   Jos22
work not to be done on the sabbath   De5

NEW TESTAMENT

alms before men, take heed that ye do not your   Mw6
apostles, the twelve   Mw10
arguments of the wise are futile   PCF3
arrogant, God sets his face against the   LPF5
assembly, dealt with by statutory   A19
astrology   Mw2
authority, speak with   Tt2
barbarian, no question here of   PCo3
birthright, Esau sold his   LH12
book in John's vision, ate the   Rev10
  in the angel's hand   Rev10
  it is written of me in the volume of the   LH10
  of Hosea   Pr9
  of life   PPs4; Rev3
  of Moses, have you never read in the   Mk12
  of psalms   L20
  of the prophecies of Isaiah   L3
  sealed   Rev4f
  what thou seest, write in a   Rev1
  worthy to read the   Rev5
books, Paul's   PTS4
  were opened   Rev20
bread alone, man cannot live on   L4
bribe from Paul, Felix had hopes of a   A24
  offered the soldiers a substantial   Nw28
brotherhood, about love for our   ThF4
cast lots for his clothes   Mw27; Mk15; L23; J19
census, at the time of the   A5
  throughout the Roman world   L2
character, a balanced   LJ1

charity, do not announce   Mw6
  sell your possessions and give in   L12
  the greatest of these is   PCF13
chatter, avoid empty   PTS2
chosen race   LPF2
Christian movement   A19, 24
  of me, to make a   A26
Christianity, discussing the rudiments of   LH6
Christians, the disciples first got the name of   A11
circumcised, let him not be   PCF7
circumcision, beware of   PPs3
  is nothing, uncircumcision is nothing   PG6
  is of the heart, true   PR2
  or uncircumcision is neither here nor there   PCF7
  true, not the external mark in the flesh   PR2
  what is the value of   PR3
cleverness, bring to nothing the   PCF1
collection in aid of God's people   PCF16
commandments of men, they teach as doctrines the   Mw15
common fund for the benefit of the poor   PR15
commonwealth of Israel   PE2
concision, beware of the   PPs3
conduct in the body, due to him for his   PCS5
conscience, called in question by another man's   PCF10
  convicted on their own   J8
  love which springs from a good   PTF1
  train myself to keep a clear   A24
conversation be gracious, let your   PCo4
convert, you travel on sea and land to make one   Mw23
conviction in his own mind, should have reached   PR14
Council, a respected member of the   Mk15
  Jewish   J3
  Joseph a member of the   L23
  of elders   A22
councillors   L23
cross, doctrine of the   PCF1
custom house   Mw9
debate, full of   PR1
debater, where is your subtle   PCF1
deceit defiles the man   Mk7
deceptions, they revel in their own   LPS2

9 CULTURE AND CUSTOM

freedmen, synagogue of   A6

friend of the world, enemy of God   LJ4

friendly advice, give him   ThS3

genealogies, interminable   PTF1

  steer clear of   Tt3

Gentile origin, greetings to our brothers of   A15

    she was of   Mk7

Gentiles, a light to lighten the   L2; A13

  and Jews, he has made the two one   PE2

  deliver him to the   Mw20

  Galilee of the   Mw4

  he shall be delivered unto the   L18

  hindering us from speaking to the   ThF2

  Jerusalem shall be trodden down of the   L21

  mystery among the   PCo1

  Paul an apostle to the   PG2

  seek after all these things   Mw6

  shall deliver him to the   Mk10

  to proclaim his Son among the   PG1

  will he go to teach the   J7

gibberish to me, his words will be   PCF14

gifts we possess differ   PR12

giveth, he that, let him do it with simplicity   PR12

glory and honour, crowned with   LH2

God loves a cheerful giver   PCS9

godless world, do not set your heart on the   LJ2

gospel, Gentiles should believe the   A15

  he proclaimed the   L4

  must be proclaimed before the end   Mk13

  of God   Mk1

  of the kingdom will be proclaimed   Mw24

  set apart for the service of the   PR1

  to make known the mystery of the   PE6

  twelve whom he would send out to proclaim the   Mk3

Greek, Hebrew and Latin, inscription in   J19

  in letters of   L23

  language   A9, 21

  those who spoke   A6

greeting, do not give him a   LJS1

handwriting of ordinances, blotting out the   Pco2

philosophy, vain deceit   PCo2
plain speaking, no figure of speech   J16
prayers for appearance sake   Mk12
preaching in all the towns   A8
presbytery of elders   PTF4
proclaim the message   PTS4
profane babblings, shun   PTS3
propagandist for foreign deities   A17
proselyte, ye compass sea and land to make one   Mw23
proselytes, both Jews and   A2
   followed Paul and Barnabas, many   A13
proverbs, I have spoken in   J16
public reading of the scriptures   PTF4
   speaking and teaching, to refrain from   A4
publican, Matthew the   Mw10
publicans and sinners   Mw9
pupil content to share his teacher's lot   Mw10
purification, dispute about   J3
qualification comes from God   PCS3
race, all the runners run the   PCF9
reasoning powers become atrophied   PTF6
religion, let us hold fast to the   LH4
   men who pour scorn on   LJu1
   men who scoff at   LPS3
   points of disagreement about   A25
   the enemies of   LJu1
   who preserve the outward form of   PTS3
resurrection, Sadducees deny there is any   Mk12; L20; A23
   whose wife will she be at the   Mk12
reverence and respect, to those to whom they are due   PR13
rich man will disappear like a flower   LJ1
righteousness, the garland of   PTS4
ringleader of the Nazarene sect   A24
roll of the living   PPs4; Rev3, 13, 17, 20f, 23
Roman, rescued him, having understood that he was a   A23
Sadducean party   A5
Sadducees   Mw3, 16, 22; Mk12; L20; A4f, 23
Sanhedrin, Israeli senate of   A5
seal, delivered under my own   PR15
   of God on the forehead   Rev9
   upon us, set his   PCS1

tongue, a small member, can make huge claims LJ13
tongues of ecstasy   A19; PCF13f
  they will speak in strange   Mk16
traditions of my ancestors   PG1
  of my fathers, zealous in the   PG1
treat others as you would like them to treat you   L6
truth, be straightforward in your proclamation of   PTS2
  belong to the realm of   LJ3
  blind to the   PR11
  by our grasp of   PCS6
  loins girt about with   PE6
  lost their grip of the   PTF6
  recommend ourselves by declaring the   PCS6
  scripture has its use for teaching the   PTS3
  what is   J18
tutor, the law was a kind of   PG3
uncircumcised, you who are called the   PE2
uncircumcision or circumcision, neither here nor there   PCF7
  or circumcision is nothing   PG6
understand by instinct like brute beasts   LJu1
  pour abuse upon things they do not   LPS2; LJu1
understanding, wisdom and spiritual   PCo1
vanity, speak great swelling words of   LPS2
verbal questions and quibbles   PTF6
virtue with knowledge, supplement your   LPS1
vow, hair cut off because of a   A18
washing before the meal   Mk7; L11
wickedness defiles the man   Mk7
widow's mite   Mk12; L21
will that the universe might be brought into a unity   PE1
wisdom and spiritual understanding   PCo1
  and vision, spiritual powers of   PE1
  become a fool to gain true   PCF3
  demonic   LJ3
  fleshly   PCS1
  Greeks look for   PCF1
  I speak of God's hidden   PCF2
  if you fall short in   LJ1
  it has an air of   PCo2
  of this world is foolishness with God   PCF3

wisdom, they boast of their   PR1
wise by the standards of this passing age   PCF3
   man now, where is your   PCF1
   or clever, who among you is   LJ3
   speech, gift of   PCF12
   you are, do not keep thinking how   PR12
wit's end, I am at my   PG4
words as your sword   PE6
   gone astray in a wilderness of   PTF1
   so secret that human lips may not repeat them   PCS12
world, love of the, is enmity to God   LJ4
worldly minds, futile conceit of   PCo2
   standards have ceased to count in our estimate   PCS5
worth of everything, judge the   PCF2
wrangles, quibbles which give rise to endless   PTF6
wreath, to win a fading   PCF9
writing tablet   L1
written, what I have written, I have   J19
yoke-fellow, true   PPs4
zeal for God is an ill-informed zeal   PR10
Zealot party, member of the   Mw10
   Simon the   Mw10; Mk3; L6; A1
zealous in the traditions of my fathers   PG1

10 *Death, Burial and Mourning*

OLD TESTAMENT

anointed the bodies with spices   SF31
ashes, handfuls of   Ex9
  I repent in   Job42
  Mordecai put on   Est4
  over her, Tamar threw   SS13
  sprinkle over yourself   Je6, 25
  wallow themselves in   E27
  wallow thyself in   Je6
beds of sackcloth and ashes   SS21; Est4; Is58
bier heaped with spices   CS16
  of Abner   SS3
bones of Joseph   Ex13
    buried in Shechem   Jos24
  shall lie in the wilderness   Nu4
broke his neck, Eli   SF4
burial beneath an oak   Gen35
  carry him out for   Am6
  ground   KS23; E39
  he alone shall have proper   KF14
  I will grant you   Na1
  man of God at Bethel   KF13
  of Abdon   Ju12
  of Abijah   CS13
  of Abijam   KF15
  of Ahaz   KS16; CS28
  of Ahaziah   KS9; CS22
  of Ahithophel   SS17
  of Amaziah   KS14; CS25
  of Asa   KS15; CS16
  of Asahel   SS2
  of Azariah   KS15
  of Baasha   KF16
  of bones of Joseph   Jos24
  of David   KF2

burial of Eleazar   Jos24
  of Elisha   KS13
  of Elon   Ju12
  of Gideon   Ju8
  of the head of Ishbosheth   SS4
  of Hezekiah   CS32
  of Jacob   Gen50
  of Jair   Ju10
  of Jehoahaz   KS13
  of Jehoash   KS14
  of Jehoiada   CS24
  of Jehoshaphat   KF22; CS21
  of Jehu   KS10
  of Jephthah   Ju12
  of Joab   KF2
  of Joash   KS12; CS24
  of Joram   KS8; CS21
  of Joshua   Jos24; Ju2
  of Josiah   Ks23; CS35
  of Jotham   KS15; CS27
  of Manasseh   KS21; CS33
  of Omri   KF16
  of Reheboam   KF14; CS12
  of Samson   Ju16
  of Samuel   SF25
  of Sarah   Gen23
  of Saul and his sons   SF31; SS21
  of Saul's bones   CF10
  of Solomon   KF11; CS9
  of Tola   Ju10
  of Uzziah   CS26
  place among the refuse of mankind   Is53
    of David   Ne3
    of Moses unknown   De34
buried at Topheth   Je7
carcase trodden under feet   Is14
common grave   Je26
corpse trampled underfoot   Is14
corpses lay like offal in the streets   Is10
day of wrath   Je26
dead and living, Aaron stood between   Nu16

death of Baasha   KF16
  of Balaam   Nu31
  of Bathsheba's son   SS12
  of Chilion   Ru1
  of David   KF2; CF29
  of Elah   KF16
  of Eleazar   Jos24
  of Eli and his sons   SF4
  of Elimelech   Ru1
  of Elisha   KS13
  of Ezekiel's wife   E24
  of Goliath   SF17; SS21
  of Hanamiah   Je28
  of Hazael   KS13
  of Hezekiah   KS20; CS32
  of Ishbosheth   SS4
  of Jehoahaz   KS13, 23
  of Jehoash   KS14
  of Jehoiada   CS24
  of Jehoiakim   KS24
  of Jehoram   KS9
  of Jehoshaphat   KF22; CS21
  of Jehu   KS10
  of Jezebel   KS9
  of Joab   KF2
  of Joash   KS12; CS24
  of Job   Job42
  of Jonathan   SF31; CF10
  of Joram   KS8; CS21
  of Joshua   Jos24; Ju2
  of Josiah   KS23; CS35
  of Jotham   KS15; CS27
  of Mahlon   Ru1
  of Malchishua   SF31; CF10
  of Manasseh   KS21; CS33
  of Menahem   KS15
  of Miriam   Nu20
  of Moses   De34
  of Nabal   SF25
  of Naboth   KF21
  of Nadab   KF15

death of Omri   KF16
  of Reheboam   KF14; CS12
  of Rezin   KS1
  of Samuel   SF25
  of Saul   SF31; SS1; CF10
  of Saul's sons   SS21
  of Sennacherib   CS32
  of Shallum   KS15
  of Sheba   SS20
  of Shimei   KF2
  of Shophach   CF19
  of Solomon   KF11; CS9
  of Tibni   KF16
  of Uriah   SS11
  of Uzza   CF13
  of Uzzah   SS6
  of Uzziah   CS26
  of Zechariah   KS15
  of Zimri   KF16
    shadow of   Job16; Ps23, 44, 107
    sleep the sleep of   Ps13
    terrors of   Ps55
    valley of the shadow of   Ps23
die, a time to   Ec3
  on the same day, Hophni and Phinhas shall   SF2
  you shall not rise from your bed; you will   KS1
died, on the seventh day the boy   SS12
dirge, harp tuned for a   Job30
  I will chant over the desert pastures   Je9
  sing it as a   E24
  teach one another this   Je9
  they will raise over you   E26ff
    those skilled in the   Am5
dirges and laments   E2
dust on his head   SF4
  sprinkle yourselves with   Mi1
earth on their heads   Ne9
embalmer   Am6
embalming of Jacob   Gen5o
  of Joseph   Gen50

fast, proclaim a   KF21
fasted, Ahab   KF21
  and lamented   Ju20
  for the child, David   SS12
  three days in mourning   SF31
  till evening   SS1, 3
fasting, weeping and beating of the breast   Est4
garden-tomb   CS33
  at Uzza   KS21
gash himself in mourning   Je16
grave, cruel as the   So8
  common   Je26
  dug yourself a   Ps49
  eternal home   Ps49
  I will ransom them from the power of the   Ho13
  jealousy as cruel as the   So8
  lying in the quiet   Job3
  never satisfied   Pro30
  set in the recesses of the abyss   E32
  sleep in the   Ps88
  swallow them alive as the   Pro1
  the silent   Ps94
  their jaws are a   Je5
  there is no knowledge or wisdom in the   Ec9
  those who go down to the   Ps22
  touching, cleansing after   Nu19
  whither thou goest   Ec9
  with the wicked, assigned a   Is53
graves, bring the bones out of their   Je8
  I will open your   E37
  keeping vigil crouching among   Is65
  those long in their   Is26
  took the bones from   KS23
hair, O Jerusalem, cut off your   Je7
  tear out their   E27
hanged himself, Ahithophel   SS17
hewed him out a sepulchure   Is22
keening, skilled in   Je9
lament for Abner   SS3
  for Jacob   Gen50

lament in thy book, enter my   Ps56
  of David   SS1
  of Jeremiah   CS35
  raise upon the high bare places   Je7
  teach your daughters the   Je9
  thrice told   Mi2
lamentation, a place of   Mi1
  the people broke into   SF11
  the princes broke into   SS13
  there shall be   Am5
  turn your songs into   Am8
lamented and fasted till evening   Ju20
  the people at Bethel   Ju21
laments and dirges   E2
  turned into dancing   E2
mourned for Absalom, David   SS13
  for Amnon, David   SS13
  for the man of God   KF13
  three whole weeks, Daniel   D10
mourner, go like a   Ps42
  professional   Je9
mourning, a time for   Ec3
  beat their breasts in   Je34
  cover upper lips in   E24
  enter not into the house of   Je16
  feast   Je16
  for Bathshua   Gen38
  for Jacob   Gen50
  for Joseph   Gen37
  for Sarah   Gen23
  for the offence   Ez10
  harp tuned to   Job30
  I will turn your pilgrim-feasts into   Am8
  in Jerusalem, a great   Z12
  Judah had finished   Gen38
  lay prostrate in   Ps35
  like doves of the valleys   E7
  of Abraham   Gen23
  of Egyptians   Gen50
  of Jacob   Gen37

10 DEATH, BURIAL AND MOURNING

mourning of Joseph   Gen50
  our dances turned to   La5
  patches on our head   Le21
  rites   Je16
  shave your head in   Je16, 48; Mi1
perish, if I   Est4
remembrance, day of   Ex12
rent clothes and dust on his head   SF4
  her robe, Tamar   SS13
  his clothes, Ahab   KF21
    David   SS1, 13
    Hezekiah   Ks19; Is37
    Job   Job1
    Josiah   KS22
    Mordecai   Est4
    the king of Israel   KS5
  his mantle in two, Elisha   KS2
  their clothes, all the people   SS3
sackcloth   Gen37; SS3; KF20ff; CF21; Ne9; Est4; Job16; Ps30, 35, 69; Is3, 15, 20f, 32, 37,
    50; Je6, 49; La2; E7, 27; D9; Joel1; Am8; Jon3
  Ahab put on   KF21
  and ashes, a bed of   Est4
    make his bed on   Is58
  as a bed   SS21
  clothed themselves in   La2
  David wore   CF21
  Israelites clothed in   Ne9
  Mordecai put on   Est4
  put on   SS3; E27; Je4
  round your waist   Am8
  sat in ashes and put on   Jon3
  stitched together   Job16
  the king wore   KS6
  they will go in   E7
  wrap yourself in   Je6
  wrapped himself in, Hezekiah   KS19; Is37
sepulchre, an open   Ps5; Je5
  hewed him out a   Is22
  of Ahaziah at Jerusalem   KS9
  of David   Ne3

NEW TESTAMENT

burying, anoint my body to the   Mk14
cave tomb   J11
cemetery for aliens   Mw27
Christian dead will rise   ThF4
cloud of death, those who live under   L1
corpse,vultures gather by the   L17
corpses, desert was strewn with their   PCF10
corruption, that his flesh never suffered   A2
cross, took the body of Jesus down from the   Mw27; Mk15; L23; J19
dead are raised to life, how the   L7
  but sleepeth, the maid is not   Mw9
  Christ was raised from the   PCF15
  first-born from the   Rev1
  four days, Lazarus has been   J11
  God raised him from the   A3
  in Christ shall rise first   ThF4
  judged according to their   Rev20
  raised from the   Mw17
  receiving baptism on behalf of the   PCF15
  resurrection of the   PCF15
  shall be raised incorruptible   PCF15
  standing before the throne   Rev20
  until the Son of Man had risen from the   Mk9
  will rise immortal   PCF15
death and mourning, an end to   Rev21
  at his command, him who had   LH2
  broken the power of   PTS1
  crossed over from   LJF3
  has no claim, on such the second   Rev20
  hold the keys of   Rev1
  in our body, wherever we go, we carry   PCS4
  in tasting, he should stand for us all   LH2
  is gain to me   PPs1
  it is written that the Messiah shall suffer   L24
  lake of fire is the second   Rev20
  last enemy to be abolished is   PCF15
  no longer under the dominion of   PR6
  obedient unto   PPs2
  of Herod   Mw2; A12
  of Jesus   Mw27; Mk15; L23; J19

death of Stephen   A7

  on a cross, accepted even   Pps2

  passed from, to life   J5; LHF3

  powers of, shall never conquer it   Mw16

  ready to go with you to   L22

  second   Rev2

  showed himself after   A1

  sinking towards   PE4

  stayed in Egypt until Herod's   Mw2

  the rider's name was   Rev6

  the wages of sin is   PR6

  thou wilt not abandon my soul to   A2

  unto death, the savour of   PCS2

  where is your victory?   PCF15

  will seek but not find   Rev9

death's domain, the keys of   Rev1

decay, though our outward humanity is   PCS4

depart, and be with Christ   PPs1

died and rose again, Jesus   ThF4

  as Christians, those who   ThF4

  every living thing in the sea   Rev16

  for us that we might live   ThF5

  Herod was eaten up with worms and   A12

  Jesus gave a loud cry and   Mw27; Mk15; L23; J19

  my daughter has just   Mw9

  of poisoned water, great numbers of men   Rev8

  Tabitha fell ill and   A9

  with these words he   L23

dropped dead at his feet, Sapphira   A5

   when Ananias heard these words he   A5

dust on their heads, threw   Rev18

dying we still live on   PCS6

follow me, and leave the dead to bury their dead   Mw8

foreigners, a burial place for   Mw27

funeral, met a   L7

  pall, black as a   Rev6

gave up the ghost, Jesus   Mw27; Mk15; L23; J19

grave, able to deliver him from the   LH5

  all who are in the, shall come out   J5

  rock   Mw27

grave, their throat is an open   PR3
grave-clothes   J11
graves opened, rocks split and   Mw27
  shall not suffer their dead bodies to be put in   Rev11
  unmarked   L11
grief will be turned to joy   J16
  you are plunged into   J16
grieve like the rest of men, you should not   ThF4
guard at the tomb of Jesus   Mw27; Mk15; L23; J19
Lazarus has fallen asleep, but I shall go and wake him   J11
let the dead bury their dead   Mw8; L9
linen wrappings   Mw27; Mk15; L23f; J19f
mourn with the mourners   PR12
mourning, turn your laughter into   LJ4
myrrh and aloes   J19;
    oil of   L7
perfumes, prepared spices and   L23f
raised from the dead, he has been   Mw28
  to life again, the dead are   L20
raises from the dead and gives them life   J5
raising of the dead, scoffed when they heard about   A17
realm of death, who does not love is in the   LJF3
resurrection, entered the Holy City after his   Nw27
  from the dead, finally arrived at the   PPs3
  of the dead   Mw22
rise from the dead, when good people   L14
    he must   J20
    on the third day   L24
    the Son of Man to   Mk8
rising from the dead, discussed among themselves   Mk9
sackcloth and ashes   Mw11
    sitting in   L10
  dressed in   Rev6
sepulchre, found the stone rolled away from the   Mw28; Mk16; L24; J20
  hewn in stone   L23
  in the garden was a new   J19
  laid him in a   A13
  of David   A2
  rolled a great stone to the door of the   Mw27; Mk15
  their throat is an open   PR3
  they came to the   Mk16

sepulchre, taken the Lord out of the   J20
  whitewashed   Mw23
sepulchres of the prophets, ye build the   L11
  of the righteous, garnish the   Mw2
shroud of Jesus   Mw27; Mk15; L23f; J19f
  of Lazarus   J11
sleep in death, those who   ThF4
spices, they prepared sweet   Mk16; L23f
spirit, he bowed his head and gave up his   Mw27; Mk15; L23; J19
  Lord Jesus, receive my   A7
stinketh, by this time he   J11
three days after being killed he will rise again   Mk9
tomb, already been four days in the   J11
  cut out of the rock   Mw27; Mk15; L23
  David's   A2
  found the stone rolled away from the   Mw28; Mk16; L24; J20
  laid him in a   A13
  Jesus laid in the   J19
  laid the body of John the Baptist in a   Mk6
  Mary came to the   J20
  of Jesus   Mw28
  they went into the   Mk16
tombs, came from among the   Mk5
  covered with whitewash   Mw23
  he stayed among the   L8
  of the prophets   M23; L11
  two men who came out from the   Mw8
touch me not; for I am not yet ascended   J20
vultures gather where the corpse is   L17
weep not; she is not dead, but sleepeth   L8
weeping, Mary stood at the tomb outside   J20
wormwood, water turned to   Rev8

11 *Divination and Witchcraft*

OLD TESTAMENT

11 DIVINATION AND WITCHCRAFT

diviners see false signs   Z10
  stripped of all   Is3
enchanters   Is3
  let none be found   De18
enchantments   KS17; CS33; Ls47
  Balaam did not seek   Nu24
En-dor, witch of   SF28
evil spirits would seize Saul   SF16ff
exorcists, Babylonian   D1, 5
false prophets, I frustrate them   Is44
  visions   E13
familiar, let none consult a   De18
  spirit   KS21ff; CS33; Is8, 19, 29
    a woman who has a   SF28
fate, god of   Is65
foretell the future month by month   Is47
fortune, in honour of   Is65
gash not yourselves   De14
ghost   Is8, 29
  of Samuel   SF28
ghosts and spirits   Is19
    got rid of those who called up   KS23; SF28
    who traffic with   SF28
  dealt with   CS33
  let none traffic with   De18
  resorting to   Le19ff
  Saul had resorted to   CF10
  who dealt with   KS21
ghostly form coming up from the earth   SF28
herbal magic   Job18
lots, the king of Babylon cast   E21
magic wrist-bands   E13
  pursuit of souls   E13
magicians   Is47
  Babylonian   D1, 4ff
  Belteshazzar, chief of the   D4
  of Darius   D5
  of Pharaoh   Ex7
necromancers, let none be found   De18
observing times,   CS33

11 DIVINATION AND WITCHCRAFT

oracle, oracles, Balaam uttered   Nu23ff
  Benjamites sought   Ju20
  concerning Jerusalem, Ezekiel's   E12
  from God   Is14
  of Damascus   Is17
  of Dumah   Is21
  of Egypt   Is19
  of Habbakuk   H1
  of Isaiah   Is13
  of Malachi   Ma1ff
  of Moab   Is15
  of Tyre   Is23
  of the Arabs   Is21
  of the Beasts of the South   Is30
  of the valley of vision   Is22
  of the wilderness   Is21
  of Zechariah   Z9, 12
  seal the   Is8
oracle-mongers   Is19
prognosticators, monthly   Is47
Samuel's ghost   SF28
seers and diviners shall blush for shame   Mi3
soothsayers   Is2, 57
  among you, there shall be no more   Mi5
  Babylonian   D2, 4ff
  do not listen to your   Je27, 29
  let none be found   De18
  like the Philistines   Is2
  thou shalt have no more   Mi5
soothsaying   KS21; CS33
  prohibition of   Le19
sorcerers, Babylonian   D2
  do not listen to your   Je27
  I will destroy your   Mi5
  I will testify against   Ma3
  let none be found   De18
  Pharaoh's   Ex7
sorceress   Is57
  Jezebel's   KS9
sorcery   CS33
  mistress of   Na3

spells, gift of unbinding   D5
  let none cast   De18
  magic   Is47
spirits, dealt with   KS21; CS33
  familiar   SF28; CS33
  resorting to   Le19ff
  those who call up   SF28
  traffic with, let none   De18
stargazers   Is47
staves in Zechariah's oracle   Z11
times, an observer of   De18
vision is false, their   E22
  oracle of Isaiah   Is13
wise men of Darius   D5
  women, do not listen to your   Je27
witch, let none be found   De18
  of En-dor   SF28
witchcraft   CS33
  I will cut off   Mi5
  mistress of   Na3
  of Jezebel   KS9
wizards   SF28; KS21ff; CS33; Is8, 19
  let none be found   De18
year for a day   E4

NEW TESTAMENT

astrologers from the east   Mw2
bewitched, you must have been   PG3
curious arts, those who used   A19
day of the Lord is already here, alleging the   ThS2
demonic wisdom   LJ3
devil's sign, conscience branded with the   PTF4
divination, damsel possessed with a spirit of   A16
doctrines inspired by devils   PTF4
elemental spirits   PG4
exorcism   A19
exorcists, some strolling Jewish   A19
fortunes, brought a large profit by telling   A16

great power of magic   A8

lie, signs and miracles of the   ThS2

magic books publicly burnt   A19

   great power of   A8

   Samaritans were carried away by Simon's   A8

   those who formerly practised   A19

magical arts, Simon practised   A8

   spells   A19

magician, Simon   A8

oracles, the ABC of God's   LH5

oracular utterance   A16

powers of the air, spiritual   PE2

sign, conscience branded with the devil's   PTF4

signs and miracles of the lie   ThS2

slave-girl who was possessed   A16

soothsaying, brought her masters much gain by   A16

sorcerer, Bar-Jesus by name   A13

sorcerers, outside are   Rev22

sorceries, bewitched them with   A8

sorcery and idolatry belong to the lower nature   PG5

   deceived all nations, your   Rev18

   Simon used   A8

spirit of divination   A16

   possessed by an oracular   A16

spirits, ability to distinguish true from false   PCF12

   elemental   PG4

we observed the rising of his star   Mw2

wisdom, demonic   LJ3

wise men, three   Mw2

witchcraft, work of the flesh   PG5

12 *Divinity*

Amen, God whose name is   Is65
Ancient of Days   D7
beauty of holiness   CS20
cherubim, enthroned on the   Is37
city of God   Ps46, 48, 87
  of the Lord   Is60
creator   Ps75, 78
  of the wide world   Is40
Eden, Garden of   Gen2; Joe2
  garden of God   E28, 31
    of the Lord   Is51
God, city of   Ps46, 48, 87
  house of   Ps42, 92
  know that I am   Ps46
  of gods, your god is indeed   D2
  of heaven   Jos2
  of Hosts   Je15
  of Israel   Je7f, 11ff
  of Jacob   Is2
  the mystery of   Job11
  whose name is Amen   Is65
heaven   Ps2, 11, 14, 19, 33, 36, 53, 57, 65, 76, 80, 85, 103, 113, 115, Ps123, 135f, 146;
          Pro30; Is24
  highest   Ps71, Is7
  of heavens   Ps148
  God of   Jos2
holiness, the beauty of   CS20
  the splendour of   Ps29
holy city   Is48
  dwelling   Ps46; Z2
  ground   Ex3
  habitation   Je25
  hill   Ps43, 48, 99; Is56ff
    flaunt your pride on my   Zp3
    God's   E28

holy hill, the lofty hill of Israel   E20
   who shall dwell in thy   Os15
   worship at his   Ps99
   Zion   Joe2
  is the Lord of Hosts   Is6
  land   Z2
  mountain   Ps78; Is66; Je31; Joe2ff; Ob1; Z8
   of Jerusalem   Is27
  name   Le24
  of Holies in Ezekiel's vision   E41ff
  One   Is40ff
   of Israel   Is10f; Je51
   of Jacob   Is29
  place   Ps68, 74, 150
   in Ezekiel's vision   E41ff
   Most   KF6ff; CS2ff; D9
  Spirit from me, take not thy   Ps51
  temple, my prayer reached thee in thy   Jon2
   the Lord from his   Mi1
   the lord is in his   H2
Immanuel   Is7ff
Jehovah   Ex3ff
  my name is   Ex6
  the Lord is   Is12, 26
  whose name is   Ps83
living God, sons of the   Ho1
Lord appeared in a burning bush   Ex3
  blessed be the   KF1
  cloud filling the house of the   KF8
  God of Abraham, Isaac and Israel   CS30
   of Hosts   Je5; Am3; Ho12; Am4ff, 9
   of Israel   KS22
  is witness   SF12
   of Hosts   SS5ff; KS3; CF17; Ps46, 48, 59, 69, 80, 84, 89; Is1f; Je6ff, 20, 23, 25,
     29ff, 48ff; Mi4; Na3; H2; Hg1ff; Z1ff; Mal1ff
  city of the   Ps48
  enthroned upon the cherubim   SF4
  God of Israel   Je16, 19, 27ff, 32ff, 39, 42f, 46, 48, 50; Zp2
  holy is the   Is6

Lord of hosts, praise the   Je33
   was with him   CF11
  seeth not as man seeth   SF16
  spirit of the   Ju3; CS15, 20, 24
  the God of heaven   Jon1
    of Israel   Je35
  the Holy One of Israel   Je50
  the mountain of the   Mi4
  worship the   Ps96
  your God consuming fire   De4
Lord's house   Joe3
  pillars of the earth are the   SF2
love which never fails   Is54
Messiah the Prince   D9
Mighty One of Jacob   Is49, 60
redeemer liveth, I know that my   Job19
refuge, the Lord is a sure   Na1
robe of light   Ps104
splendour of holiness   Ps29
still small voice   KF19
watcher, a Holy One   D4
Zion, building in bloodshed   Mi3
  city of   Ps48
  holy hill   Joe2
  nobody's friend   Je30
  palaces of   Ps48
  this is   Je30
  which abideth forever   Ps125
  which cannot be moved   Ps125

NEW TESTAMENT

Alpha and Omega, the First and the Last   Rev1f, 21f
ascended, I have not yet   J20
behold the Lamb of God   J1
Blessed One, son of the   Mk14
Christ of God, Peter answering said the   L9
  Jesus which is called   Mw27
  Son of the living God   Mw16
  they knew that he was   L4

12 DIVINITY

Christ, thou art the   Mk8
dayspring from on high hath visited us   L1
divine secret kept in silence for long ages   PR16
   Emmanuel, he shall be called   Mw1
  which being interpreted is, God with us   Mw1
eternal kingdom, full and free admission into the   LPS1
  life, harvest of   PG6
    I give them   J10
    inner spring welling up for   J4
    shall possess   J6
    the end is   PR6
    the righteous will enter   Mw25
Father, comes in the glory of his   Mk8
  heavenly   Mw5f
  in heaven, give praise to your   Mw5
    our   Mw6, 10
  into thy hands I commit my spirit   L23
  who sees what is secret   Mw6
First and Last, Alpha and Omega   Rev1f, 21f
glory as befits the Father's only son   J1
God alone is good   Mk10; L18
  descended like a dove, the Spirit of   Mw3
  has never been seen   LJF4
  is love   LJF4
  is with us   Mw1
  of Abraham, I am the   Mw22; Mk12
  of Isaac, I am the   Mw22; Mk12
  of Israel, give praise to the   Mw15
  of Jacob, I am the   Mw22; Mk12
  of love and peace will be with you   LCS13
  our Father   PCo1; ThS1
  the Father   PE1; PPs1; PTS1; ThF1; LPF1
  the Son of   Mw4
  they shall see   Mw5
  with us, Emmanuel   Mw1
Godhead, complete being of the   PCo2
God's chosen, for the sake of   Mw24
   One   J1
  Messiah   L9, 23
  secret is Christ himself   PCo2

12 DIVINITY

gospel of God's grace   A20

grace of God, hold fast to the   A13

heavenly Father gives to those who ask   Mw7

   it was revealed to you by my   Mw16

   the will of my   Mw7, 18

Holy Ghost   Mw1, 3, 8, 12, 28; Mk1; L10; J14; A2, 11; PR9, 14f; PCF6; PCS6; PE1;
      LH3, 6, 10

   kingdom of God is joy in the   PR14

   his name is   L1

   holy, holy, Lord God Almighty   Rev4

   One of God   Mk1; L4; J6

   who art and wast the   Rev16

Holy Spirit   Mw1, 3, 8, 12, 28; Mk1; L10; J14; A2, 11; PR9, 14f; PCF6; PCS6; PE1;
      LH3, 6, 10

   by the power of the   PR15

   he received from his Father the   A2

   he will baptize you with the   Mw3

   the indwelling   PCF6

   Jesus exulted in the   L10

I am with you always, to the end of time   Mw28

immortal, invisible, the only God   PTF1

Jesus Christ is in you   PCS13

King eternal, the only wise God   PTF1

   of kings and Lord of Lords   PTF6; Rev17, 19

Kingdom of God, accept like a child the   L18

   already come to power, before they have seen the   Mk9

   already come upon you   Mw12; L11

   belongs to such as these   Mk10

   flesh and blood can never possess the   PCF15

   is joy inspired by the Holy Spirit   PR14

   is like a mustard seed   L13

   is like this   Mk4

   is like yeast   L13

   is upon you   Mk1

   is within you   L17

  of heaven is theirs   Mw5

   is upon you   M4, 10

   keys of the   Mw16

   parables of the   Mw13

   the least in the   Mw11

Kingdom of heaven, to know the secrets of the   Mw13
Lamb of God   J1
light of the world, I am the   J9
Lord has risen, it is true   L24
   of lords and King of kings   PTF6; Rev17, 19
   your God, put to the test   Mw4
Lord's prayer   Mw6, 11
love, God-given   PCo1
many who are first will be last, and the last first   Mw19
Messiah   Mw1f, 16, 22, 27; Mk8, 14; L2, 4, 22; J1; A2, 8; PR9
   are you the   Mk14; L2
   from the patriarchs in natural descent sprang the   PR9
   Jesus called the   Mw1, 27
   proclaiming the   A8
   resurrection of the   A2
   Son of the living God   Mw16
   the Lord   L2
   they knew that he was the   L4
   we have found the   J1
   what is your opinion about the   Mw22
   you are the   Mk8
Most High God, Jesus Son of the   L8
   you will be sons of the   L6
mystery of the kingdom, given to know   Mw13; Mk4, 12; L8
One God, and one mediator between God and man   PTF2
   who sat upon the great white throne   Rev20
parable of the alert servants   L12
   bad servant   Mw24
   bags of gold   Mw25
   banquet   L14
   beam in the eye   Mw7
   beggar Lazarus   L16f
   birds   Mw6
   blind guides   Mw15, 23; L6
   bridegroom   Mw9; Mk2; L5
   bullying servant   L12
   buried treasure   Mw13
   bushel   Mw5
   camel and needle   Mw19
   candle   Mw5; L8, 11

resurrection, preaching about Jesus and the   A17
revelation of Jesus Christ   PG1
  of the glory of God   PCS4
Righteous One, appointed you to see the   A22
risen from the dead   PTS2
Saviour, Jesus Christ   Mw1
  of the world, we know that he is   J4
secret, kept the divine   PR16
  of Christ, I understand the   PE3
Son made heir to the whole universe   LH1
  of God, if you are indeed the   Mw4, 27
    Jesus Christ the   Mw4; Mk1
    shouting you are the   L4
    truly you are the   Mw14
  of Man coming on a cloud   L21
    is come to save that which was lost   Mw18
    is glorified, now the   J13
    is not come to destroy, but to save   L9
    seated at the right hand of God   Mk14
    standing at the right hand of God   Mk14; A7
    to be glorified, hour has come for thee   J12
    to stand in the presence of the   L21
    who do men say is the   Mw16
    will be seated at the right hand of God   L22
  of the Most High, he will bear the title   L1
soul, shepherd and guardian of your   LPF2
Spirit, divine dispensation of the   PCS3
  of God   Mw3, 12
    knows what God is, only the   PCF2
throne for ever and ever   LH1
  of God   LH12
  of grace, let us come boldly unto the   LH4
thou art my Son, my Beloved   L3
truly this man was a Son of God   Mk15
universal giver of life   A17
wise, to God only   PR16
Word of God is divine and active   LH4
  was with God at the beginning   J1
worship, it is God you must   Rev19
you did not choose me: I chose you   J15

13   *Dreams and Visions*

OLD TESTAMENT

13 DREAMS AND VISIONS

NEW TESTAMENT

alive for evermore, now I am   Rev1
angel appeared to Joseph in a dream   Mw1f
  of God, vision in which he saw an   A10
angels, seen a vision of   L24
Babylon the great, the mother of whores   Rev17
beast, all on earth will worship the   Rev13
  from the mouth of the   Rev16
  full of eyes   Rev4
  scarlet, in John's vision   Rev17
breastplates of brimstone and jacinth   Rev9
cataclysm in John's vision   Rev8
chain in his hand, a great   Rev20
clouds, Son of Man coming on the   Mw26; Mk14; L21
creature with a human face   Rev4
crown of life   Rev2
crowns lay before the throne   Rev4
Day of Christ   PPs1f
  of God will set the heavens ablaze   LPS3
  of the Lord comes like a thief in the night   ThF5
door in heaven   Rev4
dream, angel of the Lord appeared in a   Mw1f
  warned not to go back to Herod in a   Mw2
dreams lead them to defile the body   LJu1
  your old men shall dream   A2
earth lit up with the angel's splendour   Rev18
eyes all over, inside and out   Rev4
  flamed like fire   Rev1
Faithful and True, the rider's name was   Rev19
fallen is Babylon the great   Rev18
furnace, smoke rose like a great   Rev9
garden of God   Rev2
ghost, they thought they were seeing a   L24
glass, a sea of   Rev4
God's right hand, Stephen saw Jesus standing at   A7
hair on his head was white as snow-white wool   Rev1
heaven, new Jerusalem coming down out of   Rev3
horsemen of the Apocalypse   Rev6

horses had lions' heads   Rev9

key of David   Rev3

kingdom of the beast   Rev16

Lamb of God   Rev5ff, 14, 17

lake of fire in John's vision   Rev19f

last trump   PCF15

light from heaven, shined round him a   A9

  of day failed, a third of the   Rev8

living creatures covered with eyes   Rev4f

  one, the first and the last   Rev1

marriage of the Lamb   Rev19

martyrs, drunk on the blood of   Rev17

Mount Zion, vision of   Rev14

new heavens and a new earth   LPS3

  name known to none but him that receives it   Rev2

old order has passed away   Rev21

One who sits on the throne   Rev4

paradise of God, tree of life in the midst of the   Rev2

Pergamum, home of Satan   Rev2

pillar of cloud   PCF10

portent in heaven, great and astonishing   Rev15

revelation granted by the Lord   PCS12

  his secret was made known to me by a   PE3

  of John   Rev1ff

sea of glass shot with fire   Rev15

seal of the living God   Rev7

secret hidden for long ages   PCo1

serpent of old that led the world astray   Rev12

   the dragon, that   Rev20

shadows, with him there is no play of passing shadows   LJ1

sign from heaven, asked him for a   Mk8

  that heralds the Son of Man   Mw24

signs and portents, believe without seeing   J4

snakes, horses' tales like   Rev9

Son of God whose eyes flame like fire   Rev2

Spirit carried me away to a high mountain   Rev21

  I was caught up by the   Rev4

spirits, before his throne stood seven   Rev1ff

splendour of the Lord, possess for your own the   ThS2

synagogue, Satan's   Rev2f

throne in heaven   Rev4

trance, Peter fell into a   A10f

tree of life, the right to eat from the   Rev2

trump of God   ThF4

vengeance of the Lamb   Rev6

victory to our God who sits on the throne   Rev7

vision, Ananias had a   A9

  angel's intervention he thought was just a   A12

  Cornelius had a   A10

  heavenly, I did not disobey the A26

  in which he saw an angel of God   A10

  Lord spoke to Paul in a   A18

  of a Macedonian came to Paul   A16

  of angels, they had seen a   L24

  of the holy city   Rev21

  of the sheet full of creatures   A10f

  of the transfiguration   Mw17

  of their own, try to enter some   PCo2

  Peter puzzling over the meaning of the   A10

  realized that he had seen a   L1

  Saul had a   A9

  spiritual powers of wisdom and   PE1

visions granted by the Lord   PCS12

  your young men shall see   A2

voice, from the cloud came a   Mk9; L9

washed in the blood of the Lamb   Rev7

wedding day of the Lamb   Rev19

white stone   Rev2

wife of the Lamb   Rev21

winepress of God's wrath   Rev14

worthy is the Lamb that was slain   Rev5

14   *Farming*

OLD TESTAMENT

acres, vineyard of five   Is5
asses, Job owned five hundred   Job1
  latterly Job owned a thousand   Job42
  set in charge of   CF27
barley   Ex9; KF4; CF11; CS32; Job31; Is28; Je41; E4, 13, 45; Ho3; Joe1
  harvest   Ru1ff; SS21
  land of   De8
barn   Job39; Ps144; Pro3; Joe1; Hg2
  floor   KS6
  storage   CS32
basket for another's grapes   De23
  of first fruits   De26
beans   E4
blasting, plant disease   Ps105; Am4; Hg2
blight, black and red   Am4; Hg2
  curse of   De28
breeding, selective   Gen31
briars   Mi7; Na1
broadcast sowing   Is28
budding, vine   Is18
buffalo, domestic   E39; Am5
bull   Is10; Je50; E39, 43, 45
bullock   Is34, 65; Je50; E39, 43
  fatted   Is5; Je46
  unaccustomed to the yoke   Je31
bulls, herd of   Ps22
bushels, ten of seed shall return only a peck   Is5
calf   Is11, 27; E1; Am6; Mi6
  stall-fed   Je46
  unbroken to the yoke   Je31
calves released from a stall   Ma4
  stalled   SF6
camel pasture   E25
camels, in charge of   CF27
  Job owned 3000   Job1

147

camels, latterly Job owned 6000   Job42

cartwheels to crush corn   Is28

cattle   SS17; Ps49ff, 147ff; Ec2; Is11, 22, 46, 63; Je31; E14, 32, 34, 38; Ho5, 14; Joe1ff;
        Jon4; H3; Hg1; Z2, 13

  grew fat   Is5

  herds in the plains   CS26

  I had more than any   Ec2

  levied   Nu19

  lost to plague   Ps78

  of Jericho, slaughtered   Jos6

  pen   Ju5; Ho14

· stalls   Cs32

  vast herds of   Je49

chaff   Is5, 17, 29, 33, 40ff, 47

  as flames consumeth   Is5

  before the wind   Ls17, 41

  blown from the threshing floor   Ho13

  carried off   Is40

  driven by the desert wind   Je13

  fly lie   Is29

  gone like   Is47

  swept away like   D2

  vanish like   Zp2

churn   Pro30

cleaving wood   Ec10

corn   De33; CS31, 32; Job28; Ps4, 65, 72; Pro3; Is17, 55, 62; Je31; La2, 5; E36;
        Ho2, 7f, 10, 14; Joe2; Am8ff; Hg1ff; Z9, 12

  and wine, a land of   De33

  beginning to sprout   Am7

  contributions of   Ne10

  every hill shall wave with   Am9

  floor   Ho9

  grinding   La5

  land of   Is36

  late   Am7

  pluck ears to rub   De23

  ruined crop of   Joe1

  sprouting   Am7

  they shall eat your   E25

corn, those who bring in the Is62
  threshing Is21
  tithe of CS31
cornfields SF8
cottage in a vineyard Is1
cow Nu19; SF6; Job21; Is7, 11; Am4
  of Bashan Am4
crib, ox and ass Is1
crook, shepherd's Ps23; Mi7
crop will be scorched Is17
crops destroyed by eastern tribes Ju6
  early Ps72
  forgo the seventh year Ne10
  make the ground yield heavy E36
  rain falling upon Ps72
cucumbers, field of Is1
  plot of Je10
cummin, beaten out with a rod Is28
  scatter seed of Is28
cuttings, strike Is17
dealer, animal Z11
dew heavy at harvest time Is18
digged, not pruned nor Is5
dill seed sown broadcast Is28
ditch Is22
dovecote Is60
dresser of sycomore figs Am7
drought, curse of De28
  I have proclaimed Hg1
  scorching *Is25*
  summer Ps32
dunghill Ps113; La4; Am4
  straw trodden for a Is25
dyke Joe1
ear of corn Job24, Is17
ewe Ps78; Is7
  before the shearers Is53
  fresh from dipping So6
  lead to water Is40
  shorn So4
fallow, break up your Ho10

fallow, land in seventh year to lie   Ex23; Le25

fan, threshing   Is41

fanner, winnowing   Je51

farm   Pro24

  land from the wilderness   Je4

  of Joshua   SF6

farmer   CS26; Je14; Am1, 5

farmers, prosperous, utterly ruined   Is16

farming villages, tithes of   Ne10

farms, they made off to their   Ne13

fatling   Is11; E39

fatten the flock for slaughter   Z11

fence   Ps26

  vineyard   Is5

field   Pro24; Joe2

  all the valley and every   Je31

  edges, harvest left for the poor   Le19f

  fuller's   KS18

  of barley   SS14

  of cucumbers   Is1

  of lentils   SS23

  ruined   Joe1

  to field, you who join   Is5

fields   Ps50, 107, 144; So7; Is32

  flocks in her green   E34

  invaders shall devour their   Ho5

  mortgaged   Ne5

  of Heshbon   Is16

  parcelled out   Mi2

  ploughed   Je26; Mi3

  sale and purchase of   Je32

  sow   Ps107

  teeming life of the   Ps50

figs killed by heavy rain   Ps78

fig-tree   Mi4; Na3; H3; Z3

fig-trees, a land of   De8

first-born of flocks and herds   De12

first-fruits, sacrifice of   De26

fitch beaten out with a staff   Is28

  mixed in a bowl   E4

flax   Ex9, Jos2, Is19; Ho2
flock   Is13, 17, 40; Je5ff, 25, 49ff; E24ff, 34, 45; Joel; Am6ff; Jon3; Mi5, 7; Z10ff
  round it up, with no man to   Is13
  where is my beautiful   Is13
flocks   Job24; Ps77, 79ff, 100, 107; Pro27; So1; Ho5; Zp2
  a couching place for   E25
  a refuge to fold   Je33
  as a shepherd watches his   Je31
  a pasture, scattered   Je10
  carry off their   Je49
  graze their   Is14
  herds and   SF8, 27, 30
  I had more than any   Ec2
  in charge of   CF27
  of Kedar   Is60
  scattered   Je23, 50
  shall couch there   Zp2
flock-master   Je14, 25; Na3
fodder, well-seasoned   Is30
fold bereft of its flock   H3
folds, goat   Ps50
  sheep   Nu32
forest of the Perizzites, clear for yourselves   Jos17
fruit of your land, bless the   De7
  they shall eat thy   E25
  trees   Ne9; Ps148
    planted all kinds   Ec2
fruitful land turned into salt waste   Ps107
furrow, plough   Ps129
  water   Ps65
furrows of the fields   Ho10
garden   So4ff; Is66
  by a river   Nu24
  close-locked   So4
  lodge in a   Is1
  of nut trees   So6
  of Uzza   KS21
  the king's   KS25
  royal   Est7
  Persian court   Est1

garden, plant in exile   Je29
  plant your   Is17
  vegetable, irrigated your land like a   De11
  watered, like a   Je31
  well-watered   Is58
gardens   KS5
  laid waste   Am4
  make   Am9
  orchards and, I made   Ec2
garner   Joe1
gather stones, a time to   Ec3
glean, in the cornfields   Ru2
  leaving loose ears   Le19f
gleaners, reserve edges of harvest for poor   Le19f
gleanings   Is17; Je49; Ob1
  last of the vintage   Mi7
goat   Gen30; Ps50, 66; Pro27, 30; So4, 6; Is13; E27, 34, 39, 43
grain   Joe2
  beat out the   Is27
  land of   KS18; Is36
  making offerings of   Ex29ff
  parched   Jos5
  sift but get no   Je12
  stored   Gen41
  this year you shall eat shed   Is37
  to feed your foes   Is62
granary   Pro3; Je50; Joe1
grapes, eat another's   De23
  gleaning   Is17, 24
  leave gleanings of   De24
  treading   Je25; Joe3; Mi6
  you shall tread, but not drink the wine of   Mi6
grape-gatherers   Je6, 49; Ob1
grass   Ps37, 58, 72, 90, 102f, 147; Is51
  clothes the hills with   Ps147
  ephemeral   Ps103
  fade like   Ps90
  field, in every man's   Z10
  mower   Ps129
  new   Pro27

grass, fresh as spring   Is66
  withered   Ps102
grazing flock which stampedes   Mi2
  good, in Midianite country   Nu32
  ground, flocks on   E34
  they shall find on the dunes   Is49
grinding meal   Ec12
grub, curse of the   De28
hamlets with surrounding fields   Ne11
harness, ox   SS24
harnessed two milch cows to the wagon   SF6
harrow   SS12
  the furrows   Job39
  the land   Ho10
harvest   Pro10, 12, 20, 25ff; Is16, 18, 23; Je5, 8; Ho2, 6; Joe2ff; Am4; H2
  barns for   CS32
  blasted   Hg1ff
  dew heavy at   Is18
  disappointed of their   Je12
  first fruits of   Je2
  fixed seasons of   Je5
  land shall yield its   Ps85
  leave a swathe for the gleaners   De24
  lost to drought   Joe1
    to locusts   Ps78
  offering the rites of   Le23
  rain at   Pro26
  reap a fruitful   Ps107
  snow at   Pro25
  thanksgiving   Ex23
  time   Je50ff
harvesters   Ps129; Is16f; Je48
harvesting wheat   SF6
harvestman   Je9
hay   Pro27; Is15
heath, flock that dwells on meadow and   Mi7
  rough   Je26; Mi1, 3
hedge   Ps80; Je49; E13; Na3
  of thorns   Ho2
  whoso breaketh a   Ec10

heifer   Is15; Je46, 48, 50; Ho4, 10
heifer on a rope   Is5
herb garden   KF21
herbs of every field wither   Je12
  shrivel all their green   Is42
herds   Ps107; Pro27; So1; Je5, 31; Ho5; Jon3; H3
  divided   Gen32
  in charge of   CF27
  laden with great   Jos22
  vast   Je49
herdsman, herdsmen   SF21; Am1, 7
  ancestor of all   Gen4
hoed, neither pruned nor   Is5
homesteads   Ps79
honey, tithe of   CS31
hurdle   Job18
husbandman   KS25; Je32, 51ff; Joe1; Am5; Z13
hut, shepherd's   So1; Zp2
irrigate a grove of growing trees   Ec2
keeper of the royal forests   Ne2
kids   So1; Is11; E43
  shall graze broad acres   Is5
kine of Bashan   Am4
lamb   Gen30; Ps144; Pro27; So4, 6; Is11, 16, 65; E27, 39, 45; Ho4; Am6
  carry in his bosom   Is40
lambs to the slaughter   Je51
land, ancestral, Naboth's vineyard   KF21
  littered with stones   KS3
  on which you had not laboured   Jos24
lentil   E4
lodge in a garden   Is1
logging raft   KF5
locusts   KF8; CS6; Job39; Ps78, 105; Je46, 51; Joe1ff
  curse of   De28
  east wind bringing   Ex10
  plague of   Ex8, 10
  swarm hatched out   Am7
  west wind dispersing   Ex10
mattock   SF13; Is2, 7; Joe3; Mi4
meadow   Ps65; Is16

meadow, graze flocks in my   Is14
  lambs in a broad   Ho4
meadows of Moab   Je48
mildew   Am4; Hg2
millet   E4
mower, grass   Ps129
mowing   Am7
muzzle the threshing ox, do not   De25
nursery-ground   E17
nut trees, garden of   So6
oil, pressing olive   Job24
olive   Ho14; Am4
  crop   H3
  drop, the curse of   De28
  groves   De6
    mortgaged   Ne5
    which you did not plant   Jos24
  oil, pressing   Job24
  tree   Z4
    beaten and stripped   Is24
    do not strip the   De24
  yards   SF8; Ne5
olives, a land of   De8
  you shall press, but not use the oil   Mi6
orchard, orchards   H3
  pomegranate   So4
  and gardens, I have made   Ec2
  of Heshbon   Is16
ox goad   Ju3
 ploughing   KF19
oxen   KF1, 4, 8, 19; Ne5; Ps8, 66; Is7, 22, 30; E1; Am6
  Job owned five hundred yoke of   Job1
palm trees, vale of   De34
pastor   Je1
pasture   Ps23, 37, 65, 83; Is32; Je49ff; La1; Ho13; Joe1ff; Am1
  broad   Is30
  cattle, in the vale of Achor   Is65
  desert   Je9
  each grazing his own strip of   Je6
  flocks at   Je10

pasture by the sea   Zp2
  in the desert sands   Is49
  perennial   Je49f
  ravaged rich   Z11
  shall be in all high places   Is49
  wild, have all dried up   Je23
pastured fat bullocks   Is5
peck, ten bushels shall return only a   Is5
pen, cattle   Ho14
pests to destroy your produce   Ma3
pestilence, beasts killed by   Ps78
  of camels   Ex9
  of cattle   Ex9
  of horses   Ex9
  of sheep   Ex9
plant anew the waste land   E36
plantations   E34
  watered by the furrows   E17
plot of cucumbers   Je10
plough, plow   Ju14; Pro20ff
  for the sowing   Is28
  furrows   Ps129
  with oxen   Am6
ploughed field   J26; Mi3
  heaped stones beside a   Ho12
ploughlands of Gilead   Am1
ploughman   Ps129; Is28, 61; Je14, 51; Am9
ploughing ox   KF19
ploughshare, plowshare   SF13; Is2; Joe3; Mi4
pomegranates, a land of   De8
  orchard of   So4
press, oil   Job24
  wine   Job24; Pro3
produce lost to grubs   Ps78
provender, clean   Is30
pruned nor hoed, neither   Is5
pruning hook, pruning knife   Is2, 18; Joe3; Mi4
rain at harvest   Pro26; Ps72
rains, failed   Joe1
rams   Gen30; E27, 34, 39, 43, 45; Is5; Je49f; Mi6

sheep walk   E25
  without a shepherd, Israel is like   CS18
sheepcote   SS6
sheepfold   Ju5; SF24; CS32; Ps68, 78; Is13; Je50; Mi1; Zp2
sheepmaster   KS3
shed in a field of cucumbers   Is1
shepherd   Gen4; Job24; Ps23, 28, 49, 78ff, 95, 100; So1; Is13; Je2, 6, 10, 12, 25, 31, 43,
          49ff; E34; Ho12; Am1, 3; Mi5, 7; Na3; Zp2; Z10ff
  Abel was a   Gen4
  abomination in Egypt, held to be   Gen46
  boys, turn my hand against   Z13
  foreigners shall serve as   Is61
  who lets the flock scatter   Je23
  worthless, who abandons his sheep   Z11
shepherdess, Rachel was a   Gen29
shepherd's hut   KS10; Zp2
sickle   SF13; Je50; Joe3
  for another's corn   De23
sift but get no grain   Je12
sifting wheat   SS4
slaughter, fatten stock for   Z11
sledge, threshing   Is28
slips of cedar set in soil   E17
  set   Is17
snow at harvest   Pro25
soil, Uzziah loved the   CS26
sow but not reap, you shall   Mi6
  thy seed in the morning   Ec11
sowed much but reaped little   Hg1
sower in Babylon, every   Je50
sowing seed   Am9
    broadcast   Is28
spelt   Ex9; E4
spring rain failed   Je3
stable   KF110; E25
stall, ass knows its master's   Is1
  calves'   Am6; Ma4
  cattle   CS32; Job39; H3
stall-fed calves   Je46
sterile land   KF9

vine   Gen9, 49; Ju9; Nu20; KF4; KS4, 18; Ps78, 80, 105, 128; Job15; So6ff; Je6, 8, 31, 48;
        Is1, 3, 5, 7, 16, 18, 24, Is27, 32, 34, 36ff, 61; La2; E15, 17, 19; Joe1f; Mi1, 4;
        Na2; H3; Hg2; Z3, 8; Ma3
    choice red   Je2
    leaf withers from the   Is34
vine-dressers   KS25; CF27; CS26; Is61; Je39, 52; Joel
vines, aliens shall tend your   Is61
    killed by hailstones   Ps78
    land of   De8
    of Sibmah   Is16
    place for planting   Mi1
    red   Is5
    sicken   Is24
vineyard   SF8; KF4, 21; KS5, 18; CF27; Ne9; Job24; Pro24, 32; So1, 7ff; Is3, 5, 16, 18,27;
        Ho2; Je12, 31, 35; Am5, 9; Mi1
    buying and selling a   Je32
    by the waterside   E19
    cottage in a   Is1
    five acres of   Is5
    mortgaged   Ne5
    Naboth's   KF21
    new, unused   De20
    no second crop   De22
    Noah's   Gen9
    of En-gedi   So1
    shelter in a   Is1
    wall of a   Pro24
vineyards at Timnath   Ju14
    derelict   Is5
    I planted   Ec2
    laid waste   Am4
    land of   Is36
    of red wine   Is27
    pillaged their   Na2
    plant   Ps107; Is37; E28
        but shall not drink the wine of   Zp1
    planted pleasant   Am5
    which you did not plant   De6; Jos24
vintage   Je48; Ho2; Joel; Am9
    last gleanings of the   Mi7

vintagers   Je6, 49; Ob1
walls, vineyard   Pro24; Is5
watering herds at time of drought   KF18
watermelons   Nu11
wheat   Ex9; SF12; KF5; CS2; Pro27; So7; Is28; Je12, 31, 41; E4, 27, 45; Joe1; Am5, 8
  harvest   SF6, 12
    time of   Ju15
  land of   De8
  men sow, and reap thistles   Je12
winepress   KS6; Job24; Is63; La1; Joe3; Z14
  hewed out of stone   Is5
  of Moab   Is16
winnowers   Je51
  barley   Ru3
  wind too strong   Je4
woodman   CS2; Ps74
wool production   KS3; Is1, 51; D7; Ho2
yield, a mere gallon from five acres of vineyard   Is5
  a mere peck from ten bushels of seed   Is5
yoke   KF19; La1, 5; Mi2; Na1
  of iron   De28
  of oxen   Je51
  ox and ass separately   De22
  ploughing   Ho10f

NEW TESTAMENT

barley   J6
  measures of   Rev6
barn, barns, collect the wheat into my   Mw13
  ravens have no   L12
  pull down and build greater   L12
brushwood   Mk11
bull   LH9f
calf   LH9
  fatted   L15
cattle, dealers in   J2
  fattening yourselves like   LJ5
  feeding   L17

chaff, he will burn on a fire   Mw3; L3
corn   Mw12f; Mk4; L6, 12, 17; A7, 27; PTF5, 9
  ears of   Mk2, 4; L6
  in Egypt   A7
  ox that treadeth out the   PCF9; PTF5
  storehouses for   L12
  two women grinding   L17
  was scorched   Mk4
cornfield, cornfields   Mk2; L6
  Jesus went through the   Mw12
crop, farmer has first claim on the   PTS2
  his land may yield precious   LJ5
  I sent you to reap a   J4
  is heavy, but labourers are scarce   Mw9f
  send labourers to harvest his   L10
crops in their seasons, he sends you   A14
  land yielded heavy   L12
  once more the land bore   LJ5
darnel sowed among the wheat   Mw13
ditch   Mw12, 15
  both fall in the   L6
dung and dig about the fig tree   L13
  heap, useless on the   L14
  hill   L14
ears of corn, began to pluck   Mk2
    plucking   L6
fan, winnowing   Mw3; L3
farm   Mk6; L9, 15
  elder son was out on the   L15
farmer   PTS2
  can only wait in patience   LJ5
fat beasts   Mw22
fatling   Mw22
fatted calf   L15
field, darnel in the   Mw13
  flower of the   LPF1; LJ1
  if a man is in the   Mk13
  is the world   Mw13
  like treasure buried in a   Mw13
  lilies of the   Mw6; L12

162

reapers, unpaid   LJ5
reaping, sparse sowing, sparse   PCS9
seed fell along the footpath, some   Mw13; Mk4; L8
  fell on stony ground, some   Mw13; Mk4; L8
  for sowing, he who provides the   PCS9
  I planted the   PCF3
shearer   A8
sheep   Mw9, 12, 15; L17; J2, 5, 10, 21; A8; PR8; Rev18
  a servant minding   L17
  and cattle, cargoes of   Rev18
  dealers in   J2
  fold   J10
  for slaughter   PR8
  he calls by name   J10
  hears his voice   J10
  lost   Mw15
  market   J5
  of my flock   J10
  straying like   LPF2
  tend my   J21
  which fell into the ditch   Mw12
  without a shepherd   Mw9
shepherd   Mw2, 9, 25f; Mk6, 14; L2; L10; A20; LPF2, 5; LJu1
  I am the good   J10
  of my people Israel   Mw2
  of the church   A20
  of the sheep, great   LH13
  the Lamb will be their   Rev7
sickle   Mk4; Rev14
slaughter, the day for   LJ5
slaughtered, led like sheep to be   A8
sow and reap and store in barns   Mw6
  birds of the air do not   Mw6
  bountifully, reap bountifully   PCS9
  reap what you did not   L19
  seed in the field of his lower nature   PG6
sower   Mk4; J4
  parable of the   Mk4
  went out to sow   Mw13
sowing, sparse reaping, sparse   PCS9

15 *Feasts, Fasts and Festivals*

OLD TESTAMENT

ablution ritual   Ex30ff
abstention from wine and strong drink   Nu6
abstinence, appoint a day of   Joe1f
acclamation, day of   Nu29
anointing, rites of   Ex25ff; Le8
appointed seasons, commemoration of   Ne10; La2
assemblies   Is1
assembly, citizens in   Mi6
atonement, day of   Le24
banquet, Esther's   Est5ff
  in honour of Esther   Est2
  is set out   Is21
  of Ahasuerus   Est1
  of Balshazzar   D5
  of Nabal   SF25
  royal, for the women   Est1
banqueting hall, Balshazzar's   D5
blood not to be eaten   Le3, 17
bread from heaven   Ne9
ceremonial, sacred   Am5
ceremonies   Is1
circumcise your hearts   De10, 30; Je4
circumcised, Israeli people again   Jos5
  those born in the wilderness   Jos5
circumcision for every male   Ex13
  of Moses   Ex4
  of Shechem's men   Gen34
  rite of   Le12
  sign of   Gen17
consecrated from birth   Ju13
convocation, holy   Le24
danced for Joy, David and all Israel   SS6
dancers of King Saul   SF18
day of atonement   Le24
  of acclamation   Nu29

drunk, David made Uriah   SS11

fast, Daniel's three-week   D10

    day, read the words of the Lord on the   Je36

    earth on their heads for the   Ne9

    people of Ninevah ordered a public   Jon3

    proclaim a solemn   Joe1f

    the Israelites assembled for a   Ne9

    why do we   Is58

fasted all day, confessing   SF7

fasting, Daniel spent the night   D6

   in sackcloth and ashes   D9

   in the fifth and seventh months   Z7

   in the fourth, seventh and tenth months   Z8

fatted calves, feasting on   Am6

feast, Absalom prepared a   SS13

  annual appointed   CS8

  at the hill shrine   SF9

  days, I despise your   Am5

    ritual of   E46

  David gave for Abner   SS3

  for seven days they kept the   Ne8

  for the Aramaean army   KS6

  instead of mourning   Is22

  live in leafy arbours during the   Ne8

  of fatlings   Is25

  of Hezekiah   CS8

  of Job's sons   Job1

  of new moons   SF20; KS4; CS2, 8; Ez3; Ne10; Ps81; Is1, 66;   E45f; Am8

  of tabernacles   CS8

  of the Passover   Le23; Nu28; De16; Jos5; CS7, 30, 35; Ez6; E45

  of the seventh month   Ne8

  of unleavened bread   CS8, 30, 35

  of weeks   CS8

  on the fourteenth and fifteenth day of Adar   Est9

  pilgrim   Ex5, 10, 23; Le23; Nu28ff; De31; KF8, 12;CS5, 8, 30, 35; Ez3, 6; Ps81; Is29; E45; Ho9; Am5, 8; Z14; Ma2

  Zion, city of our solemn   Is33

feasts, all the set   Ez3

  appointed   Is1, 5

NEW TESTAMENT

anoint with oil in the name of the Lord   LJ5
banquet, Herod's   Mk6
  not one of those who were invited shall taste my   L14
baptism , accepted John's   L7
  an appeal made to God   LPF3
  as a token of repentance   A13, 19
  in the one Spirit   PCF12
  Noah's flood prefigured the water of   LPF3
  of Jesus Christ   Mw3
  of John the Baptist   Mk1; L20
    was it from God, or from man?   Mk11
    Whence was it   Mw21
  of the doctrine of   LH6
  on behalf of the dead   PCF15
  that I am baptized with   Mw20
  they all received   PCF10
  you were buried with him in   PCo2
baptize in the name of the Father   Mw28
  in water   J1
  you with the Holy Spirit and with fire   L3
baptized, bishop must not be newly   PTF3
  in the river Jordan   Mw3
  Jesus, John the Baptist   Mw3
  many Corinthians were   A18
  Saul was   A9
  the eunuch, Philip   A8
  when Jesus too had been   L3
  with water, John   A1
birthday, Herod's   Mk6
blood, abstain from   A15, 21
bread is my own flesh   J6
circumcise on the sabbath   J7
circumcised, is happiness confined to the   PR4
  they must be   A15
  those who were not   A15
  Timothy out of consideration for the Jews   A16
circumcision, Christ's way of   PCo2

Sabbath, day before the   Mk15
   daybreak after the   Mw28; Mk16, forbidden on the   Mw12
   he began to teach on the   Mk1
   he was not only breaking the   J5
   observance of the   PCo2
   pray it may not be the   Mw24
   rest awaits the people of God   LH4
   Son of Man is sovereign over the   Mw12; L6
   was a day of great solemnity   J19
   was made for man, not man for the Sabbath   Mk2
   why are they doing what is forbidden on the   Mk2
   you are not allowed to carry your bed on the   J5
seats of honour in the synagogues   L11
shave their heads in ritual purification   A21
strangled, abstain from anything that has been   A15, 21
supper in Jesus's honour   J12
   last   Mk14; L22
   Lord's   PCF11
   Passover   Mw26; Mk14; L22
sworn not to eat or drink   A23
Tabernacles, feast of   J7
table, may eat and drink at my   L22
take this and eat, this is my body   Mw26; Mk14
this is my blood, the blood of the covenant   Mw26; Mk14
Unleavened Bread, festival of   Mw26; L22; A12, 20
wedding feast is ready   Mw22
Whitsuntide   PCF16

16 *Food, Drink and Spices*

allowance of food, daily   Ne5; Je40; E4; D1
almond   Je1
apple   So2, 7ff; Joe1
apricot   So2, 7
banquet of Adonijah   KF1
  of Nabal   SF25
banqueting house   So2
barley   Ex9; SS14, 17; KF4; CF11; CS2; Job31; Ls28; Je41; E4, 13, 45; Ho3; Joe1
  cake   Ju7; E4
  loaf   KS4
beans   SS17; E4
bitter-apples   KS4
blood, on no account eat   De12
  they ate meat with the   SF14
bread   SF16f, 21, 28; SS6; KS4; CF16; Ne5; Job42; Ps14, 37, 53, 78, Ps80, 102, 104,
          127,132ff; Pro4, 25, 28; Ec9; Is3ff, 55, 58; Je5, 37ff, 41ff, 52; La1, 4f; E4f, 12ff,
          24, 44ff; D10; Ho2, 9; Am4, 8; Hg2; Ma1
  alone, man cannot live by   De8
  bakes on the fire   Is44
  brought by ravens   KF17
  clean and unclean   E4
  corn   Is28
  daily   Ps105
  from heaven   Ex16; Ps105
  land of   Is36
  of angels   Ps78
  of the Presence   Ex25ff, 35
  shall not lack   Is51
  unleavened   E45
broth   Gen25; Ju6; KS4; E24; Hg2
butter   SS17; Job20; Ps55; Pro30; Is7
  in a lordly dish   Ju5
butter-cake, manna tasted like   Nu11

cake   SS13; CF23; Ho7
  baked on hot stones   KF19
  barley   E4
  crescent   Je7, 44
  fig   CF12
  of dried figs   SF25
  of manna   Nu11
  of unleavened bread   SF28
  make a small   KF17
  Nazirite offering of   Nu6
  raisin   CF12, 16; Ho3
  unleavened   Le23; Ju6
    and bitter herbs   Nu9
cheese   SF17; SS13; Job10
corn   De33; KS4, 18; CS31ff; Job28; Ps4, 65, 72; Pro3; Ne5; Is17, 55, 62; Je31; La2, 5;
      E36; Ho2, 7f, 10, 14; Joe2; Am8ff; Hg1ff; Z9, 12
  ears in the husk   KS4
  they shall eat your   E25
  those who bring in the   Is62
cracknels   KF14
cream   Job20
cream-cheese   SF17
crops destroyed by eastern tribes   Ju6
cucumber   Nu11; Is1; Je10
curds   SS17; Job20; Is7
dates   So7
donkeys head as siege food   KS6
dough   SS13; Ne10; E44
  kneading   Je7; Ho7
"doves' dung", locust beans   KS6
drink, strong   De14
drunk, Ben-hadad became   KF20
  king Elah became   KF16
  Nabal became   SF25
  Noah became   Gen9
  with a bitter draught   Ps60
drunkards   Ps69
fat not to be eaten   Le3
fatted calf   SF28; Am6
feast of Abimelech   Gen26

176

16 FOOD, DRINK AND SPICES

loaf, barley   KS4
  daily ration of one   Je37
locust beans   KS6
manna ceased at Gilgal   Jos5
  like coriander seed   Nu11
  rained down   Ps78
  tasted like butter-cake   Nu11
  they called the food   Ex16
marrow, fatling   Is25
meal   SF1, 28; SS17; KF4; KS4; CF12; Is47; E27
  women grinding   Ec12
meat   SS6; Ps78, 106; Pro30; E24
  brought by ravens   KF17
  "give us to eat"   Nu11
  portion of   CF16
  roast   Is44
  rules for eating   De12
  with the blood in it   SF14
melon   Nu11
milk   Job10, 29; So4ff; Is7; Je11, 32; La4; E20, 25; Joe3
  and honey, flowing with   Ex3; Le20; Nu13; De11, 26ff
  churning of   Pro30
  goat's   Pro27
  mother's, do not boil a kid in its   De14
  sheep's   E34
  skin full of   Ju4
millet   E4
mulberry   Is40
nitre upon vinegar   Pro25
nuts   So6
oil   KF17; SF9, 10, 16; KS18; CF12; CS2, 31ff; Ez6; Ne5, 10; Job24, 29; Ps55, 109;
      Pro21; Is39, 57, 61; Je31, 40ff; E27, 45; Ho2, 12; Joe1ff; Am6; Mi6; Hg1f
olive   SF8; Ps128; Ho14; H3; Hg2
  oil   Ex30ff; KF5; E16
  pounded   Ex27f; Nu28
onions   Nu11
parched grain   SS17
pastry   CF23
pigs, those who eat the flesh of   Is66
poison of dragon is their vine   De32

pomegranate   SF4; So4, 6, 8; Je52; Joel; Hg2
  juice   So8
pottage   Gen25; KS4; Hg2
  sold his birthright for a mess of   Gen25
provender and straw for the asses   Ju19
pulse   D1
raisins   SF30; KF14; CF12, 16; So2
  cake of   SS6; Ho3
  clusters of   SS16
  ration, daily   Ne5; Je40; E4; D1
rats, those who eat the flesh of   Is66
salt   KS2, 14; Ez4, 6ff; Job6, 32; E43, 47
  sowed the site with   Ju9
shewbread   Ex25ff; Nu4
skin full of milk   Ju4
spice   KF10; KS20; CS9, 32; Ps75; So4f, 8; Is39; Je6; E24
  choicest   E27
  golden   Is60
  powdered   So3
spices, aloe   Ps45; So4
  balm   Gen37; E27
  balsam   Gen43; Ex25ff; So6; Ez7
  calamus   Ex30; So4; E27
  camphire   So1, 4
  caper bud   Ec12
  cassia   Ex30f; Ps45; Pro7; E27
  cinnamon   Ex30f; Pro7; So2, 4
  coriander seed   Nu11
  cummin   Is28
  dill   Is28
  frankincense   So3ff
  henna   So4, 7
  myrrh   Gen37, 43;
    a bunch of   So1
  saffron   So4
  spikenard   So1, 4
spice-bearing mountains   So8
spiced wine   Ps75; Pro9; So7f; Is65
spelt   E4
starvation, curse of   De28

stew   E24

stewing meat   SF2

strong drink, addiction to   Is28

summer fruits   SS16; Is16; Je40; Am8; Mi7

sweet cane   So4; Is43; Je6; E27

swine's flesh, eating   Is65

syrup   KF14; Ps19; So4f; E27

thirst, curse of   De28

topers, confirmed   Is28

unleavened cakes   Le8; Jos5

  bread   Ex12; KS23

vegetables to eat, give us only   D1

venison for Isaac   Gen27

vinegar   Nu6; Ps69; Pro10, 25

  shall drink no   Nu6

water to drink, give us only   D1

watermelon   Nu11

wax   Ps68, 97

wheat   Ex9; SF12; SS17; KF5; CS2; Ez6; Pro27; So7; Is28; Je12, 31, 41;E4, 27, 45; Joe1;
      Am5, 8

  flour   Ps81

wine   Gen9; Nu18; De14; Ju13; SF1, 10, 16, 25; SS6, 16; KS6, 18; CF9, 12, 27; CS2, 31ff;
      Ez6; Ne2, 5, 10, 13; Est1; Ps4, 60, 75, Ps78; Pro3ff, 20ff, 31; Is5, 22, 24, 27ff,
      36, 49, 51,56, 65; Ec9; So1, 4ff, 7; J13, 23, 25, 31, J35, 40, 48, 51; La2; E27, 44;
      D5, 10; Ho2f, 7, 9; Joe1ff; Am2, 9; Mi2; H2; Zp1; Hg1ff; Z9ff

  addicted to   Is28

  daily allowance of   D1

  drink with rejoicing   De14

  let foreigners drink the new   Is62

  mixed with water   Is1

  mulled   So8

  offering of   Le23

  on the lees, well refined   Is25

  produce of the press   Nu18

  prohibited in the tent of the Presence   Le10

  settled on its lees   Je48

  spiced   Ps75; Pro9; So7f; Is65

  wash robes in   Gen49

  well matured, strained clear   Is25

16 FOOD, DRINK AND SPICES

wine-cellar   CF227
wine-garden   So2
wine-press   Nu18; KS6; Job24; Ls63; La1; Joe3; Z14

NEW TESTAMENT

anise   Mw23
appetite, all that panders to the   LJF2
  is their god   PPs3
baking, bread of a new   PCF5
  meal   Rev6
  measure   Rev6
bread   Mw4, 6f, 12, 14ff, 26; Mk2, 6ff, 14; L4, 6f, 9, 11, 14f, 22, L24; J6, 13, 21;
        A2, 12, 20, 27; PCF5, 10f; PCS9; ThS3; LH9
  a stone when he asks for   Mw7
  alone, man cannot live by   Mw4; L4
  are we to spend twenty pounds on   Mk6
  daily   M6; L11
  dipped in the dish   J13
  during supper he took   Mk14
  enough and to spare, hired servants have   L15
  forgotten to take   Mw16; Mk8
  from heaven, he gave them   J6
  give us each day our daily   M6; L11
  he broke   L24
  he who eats   J13
  he who provides the   PCS9
  I was not speaking about   Mw16
  if a son should ask for   L11
  Jesus took   Mw26
  of a new baking   PCF5
  of life   J6
  sacred   Mk2
  take no   Mk6
  tell these stones to become   Mw4; L4
  they had forgotten to take with them   Mw6; Mk8
  they wash not their hands when they eat   Mw15
  to eat, took sacred   L6

bread, to take the children's   Mk7
  unleavened   L22; A12; PCF5
  where are we to buy   J6
  with unwashed hands, eat   Mk7
  work, and eat their own   ThS3
cinnamon and spice, cargoes of   Rev18
cummin   Mw23
dill   Mw23
dinner   L14
dough, consecrated   PR11
  leaven in the   PG5
  leavens all the   PCF5
drinker, a bishop must not be a   Tt1
drinking, not given to excessive   PTF3
  they have been   A2
drunkards are drunk at night   ThF5
  no grabbers or   PCF6
drunkenness, do not give way   PE5
  revelry and tippling, you lived in   LPF4
eat and drink, for tomorrow we die, let us   PCF15
  or drink, sworn not to   A23
    take you to task about what you   PCo2
  who will not work shall not   ThS3
  without raising questions of conscience   PCF10
eating food with defiled hands   Mk7
eats and drinks judgement on himself   PCF11
egg, offer a scorpion when he asks for an   L11
fig   Mw7, 21, 24; Mk11; L6, 13; LJ3; Rev6
fish, broiled   L24
  a few small   Mw15; Mk8
  five loaves and two   Mw14; Mk6; L9; J6
  offer a snake when he asks for   L11
  offered him a piece of   L24
flour   Mw13; L13; Rev6, 18
  and wheat, cargoes of   Rev18
food and drink, put away anxious thoughts about   Mw6; L12
  and good cheer in plenty, he gives you   A14
  anyone who has must share   L3
  consecrated to heathen deities   PCF8
  is for the belly and the belly for food   PCF6

food of eternal life   J6
  the Son of Man will give you   J6
  they ate the same supernatural   PCF10
  they had gone a long time without   A27
  was locusts and wild honey, John's   Mw3
fruit of the vine   L22
glutton, lazy   Tt1
grape   Mw7; L6; Rev14
greed, never been a cloak for   ThF2
herbs, all manner of   L11
  another who is weak eateth   PR14
  tithes of   Mw23
honey, his food was wild   Mw3; Mk1
  sweet as   Rev10
honeycomb   L24
hyssop   LH9
leaven   Mw13; Mk8; L13; PCF5; PG5
  hid in three measures of meal   L13
  of Herod, beware the   Mk8
  of the Pharisees, be on your guard against   Mk8
leavened bread   PCF5
locusts, fed on   Mw3; Mk1
loaf   Mw14f; Mk8; L9, 11; PCF10
  they had only one, in the boat   Mk8
loaves and two fishes, five   Mw14; Mk6; L0; J6
  how many have you?
lunch   L14
manna, I will give you hidden   Rev2
  jar containing   LH9
  our ancestors had   J6
marjoram   J19; LH9
meal, leaven in   Mw13; L13
  wait on me while I have my   L17
meat, he who abstains from eating   PR14
  he who eats   PR14
  that has been offered to idols   A15
milk instead of solid food   PCF3; LH5
  tend a flock without using its   PCF9
mint   M23; L11
new wine must be put in new bottles   Mw9; Mk2

oil, olive   L16; Rev6

olives   LJ3; Rev6

rations at the proper time, issue their   L12

rue   L1

salt   Mw5; Mk9; L14; PCo4

sober, keep awake and   ThF5

  temperate, leader must be   PTF3

sop, he dipped the   J13

sour wine   Mw27; Mk15; L23; J19

spice and cinnamon, cargoes of   Rev18

spices   J19

strong drink, he shall never touch   L1

   slaves to   Tt2

supper, Passover   Mw26; Mk14; L14; J13

table, he took his place at   L7

unleavened bread   L22; A12; PCF5

vegetables, who eats only   PR14

vinegar, offered him a sponge full of   Mw27; Mk15; L23; J19

wheat, measure of   Rev6

wine   Mw9, 11, 26f; Mk2, 15; L1, 5, 7, 10, 23; J2, 19; A2; PR14; PE5; PTF3, 5; LPF4;
      Rev6, 14, 16, 18

  cargoes of   Rev18

  fierce   Rev16, 18

  for thy stomach's sake   PTF5

  he shall never touch   L1

  he was offered drugged   Mk15

  mingled with myrrh   Mk15

  mixed with gall   Mw27

  new   Mk2

  not given to   PTF3

  offered him their sour   L23

  sour   Mw27; Mk15; L23; J19

  sponge soaked in sour   Mw27; Mk15; L23; J19

  take a little   PTF5

  these men are full of new   A2

  to abstain from drinking   PR14

  water turned into   J2

  wherein is excess   PE5

yeast   Mw13, L13

17   *Geographical Features*

OLD TESTAMENT

bitumen as mortar   Gen11
  pits of Siddim   Gen14
brimstone   Is30, 36
cave at Makkedah   Jos10
  at Mount Horeb   KF19
  Elijah's   KF19
  in the Rock of Etam   Ju15
  of Abraham's tomb   Gen23
  of Adullam   SF22; SS23; CF11; Mi1
  of Lot   Gen19
  of Machpelah   Gen23
  of Sarah's tomb   Gen25
  prophets hidden in the   KF18
  robbers'   Je7
  Saul went to relieve himself in the   SF24
caves, forced to find themselves   Ju6
  in the rocks   Is2
clay   Na3
  in the brick kiln   Je43
crag, towering   Ps71
earth trembled, heaven quaked   Ju5
  two mule loads of   KS5
earthquake blocking the valley   Z14
fen, a waste of   Is14
flint   Is5, 50; Je5; E3
forest of Hareth   SF22
gorge of Arron   KS10
  of the Arabah   Am6
  of the Kidron   SS15; KF2, 15; KS23; CS15; 29ff; Je31
  of Shittim   Joe3
gullies   Ps104
heath   Mi1, 3
  open   Is32
hill of Bashan   Ps68
  of Gareb   Je31

hill of Mizar   Ps42f
  of Samaria   Am4, 6
lime   Am2
Mount Carmel   Am1, 9
  of Esau   Ob1
  of Olives   Z14
  Paran   H3
  Zion   Ob1; Mi4
mountain   Ps2, 11, 15, 18, 24, 30, 65, 104, 144
  Abarim   De32
  Amana   So4
  Baalah   Jos15
  Baal-hermon   Ju3
  Carmel   KF18; KS2
  Ebal   De11, 26ff; Jos8
  Ephraim   Je4
  Ephron   Jos15
  Gaash   Jos24; Ju2
  Galud   Ju7
  Gerizim   De11, 27; Jos8; Ju9
  Gilboa   SF31; SS1; CF10
  Gilead   So4, 6
  Heres   Ju1
  Hermon   Los11ff; CF5; Ps42, 89, 133; So4
  Hor   Nu20; Ps106
  Horeb   KF19; Ps106
  Jearim   Jos15
  Lebanon   Ju3
  like the lofty   Ps36
  Moriah   CS3
  my holy   Is65
  Nebo   De32, 34
  of the Lord's house   Is2
  Paran   De33
  Perazim   Is28
  Pisgah   De34
  Seir   Jos15
  Senir   So4
  Sinai   Ne9; Ps68
  Tabor   Ju4; Ps89; Ho5

mountain, your holy   Je31
  Zalmon   Ju9
  Zion   Ps48, 74, 125f, 128f; Is8, 10, 18, 24, 29, 31, 37
mountains of Bether   So2
  of Israel   E33ff
  of Samaria   Am3ff
  of Seir   E35
  shudder   Is54, 64
  spice-bearing   So8
nitre   Pro25
oil, a land of   De8
  from the flinty rock   De32
ore   Je6
pass of Michmash   SF13
pitch, ark coated with   Gen6
plain full of bones   E37
  of Dura   D3
potash   Is1
ravine, break a heifer's neck in a   De21
  of Besor   SF30
  of Kerith   KF17
ravines, land of many   De10
  of Gaash   SS23; CF11
rock, dividing   SF23
  of Bozez   SF14
  of Oreb   Is10
  of the wild goats   SF24
  Seneh   SF14
  strike the   Ex17
salt, pillar of   Gen19
saltpit   Zp2
sand dunes   Is41
slime pits   Gen14
spice-bearing mountains   So8
thickets, Jordan's dense   Z11
vale of Achor   Is65
  of Aven   Am1
  of Elah   SF17, 21
  of Gibeon   Is28
  of Jezreel   Ho1

vale of Jordan   SF31
  of Megiddo   CS35; Z12
  of Rephaim   SS5, 23; CF11, 14; Is17
  of Trouble   Ho2
valley   Ps23, 65, 104
  blocked as by an earthquake   Z14
  of Abarim   E39
  of Achor   Ho2
  of Ben-hinnom   KS23; CS28, 33; Je7, 19, 32
  of Berakah   CS20
  of Blessing   CS20
  of Craftsmen   Ne11
  of Decision   Joe3
  of Gog's Horde   E39
  of Hamon-gog   E39
  of Hinnom   Ne11
  of Jehoshaphat   Joe3
  of Jordan   SF31
  of Megiddon   Z12
  of Rephaim   SS5, 23; CF11, 14; Is17
  of Salt   KS14; CF18; CS25
  of Slaughter   Je7, 19
  of Succoth   Ps108
  of the Dead Bodies   Je31
  of the Lord's Judgement   Joe3
  of Vision   Is22
  of Woods   Ne11
  of Zeboim   SF13
  of Zephathah   Cs14
valleys shall be lifted up   Is40

NEW TESTAMENT

bay with a sandy beach   A27
cave, robbers'   Mw21; Mk11; L19
caves, hiding in   LH11; Rev6
clay, potter's   PR9
creek into which to thrust the ship   A27

17 GEOGRAPHICAL FEATURES

desert, time of testing in the   LH3
  was strewn with their corpses   PCF10
earthquake, a violent   Rev6, 8, 11
earthquake like none before in human history   Rev16
  suddenly there was a violent   A16
hill called Olivet   L19
  shall be brought low   L3
hills, seven, on which the woman sits   Rev17
  take to the   L21
hillside, went to pray up the   Mk6
Mount of Olives   Mw21, 24, 26; Mk11, 13f; L19, 21f; J8; A1
  sermon on the   Mw5
  Sinai   Mw5; A7; PG4; LH12
  Zion   PR9, 11; LH12; LPF2; Rev14
mountain and island moved from its place   Rev6
  blazing, hurled into the sea   Rev8
  in Galilee   Mw28
  led them up a high   Mw17; Mk9
  our fathers worshipped on this   J4
  sacred   LPS1
  Spirit carries me to a high   Rev21
  the devil took him to a very high mountain   Mw4
mountains and crags, fall on us   Rev6
  fall on us, then shall they say   L23
  seven   Rev17
quicksands   A27
Ravine of Kedron   J18
uplands of Juday   L1
valley, Jordan,
  shall be filled, every   L3
wilderness, Jesus in the   Mw4; Mk1; L1
  Judaean   Mw3

18   *Health and Longevity*

OLD TESTAMENT

affliction, bound in   Ps107
age of king Ahaz   KS16
    Amaziah   KS14
    Amon   KS21
    Azariah   KS14f
    Darius   D5
    David   SS5
    Hezekiah   KS18
    Ishbosheth   SS2
    Jehoahaz   KS23
    Jehoiachin   KS23
    Jehoiada   CS24
    Jehoiakin   KS24
    Jehoshaphat   KF22
    Jeroboam   KF15
    Joash   KS12
    Joram   K38
    Josiah   KS21
    Jotham   KS15
    Manasseh   KS21
    Reheboam   KF14; CS12
    Saul   SF13
    Zedekiah   KS24
    of matriarch Sarah : 127 years   Gen23
    of patriarch Aaron : 123 years   Ex7; Nu33
    Abraham : 175 years   Gen25
    Adam : 930 years   Gen5
    Amram : 137 years   Ex6
    Arphaxad : 438 years   Gen11
    Eber : 464 years   Gen11
    Enoch : 365 years   Gen5
    Enosh : 905 years   Gen5
    Isaac : 180 years   Gen35

190

age of patriarch Ishmael : 137 years   Gen25
    Jacob : 147 years   Gen47
    Jared : 962 years   Gen5
    Job : approx 200 years   Job42
    Joseph : 110 years   Gen50
    Joshua : 110 years   Jos24; Ju2
    Kenan : 910 years   Gen5
    Kohath : 133 years   Gen5
    Lamech : 777 years   Gen5
    Levi : 137 years   Ex6
    Mahalalel : 895 years   Gen5
    Methuselah : 969 years   Gen5
    Moses : 120 years   Ex7; De31, 34
    Nahor : 138 years   Gen11
    Noah : 950 years   Gen9
    Peleg : 239 years   Gen11
    Reu : 239 years   Gen11
    Serug : 230 years   Gen11
    Seth : 912 years   Gen5
    Shelah : 433 years   Gen11
    Shem : 600 years   Gen11
aged, honour the   Le19
ague, burning   Le26; De28
baldness, infectious   Le13
bandage   Is1; E30, 34
blind, debarred   Le21
  respect the   Le19
blindness   De28; SS5; KF14; KS6; Je31
boil, poulticed   KS20; Is38
boils   Ex9; De28; KS20; Job2; Is38
bowels, anguish of   La1
  disease of   CS21
  prolapse of   CS21
breath, noisome   Job19
consumption   Le26; De28
corpse, touching an unclean   Nu6, 19; De21; Hg2
crippled feet   SS4; KF15
deaf, respect for the   Le9
deafness   Ps38
deformities   Le21

ulcers   De28; Je16
unclean condition   Le5, 22
  cry   Le13
under-grown people   Le21
washing before the meal   L11
waste away, fat on his limbs shall   Is17
wasting disease   Le26; De28; Ps106; Is17
wounds, binds up our   Ho6
  dressed with vinegar   Pro25

NEW TESTAMENT

age of Abraham   PR4
  of Jesus Christ   L2
  of the girl raised by Jesus   Mk5
  of the widow Anna   L2
ailment and disease, curing every kind of   Mw9
ailments, take a little wine for your frequent   PTF5
anointed with oil, sick people   Mk6
bandage   L10
bed-ridden with paralysis   A9
bent double, she was   L13
blind beggar   Mk10
  for a time   A13
  from birth   J9
  man at the gate   Mw20
    at the roadside   L18
  men, Jesus was followed by two   Mw9
  people, he restored sight on many   L7
  recover their sight, tell him how they   L7
  to announce recovery of sight   L4
bloody flux   A28
clay of the spittle, made   J9
convulsions, threw the boy into   Mk9
crippled folk cured   A8
  for eighteen years   L13
  from birth   A3
  man lame from birth   A14
cure his son, begged him to   J4

cured, saw that he had the faith to be   A14
  sufferers from every kind of illness   Mw4
  you, your faith has   L17
dangerously ill, he was   PPs2
deaf and dumb   Mk9
  brought him a man who was   Mk7
  hear, tell him how the   L7
digestion, take a little wine for your   PTF5
disabled limb will regain its former powers   LH12
disease, power to cure   L9
  suffering from one or another   L4
diseases, cured many sufferers from   L7
  divers   Mw4
  he lifted from us   Mw8
  were rid of their   A19
dropsy, a man suffering from   L14
dull of hearing   LH5
dumb man began to speak   L11
  man who was   Mw9; Mk7
dysentery   A28
epilepsy   Mw4, 17
epileptic, my son is   Mw17
faith has cured you,   Mw9; Mk5; L8, 17; A14
  to be cured, saw that he had the   A14
feeble minded, comfort the   ThF5
fever, he stood over her and rebuked the   L4
  left her and she waited upon them   Mk1
  left him at the exact time   J4
  mother in law in bed with   Mw8; Mk1
  recurrent bouts of   A28
fits, epileptic   Mw17
foams at the mouth, grinds his teeth, and goes rigid   Mk9
gangrene   PTS2
haemorrhages, suffered from   Mw9; Mk5; L8
healed him, laid his hands upon him and   A28
healers, God has appointed   PCF12
healing all manner of sickness   Mw4
  for all mankind   Tt2
  the gift of   PCF12
  went about doing good and   A10

19   *Heavens and Hell*

Abaddon   Job26; Pro15, 27
abyss   Ps36, 143; Pro1; Is38
   fire to devour the great   Am7
   go down to the   Ps28
   gone down to the stony   Is14
   sinking into the   Ps30
   swallow me up   Ps69
   those that go down to the   E26, 31ff
   thou hast plunged me into the lowest   Ps88
   to the depths of the   Is14
Adversary, Satan the   Z3
Aldebaran   Job9, 38
Amanus, the southern sky   Ps150
Arcturus   Job9
Azazel   Le16
Belial, a man of   SS20
   certain sons of   Ju19
   Eli's sons were sons of   SF2
   sons of, bore witness against Naboth   SF21
   this man of   SF25
brimstone   Is30, 34
Capella   Am5
chambers of the south   Job9
circle of southern stars   Job9
constellations   Is13
crescent-cakes offered to the queen of heaven   Je7, 44
day darkened into night   Am5
demon of the night   So3
dog-star   Job38
drink offerings poured to the queen of heaven   Je44
earth, arches his ceiling over the   Am9
eclipse of the sun   Am5, 8

heaven   Ps2, 11, 14, 19, 33, 36, 53, 57, 65, 76, 80, 85, 103, Ps113, 115, 123, 135f, 146;
Pro30; Is24
cover the, and make the stars go dark   E32
every activity under   Ec3
four quarters of   Je49
highest   Ps71; Is7
host of   Ps33
of heavens   Ps148
vault of   Ps150
heavenly host in Daniel's vision   D8
heavens   Ps8, 19, 33, 50, 57, 89, 96, 104, 108, 136, 138; Pro3; Je10
builds his stair up to the   Am9
creator of   Is45
grow murky as smoke   Is51
he roars across   Je25
if man could measure the   Je31
if they climb up to   Am9
lift your eyes to the   Is40
limits to the   Is40
music of the   Ps19
new   Is66
rain righteousness   Is45
signs in the   Je10
the ancient   Ps68
turn black   Je4
hell, Job11; Ps9; Pro7; Is14, 28
casteth down to   E31
though they dig into   Am9
horse statues in honour of the sun   KS23
host of heaven   KS17, 21, 23; Ps33; Is24; Je8
altars for   CS33
aspired to be as great as   D8
bow down on the housetops to worship   Zp1
burned incense to, priests of Baal   KS23
incense burned to in Judah   Je19, 44
innumerable   Je33
lest thou lift up thine eyes unto   De4
sacrifices to   Je19
those who worship the   Zp1
worships the Lord God   Ne9

19 HEAVENS AND HELL

Lucifer, morning star   Is14
Mazzaroth   Job38
moon   Ps8, 72, 74, 89, 136, 148; Ec12; Is13, 24; Je8
  and stars for a light by night   Je31
  beautiful as the   So6
  burned incense to the   KS23
  nor raise your eyes to the   De4
  precious things put forth by the   De33
  sacrifices to the   KS23
  shall grow pale   Is24
  shall not give its light   E32
  stand in the vale of Aijalon   Jos10
  to measure the year   Ps104
  turned to blood   Joe2
morning star   Is14
music of the heavens   Ps19
Navigator's Line   Job38
new moon, ceremony of the   Ho2; Am8
   commemoration of the   Ne10
   feast of the   SF20; CS2, 8; Ps81; Ez3; Is1; E45ff
   month by month at the   Is66
   sabbaths and appointed seasons   CF23
Orion   Job9; Am5
Orion's Belt   Job38
pit   Ps16, 94; Pro1, 28; Is14
  go down into the   Ps30
  of death   Ps49, 103, 107
  of destruction   Ps55
  sending you down to the   E28
  them that descend to the   E26
  then didst bring me up alive from the   Jon2
  went down alive to the   Nu16
planets, burned incense to the   KS23
Pleiades   Job9, 38; Am5
portents in the sky   Joe2
queen of heaven   Je7
   bake crescent-cakes for   Je7, 44
   burn incense to   Je44
   pour drink offering to   Je44
rising sun, prostrating themselves to the   E8

sacrifices to the host of heaven   Je19
  to the queen of heaven   Je44
Satan   CF1; Job1ff; Ps109
  the Adversary   Z3
seven stars   Am5
Sheol   Job7, 11, 14, 17, 21, 24, 26; Ps6, 9, 16, 18, 30f, 49, 55, 86, Ps88f, 116, 139, 141;
        Ec9; Pro1, 5, 7, 15, 27; Is5, 14, 28, Is38; Je7, 19; H2
  burns to the depths of   De32
  gates of   Is57
  go down to alive   Nu16
  he sends down to   SF2
  if they dig down to   Am9
  oh, for your sting!   Ho13
  out of the belly of   Jon2
  shall I redeem him from   Ho13
  the lowest   Is7
  warrior chieftains in   E32
  went down to   E31
shooting star   Is5
signs in the havens, do not be awed by   Je10
star, of your god which ye made   Am5
  shines forth out of Jacob   Nu24
stargazers   Is47
starry heavens, majestic as the   So6
stars   Ps8, 147ff; Is13
  as numerous as   De1
  forbear to shine   Joe2f
  grow dim   Ec12
  nor raise your eyes to the   De4
  the seven   Am5
  to rule by night   Ps136
  withdraw their shining   Joe2
sun   Ps19, 72, 74, 89, 104, 136, 148; Ec12; So6; Is13, 24; Je8
  burned incense to the   KS23
  for a light by day, who gave the   Je31
  from the rising to the setting   Ps50, 113
  hides its face in shame   Is24
  prostrating themselves to the rising   E8
  rises, and rises again   Ec1
  sacrificed to the   KS23

sun and moon darkened   Joe2f
  shall be turned into darkness   Joe2
  stood still   Jos10
  toil under the   Ec1
  veil with a cloud   E32
Taurus   Am5
Teman, the south, turn your face towards   E20
three days of darkness   Ex10
Tophet   KS23; Is30; Je7, 19
vault of heaven, shine like the bright   D12
vaulted roof of the earth   Is40
Vintager constellation   Am5
Zaphon, northern sky   Ps89
zodiac, can you bring out the signs of the   Job38

NEW TESTAMENT

Abaddon, angel of the abyss   Rev9
abyss, angel given the key of the   Rev9
  angel of the   Rev9
  beast that comes up from the   Rev11
  begged him not to banish them to the   L8
  threw him into the   Rev20
  who can go down to the   PR10
  yet to ascend out of the   Rev17
angels in heaven will not know   Mk13
  the devil and his   Mw25
Apollyon, angel of the abyss   Rev9
antichrist, the arch-deceiver   LJS1
  the spirit of   LJF4
  was to come, you were told   LJF2
beast, armies of the   Rev19
  had not worshipped the   Rev20
  scarlet   Rev17
  thrown into the lake of fire   Rev19
Beelzebub   Mw10, 12
  he is possessed by   Mk3
  prince of devils   L11
Belial   PCS6
blood, fire, and drifting smoke, signs on earth   A2

brimstone, lake of fire and   Rev20
  rained fire and   L17
celestial bodies   PCF15
cosmic powers, our fight is against   PE6
created, everything that God   PTF4
creation under heaven, the whole   PCo1
darkness, bound beneath the   LJu1
  his kingdom was plunged in   Rev16
  is passing and the real light already shines   LJ2
  let light shine out of   PCS4
  those who live in   L1
  to light, turn them from   A26
day like a thousand years with the Lord   LPS3
demonic earth-bound sensual wisdom   LJ3
demons, a dwelling place for   Rev18
  partners with   PCF10
  sacrifice to   PCF10
  table of   PCF10
destroyer, destroyed by the   PCF10
  the angel of the abyss   Rev9
devil, a man possessed by the   L4
  anything beyond "yes" and "no" comes from the   Mw5
  came out and the dumb man began to speak   L11
  carries off the word from their hearts   L8
  child of the   LJF3
  dashed him to the ground   L9
  devices of the   PE6
  entered Judas   J13
  gone to the   PTF5
  had death at his command   LH2
  he hath a   J10
  healing all who were oppressed by the   A10
  his angels   Mw25
  in debate with Archangel Michael   LJu1
  Jesus rebuked the   Mw17
   tempted by the   Mw4
  judgement contrived by the   PTF3
  leave no loop-hole for the PE4
  Michael in debate with the   LJu1
  now we know that thou hast a   J8

devil, one of you is a   J6
  possessed with the   Mk5
  seducer   Rev20
  set him on a parapet of the temple,   Mw4
  sinneth from the beginning   LJF3
  stand up to the   LJ4
  tempted by the   L4
  tempting Jesus   Mw4
  that he might destroy the works of the   LJF3
  that serpent of old   Rev20
  thou child of the   A13
  thou hast a   J7
  thrown down to earth   Rev12
  took him to a very high mountain   Mw4
  was cast out   Mw9
  wiles of the   PE6
  your adversary the   LPF5
  your father is the   J8
devils, a commission to drive out   Mk3
  a man who was possessed by   L8
  authority to overcome   L9
  Beelzebub, prince of the   L11
  by the finger of God that I drive out   L11
  by the prince of devils he drives out   Mk3
  cast out   Mw10
    in your name   M7
  drove out many   Mk1
  habitation of   Rev18
  had cast out seven   Mk16
  had come out of Mary Magdalene, seven   L8
  had taken possession of him, so many   L8
  have faith like that   LJ2
  in your name, we saw a man driving out   Mk9; L9
  possessed by   Mw4, 8
  snare   PTS2
  submit to us in your name   L10
  subversive doctrines inspired by   PTF4
  the table of   PCF10
  they drove out many   Mk6
  they sacrifice to   PCF10

heaven, a light from   A26
  a voice sounded from   A12
  and earth and sea, God who made   A14
  and earth, Lord of   A17
  and on earth, brought into unity, all in   PE1
  as it is in   L11
  asked him for a sign from   Mk8
  bread from   J6
  coming with the clouds of   Mk14
  demanded a sign from   L11
  door opened in   Rev4
  eternal house in   PCS5
  first-born citizens of   LH12
  from the farthest bounds of   Mk13
  glory to God in highest   L2
  great is your reward in   Mw5
  has no favourites, master in   PE6
  he was parted from them and carried up into L24
  he was to be taken up to   L9
  hope stored up for you in   PCo1
  inheritance kept for you in   LPF1
  is my throne and earth my footstool   A7
  is theirs, kingdom of   Mw5
  it was not David who went up to   A2
  Jesus looked up to   Mk6; J17
  living bread come down from J6
  Lord Jesus was taken up into Mk16
  many will come to the feast in the kingdom of   Mw8
  may we call down fire from   L9
  morning sun from   L1
  never-failing treasure in   L12
  opened and the Holy Spirit descended   L3
    at that moment   Mw3
  our Father which art in   L11
  over one sinner that repenteth, joy shall be in   L15
  rained fire from   L17
  rejoice, because your names are written in   L10
  retribution revealed from   PR1
  roar of a vast throng in   Rev19
  shall be shaken, the powers of   L21

silence in   Rev8
store up treasure in   Mw6
swear not by   M5
symbol of Diana which fell from   A19
heaven, the angels in   Mw22
  the kingdom of   Mw5
  the Lord himself will descend from   ThF4
  there came a voice from   L3
  third   PCS12
  this voice from   LPS1
  to swear by   Mw23
  until he was taken up to   A1
  voice from   L3; J12; Rev18
  voices heard in   Rev11
  war broke out in   Rev12
  we are citizens of   PPS3
  when your Lord is revealed from   ThS1
  who can go up to   PR10
  wide open, I saw   Rev19
    you shall see   J1
  you have a rich reward in   Mw5
    will have riches in   L18
  your Father in   Mw23
heavenly bodies, the splendour of   PCF15
  country   LH11
  host, a great company of the   L2
  realms, enthroned him in the   PE2
    every blessing in the   PE1
heavens ablaze, day of God will set the   LPS3
  forces of evil in the   PE6
  Hosanna in the   Mk11
  new, and a new earth   LPS3
  shall pass away but thou endurest   LH1
  will disappear with a great rushing sound   LPS3
hell and the unquenchable fire   Mk9
  better to lose one part, than be thrown into   Mw5
  consigned to the dark pits of   LPS2
  fire, shall be in danger of   Mw5
  fit for   Mw23
  followed by death   Rev6

pit, key of the   Rev9
portents will appear in sun, moon and stars   L21
possessed by devils   Mw4, 8f; Mk1, 5, 16; L4, 8ff
prince of devils   Mw9; Mk3
  of the power of the air   PE2
realm above, aspire to the   Pco3
realm, higher   PCo3
  of light, God's people in the   PCo1
revelation, the light of   PCS4
Satan, away with you   Mw16; Mk8
  begone   Mw4
  beneath your feet, will crush   PR16
  bruise under your feet   PR16
  comes and carries off the word   Mk4
  consigned to   PTF1
  deep secrets of   Rev2
  divided against himself   Mw12; L11
  drive out Satan, how can   Mk3
  entered Judas Iscariot   L22; J13
  fell like lightning out of the sky   L10
  filled thy heart to lie to the Holy Spirit   A5
  get thee behind me   Mw4, 16; Mk8; L4
  has his throne   Rev2
  himself masquerades as an angel of light   PCS11
  if Satan casts out   Mw12
  keep prisoner by   L13
  let loose from his dungeon   L20
  messenger of   PCS12
  must not get the better of us   PCS2
  possessed your mind   A5
  sifts you like wheat   L22
  tempted by   Mk1; PCF7
  that serpent of old   Rev20
  the work of   ThS2
  this man is to be consigned to   PCF5
  thrown down to earth   Rev12
  thwarted us   ThF2
  to God, from the dominion of   A26
  turned aside after   PTF5
Satan's synagogue   Rev2f

seducing spirits   PTF4
serpent called the devil, that old   Rev12
shaft of the abyss   Rev9
sky, terror and great portents in the   L21
   vanished   Rev6
sound from heaven as of a mighty rushing wind   A2
spirit, Jesus rebuked the unclean   L9
   open men's eyes, could an evil   J10
   possessed by an unclean   Mk5, 7, 9; L4
   unclean, commanded to come out   L8
spirits begged him to let them go into the pigs   L8
   evil, cured many suffering from   L7
   of the universe, elemental   PCo2
   seducing   PTF4
   unclean, like frogs   Rev16
     would fall at his feet   Mk3
star called wormwood   Rev8
   fallen from heaven to earth   Rev9
   great, shot from the sky   Rev8
   I am the bright   Rev22
   in glory, one differeth from another   PCF15
   of dawn   Rev2
   we observed the rising of his   Mw2
   went ahead of them until it stopped above the place   Mw2
stars fell to earth   Rev6
   have a splendour   PCF15
   in a dark world, shine like   PPs2
   in his right hand he held seven   Rev1
   in the firmament   PPs2
   portents will appear in   L21
   seven   Rev2f
   third part struck   Rev8
   twelve, a crown of   Rev12
   will fall from the sky   Mw24; Mk13
   wandered from their course   LJu1
sulphur, rained fire and   L17
sun allowed to burn men with its flames   Rev16
   has a splendour of its own   PCF15
   his face shone like the   Mw17; Rev1
   light more brilliant than the   A26

sun or moon, city had no need of   A26
  or stars, no sign of, for days on end   A27
  portents will appear in the   L21
  righteous will shine as brightly as the   Mw13
  rise on good and bad alike   Mw5
  shall be turned to darkness   A2
  third part will be struck   Rev8
  will be darkened   Mw24; Mk13
  woman robed in the   Rev12
sun's light failed   L23
temptation of Jesus   Mw4
tempted by the devil   Mw4
tempter approached him   Mw4
  tempted you   ThF3
thousand years like a day with the Lord   LPS3
throne of the beast   Rev16
torment, Hades place of   L16
unclean spirit, a haunt for every   Rev18
  commanded to come out of the man   L8
  Jesus rebuked the   Mk9; L9
  possessed by an   Mk1, 5, 7; L4
  wanders over the deserts   L11
  spirits came out with a loud cry   A8
  gave them authority to cast out   Mw10; Mk6
  harassed by   A5
  he gives orders to   L4
  like frogs   Rev16
  would fall at his feet   Mk3
universe created through him and for him   PCo1
wailing and grinding of teeth   Mw8, 13
wandering stars   LJu1
weeping and gnashing of teeth   Mw8, 13

20 *Household*

awl   De15
axe   De15, 19
ball, children's   Is22
barrel   KF17
basin   SS17; CS4; Je52
  bronze   Ex30ff; KF7
  gold   Ez1
  silver   Ez1
basket   De23; KS10; Ps81; Je6, 24; Am4, 8
  rush   Ex2
  watertight   Ex2
bed   SK19; SS13; KF17; KS4; Ps6, 36, 132; Pro7, 26; So3; Is28, 57; E23; D4, 7; Ho7;
      Am3, 6; Mi2
  perfumed   Pro7
bedchamber   Ec10
bed-covering   Is28
bedroom   Ec10
bell   Ex28ff
bellows   Pro26
bench   E27
besom   Is14
bit   Ps32
blanket   SS11, 17; Ks8; Is28
bolts and bars   Ne3
bottle   SS16; Je13, 48; Ho7
  earthen   Je19
bowl   SS17; KS2, 16; Is22, 51, 65; Je35, 52; Am6; Z9, 14
  golden   Ex25ff; Ez1, 8; Ec12
  mixing   E4
  silver   Nu7
  table of the Presence   Nu4
  tossing   Ex27ff; Nu7
brazier   Je36; Z12
bridle   Ps32; Pro26

bucket   Is40

candle   Pro24, 29, 31; Je25; Zp1

candlestick   Nu4; KS4; Je52; D5

  gold   Rx25ff

  seven branch   Z4

canopy, wedding   Ps19

carding, weaving and spinning   Is19

cask   E27

cauldron   SF2; CS35; Job41; Is65; Je1, 52; E11, 24; Mi3

charger, gold   Ez1

  silver   Nu7; Ez1

chest   KS12; CS24; So5

  cedar wood   E27

churn   Pro30

cistern, rock-hewn   De6; Ne9

clay, potter's   Is29, 41, 45, 64

  pot   Ps2

cleanse hands with lye   Job9

coals   Ps11, 19; La4

cord   Na1

  leather   Ho11

couch   SS11; Ps6; So1; E16; Am3, 6

  of gold and silver   Est1

coverlet   Is14

crisping pins   Is3

crucible   Ps12

cruse   KF14, 17, 19; KS2

cup   Ps11, 16, 23, 75; Pro23; Is22, 28, 51; Je25, 35, 49, 52;

  gold   Est1; Je51

  silver   KS12

curtain   So1; Is40

  rings, silver   Est1

  tabernacle   Ex26

  tent   Is54; Je4, 10, 49; H3; La4; E23; Z12

curtains, green, white and blue   Est1

dish, gold   Ex25ff

  lordly   Ju5

  silver   Nu7

  table of the Presence   Nu4

distaff   SS3; Pro31

rope   SF19; Is3, 5; Je10, 38
rug   SF19; Is21
saddle, ass   KS4
saucer   Nu4, 7; KS25; CS4, 24; Je52
  of incense   Nu7
scales   Je32
seat   KS4
shard   Job2; Ps22; Pro26; Is30; E23
shovel   Ex27f; KS25
sieve   Am4, 9
skin, wine   SF16, 25; Ne5; Job14; Ps119
snuffdish   Nu4
snuffer   KS12, 25; CS4; Je52
soap   Job9; Je2
soot   La4
spindle   Pro31
spinning   Is19
spoon   Nu7; KS25; Je52
  of incense   Nu7
stewpot   E11
stool   KF10; E16
  high   E16
sundial   Is38
table   Nu4ff; KS4; Ps23, 41, 69, 78; Is28, 65; E23, 40ff
tent covering   Je4
  curtain   So1; H3
  hangings   Je49
  peg   Z10
toilet, sign for a   De23
tongs   CS4
torch, blazing   Z12
trowel for burying excrement   De23
vat   Is63; Joe2f; Hg2
  juice from the   Nu18
  wine   Pro3; Je48
vessels, brass   E27
  bronze   KS25; Je52; E27
    or copper   CF18
  clay   Je18
  earthen   SS17; Je19

vessels, gold   KS24
  and copper   SS8
  and silver   CF18, 28
 silver   Ez8
  and gold   CS24; KF10; D11
 small bowls and pots   Is22
 storage   Je40
vial   SF6
wagon   SF6
wardrobe   Je38
wash-bowl   Ps108
water, payment for   La5
 jar   SF26
wax   Ps22, 68, 97; Mi1
weaving   Is19, 38
web and thrum, weaving   Is38
wick, smouldering   Is42
 snuffed out   Is43
wheel, potter's   Je18
whip   Na3
 horse   Pro26
wine jar   Je13
 press   Ju7; Ne13; La1; Ho9; Hg2
 skin   SF16, 25; Ne5; Job14; Ps119
 vat   Hg2; Z14
yoke   Je31; Ho11; Na1

NEW TESTAMENT

alabaster box   Mw26; Mk14; L7
baggage, packed our   A21
bandage   L10
basin   L8; J3
basket   Mw4ff; Mk6, 8; J6; A9; PCS11
bed   Mw9; Mk4, 6; L5, 8, 11, 17; J5; A5, 9, 28; LJ5
 children with me in   L11
 do you put the lamp under the   Mk4
 two men in one   L17
board and lodging   ThS3
bonfire   A28

bottle   Mw9; Mk2, 14; L5
  perfume   Mk14
  wine   L5
bowl   Mw26; Mk7; Rev15, 17
  copper   Mk7
  gold   Rev15
box, alabaster   M26; Mk14; L7
bucket   J4
candle   Mw5; Mk4; L8, 11, 15; Rev18, 22
candlestick   Mw5; Mk4; L8f, 11; Rev1f, 11
chair   Mw23
charcoal   J18
charger   Mw14; Mk6
cord   L5
couch   L5; A5
cup   Mw10, 20, 23, 26; Mk7, 9f; L11, 22; J18; PCF10f; PCS1,7; PPs2; Rev17
cushion, asleep on a   Mk4
dish   Mw23; Mk6, 14
earthenware   PCS4; PTS2; Rev2
flask of oil   Mw25; L7
footstool   Mk12; L20; LH1, 10; LJ2
glass   Rev15, 21
  looking   PCS3; LJ1
guest chamber   Mk14; L22
homes of your own, have you no   PCF11
hospitality, practice   PR12
  remember to show   LH13
house swept clean and tidy   L11
household, Caesar's   PPs4
  manages his own   PTF3
householder   Mw20
ink   PCS3; LJS1; LJT1
jar   L22; J4, 19; LH9
jug   Mk7
key   Rev1, 9
lamp   Mw5f, 25; Mk4; L8, 11f, 15; J5; A20; LPS1; Rev1f, 4, 11, 18, 22
  stand   Mk4; L8, 11; LH9
lantern   J18
lodging, board and   A10; ThS3; PTF5

looking glass   PCS3; LJ1
market place   Mk6f; L7; A16
meal-tub   Mk4
millstone   Mw18; Mk9; L17; Rev18
mirror   PCS3; LJ1
needle   Mk10; L18
oil   Mw25; L16; Rev18
oven   L12
pail   Mw13
pen and ink   LJT1
perfume bottle   Mk14
pitcher, water   Mk14; L22
plate   L11
platter   Mw23; L11
pot   Mk7; J4; PR9; PCS4; LH9
room ready for me, have a   Ph1
shop and buy some oil, go to the   Mw25
spin nor weave, they neither   L12
sponge   Mw27; Mk15; J19
stone jar   J2
   tablet   PCS3
stove   Mw6; L12
stretcher   Nk2, 6; J5; A5
sweep out the house   L15
table   Mw21; Mk7, 11, 14; L1, 7, 12, 16, 22, 24; J2, 13; PR11; PCF20; LH9; LPS2
   scraps from the rich man's table   L16
   writing   L1
tablet, writing   L1
tablets of stone   PCS3
torch   J18
   flaming   Rev4, 8
utensils of gold and silver   PTS2
   of wood and earthenware   PTS2
vessel, brazen   Mk7
   earthen   PCS4
vial   Rev5, 15ff, 21
washing hands   Mk7
water jar   Mk14; J2, 4
   pot, stone   J2
weave, they neither spin nor   L12

wick, smouldering   Mw12

wine bottle   L5

  skin   Mw9; Mk2; L5

winepress, winefat   Mw21; Mk12; Rev14, 19

  hewed out a   Mw21

wood, utensils of   PTS2

21 *Human Passions, Social Perceptions*

OLD TESTAMENT

afraid, naked and   Gen3
ambidextrous, David's men with slings and arrows   CF12
antimony, make your eyes big with   Je4
appearances, men judge by   SF16
apple of his eye   De32; Z2
baldness   Le13
beard, Aaron's   Ps133
   dribbling down his   SF21
beauty, Absalom was greatly admired for his   SS14
   display her   Est1
   surpass all mankind in   Ps45
beggar us, did you come to   Ju14
beloved of the Lord, Solomon was   SS12
bewilderment, curse of   De28
blind debarred from the altar   Le21
   respect for the   Le19
boast of Adonijah   KF1
born to trouble, man is   Job5
bribe, do not accept a   De16
broke wind, Achsah   Jos15; Ju1
brother's keeper   Gen4
brow like adamant, harder than flint   E3
   misshapen, debarring a person   Le21
choice of life and good, or death and evil   De30
churl is his name and churlish his nature   SF25
circumcision of children   Le12; Jos5
cleansing of skin disease   Le14
   ritual   Le5ff
close-fisted, be not   De15
closet, relieving himself in the   Ju3
clothes symbolizing guilt   Z3
comfort to you, is your religion no   Job4

corpse, contact with a   Hg2
  found in open country   De21
  touching an unclean   Nu6, 19
courage failed us   Jos2
  flowed away   Jos1
  melted away   Jos5
covet, you shall not   De5, 7
dead body, contact with a   Nu6, 19; De21; Hg2
deaf, respect for the   Le19
deformed animals unacceptable as offerings   Le22
  people debarred from the altar   Le21
dislocated Jacob's thigh   Gen32
dribbling down his beard   SF21
drunkard   Pro23
drunken stupor goes in rags   Pro23
ear tryeth words as the mouth tasteth meat   Job34
ears shall tingle, both his   KS21
embrace, a time to   Ec3
eye for eye   De19
eyes darker than wine   Gen49
  like doves   So1
excrement, disposal of   De23
exposed his person, David   SS6
fat, folds of   Ps73
  man, Eglon was a very   Ju3
feet dipped in the Jordan   Jos3
flowing locks, leaders in Israel had   Ju5
fool is destroyed by his own angry passions   Job5
foot for foot   De19
forelock, seized me by the   E8
friend, my own dear   Ps55
giant, an Amorite   Am2
  Benaiah killed a   CF11
  Goliath   SF17, 21; SS21; CF20
  Og, king of Bashan   De3
giants, Anakim   De9
  descendants of the Anakim   De1
  Emim, great and numerous   De2
  on earth in those days   Gen5
  Rephaim   De3

led astray by lavish gifts of wine   Job36
left-handed, Ehud son of Gera   Ju3
likeness of God   Gen5
lips moulded in grace   Ps45
love, a time to   Ec3
  your neighbour   Le19
madness, curse of   De28
man by man, come forward   Jos7
  God formed   Gen2
  in our image   Gen1
mark of Cain   Gen4
meek, Moses was very   Nu12
mortal, God is not, that he should lie   Nu23
  man is only a worm   Job25
naked and afraid   Gen3
  both were   Gen2
navel, it shall be health to your   Pro3
neighbour, love your   Le19
nostrils, eat until it comes out at your   Nu11
open-handed, be   De15
over and under grown people debarred from the altar   Le21
pisseth against the wall, every one that   KF16, 21; KS9
pompous talk is dust and ashes   Job13
poor will always be with you   De15
present, made Jerusalem a   Je40
pride fed on beautiful jewels   E7
proud, do not become   De8
renown, men of   Gen6
rib, Adam's   Gen2
ring in your nose, I will put a   KS19
sandals in holy place, take off   Jos5
scorn on princes, he heaps   Job12
shave edge of the beard   Le19f
  for ritual cleansing   Le14
  not your forelocks   De14
shaved, if my head were   Ju16
skin disease   Le13
  scorched black   Na1
sluggard   Pro6
speech, a man of halting   Ex4, 6

spit in his face   De25
spittle fall down his beard, he let   SF21
stones, wounded in the   De23
strength was their God, dismayed all whose   H1
   what gives Samson his   Ju16
stubborn, not any more   De10
stunted growth, debarred people of   Le21
sweating, I lay   Ps77
tattoo forbidden   Le19
teeth whiter than milk   Gen1
tooth for tooth   Le24; De19
trance, as a man in a   Nu24
   of Abraham   Gen15
try again. come on one and all   Job17
turned his face to the wall, Hezekiah   KS20
uncircumcised brutes   CF10
unclean, cry   Le13
  persons debarred   Le22
  state of being   Le5
vanity, all is   Ec1
washed their feet and ate and drank   Ju19
weak, if my head were shaved I should be   Ju16
wind, Achsah broke   Jos15
winebibber   Pro23
wisdom, die without ever finding   Job4
  let silence be your   Job13
  surpassed all men, Solomon's   KF4
wise, can a fool grow   Job11
wish come true is a staff of life   Pro13
wounds dressed with vinegar   Pro25
  he will bind up our   Ho6
wrestling, Jacob   Gen32

NEW TESTAMENT

affection, inordinate   PCo3
  warmth of mutual   PR12
anger, lay aside all   PCo3
animal body comes first, and then the spiritual   PCF15
anxious thoughts, put away   Mw6

appearance sake, they say long prayers for   L20

arrogance defiles the man   Mk7

athlete   PTS2

bad company is the ruin of a good character   PCF15

   language must not pass your lips   PE4

beam in thine own eye   L6

behold the man   J19

belly, whose god is their   PPs3

besides ourselves, if we are   PCS5

bewildered, we are never at our wits' end   PCS4

blind leading the blind   Mw15

boaster, the tongue is a   LJ3

boastings, you rejoice in your   LJ4

bodies are limbs and organs of Christ, your   PCF6

body, all of us form one   PR12

   animal and spiritual   PCF15

   exiles as long as we are at home in the   PCS5

   our vile   PPs3

   take no thought for your   L12

courage! the victory is mine   J16

covetousness defiles the man   Mk7

   mortify your   PCo3

crooked and warped generation   PPs2

cup of happiness   PPs2

currying favour, do you think I am   PG1

desires, foolish harmful   PTF6

   godless ways and worldly   Tt2

dishonest in little things   L16

dishonesty, renounced the hidden things of   PCS4

distress, helping others in   PR12

distribution to every man according as he had need   A4

drinker, a glutton and a   C7

drunkard, any Christian who is a   PCF5

drunkenness, do not let your minds be dulled by   L21

duty to help the weak by hard work   A20

earthly things, their minds are set on   PPs3

encourage one another   LH3

enemies, love your   L6

envy defiles the man   Mk7

evil eye defiles the man   Mk7

evil thoughts come from inside   Mk7
    why do you harbour   Mw9
eye, speck of sawdust in your   Mw7; L6
eye, the lamp of the body   Mw6
faith as a grain of mustard seed   L17
  in him, even his brothers had no   J7
  on earth? will the son of man find   L18
  you will all fall from your   Mk14
fear, shaking with   PCF2
  they were taken with great   L8
fellow workers risked their necks   PR16
flattering words, we never used   ThF2
flesh can give birth only to flesh   J3
  is weak, spirit is willing but the   Mk14
folly, bear with me in my   PCS11
forerunner, you will be the Lord's   L1
forgive the wrongs you have done   Mk11
forgiving one another   PCo3
free, truth will set you   J8
friend of publicans and sinners   L7
gentle spirit, those of a   Mk5
gentleness, patience, humility, put on the garments of   PCo3
give, and it shall be given unto you   L6
glutton and a drinker   L7
God, those who know their need of   Mw5
good and evil, to discriminate between   LH5
  deeds, widow must produce evidence of   PTF5
  none save God is   L18
goodness, must be no limit to your   Mw15
greed which makes an idol of gain   PE5
greet one another with a kiss of peace   PR16
greetings in the markets   L11, 20
grumblers and malcontents, a set of   LJu1
hair cut off, Paul had his   A18
hairs on your head have all been counted   Mw10
happy are those who hear the word of God   L11
  is the man who does not find me a stumbling-block   L7
hates his brother, if he   LJF2
hear, if you have ears to   Mk4
heart, discerner of the thoughts and intents of the   LH4

hearts at rest, set your troubled   J14
  harden not your   LH4
helping others in distress   PR12
honest in little things   L16
honest man comes to the light   J3
honour and dishonour are alike our lot   PCS6
human level of your lower nature   PCF3
  lot with all its ups and downs   PPs4
  nature, lay aside that old   PE4
  pride in the presence of God, no place for   PCF1
humble, gentle and patient, be always   PE4
humility, gentleness, patience, put on   PCO3
hypocrites make a show of charity   Mw6
inner man to be strengthened by his Spirit   PE3
innocence of our behaviour   PCS6
innocent as doves   Mw10
insults for my sake, when you suffer   Mw5
irreligious and worldly, law aimed at the   PTF1
jealousy, quarrelling, quibbles which give rise to   PTF6
joyful, be joyful with the   PR12
kingdom of God is within you   L17
kiss, greet one another with a holy   PCF16
  of love, greet one another with the   LPF
  of peace, greet all our brothers with the   PCS13; ThF5
law is spiritual, but I am carnal   PR7
least among you all, he is the greatest   L9
liar, he that saith I know him is a   LJF2
lie not to one another   PCo3
life is more than food, and body than clothes   Mw6
little man, being a   L19
lodging, Peter gave them a night's   A10
loose livers, have nothing to do with   PCF5
love and peace, pursue   PTS2
  cancels innumerable sins   LPF4
  cannot wrong a neighbour   PR13
  first, put   PCF4
  for one another   PPs2
  fortitude and gentleness, pursue   PTF6
  if I have not   PCF13
  is all sincerity   PR12

love, man who does not LJF3
  more than ordinary PCS2
  mount and overflow, let your ThF3
  one another J13; LJF3; LJS1
  rule of ThF4
  shows itself in action LJF3
  toward all men ThF3
  will never come to an end PCF13
  you have lost your early Rev2
  your enemies and do good L6
  your neighbour as yourself Mk12; PG5; LJ2
    they were told Mw5
loved, the disciple whom Jesus J13
lower nature, living on the purely human level of your PCF3
    the desires of your PG5
    those who live on the level of our PR8
malice, lay aside all PCo3
mammon of unrighteousness L16
men, made in the likeness of PPs2
mercy shall be shown to them Mw5
mind and spirit, you must be made new in PE4
morally uncircumcised PCo2
mortal part may be absorbed into life immortal PCS5
naked and ashamed for all to see Rev16
  you clothed me Mw25
nature, desires of your lower PG5
  has no claims on us, lower PR8
neighbour, who is my L10
nervous, weak and shaking with fear PCF2
novelty, hearing about the latest A17
out of his mind, people were saying that he was Mk3
parents, men with no respect for PTS3
passed by on the other side L10
passions and desires, lower nature with its PG5
patience and kindness, by our PCS6
  humility, gentleness, put on the garments of PCo3
  of Job, ye have heard of the LJ5
  of the saints Rev14
  under ill-treatment, a pattern of LJ5
patient towards all men ThF5

peace is my parting gift to you   J14

   live in   PCS13

   on earth, do you suppose I came to establish   L12

   pursue the things that make for   PR14

   such as the world cannot give   J14

   with all men, live at   PR12

   with one another, be at   Mk9

peacemakers, sons of God   Mw5

pleasure in the place of God, men who put   PTS3

pompous ignoramus, I call him a   PTF6

poor with you always   Mk14; J12

possessions held in common   A4

praise and blame are alike our lot   PCS6

pretence or sincerity, Christ is set forth   PPs1

pride defiles the man   Mk7

   he rises in his   ThS2

   in outward show and not in inward worth   PCS5

   lest being lifted up with   PTF3

   never make mere man a cause for   PCF3

   what room is left for human   PR3

proud, instruct the rich not to be   PTF6

publicans and sinners, drew near unto him all the   L15

   do not even the   Mw5

pure, to the pure all things are   TF1

   hearts, those of, shall see God   Mw5

quarrels among you, there are   PCF1

relations, make provisions for   PTF5

religion, making a show of   Mw6

reputation, they valued their   J12

respect for their parents, men with no   PTS3

riches, deceitfulness of   Mk4

riotous living, wasted his substance in   L15

salutations in the market place, who love   Mk12; L11

scorn, they laughed him to   Mw9

secret place   Mw6

   your good deed must be   Mw6

self importance, filled with   PCF4

    swollen with   PTS3

   indulgence, a widow given over to   PTF5

self mortification   PCo2

sensuality, human teaching of no use in combating   PCo2
share what you have with others   LH13
sincere love, recommend ourselves by   PCS6
Son of Man came eating and drinking   L7
 has nowhere to lay his head   Mw8; L9
 who speaks a word against the   L12
sorrowful shall find consolation   Mw5
speaking things best left unspoken   PTF5
spirit is willing but the flesh is weak   Mk14
 of God, refuses what belongs to the   PCF2
spiritual gift, I want to bring you some   PR1
spite and passion, have done with   PE4
stature, add one cubit to his   L12
staying power, they have no   Mk4
strangers to the truth   LJ1
superstition, questions of their own   A25
temperance, honesty and godliness, live a life of   Tt2
temptation, lead us not into   L11
 which shall come upon all the world   Rev3
 of those who want to be rich   PTF6
tempted, he himself has suffered being   LH2
trance, fell into a   A22
true self, he will find his   Mw16
truth, believers who have inward knowledge of the   PTF4
 fasten on the belt of   PE6
 with his neighbour, speak every man   PE4
unjust in the least, he that is   L16
vanity, no room for personal   PPs2
 speaking words of   LPS2
vegetarian   PR14
warmth of mutual affection   PR12
warped and crooked generation   PPs2
wasted his substance in riotous living   L15
watch and pray   Mw26; Mk14
way of peace, guide our feet unto the   L1
weak, nervous and shaking with fear   PCF2
weakness, sown in, raised to power   PCF15
weaknesses, able to sympathise with our   LH4
wits are beclouded, their   PE4
word became flesh   J1

22 *Hunting and Fishing*

OLD TESTAMENT

angle for fish   H1
dead-fall trap   Job18; Pro22, 26, 28; Je48; La3
deer pursued by hunter   La1
drag-net   H1
fish basket   Am4
  dying   Ex7
  for the asking in Egypt   Nu11
  in shoals   E47
fisherman   Is19; Je16; E26, 47
fishhook   E29; Am4; H1
fishing equipment   Job41
fowler   Ps91, 124; Pro6; Je5; Ho9
fowler's snare   Ps91
  trap   Ps124
gaff, fishing   Job41
gin trap   Is8; Am3
harpoon   Job41
hook, barbed   Nu33; Jos23; E29; Am4; H1
hunter   Job15; Ps91; Pro6, 12; Is13, 24; Je16, 48; La1; Ho12; Mi7
  Esau became a skilful   Gen25
  mighty before the Lord   Gen10
  Nimrod was a mighty   Gen10
hunting equipment   Job18
huntsman   Ps22
net   Pro1, 29; E12
  antelopes caught in the   Is51
  fishing   Ec9; Is19; E26, 32, 47; H1
  fowler's   Pro1, 29; Je5; Ho7
  hunter's   Job18; Mi7
  wild bull in a   Is51
noose, hunting   Job18; Pro7

partridge over the hills, as one might hunt   SF26
pit, hunter's   Job18; Pro26, 28; Is24; Je48; La3
  lion caught in a   E19
pitfall   Pro22, 26, 28
scare, hunter's   Is24; Je48; La3
snare   Ps91, 141f; Pro7, 20, 22, 29; Is8, 24
  fowler's   Ps91; Ec9; Am3
  hunter's   Job18; Je5, 48, 50
spear, fish   Job41
trap, fowler's   Ho9
  gin   Is8; Am3
  hunter's   Ps91; Is24; Je48; Am3
  metal   Job18
  toothed   Job41
trawls, fishing   H1

NEW TESTAMENT

boat, fisherman's   Mw4; Mk1
  towing a full net   J21
casting-net   Mk1
fish, a great multitude of   L5
  made a big haul of   L5
  net full of   J21
  that comes to the hook   Mw17
fishermen   Mk1; L5
  of Galilee   Mw4
fishers of men, I will make you   Mk1
fishing, I am going out   J21
  net   Mk1
hook, go to the sea and cast an   Mw17
hunted, we are never abandoned   PCS4
mending their nets   Mw4
net, fishing   Mw4; L5; J21
  let down into the sea   Mw13
nets began to split   L5
  overhauling their   Mw4; Mk1

ship, fishing   Mw4; Mk1
snare   PR11; PCF7; PTF6
  caught in the devil's   PTF3
  of the devil   PTS2
  shall it come, as a   L21
trap, a snare and a   PR11
  great day closes upon you like a   L21
traps the wise in their own cunning   PCF3

23 *Idols, Gods and Images*

feet of clay, image in Nebuchadnezzar's dream   D2
fetish, take their orders from a   Ho4
figure carved in relief   De4
fire, children made to pass through   KS17
  made his sons pass through   KS17
  not to pass through   De18
  pass through in honour of Molech   KS23
  passed his son through   KS16, 21
  you pass your sons through   E20
garden rites   Is66
  shrines   Is1
gardens, offering sacrifices in   Is65
god, bull   Je46
  cried out for help, each to his   Jon1
  daughters of a foreign   Ma2
  fashion gold and silver into a   Is46
  foreign   Ps81; Is17
  of fate   Is65
  strange   Ps81
goddess Asherah, Ashtoreth   KF11, 15; KS13
  Ashima   Am8
  of the field   So2f
  of the Sidonians   KS23
gods   Ps29, 81ff; 106, 135
  ancestral   Jos24; SF7; D11
  as many as you have towns   Je11
  banish the foreign   Jos24; SF7
  beloved of women   D11
  burning incense to his   Je48
    offerings to their   Je48
    sacrifices to other   Je19, 44
  can give the answer, none but the   D2
  Canaanite   Ju2ff
  consigned to the fire   Is37
  declare what will happen, then we shall know   Is41
  drink-offerings to other   Je19, 32
  gold calves as   KF12
  household   Z10
  I love foreign   Je2
  led astray by false   Am2

gods, made out of wood and stone   De4
    must not follow other   Jos23; Je28
    of all nations   Ps96
    of bronze and iron   D5
    of Egypt, houses of the   Je43
    of gold and silver   D5
    of metal   Le19
    of Seir, sacrificed to   CS25
    of silver and gold   Ex20
    of the earth   Zp2
    of the household, Teraphim   E21
    of wood and stone   D5
    powerless to help   Je2
    run after other, to your own ruin   Je7
    served alien   Je5
    temples of the Egyptian   Je43
    that are no gods, sworn by   Je5
    they resort to other   Ho3
    they went after other   Ju2
    trusted in false   Je13
    we will not serve your   D3
    worshipping other   De17
    you have taken my   Ju18
    you shall have no other   De5
golden calf of Aaron   Ex32
    calves, Jehu maintained the worship of   KS10
    image of Nebuchadnezzar   D3
graven images, a land of   Je50
    beaten to pieces   Mi1
    burned incense to   Ho11
    confounded by   Je10, 51
    curse on the maker of   De27
    do not make   De4
    hew down the   De12
    I will cut off your   Mi5; Na1
    molten, profitable for nothing   Is44
    of Babylon   Is21
    provoked me to anger with their   Je8
    served their   KS17
    that trust in   Is42

idol   Ps16, 31, 96, 106; Is44f, 48, 57
  and image will I hew down   Na1
  carved   Nu33
  despised broken   Je22
  every goldsmith is discredited by his   Je51
  figures of reptiles, beasts and vermin   E8
  forbidden   Le26
  gold   Is31
  king, take up the shrine of an   Am5
  set up in Dan   Ju18
  sheathed in gold   Is30
  they burn sacrifices to a mere   Je18
  to make a carved   Ju17
  what use is an   H2
  worship an   Is66
idolatry in Gilead   Ho12
idols, all who vaunt   Ps97
  Asa did away with   KF15
  banish your loathsome   Je4
  buried   Gen35
  carved round the walls   E8
  David carried off the Philistine   SS5
  defiled the land   E36
  destroy their   DE7
  erase the names of   Z13
  fashioned their silver into   Ho13
  fling down your slain before your   E6
  four kingdoms full of   Is10
  go awhoring after their   E6
  hack down their   De12
  have spoken vanity   Z10
  I will cleanse you from the taint of your   E36
  I will punish Babylon's   Je51
  Josiah got rid of   Ks23
  land filled with   Is2
  let them come forward, these   Is41
  loathsome   Je7
  make a waste heap of   Mi1
  making dumb   H2
  men of Judah worshipped   CS24

idols   never again be defiled with   E37
  of Egypt   Is19
  of gold   Is2
  of Israel   E18
of Manasseh   KS21
  of Philistines burnt by David   CF14
  of silver,   Is2, 31
  provoke me to anger with   Je25
  purged   CS34
  raisin-cakes offered to their   Ho3
  set up their loathsome   Je32
  silver and gold   Ps115, 135; Ho8
  slaughtering their sons as an offering to   E23
  suppressed by Asa   CS15
  the city that makes herself   E22
  the dead lumber of their   Je16
  their eyes have gone roving wantonly after   E6
  these people have set their hearts on E14
  they are mad upon their   Je50
  they worshipped   KS17
  to defy all wooden   E21
  turn away from your   E14
  you lift up your eyes to   E33
idol-worship, Jezebel's   KS9
image, a source of lies   H2
  and idol will I hew down   Na1
  broken down   CS34
  bull   Ps106
  calf   CS11, 13; Ps106
  carved   CS34; Ps78
  cast, Baalim   CS28
    metal   Nu33
  confounded by his graven   Je10
  gold, Nebuchadnezzar made a   D3
  graven   De4; CS34
  laid in bed   SF19
  molten   CS34
    is falsehood   Je10
  Nebuchadnezzar's dream   D2
  of a bull-calf   Ne9

images, all who worship   Ps97
  burnt offerings before carved   Ho11
  burnt one and all   Mi1
  of cast metal   Ho13
  which craftsman sets up   Is40
carved, are a sham   Je10
  cherished, profit nobody   Is44
  I will destroy your   M5
  made jewels into vile   E7
  molten gold   Is30
  of Baal, burnt   KS10
    smashed   KS11
  of Beth-shemesh, he shall break   Je43
  of cast metal   KS17
  of gods cast in metal   D11
  of Israel shall be broken   E6
  of lust at Jerusalem   E8
  pedestals of your   Am5
  sacred   Is17
  sacrificing children to   E16
  shall live without   Ho3
  shall not stand   Is27
  silvered   Is30
  under every green tree   KF14
incense   Is43, 60
  an abomination   Is1
  burnt as a token   Is66
    for idols   E8, 23
    in pagan rites   KS14ff, 22ff
    offered to Baal   Je32
    on brick altars   Is65
    on the mountains   I65
    to Baal   Je7, 11
    to Baalim   Ho2
    to gods   Je11
    to graven images   Ho11
    to his gods   Je48
    to other gods   Je1, 19, 44
  they burn up on the hills   Ho4
incense-altars   Is17, 27

poles, sacred, burn their   De12
   by every spreading tree   Je17
   cut down   CS14, 31
   I will pull down your   Mi5
power, subdue the ancient   De33
priests of the high places, slew all the   KS23
  of the hill-shrines from every class   KS17
processions, images carried in your   Is46
purge of idols   CS34
raisin-cake offered to idols   Ho3
Rimmon, Babylonian god of storms   KS5
  temple of   KS5
rites, your vile and abominable   E5
sacred groves   De12; Ju6; KF14, 18; KS11, 21; CS14ff; Is17; Je17; Mi5
 oaks   Is1
 pillars   Le26; KS3,10,17ff, 23; CS14, 31; Je43; Ho3, 110; Mi5
  broke down   KS23
  Hezekiah smashed   KS23
  I will destroy your   Mi5
  of Baal   KS3, 10
  of Beth-shemesh   Je43
  shall live without   Ho3
  smashed   CS14, 31
 poles   KF14, 16; KS10, 13, 17ff, 23; CS11, 14, 24, 31, 33; Is17, 27
  by every spreading tree   Je17
  cut down   Ju6; KS23
  Hezekiah destroyed   Ks18
  I will pull down your   Mi5
  in hill-shrines   Is6
  of Baal, burnt   KS10
sacrifice at every leafy tree   E20
 at hill-shrines   KS14ff
 child   Le20; Ju11; KS3, 16f, 21, 23; CS33; Ps106; Is57; Je7, 19, 32; E16, 20, 23; Ho13
 first-born sons, redeemed   Ex13
 offered in gardens   Is65
 on the mountain tops   Ho4
 to Baal   Je11, 19, 32
  a great   Ks10
 to Baalim   CS28
 to bull-gods   Ho12

NEW TESTAMENT

gods, slaves of beings which are no   PG4
graven by art, gold, silver, or stone   A17
great is Diana of the Ephesians!   A19
heaven, symbol of Diana which fell from   A19
host of heaven, gave them up to worship the   A7
idol, anything but an   PCF10
  bull-calf   A7
  of gain, greed which makes an   PE5
idolater, no, hath any inheritance   PE5
  no, will possess the kingdom   PCF6
idolaters, do not be   PCF10
  outside are   Rev22
  pagan   PCF5
idolatry and sorcery belong to lower nature   PG5
   city given over to   A17
  greed no less than   PCo3
  is covetousness   PCo3
  shun   PCF10
  so accustomed to   PCF8
idols, abstain from contact with   A15
   from meat offered to   A21
  Athens was full of   A17
  dumb   PCF12
  eat food sacrificed to   Rev2
  food consecrated to   PCF8
  forbidden worship of   LPF4
  little children, keep yourselves from   LJF5
  of gold, silver, bronze, stone and wood   Rev9
  of the heathen   PCS6
  what agreement hath the temple of God with   PCS6
  worship of   Rev9
  you turned from   ThF1
image in gold or silver   A17
  of Baal, not boweth the knee to the   PR11
  of the beast, to worship the   Rev13, 16
  shaped like mortal man, exchanging God for an   PR1
images like birds, beasts and creeping things   PR1
Jupiter, image which fell down from   A19
  priest of   A14
  temple of   A14

24 *Laws, Oaths, Pledges*
and Covenants

OLD TESTAMENT

bribery makes a crooked answer   De16
   the wise man blind   De16
bribes, hands full of   Ps26
  Samuel's sons took   SF8
calumnies heaped upon me   Ps109
  of the nations   Ps89
  sanctimonious   Ps94
  they spread   Ps73
census of Solomon   CS2
champion, God shall be   Ps59
  to their cause   Is19
college at Jerusalem   KS22
commandment to bless   Nu23
commandments, find joy in his   Ps112
  fix my eyes on   Ps119
  observe his   KF2
  ten, declared by Moses   Ex20
  they did not keep his   KS17
commands, do serve my   Ps89
common lands attached to cities   CS31
   surrounding towns   Nu35
compact, Jonathan and David made a solemn   SF18
compensation for wrongdoing   Nu5
complaint against Moses and Aaron   Nu16
contributions, defrauding over   Ma3
council, if they have stood in my   Je23
counsel, let us seek   KF22
  of the people   Ps33
  the Lord's   Ps33
counsellor   Is40
  like those of old   Is1
  Pharaoh's   Is19
  stripped of every   Is3
court   Ps127
  in Daniel's vision   D7
  institution of the   Ex18
  of the tabernacle   Ex27ff
  sat, and the books were opened   D7
covenant, Ahab to Ben-hadad   KF20
  anger in his heart against the   D11

judge over Israel, Tola   Ju10
  stripped of every   Is3
  swift to do right   Is16
  the earth   Ps82
judges appointed by Jehosaphat   CS19
  Ezra to appoint   Ez7
  over them, the Lord set   Ju2
  what they once were   Is1
judgement belongs to God   De1
  breastplate of   Ex18ff
  conform to my   Ps89
  every case to bring before the king for   SS15
  Lord sits high in   Is5
  of Solomon   KF3
  rising in   Ps76
  regarding who is the mother   KF3
  Valley of the Lord's   Joe3
judgements, just, are your   Ps58
justice   Ps9ff, 67, 101
  administer true   Z7
  alone pursue   De16
  always on his lips   Ps37
  and equity   Ps99
  and judgement of their own making   H1
  comes out perverted   H1
  court of   Is28
  dawns like morning light   Ho6
  do not pervert the course of   De16
  give me   Ps26
  heavens proclaim his   Ps50
  judge mankind with   Ps75
  in the courts, enthrone   Am5
  my own   Ps72
  rule with   Is32
  shall redeem Zion   Is1
  spirit of   Is28
  they went to Deborah for   Ju4
  use as a plumb-line   Is28
  wear the belt of   Is11
  when the inhabitants of the world learn   Is26

justice, who taught him   Is40
justly, to love loyalty, to act   Mi6
land, common, surrounding towns   Nu35; CS31
  register of   Jos18
  tenure by slaves   E46
land-mark   Pro22ff
law and justice, the branch of David will maintain   Je33
  book of God's   Jos24
    be ever on your lips   Jos1
  contrives a mischief under cover of the   Ps94
  grows effete   H1
  her priests have done violence to my   E22
  if his sons forsake my   Ps89
  of God   Ps37
  of Moses   KF2; KS23; CS23, 25; Ez3, 7; Ne8
    all foreshadowed by the   D9
    perform everything in the   Jos23
    turn not aside from the   Jos23
  swerve not from thy   Ps119
  stands firm, thy   Ps93
  the people assemble to study the   Ne8
  they that keep the   Pro28
  words of, inscribed   De27
lawgiver, Gad in the position of   De33
  the Lord is our   Is33
lawlessness and robbery, put an end to   E45
laws and statutes, she has rebelled against my   E5
  and teachings, you did not obey his   Je44
  Jerusalem rejected my   E5
  live humbly by his   Zp2
  of nature on earth   Job38
  of the Medes and Persians   Est1
  shame on you who make unjust   Is10
  they have broken the   Is24
  you have not kept my   E11
letters of King Ahasuerus   Est1
levies on merchandise   CS9
levy, general   Ez4, 7
  on all men of wealth   KS15
  Solomon raised forced   KF5

licence to obtain timber   Ez3

litigation spreads like a poisonous weed   Ho10

loan, pledges for a   De24

lost property, rules concerning   De22

lot, Benjamin was picked by   SF10

  territories were assigned by   Jos14

lots cast for land   Jos18

    to apportion blame   SF14

    to decide local residence   Ne11

manumission, rules of   E46

misdemeanours, wise men versed in   Est1

money lending, rules of   Ex22

mortgage, house and farm   Ne5

Moses and tables of stone   KF8

oath and solemn vow   Ps119

  binding obligation of an   Nu30

  captains put on   KS11

  David answered with an   SS4

  for the life of Rahab   Jos2

  Jonathan had not heard his father's   SF14

  laws of taking an   Nu30

  no respect for an   Ps55

  not to be broken   Ps132

  of allegiance   CS36

  of David regarding Solomon   KF1

    to Bathsheba   KF1

  of David's officers that he should never again go to war   SS21

  of Ezra   Ez10

  of Moses to Caleb   Jos14

  of Saul, that Jonathan should die   SF14

  pervert the course of justice with an   SF8

  pledged to the Gibeonites   Jos9

  trial for unfaithfulness involving an   Nu5

oaths are imposed and broken   Ho4

  are perjury, their   Ps144

offence at Peor, remember our   Jos22

oppression of the poor, strangers and widows, forbidden   Z7

orders sent to exterminate all Jews, young and old   Est3ff

ordinance, Joshua drew up an   Jos24

  of King Darius   D6

NEW TESTAMENT

Son of Man given the right to pass   J5
that you expose yourselves to   LJ5
the coming   A24
to bring all men to   LJu1
world come before you for   PCF6
judges, appointed for them   A13
judging your fellow man you judge yourself   PR2
jurisdiction of the governor   L20
justice, integrity, pursue   PTS2
of God, anger cannot promote the   LJ1
pursue   PTF6
kill, thou shalt not   L18; PR13; LJ2
law a temporary measure   PG3
and the prophets, after readings from the   A13
I believe all that is written in the   A24
that is the   Mw7
until John it was the   L16
avoid contentions and strivings about the   Tt3
bickering about your Jewish   A18
book, Moses sprinkled with blood the   LH9
brings only the consciousness of sin   PR3
brought nothing to perfection   LH7
can bring only retribution   PR4
cancelled the bond of the   PCo2
Christ ends the, for everyone who has faith   PR10
contains but a shadow   LH10
controversial matters in their   A23
converts, staunch upholders of the   A21
court, pagan   PCF6
curse of the   PG3
devout observer of the   J7
did not Moses give you the   J7
did you receive the Spirit by keeping the   PG3
do not suppose that I have come to abolish the   Mw5
doctor of   Mw5, 8, 12, 16, 20f, 23; Mk1ff, 7f, 10ff, 14; L2, 5, 9, 15, 20, 22; J8; A4ff, 23
engraved upon stone dispensed death   PCS3
flout the emperor's   A17
he annulled the   PE2
in the absence of, no reckoning is kept of sin   PR5
instructed by the, you know right from wrong   PR2

25 *Metals, Treasures and Precious Stones*

OLD TESTAMENT

bronze, cherubim   KF7
  cymbals   CF15
  door   Ps107
  fetters of   Ju16; KS25; Je39, 52
  gate-bars of   KF4
  gates   Is45
  Goliath's armour of   SF17
  great quantity of   SS8
  hooves of   Mi4
  implements   Ex30, 38
  lions   KF7
  more than can be weighed   CF22
  oxen   KF7
  pillars   Je52
    broken up   KS25
  Samson in fetters of   Ju16
  sea of   KF7ff
    broken up   KS25
    dismantled   KS16
  serpent of Moses   Nu21
  shields   KF14
  spear   SS21
  temple fitments of   Je52
  vessels of   KS25; Le52
  wall of   Je1, 15
  your shoes to be   De33
  Zedekiah in fetters of   KS25, 39; Job28; E28
carbuncle   Is54; E27ff
chrysolite   Ex28, 39; Job28; E28
copper   Ex25, 31, 35; Nu31; De8; Jos6, 22; SS8; CF18; CS2, 4, 24; Is60; Je6; E22, 24;
      D2; Z6
  beyond reckoning   CS4
  laden with   Jos22
  offering of   Ex25ff
  red   Ez8
  smelted from the ore   Job28
  vessels of   SS8
    at Jericho   Jos6
coral   Pro3, 8, 20; E27
  black   Job28; E27

gold chain   Gen41; Ex28; KF6ff; D5
 common as stones   CS1
 crown of   SS12; Ps21
 crucible for   Pro27
 cup   Je51
 dust   Job28
 earrings   Ex32; Nu31; Ju8; Job42; Pro25
 fasteners   Ex26
 from Ophir   D10
 from Sheba   Ps72
 haemorrhoids modelled in   SF6
 headrest, palanquin   So3
 hooks   Ex36
 imported from Ophir   CS8ff
 laden with   Jos22
 lamp-stand   Ex37; Nu8; Z4
 nose-ring   Gen24
 Nubian   Pro25
 of Havilah   Gen2
 of Jericho   Jos6
 of Ophir   Ps45; Is13; Je10; D10
 of Uphaz   D10
 ornaments   Ex35; Nu31; Ju8; Pro25; Je4; E16
 overlay   Ex25, 30, 36
 pendant   Nu31
 plating   Ex25; Is40
 quiver   SS8; CF18
 rats modelled in   SF6
 red   KF6, 10; CS4; Job28
 rings   Ex28, 30, 32, 39; Nu31; Ju8; Pro11, 25; So5
 rosette   Ex28ff; Le8
 sceptre   Est4
 shield   SS8; KF14
 trade in   E27
 tumours modelled in   SF6
 vessels   Ex37; SS8; KS12; D5
golden image of a bull calf, Aaron's   Ex32
 wedge of Ophir   Is13
iron   Nu31; De8, 27ff, 33; Jos6, 22; Ju1, 4; SS12; CF20, 22, 29; CS2, 18, 24; Job40ff;
       Pro27; Is10, 48, 60; Je6, 15; E4, 22, 27; D2, 4ff

iron and bronze, your bolts shall be   De33
  bands of   Je28
  bars   Ps107
  bright   E27
  chain   Ps107
  chariots   Jos15; Ju1, 4
  collar   Ps105, 107
  earth shall be   De28
  engraving   Job19
  for altar stones, no tool of   De27
  great store of   CF22
  harrows of   SS12
  horns of   KF22; CS18; Mi4
  laden with   Jos22
  ore   De8
  pen of   Je17
  pillar of   Je1
  ring   D4
  rod   Ps2
  sarcophagus   De3
  spearhead   SF17
  spikes   Am1
  tools   De27; SS12; KF6; CF20; Je17
  vessels at Jericho   Jos60
  weapons of   Job20
  whetted edge of   Ec10
  won from the earth   Job28
  wrought   E27
ivory   KF22; CS9; So7; E27; Am3, 6
  benches of   E27
  panelled with   Ps45
  plaque of   So5
jade   Ex28ff, 39; E28
jasper   Ex28ff, 39; E28
  green   Ex28
  red   Is54; E27
jewelled chain necklace   So1
jewellery, ask for   Ex11
  silver and gold   Ex3, 11
jewels   So7; Is3, 49, 54, 61; E7; Ho2; Z9; Ma3

jewels, collar of Ps73
  decked herself with Ho2
  forehead E16
  necklace of So1
  nose Is3
  of gold SS1
  precious Pro20
  wear them proudly as Is49
lapis lazuli Ex28, 39; Job28; So5; Is54; Je6; La4; E1, 10
lead Nu31; Job19; E22, 27; Z5
malachite, mosaic of Est1
marble So5
metal, cast Ex34; Nu33
    clay for KF7
  image Ex20, 32; Le10; Nu33; De9; KF12, 17; CS13, 28, 34; Ne9; Ps115, 135; Je10, 51;
        Is2, 30f, 40, 42, 46; D3, 5, 11; Ho8, 13
  foundry KF7
  precious Je52
  smelting E1, 22
money for temple repairs Ks12
mosaic pavement Est1
mother-of-pearl mosaic Est1
mould, bronze KF7
onyx Ex25ff; CF27; Job28; E28
orichale Ez8
ornaments, crafted Gen24, 35; Ex28, 32; Le8; Nu31, 37; De6, 11; Ju8; SS1; KF6; Est3f, 7;
        Job42; Ps73; Pro1, 3, 4, 7, 11, 25; So1, 4ff; Is3, 28, 37, 40, 49, 61; Je2, 4, 22, 31;
        D5; E16, 23, 28; D5; Ho2
pearls Job28
precious metal Je52
  stones Ex28, 35; SS12; KF10; CF20, 29; CS3, 9, 32; Ps68; D11
    crown set with SS12
    engraved Ex28
    in an idol's crown CF20
    trade in E27
red copper Ez8
  gold Job28
refined as silver Z13
refiner's fire Ma3

ruby   Pro3, 8, 20, 31; La4

sapphire   Ex24; Job28; So5; Ls54; La4; E1, 10, 28

  pavement of   Ex24

sardin, sardius   Ex28, 39; E28

sea of cast metal   KF7

silver   Gen24, 42f, 47; Ex3, 11f, 21f, 25f, 31, 25f, 38; Le27; Nu3, 7, 18, 22, 24, 31; De2, 7,
            De14, 29; Jos6ff, 22; Ju5, 16ff; SF9; SS8, 18, 21, 24; KF7, 10, 15, 20ff; KS7, 12,
            KS14, 16, 18, 20, 25; CF18ff, 28ff; CS1f, 15, 17, 21, CS24, 32, 34; Ez1, 8; Ne7;
            Job3, 27f; Ps12, 68, 105, 115, 119; Pro2f, 8, 16f, 22, 25ff; Ec2, 5; So1; Is2, 13,
            Is31, 39, 46, 48, 60; Je10, 32, 52; E7, 27f, 38; D2, 5, 11; Ho2f, 8f, 13; Joe3;
            Am2, 8; Na2; H2; Zp1; Hg2; Z6, 9, 14; M3

  100 pieces for parcel of ground   Jos24

  200 shekels of   Jos7

  1,000,000 talents of   CF22

  alloyed with copper, tin, iron and lead   E22

  and gold couches   Est1

  as common as stones   KF10; CS1

  beaten   Je10

  chain   Is40

  cord   Ec12

  dross from the   Pro25

  for tithes   De14

  goblet   Gen44

  great quantity of   CS17

  laden with   Jos22

  melt down   KS22; E1, 22

  melted in crucible   E22

  melting pot for   Pro27

  mines   Job28

  of Jericho   Jos6

  ornaments   E16

  palanquin poles   So3

  pieces of   SS8, 24; So8; Is7

  quarter shekel   SF9

  ransom money of   Nu3

  reckoned of no value by Solomon   KF10

  refined as   Ps66; Z13

  rings, curtain   Est1

  sockets   Ex26

silver, spurious   Je6
  studs   Is40
  thirty pieces of   Z11
  to be paid for killing the Jews   Est3
   to purchase food   De2
  turned into base metal   Is1
  vessels   Nu7; SS8; KS12; Ne7; D5
silverlings   Is7
steel   Je15
tin   Nu31; Is1; E22, 27
topaz   Ex28, 39; Job28; So5; E1, 10, 28; D10
treasure, buried   Pro2
  display of the royal   Est1
  hidden in the sand   De33
  no end to their   Is2
treasuries, royal palace   KS18
treasury of Judah   Is39
  of the Lord's house   Jos6
  the royal Persian   Est3
turquoise   Ex28, 39
  mosaic of   Est1

NEW TESTAMENT

alabaster box   Mw26; Mk14; L7
amethyst   Rev21
bank, money paid into the   L19
belt, money   Mk6
beryl   Rev21
brass, burnished   Rev1f
  merchandise of   Rev18
  to fill your purse   Mw10
brazen vessel   Mk7
bronze   Rev9
  cargoes of   Rev18
burnished brass   Rev1f
cankered, gold and silver is   LJ5
chalcedony   Rev21
chest of the temple, treasury   Mw27; Mk12; L21

copper   Mk7
  to fill your purse   Mw10
cornelian   Rev4, 21
chrysolite   Rev21
chrysoprase, chrysoprasus   Rev21
crystal   Rev4, 21f
emerald   Rev4, 21
filthy lucre, given to   Tt1
    greedy of   PTF3
    not for   LPF5
furnace, refined in a   Rev1
gold   Mw2, 10, 23; PCF3; LPF1; Rev9
  and silver have rusted away   LJ5
    is cankered   LJ5
  bedizened with   Rev17
  cargoes of   Rev18
  city of pure   Rev21
  crowns of   Rev4
  cup   Rev17
  decked out in   PTF2
  five bags of   Mw25
  I have coveted no man's   A20
  image in   A17
  lamps, seven   Rev1f
  measuring   Rev21
  offered him   Mw2
  or silver, I have no   A3
  passes through the assayer's fire   LPF1
  plated   LH9
  refined in the fire   Rev3
  rings   LJ2
  streets of the holy city   Rev21
  utensils   PTS2
  wearing of   LPF3
golden altar   LH9; Rev8
  bowl   Rev5, 15
  candlesticks, seven   Rev1f
  censer   LH9; Rev8
  crown   Rev14
  girdle   Rev15

golden jar   LH9
  pot   LH9
  vials   Rev5, 15
iron   Rev9
  cargoes of   Rev18
  gate   A12
ivory, cargoes of   Rev18
  vessels of   Rev18
jacinth   Rev21
  breastplates of in John's vision   Rev9
jasper   Rev4, 21
jewellery   LPF3
jewels and pearls, bedizened with   Rev17
    cargoes of   Rev18
  radiance of some priceless   Rev21
lapis lazuli   Rev21
lucre, filthy   PTF3; Tt1; LPF5
mammon, ye cannot serve God and   Mw6; L16
marble, cargoes of   Rev18
money and self, men will love nothing but   PTS3
  do not live for   LH13
  go with you to damnation, your   A8
  grubbing, deacons must not be   PTF3
  love of, is the root of all evil   PTF6
  Pharisees loved   L16
  thought that the gift of God may be purchased with   A8
  you cannot serve God and   M6; L16
pearl   Mw7, 13
pearls, bedizened with   Rev17
  cargoes of   Rev18
  decked out in   PTF2
  gate of, in John's vision   Rev21
precious stones   PCF3
    and pearls, decked with   Rev17
refined brass   Rev1
rich, those who want to be   PTF6
riches have rotted, your   LJ5
  of Christ, unfathomable   PE3
rusty, where treasure grows   Mw6

sapphire   Rev21
sardine stone   Rev4
sardius   Rev21
sardonyx   Rev21
silver   Mw10; PCF3; Rev9
  and gold had rusted away   LJ5
  cargoes of   Rev18
  I have coveted no man's   A20
  image in   A17
  or gold, I have no   A3
  pieces   Mk12; A19
  shrines of Diana   A19
  thirty pieces of   Mw26f
  utensils   PTS2
tax, from whom do earthly monarchs collect   Mw17
topaz   Rev21
treasure buried in a field   Mw13
  grows rusty, where   Mw6
  in heaven, thou shalt have   L18
  never-failing in heaven   L12
  on earth, do not store up for yourself   Mw6
  pots of earthenware to contain their   PCS4
  things old and new   Mw13
treasures of his glory   PE3
  of wisdom and knowledge, are hid   PCo2
  they opened their   Mw2
treasury   J8
  temple   Mw27; Mk12; L21
turquoise   Rev21
woods, scented and costly   Rev18

26   *Migration and Exile*

OLD TESTAMENT

frontiers of tribal lands   E47
fugitive, cut off at the crossroads   Ob1
half-breeds shall settle in Ashdod   Z9
Jews which dwelt in Egypt   Je44
journey from Sinai to Edom   Nu9
  Israelite, stages of the   Nu33
  to Canaan, Abram's   Gen12
land flowing with milk and honey   Ex3; E12
  in Egypt, Joseph gave his father   Gen47
  promised   Gen50
lost, rescue the   Zp3
lot, parcelled out Jerusalem by   Ob1
migrated to Asshur, Cush   Gen10
nations, they shall be no more two   E37
Negeb, Abram went from Egypt into the   Gen13
nomads from the dwellings of Jacob   Ma2
outcast, all men call you   Je30
scattered among all peoples   De28
service in the court of Nebuchadnezzar, young men for   D1
settlers from the dwelling of Jacob   Ma2
strange language, people of   Ps114
stranger in the earth   Ps119
  oppress not the   Z7
traveller pitching his tent for a night   Je14
travelling companies   Is21
tribal lands, frontiers of   E47
vagrant, wanderer, Cain a   Gen4
wandered in the wilderness of Beersheba, Hagar   Gen21
  you shall be a   Nu14
wanderers among the nations   Ho9
wilderness, for a long time you lived in the   Jos24
  forty years in the   Nu14
  journey into the   Ex3

NEW TESTAMENT

alien, settled as an   LH11

aliens, earthly monarchs collect tax from   Mw17

  in a foreign land, as   LPF2

    no longer   PE2

Claudius issued an edict that all Jews should leave Rome   A18

deportation to Babylon   Mw1

exiles, as long as we are at home in the body, we are   PCS5

leave Rome, all Jews to   A18

outcast, let him be   PG1

  who does not love the Lord   PCF16

refugees in deserts and hills   LH11

tents, living in   LH11

travellers on earth, passing   LH11

27 *Miracles and Angelic Visitations*

OLD TESTAMENT

Aaron's rod turned into a serpent   Ex7
altar was rent in pieces, Jereboam's   KF13
angel appeared to the barren wife   Ju13
  barring Balaam's way   Nu22
  before you, he will send his   Gen24
  destroying   CF21
    the people   SS24
  guardian   Ex23
  in the fiery furnace   D3
  in Zechariah's vision   Z1ff
  of God, as true as   SF27
  reassured Elijah   KS1
  said: I brought you   Ju2
  sat under the tree   Ju6
  sent to save Shadrach, Meshach and Abed-nego   D3
  sent to shut the lions' mouths   D6
  showed himself to Gideon   Ju6
  spoke to Hagar   Gen16
  stood firm, the divine   Ho12
  to cut down the fighting men, the Lord sent an   CS32
  touched Elijah   KF19
  went up with the flame   Ju13
angels, creatures of might   Ps103
  Jacob was met by   Gen32
  of the Lord   Ps35
  on guard   Ps34
  praise him   Ps148
  to guard you   Ps91
breath of life returned   KF17
brightness over the Tabernacle   Nu9ff
bulls, Elijah's miraculous sacrifice of   KF18
burning bush, him who dwells in the   De33
  Lord appeared in the flame of a   Ex3

282

chariots of fire appeared   KS2
cherub as guardian, a towering   E28
  he rode on a   Ps18
cherubim at the Garden of Eden   Gen3
  face of   E41
  glory of God rose from above the   E9
  lifted their wings   E11
  sound of the wings of   E1, 10
  stood on the right side of the temple   E10
  throned on the   Ps80, 99
  vault over the heads of   E1, 10
cloak, Elijah struck the water with his   KS2
cloud covering the Tabernacle   Nu9ff
  of smoke by day and a bright flame by night   Is4
  of the glory of God   CS6
  of the Lord   Ex40
copious supply of oil   KS4
corpse came to life on touching Elisha's bones   KS13
council of holy ones   Ps89
court of heaven   Job1; Ps82, 89, 92
creation   Gen1
creatures in semblance of human form   E1
day, first   Gen1
dew on the fleece   Ju6
ecstasy, prophetic   Nu11
Elijah was carried to heaven   KS2
Elisha breathed into the child seven times   KS4
  miraculous bones of   KS13
El-roi, Hagar's vision of   Gen16
evil spirit left Saul when David played   SF16
faces, each four-winged creature had four   E1
feeding a hundred men   KS4
fire after the earthquake   KF19
  chariots of   KS2, 6
  fell from heaven   KS1
  from heaven   CS7
  from heaven on the altar   CF21
  from the Lord   Nu11, 16; KF18
  horses of   Ks2, 6
  in the cloud   Ex40

NEW TESTAMENT

angel of the abyss, Abaddon, Apollyon   Rev9
  of the church at Ephesus   Rev2
    at Laodicea   Rev3
    at Pergamum   Rev2
    at Philadelphia   Rev3
    at Sardis   Rev3
    at Smyrna   Rev2
    at Thyatira   Rev2
  of the Lord appeared to him in a dream   Mw1
    rolled away the stone   Mw28
    spoke to Philip   A8
    struck him down   A12
    there appeared to him an   L1
    there stood before them an   L2
  opened the prison doors during the night   A5
  or spirit has spoken to him, perhaps an   A23
  rising out of the east   Rev7
  Sadducees deny that there is any   A23
  said, Do not be afraid   L2
  said to me, Write this   Rev19
  said unto them, Fear not: for behold, I bring you tidings   L2
  sent to John   Rev1
  standing in the sun   Rev19
  Stephen's face appeared like the face of an   A6
  there stood by me an   A27
  took up a stone   Rev18
  troubled the water   J5
  welcomed me as if I were an   PG4
  went down to the pool   J5
  with a rainbow round his head   Rev10
  with a sickle   Rev14
  with authority over fire   Rev14
  with great authority   Rev18
  with the keys of the abyss   Rev20
  worship   PCo2
angelic authorities and powers   LPF3
angels, a little lower than the   LH2
  a spectacle unto the world and to   PCF4
  abandoned their proper home   LJu1
  appeared and waited on him   Mw4

angels, are as the   Mw22
   ascending and descending   J1
   of the four corners of the earth   Rev7
   before myriads of   LH12
   being made so much better than the   LH1
   comes in the glory of the Father and his holy   L9
   died and was carried away by the   L16
   dressed in white   A1
   employ no insults   LPS2
   entertained without knowing it   LH13
   followed unnatural lusts   LJu1
   glory of the Father with his   Mw16
      of the holy   Mk8
   he shall put in charge of you   Mw4
   he who was seen by   PTF3
   I charge thee before the elect   PTF5
   in blazing fire, mighty   ThS1
   in charge of you, he will put his   Mw4
   in heaven, not even the   Mw24
      they are like   Mk12
      will not know   Mk13
   in white sitting there   J20
   intervention was real   A12
   law promulgated through   PG3
   long to see, things that   LPF1
   myriads upon myriads of   LJu1
   of God, joy among the   L15
      pay him homage   LH1
      the Son of Man will acknowledge before the   L12
   of the seven churches   Rev1ff
   orders to take care of you, he will give his   L4
   out of my regard for the   PCF11
   raised as far above the   LH1
   Satan's   Rev12
   seen a vision of   L24
   seven, in the presence of God   Rev8, 17, 21
   ten thousand times ten thousand   Rev5
   that he takes to himself, it is not   LH2
   the reapers are   Mw13
   the Son of Man will send out his   Mw13

fed the five thousand   Mw14, 16; Mk6; L9; J6

   the four thousand   Mw15f; Mk8

fetters unfastened, found their   A16

Gabriel, Archangel   L1

garment, young man clothed in a long white   Mk16

garments, two men in dazzling   L24

gift of God, stir into flame the   PTS1

gifts of the Holy Spirit   PCF12, 14; PCS6

God's gift, not a reward   PE2

guardian angel, it must be his   A12

   angels in heaven, they have their   Mw18

Holy Ghost, all were filled with the   A4

   and wisdom, seven men full of the   A6

   being sent forth by the   A13

   came upon them, and they spake with tongues   A19

   fell on them   A11

   filled with the   A2

   gifts of the   LH2; LJF2

   have ye received the   A19

   he shall be filled with the   L1

   he which baptizeth with the   J1

   him that blasphemeth agianst the   L12

   holy men spake as they were moved by the   LPS1

   is come upon you   A1

   it is not ye that speak, but the   Mk13

   Jesus being full of the   L4

   love of God is shed in our hearts by the   PR5

   Paul, filled with the   A13

   Peter, filled with the   A4

   saved us by the renewing of the   Tt3

   sent down from heaven   LPF1

   shall teach you what you ought to say   L12

   the disciples were filled with joy, and with the   A13

   they received the   A8

   thus saith the   A21

   was upon Simeon   L2

   which dwelleth in us   PTS1

   with joy of the   ThF1

Holy Spirit, a share in the   LH6

   all were filled with the   A2; A4

Holy Spirit, asking that the converts might receive the A8
 baptize you with the   Mw3; A1
 bestows on you his   ThF4
 came upon them   A10, 19
 comes on you   A1
 converts were filled with joy and with the   A13
 descending like a dove   Mw3
 did you receive the   A19
 distributing the gift of the   LH2
 dwelling within us   PTS1
 Elizabeth was filled with the   L1
 fill you, let the   PE5
 for him who slanders the   L12
 found she was in child by the   Mw1
 full of the   L4
 given by God to those obedient to him   L5
 given to those who ask   L11
 giving instructions through the   A1
 God showed his approval by giving the   A15
 he will be filled with the L1
 how God anointed him with the   A10
 impelled by the, spoke the word of God   LPS1
 in the power of the   ThF1
 inspired by the   PR14
 of God, do not grieve the   PE4
 Peter, filled with the   A4
 prevented from delivering the message by the   A16
 receive the   J20
 recommend ourselves by gifts of the   PCS6
 renewing power of the   Tt3
 said, Set Barnabas and Paul apart   A13
 Saul, filled with the   A9, 13
 sent from heaven   LPF1
 spoke to your fathers, how well the   A28
 Stephen, filled with the   A7
 these are the words of the   A21
 to baptize in   J1
 under the influence of the   PCF12
 was poured out   PCF12
 was upon Simeon   L2

Holy Spirit, when inspired by the   Mk12
    will come upon you   L1
    will instruct you what to say   L12
    you will receive the gift of the   A2
    your advocate   J14
    Zechariah was filled with the   L1
inspired utterance, the gift of   PR12
Jesus Christ cures you; get up and make your bed   A9
    himself came up and walked along with them   L24
    said to him, Go; your faith has cured you   Mk10
laid his hands on her and she straightened up   L13
    on them and cured them   L4
    upon him and healed him   A28
lame walk   Mw11
language of ecstasy   PCF14
lepers are made clean   Mw11
leprosy left him immediately   Mk1
  was cured immediately   Mw8
life-giving spirit, the last Adam has become a   PCF15
lifted up, as they walked he was   A1
light flashed from the sky all around him   A9
living water   J4, 7
miracle, had been hoping to see some   L23
  workers, God has appointed   PCF12
miracles, a man made known to you through   A2
  among you, when God works   PG3
  and signs, Stephen began to work great   A6
  devils with power to do   Rev16
  faith will bring with it these   Mk16
  false prophets that wrought   Rev19
  in your name, did we not perform   Mw7
  Jews call for   PCF1
  the beast worked great   Rev13
  through Paul God worked singular   A19
miraculous powers, the gift of   PCF12
  signs, by force of   PR15
opened, looking up to heaven, he said, Be   Mk7
passion, showed himself alive after his   A1
plagues, he healed as many as had   Mk3
portent in heaven   Rev12

raise him up on the last day   J6

raised from the dead, until the Son of Man had been   Mw17

   him from the dead, God   A13; PCo2

   to life on the third day   Mw20

resurrection of the dead, proclaiming the   A4

risen from the dead, remembered when he was   J2

   he is not here: for he is   Mw28

robes, a man in shining   A10

saints raised from sleep, many of God's   Mw27

Saul, Saul, why persecutest thou me?   A9, 26

sick, heal the   Mw10

sign from heaven, demanded of him a   L11

    show them a   Mw16

  Jews require a   PCF1

  of the prophet Jonah, the only   Mw12; L11

  wicked generation demands a   L11

signs and marvels through the apostles   A2

  and miracles to be worked at their hands   A14

  and wonders, wrought among you in   PCS12

  miracles and manifold works of power   LH2

  on earth, I will show   A2

  which God worked among you   A2

sight, he recovered his   L18

  instantly I recovered my   A22

soul and spirit, dividing asunder of   LH4

spirit, a man gifted with the   PCF2

  and wisdom, seven men full of   A6

  both guided by the same   PCS12

  comes out, when an unclean   L11

  coming down from heaven like a dove   J1

  dwells within you, if only God's   PR8

  eager for gifts of the   PCF14

  explores everything   PCF2

  gifts of the   PCF12

  I was caught up by the   Rev1

  I will endue even slaves with a portion of my   A2

  I will pour out on everyone a portion of my   A2

  into the wilderness, Jesus was led by the   Mw4

  Jesus, armed with the power of the   L4

    was then led away by the   Mw4; L4

spirit, measureless God's gift of   J3
  of God descended like a dove   Mw3
  of Jesus Christ is given me   PPs1
  of Jesus would not allow them to enter   A16
  ordered to come out   L8
  says expressly   PTF4
  seizes him from time to time   L9
  those who live on the level of the   PR8
spiritual power, carried conviction by   PCF2
staff, Aaron's   LH9
take up your bed and walk   J5
tongues, began to talk in other   A2
  of ecstasy, speaking in   A10
  of men or of angels   PCF13
  the gift of   PCF12
touched the man's ear and healed him   L22
transfiguration, vision of the   Mw17
transfigured, in their presence he was   Mw17; Mk9
trumpets, the angels blew their   Rev8
walked, immediately the girl got up and   Mk5
water became wine   J2
  walking on the   Mw14; Mk6
weep no more; she is not dead: she is asleep   L8
withered arm healed on the sabbath   Mw12

28 *Music*

bell, golden, sewn to clothes   Ex28ff
  inscribed 'Holy is the Lord'   Z14
Canticles; Song of Songs; Song of Solomon   So1ff
castanets   SS6
choirs, appointed two great   Ne12
cornet   SS6; Ps98; D3; Ho5
cymbals   SS6; CF13f, 25; CS5, 29; Ez3; Ne12; Ps150
  bronze   CF15
dance, daughters of Jephthah   Ju11
  girl shows her joy in   Je31
  girls of Shiloh   Ju21
  on the temple terrace, those who   Zp1
  praise his name in the   Ps149, 150
dancers chant your praises   Ps87
  merry throng of   Je31
  moves between the lines of   So6
dancing, a time for   Ec3
  turned my lament into   Ps30
dirge, I will chant over the desert pastures   Je9
  sing it as a   E32
  those skilled in the   Am5
drum   SF10
dulcimer   D3
fanfare of trumpets   KS11; Ps47, 150
fife   SF10
flute   Job21, 30; Ps150; D3
harp   SF10, 16, 18ff; SS6; KF10; CF13ff; CS5, 9, 20, 29; Job21, 30; Ne12; Is5, 16, 23, 30;
      Ps33, 43, 49, 57, 71, 81, 92, 98, 108, Ps137, 147, 149ff; E26; D3
  of algum wood   CS9
  the merry   Is24
harpist   E33
harpists, ancestor of all   Gen4

harps, we hanged on the willow   Ps137
horn   CS15; Ps81, 98; D3; Ho5; Z9
jingles, adorn yourselves with   Je31
lament, sing a   Ps30, 56
love song   Is5
lute   SF10; SS6; KF10; CF13ff; CS5, 9, 20, 29; Ne12; Ps57, 71, Ps81, 108, 150; Is5, 14; Am5ff
  of algum wood   CS9
  ten-stringed   Ps33, 92, 144
master-singers   CF25
melody of thy viols, I will not hear   Am5
minstrel   KS3; CS35; Ps68
music and singing   D3
  in the house of the Lord   CF6
  of strings   Ps45
  of the heavens   Ps19
  of your lutes, I cannot endure the   Am5
  young men have ceased from their   La5
musical instruments, invent   Am6
    of all sorts   Ec2
    of David   Ne12
musicians   CF6, 9, 15; CS34; E27; Ne4; E33, 40
  apprentice   CF25
  freed from tax   Ez7
organ   Job21, 30; Ps150
pipe   SF10; KF1; Ps81; Is5, 30; Je48; E28; D3
pipers, ancestor of all   Gen4
precentor in charge of music   CF25
procession   Ps68
psalms, honour his name with   Ps135
  praise him with   Ps47
  raise   Ju5; Ps57, 59, 68, 101, 108
  sing   Ps9f, 18. 21, 27, 30, 61, 66, 68, 71, 81, 92, 95, 98, 104ff, 138, Ps147, 149
psaltery   SF10; CF25; CS5; Ne12; Ps33, 71, 81, 92, 102, 108, 144, 150; D3
ram's horn trumpet   Ex19; Le25; Jos6
reed-pipe   Je48
sackbut   D3
sing a new song   Ps33
  of thy strength   Ps59

sing, the tongue of the dumb shall   Is35

singer   KF10; CF9, 25; CS5, 29; Ez2, 7, 10; Ne7, 10ff; Ps68, 87; Ec2; E40

singing and music   D3

  danced for joy to the sound of   CF13

  joy over thee with   Zp3

  women in the palace   Am8

sistrum   Is30

song of all songs   So1

  of Deborah and Barak   Ju5

  of Moses   Ex15; De32

  of the harlot   Is23

  sing praises, sing a new   Is42

songs as on a night of sacred pilgrimage   Is30

  clamour of your   E26

  of thanksgiving, Levites in charge of   Ne12

  of triumph, break into   Is49

  spare me the sound of your   Am5

stringed instruments, chief singer on   H3

strings   Ps150

  instrument of ten   Ps92, 144

tabor   Ps81; Is5

tabret   SF10, 18; Is5, 24, 30; E28

tambourine   Ex15; Ju11; SF18; SS6; CF13; Job21; Ps68, 149ff; Is24, 30

  daughter of Jephthah came out with a   Ju11

  Miriam and all the women danced to the   Ex15

timbrel   SS6; Job21; Ps68, 81

triangle   D3

trumpet   Ex19; Le25; Nu10; Ju3, 7; SF13; SS2, 6, 15, 20; KF1; KS9ff; CF13ff; Ez3; Ne4, 12; CS5, 13, 15, 20, 29; Job39;   Ps47, 81, 98, 150; Is18, 27, 58; Je4, 6, 42, 51; E7, 33, Ho5, 8; Joe2; Am2ff; Z9; Zp1

  Ehud sounded   Ju3

  military   Nu31; Je4, 6, 42, 51; Zp1

  of beaten silver   Nu10

  of Gideon   Ju7

  ram's horn   Ex19; Le25; Jos6

  signal calls   Nu10

viol   Is5, 14; Am5ff

zither   D3

NEW TESTAMENT

brass, sounding PCF13

cymbal PCF13

danced for the guests, daughter of Herodias Mw14; Mk6

  we have piped unto you, and ye have not L7

flute Mw9; PCF14

flute-player Mw9; Rev18

gong PCF13

harp PCF14; Rev5, 15

harper, harpist Rev14, 18

harps, the sound of Rev14

hymn, contributes a PCF14

  Passover Mw26; Mk14

hymns, sing thankfully in your hart with PCo3

  songs and psalms, speak to one another in PE5

  to thy name, sing PR15

lyre PCF14

melody in your heart, making PE5

minstrel Mw9; Rev18

music and dancing, he heard L15

musicians Rev18

pipe PCF14

piped unto you, we have L7

pipers Rev18

psalm, every one of you hath a PCF14

  stands written in the A13

psalms, book of L20; A1

  everything written about me in the L24

  hymns and songs, speak to one another in PE5

  merry, let him sing LJ5

  sing thankfully in your heart with PCo3

sang his praises, all men L4

sing and make music in your hearts PE5

  praises, he should LJ5

  thy praise in full assembly, I will LH2

  with the spirit and with the understanding also PCF14

singing a new song Rev14

  with grace in your hearts to the Lord PCo3

song of Moses Rev15

29 *Penalties, Punishments and Compensation*

OLD TESTAMENT

29 PENALTIES, PUNISHMENTS AND COMPENSATION

confined to Jerusalem   KF2
contention, water of   Nu5
death penalty by hanging   Nu25; De21; Jos8, 10; Est2, 7
  by stoning, offences calling for   De13ff
    for Achan and his family   Jos7
    for blasphemy   Le24
    for breaking the sabbath   Nu15
    for calling up spirits   Le20
    for daughters of Achan   Jos7
    for disobedient sons   De21
    for giving children to Molech   Le20
    for losing virginity before marriage   De22
    for misdemeanours   De22
    for sons of Achan   Jos7
    for worshipping other gods   De17
  for adultery   De22
  for approaching the tabernacle   Nu1
  for breaking house arrest   KF2
  for collecting sticks on the sabbath   Nu15
  for dreamers   De22
  for entering the king's presence unbidden   Est4
  for failing to foretell Nebuchadnezzar's dream   D2
  for kidnap   De24
  for losing virginity   De22
  for miscreants in general   De13
  for murder   Nu35
  for one's own sin only   De24
  for prophesying against the city   Je26
  for prophets in general   De13
  for rape   De22
  for working on the sabbath   Nu15
  for worshipping Baal-peor   Nu25
  for worshipping other gods   De17
  on all the wise men of Babylon   D2
  offences calling for   Ex21ff; Le20; Nu35
  this man must be put to   Je38
disobeying the king's edict, penalty for   Ez6
dungeon   Is24; Je37; La3; Z9
  lost to sight in a   Is42
  where they lie in darkness   Is42

NEW TESTAMENT

cord, made a scourge out of   L12

court, settle out of   L12

eternal fire, paid the penalty in   LJu1

  punishment, they will go to   Mw25

execution, Herod interrogated the guards and ordered their   A12

  led him away to   L23

fetters and prison bars   LH11

  he had broken his   Mk5

flog a Roman citizen, can you legally   A22

flogged, imprisoned, mobbed   PCS6

  in synagogues, you will be   Mk13

  ordered them to be   A16

  sent for the apostles and had them   A5

  severely, servant who will be   L12

  those who believe   A22

flogging, examine him by   A22

  had to face   LH11

  I propose to let him off with a flogging   L23

forgiveness, for speaking against the Holy Spirit, there is no   Mw12

fortitude, testing of faith breeds   LJ1

gibbet, carried our sins to the   LPF2

  hanging him on a   A5

  put to death by hanging on a   A10

  took him down from the   A13

Great Day, more bearable for Sodom on the   L10

heretic should be warned once and once again   Tt3

imprisoned, more often   PCS11

  spirit, proclamation to the   LPF3

  those who believe   A22

  we prove ourselves when   PCS6

innocent, beyond all doubt this man was   L23

insurrection, Barabbas guilty of   L23

  lay bound with them that had made   Mk15

irons, had him put in   A22

jail, constable put you in   L12

jailer   A16

judge, drag you before the   L12

  yourself. judging your fellow man you   PR2

judged, unbeliever has been   J3

  we are chastened of the Lord, when we are   PCF11

judgement, after the death comes   LH9

   man who puts his faith in him does not come under   J3

   more bearable for Tyre and Sidon than for you   L10

   now is the hour of   J12

   on the living and the dead   LPF4

   when the men of this generation are on trial   L11

   who commits murder must be brought to   Mw5

   will pay every man for what he has done, God's   PR2

lash, tied him up for the   A22

latter end is worse with them than the beginning   LPS2

murder, theft or sorcery, it must not be for   LPF4

offender, you must forgive the   PCS2

open arrest, to keep Paul under   A24

outlaws, he was counted among the   L22

perdition, man doomed to   ThS2

   waits for them with unsleeping eyes   LPS2

persecute this movement to the death, I implore you   A22

pilfer, tell slaves not to   Tt2

prison bars, fetters and   LH11

  flung them into   A16

  Herod shut John up in   L3

  Jesus heard that John was cast into   Mw4

  John the Baptist was cast in   Mw4; Mk1, 6

  many of the saints did I shut up in   A26

  Peter was kept in   A12

  Saul was sending men and women to   A8

  throw some of you in   Rev2

prisoner, not ashamed to visit a   PTS1

  released unto them one   Mk15

prisoners for punishment, Christians as   A22

  had escaped, assumed that the   A16

public flogging, they gave us a   A16

punishment, God's agents of   PR13

  of eternal ruin   ThS1

  tried by repeated   A26

put to death, I gave my voice against them when they were   A26

   in the body he was   LPF3

   Lazarus, consulted that they might   J12

   the prison keepers   A12

rebels, in custody with the   Mk15

refractory, discipline for the   PTS2

retribution, revealed from heaven, divine   PR1

reward each according to his deeds   Rev2

rod on every son, lays the   LH12

rods, beaten with   PCS11

scourge a man who is Roman, is it lawful for you to   A22

  and to crucify, deliver him to   Mw20

  made of cord   J2

scourging, examined by   A22

sentenced to death, handed over to be   L24

shackled, ordered Paul to be   A21

sin, if your brother commits a   Mw18

slander spoken against the Spirit will not be forgiven   Mw12

stocks, secured their feet in the   A16

stone him, the Jews picked up stones to   J10

  throw the first   J8

stoned, Moses commanded that such should be   J8

  once I was   PCS11

  such women are to be   J8

stripes, approving themselves in   PCS6

strokes, given thirty nine   PCS11

sword of the Spirit   PE6

  with which to smite the nations   Rev19

terrors of judgement to come   ThF1

    God has not destined us for   ThF5

test, do not bring us to the   L11

theft defiles the man   Mk7

thieves crucified with Jesus   Mw27

thongs, tied him up with   A22

tormented day and night for ever   Rev20

  in sulphurous flames   Rev14

torture, condemned the man to   Mw18

whip of cords, Jesus made a   J2

wicked man whom the Lord will destroy   ThS2

witnesses, put to death on the evidence of two or three   LH10

wrath is come upon them to the uttermost   ThF2

30   *Plants*

acacia   Ex25f; Is41
  wood, table of   Ex25f
algum   KF8; CS2, 9
almond tree   Gen43; Ec12; e1
   rods of   Gen30
almonds produced by Aaron's staff   Nu17
almug wood , sandalwood   KF8, 10
aloe   Pro7; So4
  trees   Nu24
aloes, powder of   Ps45
apple tree   So2, 8; Joe1
apricot tree   So2, 8
ash tree   Is44
aspen   SS5; CF14
asphodel   So2; Is35
balm   Je8, 46
balsam   Gen43; So6; E27
  as offering   Ex25ff
barley   Ex9; De8; E4, 13, 45; Is28; Je41; Ho3; Joe1
  meal as grain offering   Nu5
bay tree   Ps37
bean   E4
box wood   Is41, 60; E27
bramble   Is34
briar   Is5, 7, 9, 27, 34, 55; E28; Mi7; Na1
broom bush   KF19; Job30
brushwood, as fire attacks   Ps118
bulrush   Ex2; Is18, 58
bulrushes, ark of   Ex2
bush, burning   Ex3
calamus, sweet   Ex30; So4; E27
camel-thorn   Is7, 55

camphire   So1, 4
cane, aromatic   Ex30f
caper-bud   Ec2
cassia   Ex30ff; Ps45; Pro7; E27
castor-oil plant   Jon4
cedar   Le14; Nu19; SS5, 7; KS19; CF17; CF1ff, 9; Job40; Ps29, 80, 92, 104, 148;
   So1, 5, 8; Is2, 9, 14, 37, 41,44; E17, 23, 27, 31; Am2; Z11
   beside the water   Nu24
   choicest cut down   Je22
   logs   CF14
   of Lebanon   Ju7; KF4f, 9ff
   planks   So8
   plentiful as sycomore fig   KF10
   wood   So1
      without limit   CF22
chestnut   E31
   rods of   Gen30
cinnamon   Ex30ff; Pro7; So2, 4
citrus trees   Le23
coriander   Nu11
corn   Is17, 21, 36, 55, 62; Je31; La2, 5; E36; Ho2, 7ff, 14; Joe2; Am8ff; Hg1ff; Z9, 12
   neither, nor figs   Nu20
corn-cockle   Job31
cornfield   SF8
cucumber   Nu11; Je10
cummin   Is28
cypress   Is44, 60
   ark ribs of   Gen6
dill   Is28
ebony   E27
elm   Is60; Ho4
fig, neither, nor corn   Nu20
   leaves, stitched   Gen3
   tree   De8; Nu13; Ju9; SF25, 30; KF4; KS18; Ne13; Ps105; Pro27; So2; Is34, 36; Je5, 8;
      Ho2, 9; Joe1ff; Am4; Mi4; Na3; H3; Hg2; Z3
fir tree   SS6; KF5ff; KS19; CS3; So1;Is14, 37, 41, 55, 60; E27, 31; Ho14; Na2; Z11
   wood   KF5ff; So1
fitch   Is28; E4
flag iris   Ex2, 30; So4; Is19; E27

flax   Ex9; Is19, 42; Ho2

flowers of the field   Ps103

food to animals, green plants given as   Gen1

forest   Ps74, 83, 104; Is44; Ho2

  the high places of a   Je26

  they cut down her   Je46

  trees   E15

fruit trees   Ne9; Ps148

garlic   Nu11

gourd, wild   KS4; Jon4

grapes   Nu13; Ne13

  prohibited for Nazirites   Nu6

  wild   Is5

grass   Is5, 37, 51, 66

  on the roof   Ps129

gum tragacanth   Gen37, 43

hazel   Gen30

heath   Je17

hemlock   Ho10; Am6

henna   So4, 7

  blossom   So1

  bushes   So7

herbs   Is18; La3

  bitter   Nu9

  garden of   KF21

  magic   Job18

hyssop   Ex12; Nu19; KF4; Ps51

ilex   Is44

iris, sweet flag   Ex2, 30; So4; Is19; E27

juniper   KF19; Job30; Je17

leek   Nu11

lentil   Gen25; E4

lign-aloe   Nu24

lily   So2, 4ff; Ho14

  decorative metalwork   KF7

  of the valley   So2

lime, linden or teil tree   Is6

locust bean   KS6; Is1

logs, rafting   KF5

lotus   Job40; Is19

mallow   Job6, 24, 30

mandrake   Gen30; So7

marjoram   Ex12; Le14; Nu19; KF4

  cleansing ritual of   Nu19

melon   Nu11

millet   E4

mulberry   SS5; FC14; Is40

myrrh   Gen37, 43

myrtle   Ne8; Pro7; Is41, 55; Z1

nettle   Job30; Pro24; So6; Is34; Ho9; Zp2

oak   Ju6; SS18; CF10; Is6, 44; E6, 27; Ho4; Am2; Z11

  at Ophran   Ju6

  burial beneath   Gen35

  of Bashan   Is2

  sacred   Is1

oil tree   Is41

olive   Ex27f, 30ff; Nu28; De6, 8; Jos24; Ne5; Job24; Ps128; Is17, 24; Ho14; Am4; Mi6; H3

  leaf, plucked   Gen8

  tree   De24; Ju9; SS15; KS5, 18; CF27; Ne8ff; Job15; Ps52; Is24; Je11; Hg2; Z4

  wild   KF6; CF27; Ne8; Is41

    timber of   KF6

  yards   SF8; Ne5

onion   Nu11

palm   De8; Ne8; Is9, 19; Joe1

  carving of   E40ff

  fronds   Le23; So5

  tree, trees   Nu33; Job15; Ps65, 92; So7; Je10

    carvings of   KF6

    city of   Ju1f

    long rows of   Nu24

    of Deborah   Ju4

    of Elim   Ex15

    Vale of   Ju1, 3

papyrus, paper reeds   Is19

pine   KF5f, 9; KS19; CS2; Ps104; Is14, 37, 41, 55, 60; E27; Ho14; Z11

pistachio nut   Gen43

plane tree   E31

    rods from a   Gen30

pomegranate   Nu13; De8; SF14; So6, 7, 8; Joel; Hg2
   decorative carving of   KF7; KS25
   embroidered   Ex28ff
   in flower   So6
   juice of   So8
   neither, nor vines   Nu20
poplar   Gen30; Job40; Is44; Ho4, 14
   rods of   Gen30
reeds   Ex2; Job8, 40; Ps68; Is9, 11, 35, 42; Je51; E29; Ho13
   ark covered with   Gen6
   paper, papyrus   Is19
rose   So2; Is35
   of Sharon   So2
rushes   Job8; So6; Is9, 19, 35
   basket of   Ex2
rye   E9; Is28
saffron   So4
saltwort   Job30; Zp2
sandalwood, almug   KF8, 10
sap, trees full of   Ps92
shittah tree   Is41
   wood   Ex25ff
shrub, neither plant nor   Gen2
spelt, rye wheat   Ex9; Is28; E4
spikenard   So1, 4
stink-wood   Is7
sweet cane   So4; Is43; Je6; E27
sycamore   KF10; CF27; Is9; Am7
   fig   KF10; CF27; CS1, 9; Am7
tamarisk, green   Is44
   tree   SF22, 31
teil tree, lime, linden   Is6
terebinth   Gen12, 18, 35, 49; De11; Jos24; Ju6, 9; SF10; KF13; Is1, 6, 57; E6; Ho4
   at Ophrah   Ju6
   great stone beneath   Jos24
   old and propped-up   Ju9
thistle   Je12; Ho10
thistledown   Ps83; Is17
thorn   Is5, 7, 9ff, 27, 33; Je12; E28
   bush   Ju9; Ps58; Ho2, 9, 10

NEW TESTAMENT

nard   Mk14; J12

olive, wild, grafted   PR11

  spare the   Rev6

  tree   Rev11

palm   J12; Rev7

  branches   J12

pods that the pigs ate   L15

reed, beat him with a   Mw27; Mk15

  bed swept by the wind   Mw11; L7

  in his hand   Mw27

  measuring   Rev11

  snap off the broken   Mw12

rue   L11

seed fell on stony ground   Mw13; Mk4; L8

spikenard   Mk14; J12

sycamine tree   L17

sycomore fig tree   L19

tares   Mw13

thistle   Mw7, 13; Mk4; L6, 8; LH6

thorns and briars, that which beareth   LH6

  crown of   Mw27; Mk15

  do not gather figs of   L6

  grew up and choked the seed   Mk4

  some fell among   Mw13; L8

thyine wood   Rev18

timber set ablaze   LJ3

tree from a mustard seed   L13

  good, yields good fruit   Mw7

  known by its fruit   L6

  of life in John's vision   Rev22

trees, already the axe is laid to the   L3

  that bear no fruit   LJu1

  walking, men like   Mk8

  were burnt, a third of the   Rev8

vine, fruit of the   Mw26; Mk14; L22

  I am the real   J15

  spare the olive and the   Rev6

wheat   Mw3, 13; L3, 16, 22; J12; A27; RCF15; Rev6, 18

woods, scented   Rev18

wormwood   Rev8

31   *Priests and Prophets*

priests David's sons were   SS8
  deported, brought back to Samaria   KS17
  descendants disqualified   Ez2
  dismissed their foreign wives   Ez10
  families returned from exile   Ez2
  fell by the sword   Ps78
  for Reheboam's hill-shrines   CS11
  freed from tax   Ez7
  land set apart for   E48
  marriage rules for   Le21
  numbers returned from exile   Ne7
  of high places killed   KS23
  of the Lord, you shall be called   Is61
  profaned the sanctuary   Zp3
  put to the sword   SF22
  registration of   CF9
  roster of service   CS8
  rules for drinking   E44
    for hair and beard   E44
    for marriage   E44
  seek the guidance of   De17
  share of offerings   De18
  Solomon's   CS5
  who see no difference between holy and profane   E22
profane and sacred, the difference between   Le10
  both prophet and priest are   Je23
  priests who see no difference between holy and   E22
prophecy inspired with music   CF25
  of Agur   Pro30
  of Lemuel   Pro31
prophesy against Egypt   E30
    Gog   E38
    Seir   E35
    the shepherds   E34
    Tyre   E27
    Zidon   E28
  no more in the name of the Lord or we will kill you   Je11
  over the dry bones   E37
prophet, aged, of Bethel   KF13
  Ahijah   KF11, 14

thummin charm   Le8
  given to Levi   De33
  let the lot be   SF14
tithes and contributions, they defraud God with   Ma3
tokens of the Covenant   Ex25ff
urim   SF14, 28; Ez2; Ne7
  charm   Le8
  consulted by Eleazar   Nu27
  given to Levi   De33

NEW TESTAMENT

ambassador of Jesus Christ   Ph1
antichrists have appeared, many   LJF2
apostle and high priest, Jesus Christ   LH3
apostles, he chose twelve   L6
Baptist, John the   Mw3
bishop must be above reproach   PTF3
  must be of unimpeachable character   Tt1
  must not be a newly baptized convert   PTF3
bishopric, let another take his   A1
bishops and deacons at Philippi   PPs1
chief priest   Mw2, 16, 20f, 26ff; Mk8, 10f, 14f; L3, 9, 19f, 22, 24; J7, 11f, 18f; A4f, 9, 19,
      A22f, 25f
  Abiathar   Mk2
  Caiaphas   L3; J11, 18; A4
  Sceva   A19
chief priests, Herod gathered   Mw2
  rejected of the   Mk8
  suffer much from the   Mw16
council of the high priest   A5
deacon   PPs1; PTF3
deaconess must be woman of high principle   PTF3
deacons must be men of high principle   PTF3
  must not be money-grubbers   PTF3
evangelist, do the work of an   PTS4
eyewitnesses of ministers of the word   L1
false prophet, foul spirit from the mouth of the   Rev16
  thrown alive into the lake of fire   Rev19

false prophets, Israel had   LPS2

    just so did their fathers treat   L6

    you have mastery over   LJF4

gospel of the kingdom, preaching the   Mw4

herald and apostle, I was appointed   PTF2

high priest   Mw26; Mk2; L1, 3; J11, 18; A4f, 7, 9, 20 22ff; LH2f, 5, 9

    Aaron   L1; A7; LH5, 9

    Abiathar   Mk2

    Ananias   A23f

    Annas   L3; J18; A4

    apostle and   LH3

    before God   LH2

    Caiaphas   Mw26; L3; J11, 18; A4

    council of the   A5

    in the succession of Melchizedek   LH6

    of good things   LH9

    would you insult God's   A23

Holy Ghost has made you overseers of the flock   A20

Inspiration, do not stifle   ThF5

Interpret ecstatic utterance, the ability to   PCF12

Jerusalem will be trampled down by foreigners   L21

kingdom of God is yours, you who are in need   L6

last day, I will raise him up on the   J6

Levitic priesthood   LH7

meeting of chief priests and lawyers   Mw2

Messias cometh, I know that   J4

ministers of the word   L1

new age, birth pangs of the   Mw24

One who called you is holy   LPF1

oracular spirit, slave-girl possessed by an   A16

    utterance, alarm yourselves at some   ThS2

ordained you, I have chosen and   J15

ordination, not be hasty in   PTF5

phylactery   Mw23

possessed by the power of Elijah   L1

pray everywhere, I will that men   PTF2

    lifting up holy hands to   PTF2

preacher, John the Baptist   Mw3

    ordained a   PTF2

president of the synagogue   Mk5; L8

priest   Mw8; Mk1f; L1, 5, 10, 20; A4; LH2, 7
   Alexander   A4
   allowed to eat the sacred bread   Mk2
   and those whom he consecrates   LH2
   go and show yourself to the   Mw8; Mk1; L5
   Jonathan   A4
   Melchizedek   LH7
   went past on the other side   L10
   Zechariah   L1, 3, 11
priesthood, become a holy   LPF2
   Levitic   LH7
   of Jesus   LH7
   royal   LPF2
priestly course of Abijah   L1
   service, my   PR15
priests, a deputation of   J1
   accosted him   L20
   alone are allowed to eat sacred bread   L6
   go and show yourselves to the   L17
   have no right to eat at our altar   LH13
   of the sacred tent   LH13
   to serve as   Rev1
prophecies of Isaiah   L3
   shall fail   PCF13
prophecy, above all   PCF14
   daughter who possessed the gift of   A21
   I may have the gift of   PCF13
   in scripture was bound to come true   A1
   of Isaiah, to fulfil the   Mw8
   the gift of   PCF12
prophesied, spoke in tongues of ecstasy and   A19
prophesies, when he prays or   PCF11
prophesy again before many peoples   Rev10
   in your name, did we not   Mw7
   one at a time, you may all   PCF14
   your sons and daughters shall   A2
prophet, a Cretan   Tt1
   Agabus   A11, 21
   and far more than a   L7
   Daniel   Mw24; Mk13

prophets in the kingdom of God, all the   L13
  in the same way did their fathers treat the   L6
  killed their own   ThF2
  madness, put a stop to the   LPS2
  sages and teachers I send you   Mw23
  so persecuted they be   Mw5
  stories of the   LH11
  the doom proclaimed by the   A13
  they have killed my   PR11
  they have Moses and the   L16
  when your fathers murdered   L11
  will come true, all that is written by the   L18
  work will be over   PCF13
quench not the Spirit   ThF5
Righteous One, they killed those who foretold the   A7
ruler of the synagogue   Mk5
seal not the prophecy of this book   Rev22
sermon on the mount   Mw5
scripture has to be fulfilled   J17
shepherds of the church of the Lord   A20
Son of Man will be given up to the chief priest   Mk10
  will have come   Mw10
speak as if you uttered oracles of God   LPF4
spiritual endowment you possess   PTF4
  truths, because we are interpreting   PCF2
steward, God's   Tt1
stewards of the secrets of God   PCF4
temple police, officers of the   L22
wise men, three   Mw2
wonderful works done in thy name   Mw7

32   *Repentance, Hope and Atonement*

abuse, let him endure full measure of   La3
alive his own soul, none can keep   Ps22
  the Lord killeth and maketh   SF2
Amen, all the people said   CF16
  the people answered   Ne8
atonement for the offence of Korah   Nu16
  ram of the   Nu5
awe, hold the Lord in   Jos22, 24
beacon in darkness   Ps112
beat them and tore out their hair, I   Ne13
birth again, those long dead to   Is26
bitter draught, drunk with a   Ps60
cheek, let him turn his   La3
comfort ye my people   Is40
commune with your own heart and be still   Ps4
confession, expiation by   KF8
  of Daniel   D9
confusion, let us never be put to   Ps71
conscience smote him, David's   SS24
consolation, cup of   Je16
conversion of Nebuchadnezzar   D4
courage, be of good   Ps31
darkness, a beacon in   Ps112
death in victory, he will swallow up   Is25
defiled my holy place, you have   E5
desolate, no more shall your land be called   Is62
destiny, arise to your   D12
dust, ye that dwell in   Is26
evil befall thee, no   Ps91
expiation by confession   KF8
  for bloodshed   De21

live, mend his ways and   E18, 33
longing soul, satisfieth the   Ps107
love the Lord thy God   De31
   truth and peace   Z8
mends his ways, when a wicked man   E33
mercy and not sacrifice, I desire   Ho6
   endureth for ever, his   CF16; Ez3; Ps136
   great is his   Ps103
   have   Ps51
   he delighted in   Mi7
   show us thy   Ps85
mourning into gladness, I will turn   Je31
new name, you shall be called a   Is62
peace, dwelling in   Is32
   for the wicked, no   Is48
   make offer of   De20
   man of, Solomon   CF22
   offering on Mount Ebal   Jos8
   the land was at   Jos11; Ju3, 5, 8, 12; CS14
   the world is still at   Z1
   throughout Solomon's reign   KF4
peaceful, cities shall lie   Is32
power belongeth unto God   Ps62
praise, mouth shall show forth thy   Ps51
   the Lord all nations   Ps117
     all the people said   CF16
     let everything that hath breath   Ps150
punish you, though I   Je46
pure lips, I will give all peoples once again   Zp3
purged thy sin   Is6
quicken thou me   Ps119
refuge, the Lord is a sure   Na1
   thou art my only   Je17
reproach, he is filled with   La3
right and just, do what is   Pro21
righteousness cannot save his life   E33
rise again, their bodies will   Is26
rock like ours, the enemy have no   De32
   Lord is my, and my fortress   Ps18
   of his salvation   De32

NEW TESTAMENT

confessing their sins   Mw3

confession that leads to salvation   PR10

conscience enlightened by the Holy Spirit   PR9

  is called as witness   PR2

cross and follow me, take up his   Mw10; Mk10; L9, 14

crucified, the man we once were has been   PR6

cured, if I even touch his clothes I shall be   Mw9; Mk5

day of the Lord, his spirit may be saved on the   PCF5

deliverance, all mankind shall see God's   L3

denied me three times, you will have   J13

die with Christ, did you not   PCo2

died with him, we shall live with him if we   PTS2

disciplined by his Father   LH12

  by the grace of God   Tt2

doubt, wherefore didst thou   Mw14

end of all things is at hand   LPF4

enemies, love your   Mw5

eternal life, heirs to   Tt3

   take hold of   PTF6

   the believer possesses   J6

   the promise of   LJF2

   those who were marked out for   A13

   what should I do to win   Mw19; Mk10; L18

  salvation for all who obey him   LH5

everlasting life, he that believeth on me hath   J6

everyone of us shall give account of himself   PR14

everything is possible to one who has faith   Mk9

faith active in love   PG5

  be it unto you, according to your   Mw9

  because of your, so let it be   Mw8

  counted to him as righteousness   PR4; PG3; LJ2

  fight the good fight of   PTF6

  has made thee whole   L17

  holding the mystery of the   PTF3

  hope and love   PCF13

  how little you have   Mw6

  if a man is weak in his   PR14

  is the evidence of things not seen   LH11

  is too small, your   Mw17

  it is not all who have   ThS3

faith justified through   PR1, 3, 5
   nowhere have I found such   Mw8
   on earth, will the Son of Man find   L18
   run the great race of   PTF6
   strong enough to move mountains   PCF13
   the gift of   PCF12
   the shield of   PE6
   through this, you may possess life   J20
   thrown open the gates of   A14
   what is   LH11
   whom resist steadfast in the   LPF5
   with virtue, supplement your   LPS1
Father, I have sinned against heaven and before thee   L15
favour of God, we seek only the   ThF2
fear to have missed his chance   LH4
foolish, disobedient, deceived, we were sometimes   Tt3
forgive my brother, how many times am I to   Mw18
   one another as Christ forgave you   PE4
   us our sins, as we forgive   L11
forgiven us all our sins, he has   PCo2
   who speaks against the Son of Man will be   Mw12
forgiveness of sins, baptism for the   L3
    in whom we have   PCo1
    is now being proclaimed   A13
    repentance bringing the   L24
    that they may receive   A26
fortitude with piety, supplement your   LPS1
found, he was lost, and is   L15
fought the good fight, I have   PTS4
Gentiles, gift of the Holy Spirit poured out even on   A10
give thanks whatever happens   ThF5
glory, in bringing my sons unto   LH2
   of God, all come short of the   PR3
God and money, you cannot serve   Mw6
   forbid that I should boast   PG6
   has chosen what the world counts as folly and weakness   PCF1
   requires, conform with all that   Mw3
   shall call them his sons   Mw5
   who knows their need of   Mw5

gospel, I am not ashamed of the   PR1
Great Day, until the   PTS1
hanged himself, Judas went and   Mw27
Holy Ghost a witness to us   LH10
    abound in hope through the power of the   PR15
    approving ourselves by the   PCS6
    comforter which is the   J14
    made partakers of the   LH6
    my conscience bearing witness to the   PR9
    received the promise of the   A2
    ye shall be baptized with the   A11
  Spirit, conscience enlightened by the   PR9
    he will baptize you with the   Mk1
    says, today, if you hear his voice   LH3
    seal of the promised   PE1
    we had not heard that there is a   A19
    who speaks against the   Mw12
    you will be baptized with the   A11
hope keep you joyful, let   PR12
  of salvation as a helmet   ThF5
  overflow with   PR15
humble folk, go about with   PR15
humbly reckon others better than yourselves   PPs2
hypocrisies, lay aside all   LPF2
immortality, the perishable cannot possess   PCF15
imperishable, raised   PCF15
initiation which you received   LJF2
Jesus of Nazareth, this fellow was with   Mw26
  remember me when you come to your throne   L23
  son of David, have pity on me   L18
judges the secrets of human hearts, God   PR2
kick against the pricks, it is hard for thee to   A26
kingdom of God, a man who looked forward to the   Mk15
    has come close to you   L10
    must pass through hardships to enter the   A14
    no-one who keeps looking back is fit for the   L9
    not far from the   Mk12
  of heaven, I will give you the keys of the   Mw16
    should be thought of in this way   Mw18
knock, and the door will be opened   L11

last day, rise again on the   J11

  shall be first, and the first last   Mw20

lawless deeds are forgiven, happy are those whose   PR4

life and immortality brought to light   PTS1

  already passed from death to   J5

  of faith, are you living the   PCS13

  to receive it back, lay down my   J10

  vital fragrance that brings   PCS2

lives by the power of God, Christ   PCS13

living water, he would have given you   J4

Lord, I believe; help thou mine unbelief   Mk9

  if thou wilt, thou canst make me clean   Mw8

  lay not this sin to their charge   A7

  Lord, not everyone who calls me   Mw7

love, fidelity and purity, make yourself an example of   PTF4

  greatest of them all is   PCF13

  your enemies, I tell you   Mw5

  your neighbour as yourself   PR13

lower nature, have crucified the   PG5

manner of life may be worthy, so that your   PCo1

mansions, in my Father's house are many   PCo1

many be called, but few chosen   Mw20

  who are first will be last, and the last first   Mk10

mend your ways; take our appeal to heart   PCS13

merciful, I will be   LH8

mercy, disobedient in order that they may receive   PR11

Messiah, followers of the   Mk9

  I now believe that you are the   J11

  not see death until he had seen the   L2

  the Son of God, are you the   Mw26

  wondered whether John was the   L3

mind of Christ, we have the   PCF2

mystery of faith, holding the   PTF3

night is far spent, the day is at hand   PR13

offend thee, if thine eye   Mw18

    if thy hand   Mk9

one shall be taken, the other left   L17

  who is to come, are you the   Mw11

penniless, we own the world   PCS6

perfect joy is now mine   J3

resurrection of good and wicked alike   A24

   of the dead, our hope of the   A23

     the true issue is the   A24

   on the last day   J11

   this was the first   Rev20

retribution, warned you to escape from the coming   Mw3; L3

salvation, a sign of your   PPs1

   all men should find   PTF2

   as a helmet   PE6

   author of eternal   LH5

   God destined us for   ThF5

   he who brought us   PTS1

   in the Spirit, God chose you to find   ThS2

Saul, Saul, why persecutest thou me?   A22

save yourselves from this crooked age   A2

saved, everyone who invokes the name of the Lord   PR10

   he that endureth to the end shall be   Mw10, 24

   what must I do to be   A16

   who then can be   L18

   will have all men to be   PTF2

saw the light, my companions   A22

scales fell from his eyes   A9

seal of the Holy Spirit   PE1, 4

secret is this: Christ in you   PCo1

seek and you will find   L11

selected few have received it   PR11

sell your possessions, and give to the poor   Mw19

shine as lights in the world   PPs2

sin, he that is dead is freed from   PR6

   no more, go and   J8

   shall no longer be your   PR6

   shall we persist in   PR6

   slaves of, no longer   PR6

sinful self, destruction of the   PR6

sinless, if we claim to be   LJF1

sinner, God be merciful to me a   L18

   make your hands clean   LJ4

sins and wickedness, dead in your   PE2

   are forgiven you, Jesus said, your   Mw9; L5

     through the shedding of his blood   PE1

33 *Roads, Paths and Ways*

OLD TESTAMENT

ancient paths, look for the   Je6
  ways   Ps139
byways and unmade roads   Je18
  they take to   Je18
  we take to   La4
cairns, to mark your way built   Je31
causeway at the Upper Pool   Is7
  called the Way of Holiness   Is35
clear boulders to build a highway   Is62
crossroads, do not wait at the   Ob1
  stop at the   Je6
  wisdom stands at the   Ob1
guide them, he shall   Is49
guides lead you astray   Is3
heaps, make thee high   Je31
highway across the desert   Is40
  between Egypt and Assyria   Is19
  build a   Is62
  build up a   Is57
  called the Way of Holiness   Is35
  deserted   Is33
  embankments for the   Is49
  forks, signposted   E21
  the road of the diligent   Pro15
king's highway, we will keep to the   Nu20, 21
main road, we will keep to the   Nu20
path, a level   Ps27
  a tangle of weeds   Pro15
  before me, my messengers to clear a   Ma3
  drink from the torrent beside the   Ps110
  every hill a   Is49
  feet go downwards on the   Pro5

338

path in the barren desert   Is43
  in the great waters   Ps77
  make sure of the   Je31
  of life   Ps16
  of the sluggard   Pro15
  of thy instruction   Ps119
  prescribed in thy laws   Is26
  shall turn slippery beneath their feet   Je23
  strayed from thy   Ps44
  to death   Pro5
  which no fowl knoweth   Job28
  will be smooth   Je31
  you should take, confused the   Is3
paths drop fatness, thy   Ps65
  familiar with all   Ps139
  known to me, make thy   Ps25
  look for the ancient   Je6
  teach me thy   Ps25
  the ancient ways   Je18
  they do not know   Is42
  they stumble in their   Je18
pilgrimage, a night of sacred   Is30
pilgrims, line of   Ps84
pilgrim's way   Is35
road, if you stray from the   Is30
  lead you back along the   Is37
  make sure of the   Je31
  of no return   Job16
  of the diligent   Pro15
  prepare for my people a   Is62
  start on the right   Pro22
  watch the   Na2
roads, no traveller treads the   Is33
  straighten their twisting   Is42
  they take to unmade   Je18
roadway for passers-by   Is51
signpost, carved   E21
  set up   Je31
streets, we avoid the public   La4
track, clear the   Is57

trackless waste, wandering in a   Ps107
way, build cairns to mark your   Je31
  dark and slippery   Ps35
  follow it, this is the   Is30
  he made the   Job28
  I lead blind men on their   Is42
  is in the sea, thy   Ps77
  make straight my   Ps5
  misses his   Pro19
  no bird of prey knows the   Job28
  of holiness   Is35
  teach me thy   Ps86
  that leads to good   Je6
  to it, no man knows the   Job28
  wandering in the trackless   Ps107
  where is the   Je6
ways are not your ways, my   Is55
  directed to keep thy statutes   Ps119
  they stumble in the ancient   Je18
waymarks, set up   Je31

NEW TESTAMENT

ends of the earth, away to the   A1
falsifying the straight ways of the Lord   A13
footpath, seed sown along the   Mw13; Mk4; L8
Gentile lands, do not take the road to   Mw10
highway, sat by the   Mk10
  the Lord's   J1
highways, go out on to the   L14
journeys in the dark, he who   J12
make straight the way of the Lord   J1
path, clear a straight   Mw3
  of life, set our feet upon the new   PR6
  some seed fell on the   Mw13; Mk4; L8
paths for your feet, make straight   LH12
  make straight   Mw3; L3
  ruin and misery lie along their   PR3
perdition, on the way to   PCS4

34 *Rulers, Judges and Lawgivers*

OLD TESTAMENT

annals of Solomon   KF11
  of the kings of Israel   KF15f, 22; KS1, 10, 13ff
  of the kings of Judah   KF15, 22; KS8, 12ff, 20ff
  of the kings of Judah and Israel   CS20, 24f, 27f, 32, 35ff
anoints you prince over Israel, the Lord   SF10
bodyguard, king's   KS25; Je52
canopy, throne   Je43
chapel, the king's   Am7
child king Amon   KS21
      Azariah   KS15
      Joash   KS12
      Josiah   KS22
consort, queen   Ne2
coronet   Is3; E16
counsellor, David's   SS15
court, Bethel is the king's   Am7
  new, of Jehoshaphat   CS20
courtiers   Je36
  retinue of   Je22
crown   SS1, 12; KS11; Ps21, 132; Ls62
  golden   Est7; Ps21
  jewelled   Z9
  lay aside your   E21
  prince Abijah   CS11
  put on Joash's head   KS11
  Queen Vashti's   Est1
  royal Persian and Median   Est1ff, 6
cupbearer, the king's   Ne2
deputy, king's   Je36
diadem   Is28; E21
  kingly   Is62
effigies of kings in the temple   E43
inner court, royal   Est4

judge over Israel, Abdon   Ju12
    Abimelech   Ju8ff; SS11
    Barak   Ju4; SF9
    Ehud   Ju3; CF7ff
    Eli   SF1ff, 14; KF2
    Elon   Ju12
    Gideon   Ju6ff
    Hoshea, Joshua   Ex17, 24; Nu13, 26, 32; De3, 31; Ju2; Jos1ff; KF16; KS23; CF7; Ne8
    Ibzan   Ju12
    Jair   Ju10; CF2
    Jephthah   Ju11f; SF12
    Joshua, Hoshea   Ex17, 24; Nu13, 26; 32; De3, 31; Ju2; Jos1ff; KF16; KS23; CF7; Ne8
    Othniel   Jos15; Ju1, 3; CF4, 27
    Samson   Ju13ff; SF12
     sons of, appointed   SF8
    Tola   Ju10; CF7
judgement of Solomon   KF3
judges appointed by Jehoshaphat   CS19
king Abijah of Judah   KF14; CS11, 13, 29
  Abijam of Judah   KF14
  Abimelech of Gerar   Gen20f, 26
   the judge was declared   Ju9
  Ahab of Israel   KF16ff; KS3, 8ff, 21; CS18, 21ff; Mi6
  Ahasuerus, Xerxes I of Persia   Ez4; Est1
  Ahaz of Judah   KS15ff; CF3, 8ff; CS27ff; Is1, 7, 14, 38; Ho1; Mi1
  Ahaziah of Israel   KF22
   of Judah   KS1, 8ff; CF3; CS20ff
  Amaziah of Judah   KS12ff; CF3ff; CS24
  Amon of Judah   KF22; KS21; CF3; CS18, 33; Ne7; Je1, 25; Zp1
  Arioch of Ellasar   Gen14
  Artaxerxes of Persia   Ez4ff; Ne2, 5, 13
  Asa of Judah   KF15; CF3, 9; CS14, 20ff; Je41
  Azariah, Uzziah, of Judah   KS14f; CS26ff; Is1, 6ff; Ho1; Am1; Z14
  Baalis of Ammon   Je40
  Baasha of Israel   KF15, 21; KS9; CS16; Je41
  Baladan of Babylon   KS20; Is39
  Balak of Moab   Nu22; Jos24; Ju11; Mi6
  Bela of Edom   Gen36
  Belshazzar of Babylon   D5, 7
  Ben-hadad of Syria   KF15, 20; KS6, 8, 13; CS16; Am1

kings of Arabia, tribute of   KF10
  of Midian, capture of   Ju8
  shall present their tribute   Ps72
  table, Mephibosheth had a place at   SS9
law and justice, David maintained   SS8
  of Moses   De27; Jos23; KF2, 8; KS23; CS23; Ez3, 7; Ne8; Ps93, 119; Pro28
laws for Israeli kings   De17
Moses   Ex2ff; Le1ff; Nu1ff; De1ff; Jos1ff; 13, 24; Ju18; SF12; KF8; KS14, 18, 23; CF6,
      23, 26; CS23, 25, 33ff; Ez3, 6ff; Ne1, 8ff; Ps77, 99, 103, 106; Is63; Je15; D9;
      Ma4
palace, Babylonian royal   D4
  in Ashdod   Am3
  in Egypt   Am3
  ivory   Ps45
  of Benhadad   Am1
  of Bozrah   Am1
  of Gaza   Am1
  of Jerusalem   Ne2; Am2
  of Kerioth   Am2
  of Solomon   CS2
  of Tyre   Am1
  Pharaoh's   Je43
  royal   KF16; Am7
Pharaoh   Gen12ff; De11; SF2; KF3, 9, 11; KS17ff, 23; CF4; Ps135ff; So1; Is19, 30, 36;
      E17, 29f; Je25, 37, 43f, 46ff
  called king bombast   Je46
  the great dragon   E29
pretender to the throne, Adonijah   KF1
prince, appoint Saul   SF9
  Jotham made regent   KS15
prince, royal   Je36
princes of Canaan   Ps135
  of Midian captured   Ju7
  of Persia to advise the king   Est1
  of the Philistines, five   SF6
  of Zoan   Is19
provinces under Persian rule   Est1
queen Athalia of Judah   KS8, 11; CF8; CS22ff
  Esther proclaimed   Est2

queen mother   Je13, 29
   Hamutal   KS23ff; Je52
   Maacah   CS13
  of Sheba   KF10; CS9
  Vashti of Persia   Est1
regency of Jotham for Azariah   KS15
regent   CS26
reigned, Abijam, 3 years   KF15
  Ahab, 22 years   KF16
  Ahaz, 16 years   KS16; CS28
  Ahaziah of Israel, 2 years   KF22
   of Judah, 1 year   KS8; CS22
  Amaziah, 29 years   KS14; CS25
  Amon, 2 years   KS21; CS33
  Asa, 41 years   KF15
  Athaliah, 7 years   KS11
  Azariah, 52 years   KS15
  Baasha, 24 years   KF15
  David, 40 years over Israel   SS5; KF2; CF29
   7½ years over Judah   SS2
  Elah, 2 years   KF16
  Hezekiah, 29 years   KS18; CS29
  Hoshea, 9 years   KS17
  Ishbosheth, 2 years   SS2
  Jehoahaz, 17 years over Israel   KS13
   3 months over Judah   KS23; CS36
  Jehoiachin, 3 months   KS24; CS36
  Jehoiakim, 11 years   KS23; CS36
  Jehoram, 12 years   KS3
  Jehoshaphat, 25 years   KF22
  Jehu, 28 years   KS10
  Jeroboam I, 22years   KF14
Jeroboam II, 41 years   Ks14
  Joash, 40 years   KS12; CS24
  Joram, 8 years   KS8; CS21
  Josiah, 31 years   KS22; CS34
  Jotham, 16 years   KS15; CS27
  Manasseh, 55 years   KS21; CS33
  Menahem, 10 years   KS15
  Nadab, 2 years   KF15

NEW TESTAMENT

remitted the case to Herod   L23
rival king, Jesus   A17
rod of iron, rule with a   Rev2
rod, shall come unto you with a   PCF4
Roman emperor   Mk12
rostrum, Herod seated on the   A12
royal chamberlain   A12
  house   Rev1
  priesthood   LPF2
  robes   A12
rule my people Israel   Mw2
rulers are not a terror to good works   PR13
Sanhedrin senate   A5
sceptre of justice   :LH1
sergeants, magistrate's   A16
sovereign, submit yourselves to the   LPF2
tetrarch, Herod Antipas   Mw14, 22; Mk3, 6, 8, 12; L3, 8f, 13, 23; A4
  Lysanias   L3
  of Abilene   L3
  of Galilee   L3
  of Ituraea   L3
  Philip   L3
throne, descendant should sit on his   A2
  Herod sat upon his   A12
  in John's vision   Rev20
  of David   L1
tribunal, emperor's   A25

35 *Sacrificial Procedures*

OLD TESTAMENT

sacrifice at hill-shrines   KF3, 22
  at Zoheleth   KF1
  beasts enough for a   Is40
  bring there   De12
  by Abram   Gen15
  by Abraham, Abram   Gen15, Gen22
  by Ahaz   KS16
  by Balaam   Nu23
  by David, abundant   CF29
  by Elkanah   SF1
  by Hezekiah   CS29
  by Jacob   Gen31
  by Job for his sons   Job1
  by Job's companions   Job42
  countless, what are they to me?   Is1
  dash from his mouth the blood of   Z9
  do him service with   Is19
  find fault with your   Ps50
  for the morning, bring your   Am4
  great altar not for   Jos22
    of Gog's horde   E39
  human   Ju11; KS3; Ps106; Is57; J7, 19, 32; E16, 20; Ho13
    bones, he will burn   KF13
  I will not accept   Je14
  in Bozrah   Is34
  in the house of the Lord, all who   Z14
  let them kill   Is29
  look with favour on your   Ps20
  Moabites invited to   Nu25
  mourning   Ps5
  of 33 bulls   CS35
  of 100 rams   CS29
  of 200 lambs   CS29
   of 500 bulls   CS35
  of 670 bulls   CS29
  of 700 oxen   CS15
  of 1,000 lambs   CF29
  of 1,000 oxen   CF29
  of 1,000 rams   CF29
  of 2,600 beasts   Cs35

sacrifice of 7,000 sheep   KF8
  of 20,000 sheep   KF8
  of 30,000 beasts   CS35
  of 120,000 sheep   CS7
  of beasts beyond reckoning   CS5
  of buffalo   SS6; Am5
  of bull by Gideon   Ju6
  of bullocks   E43
    in Gilgal   Ho12
  of bulls   Ex24, 29ff; CF15; CS29, 35; E43, 45; Ez6
    and rams by David   CF15
  of calves   Mi6
  of cattle   Ho5
  of consecration   Ex29ff
  of fatlings   SS6
  of goats   Le3, 16; Nu7; CS29; Ez6ff; Ps50, 66; E43
  of Isaac, intended   Gen22
  of Jephthah's daughter   Ju11
  of kids   E43
    by Gideon   Ju6
    by Manoah   Ju13
  of lambs   Ex12; Nu28; De16; SF7; CF29; CS29; Ez6; E45; Ez6, 8
  of miraculous fire   Ju6; CS7
  of oxen   SS6; KF8; CF8, 29; CS7; Ps66
  of Passover   Ex12; CS35
  of rams   Ex29ff; CF15, 29; CS29; E43, 45; Ez6, 8
  of sheep   CS7, 15, 29; KF8; Is1, 43; E36, 46; Ho5
  offer fat beasts as a   Ps66
  offer thee a willing   Ps54
  offered by Saul   SF13
  only to the Lord   KS5
  Passover   CS7, 35
  rules for   Ex29ff; Le1ff; De12
  sailors offered   Jon1
  sheep and oxen past counting   KF8
  sweet-cane   Is43
  the Lord has prepared a   Zp1
  they brought into contempt   SF2
  thou didst desire   Ps40

NEW TESTAMENT

sacrifice and offering thou didst not desire   LH10
   if any life-blood is to crown that   PPs2
   managed to prevent the crowd from offering   A14
   needeth not daily to offer up   LH7
   of the lamb in John's vision   Rev12
   offered up himself as   LH7
   Passover   PCF5
   priest of Jupiter about to offer   A14
   spiritual and eternal   LH9
   their share of the   PCF9
   to devils they   PCF10
   whose fragrance is pleasing to God   PE5
   yourselves as a living   PR12
sacrificed himself for our sins   PG1; PTF2; Tt2
   to idols, food   Rev2
sacrifices, a pair of turtle doves or two young pigeons   L2
   cannot give inward perfection   LH9
   for sins, to offer   LH5
   heavenly things require better   LH9
   spiritual   LPF2
   that is far more than any   Mk12
   their blood mingled with their   L13
   to demons   PCF10
   which can never remove sins   LH10
sacrificial bull   LH9f
   calf   LH9
   death, expiating sin by his   PR3
     justified by Christ's   PR5
   goat   LH9f
   heifer   LH9
   meal   PCF10
self-mortification, people who go in for   PCo2
shewbread, David ate the   Mw12; Mk2; L6
   in a material sanctuary   LH9
sin-offering, animals whose blood is a   LH13
    for himself   LH5
sins, brought about the purgation of   LH1
   of the people, to expiate the   LH2
slaughtered, Passover victim   L22

36 *Servitude and Tribute*

act of freedom for slaves   Je34
attendants, the king's   Est2ff
awl to pierce a slave's ear   De15
bondage, fulfilled her term of   Is40
bondmen, takes my sons to be   KS4
bonds, I will burst asunder thy   Na1
butler, Pharaoh's   Gen40
captive, 100,000 Hagarites taken   CF5
  comely women taken   De21
  women and children of Ziklag taken   SF30
captives at Babylon   Ez2
  into exile, the train of   Na2
  of the Philistines forty years   Ju13
  proclaim liberty to   Is61
  returned   Ez2
captivity by their enemies, herded into   Am9
  curse of   De28
  for Israelites for eight years   Ju3
  Gilgal shall go into   Am5
  of Jerusalem   Je1ff
capture the girls of Shilon   Ju21
captured, King Zebekiah   KS25
  the kings of Midian   Ju8
  the princes of Midian   Ju7
cell, measurement of   E40
chains, broke their   Ps107
  prison   Ps149
chamberlains, king's   Est1ff
collar, iron   Ps105
concubines, eunuch in charge of the   Est2
covenant of Zedekiah proclaiming freedom for slaves   Je34
dungeon   La3; Z9
ear pierced with an awl, slave's   De15

sell the innocent for silver   Am2, 8
  the poor for a pair of shoes   Am2, 8
servant and master   Is24
servant, Gehazi   KS4
  honoureth his master   Ma1
  little captive girl   KS5
  of Saul's family   SS8
  Ruth, I am your   Ru3
servants, a spoil to their   Z2
  born in my house   Ec2
  have ruled over us   La5
  pour my spirit upon   Joe2
  slave-girls of   SS6
  will be wicked   Pro29
service in the court of Nebuchadnezzar, young men for   D1
shave captive woman's head   De21
slave, an Egyptian   SF30
  chop wood as a   Jos9
  do not force to surrender a   De23
  draw water as a   Jos9
  eyes of a   Ps123
  freed in seventh year   De15
  goes in fear of his master   Ma1
  I will not be your   Je2
  Joseph as a   Gen37ff
  of slaves   Gen9
  pamper a   Pro29
  pierce the ear of, with an awl   De15
  to command, I am his   SF25
  Tobiah an Ammonite   Ne2
slave-girl, brought back a little   KS5
  displacing her mistress   Pro30
  eyes of a   Ps123
  intercourse with a   Le19
  not treat me as a   Ru2
  of servants   SS6
  Sarai's   Gen46
  the sons of Gideon's   Ju8ff
slave-girls carried off   Na2
  pour out my spirit upon   Joe2

slave-mark, setting a   Job13
slavery, Gibeonites held in   Jos9
  I ransomed you from a land of   Mi6
  sold into   Ps105those who had been freed forced back into   Je34
  was he born in   Je2
slaves, a creditor has come to take my boys as   KS4
  a large number owned by Job   Job1
  a plunder for   Z2
  become rulers   La5
  both men and women, he will seize   SF8
  commerce in   E27
  covenant to proclaim freedom for Hebrew   Je34
  for six years   Ex21
  gift of land to   E46
  Hebrew, to be set free   Je34
  import of   E27
  Israelite   Ex1; Ez2
  male and female, I bought   Ec2
  pour out my spirit upon   Joe2
  ran away   KF2
  redemption of   Le25
  released   Ex21
  rights of   Ex21; Le22, 25
  shall be your   Is45
  to serve your enemies as   Je17
  you may buy   KS5
sold to the king of Aram-naharaim, the Israelites were   Ju3
  to Jabin the Canaanite king, the Israelites were   Ju4
subjection of Israelites to Cusham-rishathaim   Ju3
   to Eglon king of Moab   Ju3
   to Jabin   Ju4
   to Midian   Ju6
   to the king of Aram-naharaim   Ju3
  of Moab to Israel   Ju3
taken prisoner, 200,000 women and children   CS28
taxes, a raiser of   D11
tribute, an officer to extort   D11
  Aramaeans paid to David   CF18
  by Aramaeans   SS8
  Ehud send to pay   Ju3

NEW TESTAMENT

chains, for the sake of the hope of Israel, I am in   A28
eunuch, an Ethiopian   A8
fellow-servant, I am but a   Rev19
free man, I am not a   PCF9
   men, live as   LPF2
freedman, the Lord's   PCF7
handmaiden, regarded the lowliness of his   L1
homage, if you fall down and do me   Mw4
   to the Lord your God   Mw4
maid answered his knock   A12
   said to Peter   J18
master in heaven, you both have the same   PE6
   sin shall no longer be your   PR6
   standeth or falleth by his own, a servant   PR14
masters, be just and fair to your slaves   PCo4
   give up using threats   PE6
   no man can serve two   Mw6; L16
minister, let him who would be great be your   Mw20
pay Caesar what is due to Caesar   L20
prisoner of Jesus Christ   PE3f; Ph1
   of the Lord   PTS1
   whoever is made to be   Rev13
prisoners, to proclaim release for   L4
ransom for many, to give up his life as a   Mw20
registration throughout the Roman world   L2
servant and apostle of Jesus Christ   LPS1
   another man's   PR14
   called in the Lord   PCF7
   cannot serve two masters   Mw6; L16
   centurion had a   L7
   doth he thank that   L17
   God raised up his   A3
   he that is greatest among you shall be your   Mw23
   his discharge in peace, thou givest thy   L2
   I am the Lord's   L1
   ill and near death   L7
   is not greater than his master   J13
   Israel, he hath holpen his   L1
   Jesus thy holy   A4
   judgest another man's   PR14

servant not now as a   Ph1
  now lettest thou thy, depart in peace   L2
  of all, he must make himself   Mk9
  of God   LJ1; Rev15
  of Jesus Christ, a good   PTF4
     I should be no   PG1
     Jude   LJu1
     Paul   PR1of Jesus Christ, who shows himself a   PR14
  of sin, whosever commits sin is a   J8
  of the high priest   Mk14; L22; J18
  of the Jewish people   PR15
  one of my father's paid   L15
  sent to the tenants   Mk12
  suppose one of you has a   L17
  the chief of you like a   L22
  to pass judgement on someone else's   PR14
  to the younger, the elder shall be   PR9
  took upon him the form of a   PPs2
  unto all, made myself   PCF9
  who is the trusty   Mw24
  whoever wants to be great must be your   Mw20; Mk10
  will be cured, say the word and my   L7
  with a message, sent a   L14
servants, accept the authority of your masters   LPF2
  and handmaidens, pour out my spirit on   A2
  at the wedding   J2
  be obedient to your masters   PE6
  called his ten   L19
  gave authority to his   Mk13
  land owner's   Mw21
  met him with the news   J4
  no longer, I call you   J15
  obey in all things your masters   PCo3
  of Christ   PE6
  of the living God   ThF1
  of the supreme God   A16
  of the vineyard owner   L20
  seal the foreheads of his   Rev7
  to be obedient, exhort   Tt2
  to one another in love, be   PG5

servants, treat me as one of your paid   L15
  under the yoke   PTF6
  whom the master finds alert   L12
serve, Son of Man did not come to be served but to   Mw20; Mk10
  the Lord in ardour of spirit   PR12
service, brothers in Christ's   Rev6
serving-maid, high priest's   Mw26; Mk14; L22
servitude for fear of death   LH2
slave, Abraham's   PG4
  and freeman, no question here of   PG3; PCo3
  assuming the nature of a   PPs2
  everyone who commits sin is a   J8
  girl who was possessed by an oracular spirit   A16
  in the service of Christ   PCF7
  no longer, but as a son   PG4; Ph1
  of all, must be the willing   Mw20; Mk10
  of two masters, no servant can be   L16
  to the law of sin   PR6f
  when you were called   PCF7
  who commits sin is a   J8
  woman's son born by the course of nature   PG4
slavery, all who wear the yoke of   PTF6
  sold Joseph into   A7
  we have never been in   J8
  woman bearing children into   PG4
slaves, cargoes of   Rev18
  endue with a portion of my spirit   A2
  give obedience to your masters   PCo3
  in God's service   LPF2
  masters, be just and fair to your   PCo4
  not to answer back   Tt2
  obey your earthly masters with fear and trembling   PE6
  of beings which are no gods   PG4
  of Christ   PE6; PCo3
  of corruption, themselves   LPS2
  of righteousness   PR6
  or freemen, whether   PCF12
  to elemental spirits   PG4
  to passions and pleasures   Tt3
  to respect their master   Tt2

steward at the wedding   J2
  to manage his servants   L12
submission, his prayer was heard because of humble   LH5
submit to every institution   LPF2
tax and toll, pay   PR13
  to the Roman emperor   Mk12
taxed, all went to be, each into his own city   L2
  the world to be   L2
taxes, Roman   Mw22; L20
  superintendent of   L19
  this is why you pay   PR13
  to Caesar, opposing the payment of   L23
taxing, days of the   A5
tenants, vineyard   Mk12
tithe, Abraham gave Melchizedek a   L23
  the people, Levites commanded to   LH7
tithes of every garden herb   L11
  of mint and dill and cummin   Mw23
    and rue   L11
  on all I get, I pay   L18
tribute, does your master pay   Mw17
  to Caesar, is it lawful for us to give   Mw22; Mk12; L20
votive offerings adorn the temple   L21
wait at table   A6
wash his disciples' feet   J13
yoke, bend your neck to my   Mw11
  of slavery   PTF6

37   *Sex and Marriage*

OLD TESTAMENT

widow, do not oppress the   Z7
  those who wrong the   Ma3
  Zion personified as a   La1
widows and orphans, justice for   De10, 24
widow's weeds   Is47
wife, deserted   Is54
  for Samson   Ju14
  groomsman given Samson's   Ju14
  of your youth, unfaithful to the   Ma2
  Pharaoh's daughter as Solomon's   CS8
  pledged but not taken   De20
  take a wanton for a   Ho1
wives, Abijah had fourteen   CS13
  David took more   SS5
  foreign, to be dismissed   Ez10
  Gideon had many   Ju8
  in battle, capture of   Ju21
  of offending husbands thrown to the lions   D6
  Reheboam had eighteen   CS11
  Solomon had 700   KF11
woman, Deborah was a spirited   Ju4
  in labour, anguish of   Je6, 50
    cry like a   Is42
    gripping his sides like a   Je30
    pangs of a   Is21; Je13, 22
  taken from man   Gen2
  with child when her time is near   Is26
womb, never satisfied, a barren   Pro30ff
  shall I who deliver close the   Is66
  the Lord had shut up her   SF1
women, blessed above, be Jael   Ju5
  in labour   Je31
  surpassing the love of   SS1
  take for yourself   De20
  with child   Je31
  year's preparation for the royal   Est2

NEW TESTAMENT

adulterers and adulteresses   LJ4
  and sinful generations   Mk8
adultery, anyone who marries a divorced woman commits   Mw5
  defiles the man   Mk7
  do not commit   L18; PR2
  eyes full of   LPS2
  free of the law of   PR7
  if a man divorce his wife he commits   Mw19
  in his heart, he has already committed   Mw5
  none who are guilty of   PCF6
  they were told, do not commit   Mw5
  thou shalt not commit   Mw19; PR13; LJ2
  who marries another commits   Mk10; L16
  woman caught in the act of   J8
allure through lusts of the flesh   LPS2
barren, Elizabeth was   L1
  happy are the   L23
  woman, rejoice   PG4
body's desires, obedience to the   PR6
breast that never fed a child, happy the   L23
bride and bridegroom, voice of the   Rev18
bridegroom   Mw9; Mk2; L5
  to whom the bride belongs   J3
  went out to meet the   Mw25
bridegroom's voice, hears the   J3
brother's wife, you have no right to your   Mk6
carouse in broad daylight   LPS2
celibacy, I have no instructions on   PCF2
celibate woman cares for the Lord's business   PCF7
chaste virgin, present you as a   PCS11
chastity for the sake of the kingdom of heaven   Mw19
conceive, Sarah received strength to   LH11
conceived a child by the Holy Spirit   Mw1
  a son in her old age, Elizabeth   L1
concubine, Abraham's   PG4
concupiscence, evil   PCo3
  in the lust of   ThF4

harlot   Mw21; PCF6
  Rahab   LH11; LJ2
harlots, devoured their living with   L15
  the mother of   Rev17
homosexual perversion   PCF6
husband, a heathen   PCF7
  cannot claim his body as his own   PCF7
  man you are living with is not your   J4
  must not divorce   PCF7
  must pay honour to the woman's body   LPF3
husbands at home, let them ask their   PCF14
  love your wives   PE5; PCo3
immorality among you, reports of sexual   PCF5
  because there is so much   PCF7
  such as even pagans do not tolerate   PCF5
indecency defiles the man   Mk7
  put to death   PCo3
inordinate affection, mortify your   PCo3
intercourse, exchange of natural for unnatural   PR1
  with her, until her son was born, he had no   Mw1
lasciviousness defiles the man   Mk7
  repented of the   PCS12
  when we walked in   LPF4
learner, a woman must be a   PTF2
lewd fellows of the baser sort   A17
loving his wife, a man loves himself   PE5
lust conceives and gives birth to sin   LJ1
  has infected the world with corruption   LPS1
  not giving way to   ThF4
  put to death   PCo3
lustful eye, if a man looks on a woman with a   Mw5
lusts, deluded by   Pe4
  denying ungodliness and worldly   Tt2
  flee youthful   PTS3
  follow their abominable   LPS2
    their own godless   LJu1
  of our flesh in times past   PE2
    abstain from the   LPF2
  silly women led away with divers   PTS3

male and female all one person in Christ   PG3
males behave indecently with males   PR1
man is the head of the woman   PE5
marriage bond inviolate   LH13
   contract, Joseph desired to set aside   Mw1
   incapable of   Mw19
   is honourable   LH13
   law, obligations of the   PR7
   Mary and Joseph   Mw1
   nature of   Mk10
   Paul's views on   PCF7
   renounced for the sake of the kingdom of heaven   Mw19
   they forbid   PTF4
   young widows hanker after   PTF5
married man cares for worldly things   PCF7
   woman aims to please her husband   PCF7
marry again, young widows should   PTF5
   at the resurrection men and woman do not   Mw22
   found that she was in child by the Holy Spirit   Mw11
   if that is the position, it is better not to   Mw19
   than to burn, better to   PCF7
   the men and women of this world   L20
   when they rise from the dead, they do not   Mk12
   will have pain and grief, those who   PCF7
men burn with lust for one another   PR1
moral law, teachers of   PTF1
morality, observe high standards of   PTF2
mother-in-law, Simon Peter's   Mk1; L4
motherhood, woman will be saved through   PTF2
mother's pangs, who never knew a   PG4
pain and grief, those who marry will have   PCF7
pangs that come upon a woman with child   ThF5
passion, lay aside all   PCo3
passions and pleasures, slaves to   Tt3
perversion, the fitting wage of such   PR1
pregnant cried out to be delivered   Rev12
prostitute, Rahab the   LH11; LJ12
prostitutes are entering the kingdom of God   Mw21
resurrection, whose wife is she at the   Mw22; L20
rules of conduct, leads them to break all   PR1

wife, since seven married her, whose will she be?   Mk12
wives and mothers, loving   Tt2
   be subject to your husbands as to the Lord   PE5; PCo3
   chaste and reverent behaviour of their   LPF3
woman learn in silence with all subjection, let a   PTF2
   must not domineer over man   PTF2
   must pay her husband all respect   PE5
   to be a teacher, I do not permit a   PTF2
   with child, pangs that come upon a   ThF5
   who fell into sin   PTF2
   who was living an immoral life   L7
woman's need is man   PCF11
womb, contemplated the deadness of Sarah's   PR4
wombs that never bore a child, happy are the   L23
women burdened with a sinful past   PTS3
   eyes for nothing but   LPS2
   have exchanged natural intercourse with unnatural   PR1
   men who did not defile themselves with   Rev14
   must accept the authority of their husbands   LPF3
   of high principle, deacon's wives   PTF3
   older, should school the younger   Tt2
   Paul's views on   PCF11, 14
   should not address the meeting   PCF14
   should respect the authority of their husbands   Tt2
   who are with child, alas for   L21

38   *Significant Numbers*

OLD TESTAMENT

2 anointed ones   Z4
2 olive branches   Z4
3 cities in the east   De4
3 daughters, Job had   Job42
3 days and 3 nights Jonah was in the fish's belly   Jon1
   darkness   Ex10
   hid in the hills   Jos2
   journey across Nineveh   Jon3
   neither eat nor drink for   Est4
3 men, appoint as emissaries   Jos18
3 things the earth is disquieted at   Pro30
   there are which are stately in their stride   Pro30
   there are which are too wonderful for me   Pro30
   there are which will never be satisfied   Pro30
3 times a year, to the Presence   De16
4 chariots in Zechariah's vision   Z6
4 things there are which are smallest on earth yet wise   Pro30
   there are which are stately as they move   Pro30
   there are which I do not understand   Pro30
   there are which never say 'enough'   Pro30
   there are which the earth cannot bear   Pro30
5 cities of Egypt speaking the language of Canaan   Is19
5 lords of the Philistines   Jos13
6 days, circuit Jericho   Jos6
   shalt thou work   Le23
6 men with battle-axes, vision of   E8
6 things the Lord hates   Pro6
6 years, set free a slave who has served you   Je34
7 altars of Balaam   Nu23
7 branched candlestick, lamp-stand   Z4
7 days at the tend of the Presence   Le8
   feast at the royal pavilion   Est1
   I stayed dumbfounded   E3

7 days light in one   Is30

    Nile flowed with blood   Ex7

    pilgrim feast   E45

    purge and purify the altar   E43

    they kept the feast   Ne8

    unleavened cakes   Nu28ff

7 ears of corn   Gen41

7 eunuchs in attendance on the king   Es1

7 eyes in the stone in Zechariah's vision   Z4

7 kine, cows   Gen41

7 locks of Samson's hair   Ju16

7 maids picked for Esther   Est2

7 months Israelites shall bury Gog's dead   E39

7 pillars of wisdom   Pro9

7 priests in front of them   Jos6

7 princes of Persia to advise the king   Est1

7 sons grows faint, mother of   Je15

    Job had   Job42

    of that man, hand over   SS21

7 things are detestable to him   Pro6

7 times a day do I praise thee   Ps119

    his wonted brightness, the sun shall shine with   Is30

    pass over him, let   D4

    punishment   Le26

    seven years   Le25

    sprinkle oil   Le8

    sprinkled blood   Nu19

    the child revived by Elijah sneezed   KS4

    the usual heat of the furnace   D3

    wash in the Jordan   KS5

7 tribes remaining   Jos18

7 trumpets of ram's horn   Jos6

7 weeks pilgrim-feast   De16

7 years famine decreed   KS8

    in the hands of Midian   Ju6

    kindle fires with their discarded weapons   E39

    of famine   Gen41

    read the law every   De31

    set free any Hebrew slave within   Je34

    to build the Temple of Solomon   KF6

sevenfold, turn it back on their own heads   Ps79
seventh day blessed   Gen1
   blow the trumpets   Jos6
   closing ceremony   De6
   of rest   Le23
   of the feast   Ju14
   sabbath   De5
   shall do no work on the   Ex23ff
   the battle was joined   KF20
   the boy died   SS12
  year, slaves freed   De15
9 tribes   Nu34
10 commandments   De4ff, 10
10 horns of the beast in Daniel's vision   D8
10 men from nations of every language   Z8
10 years Judah was at peace under Asa   CS14
12 men, choose   Jos3
12 one from each tribe   De1
12 stones, set up   Jos4
thirteenth day, the lot fell on the   Est3
30 daughters of Ibzan   Ju12
30 pieces of silver, wages in Zechariah's oracle   Z11
30 sons of Ibzan   Ju12
30 sons of Jair   Ju10
30 young men to escort Samson   Ju14
40 days and 40 nights, Elijah in the wilderness   KF19
     Moses was up the mountain   De9
      on Mount Sinai   Ex24
   lie on your right side   E4
   Nineveh shall be overthrown   Jon3
   on the mountain   De10
   presented himself, Goliath   SF17
   rain   Hen7
40 sons of Abdon   Ju12
40 years Egyptian cities shall lie derelict   E29
   I was indignant   Ps95
   in the wilderness   Nu14; Am2, 5
   long thou didst sustain them in the wilderness   Ne9
   long was I grieved with this generation   Ps95
   the land was at peace   Ju3, 5, 8, 12

42 children mauled by bears   KS2
42 kinsmen of Ahajiah murdered   KS10
fiftieth year hallowed   Le25
52 days to rebuild the walls of Jerusalem   Ne6
60 cities, inhabitants of, killed by Moses   De3
    of Bashan allotted   Jos13
70 elders of Jerusalem stood in front of the carved idols   E8
70 kings whose thumbs and toes were cut off   Ju1
70 pilgrims murdered   Je41
70 sons of Gideon   Ju8
70 weeks marked out, then shall sin be brought to an end   D9
70 years has passed over Babylon, when a full   Je29
    I will punish Babylon at the end of   Je25
    is the span of life   Ps90
    Israel lay desolate   CS36
    this country shall be a scandal and a horror for   Je25
    to pass while Jerusalem lay in ruins   D9
    Tyre shall be forgotten   Is23
    vented thy wrath   Z1
80 pilgrims waylaid   Je41
80 years if our strength holds   Ps90
    the land was at peace   Ju3
180 days, royal treasures on display   Est1
190 days, lie on your left side   E4
900 chariots of iron   Ju4
1100 pieces of silver to betray Samson   Ju16
1335 days, happy the man who lives to see the completion of   D12
2000 horses I will give you if you can find riders   Is36
3000 men came to take Samson   Ju16
3000 people killed by Levites   Ex32
10,000 men came to Mount Tabor   Ju4
10.000 people stayed   Ju7
22,000 people went back home   Ju7
120,000 who cannot tell their right hand from their left   Jon4
185,000 Assyrians struck dead overnight   Is37

NEW TESTAMENT

2 fishes and five loaves   Mw14; Mk6; L9; J6
2 horns like a lamb's, a beast which had   Rev13
2 prophets a torment to the whole earth   Rev11
second death, this is the   Rev2
3 and six in the morning, between   Mw14; Mk6
3 days and three nights in the bowels of the earth   Mw12
    have been with me   Mk8
    I will raise it up in   J2
    in the sea-monster's belly   Mw12
    later, to rise   Mk8
    they found him sitting in the temple after   L2
    to be raised after   Mw27
    with nothing to eat   Mw15
    without sight, and neither did eat nor drink   A9
3 foul spirits like frogs   Rev16
3 times beaten with rods   PCS11
    I begged the Lord to rid me of it   PCS12
    you will disown me   Mw26
third day, God raised him to life on the   A10
    he shall rise again on the   Mk10; L9; PCF15
    heaven, caught up as far as the   PCS12
    hour they crucified him   Mk15
    of living creatures died   Rev8
    of mankind, four angels let loose to kill a   Rev9
    of rivers and springs poisoned   Rev8
    of the earth was burnt   Rev8
    of the sea turned to blood   Rev8
    of the ships foundered   Rev8
    of the stars flung to earth   Rev12
    of the trees were burnt   Rev8
    part of the sun, moon and stars went dark   Rev8
    time Jesus appeared after his resurrection   J21
3½ days, life came into them after   LJ5
3½ years, no rain fell for   LJ5
    the skies never opened   L4
4 angels held bound at the Euphrates   Rev9
    let loose to kill a third of mankind   Rev9

4 corners of the earth   Rev7

4 days, he has been dead   J11

4 living creatures in front of the heavenly throne   Rev4f, 14f, 19

fourth watch of the night he came walking on the water   Mw14; Mk6

5 foolish virgins   Mw25

5 loaves to feed the five thousand   Mw14, 16; Mk6; L9; J6

5 months, Elizabeth lived in seclusion for   L1

   they were allowed to torment for   Rev9

5 times given me the thirty nine strokes   PCS11

5 wise virgins   Mw25

5 words with my understanding, rather speak   PCF14

6 in the morning, between three and   Mw14; Mk6

6 wings, each of the four creatures had   Rev4

sixth hour, there was darkness over the land from the   Mw27; Mk15; L23

   month, Gabriel was sent from God in the   L1

7 angels that stand in the presence of God   Rev8, 17, 21

   with seven plagues   Rev15

7 baskets filled with left-overs   Mw15; Mk8

7 bowls of God's wrath   Rev16f

   of plagues   Rev21

7 churches in the province of Asia   Rev1

7 days, abode in Troas   A20

7 devils cast out from Mary Magdalene   Mk16; L8

7 diadems on the dragon's head   Rev12

7 emperors   Rev17

7 eyes, the lamb had   Rev5

7 flaming torches   Rev4

7 golden bowls of wrath   Rev15ff

   candlesticks   Rev1f

   lamps   Rev1f

   vials   Rev15ff

7 heads, dragon with   Rev12

   of the scarlet beast   Rev13, 17

7 hills on which the woman sits   Rev17

7 horns, the lamb had   Rev5

7 kings of whom five have fallen   Rev17

7 lamps of fire   Rev4

7 loaves to feed the four thousand   Mw15f; Mk8

7 men to deal with these matters, appoint   A6

   of whom Philip was one   A21

7 plagues   Rev15, 21

7 seals   Rev5

7 sons of Sceva   A19

7 spirits before the throne   Rev1
    of God   Rev3ff

7 other spirits more wicked than the first   Mw12; L11

7 stars, he held   Rev1ff

7 thunders spoke   Rev10

7 times am I to forgive my brother   Mw18
    if he trespass against thee   L17

7 trumpets, they were given   Rev8

7 vials of plagues   Rev16f, 21

seventh day, God rested on the   LH4

8 years, bedridden for   A9

ninth hour, from the sixth hour there was darkness until the   Mw2; Mk5; L23

10 days you will suffer cruelly   Rev2

10 horns, beast with   Rev13
    dragon with   Rev12
    of the scarlet beast   Rev17

10 kings not yet begun to reign   Rev17

tenth of the city fell   Rev11

11 were at the table, the   Mk16

12 angels at the holy city   Rev21

12 apostles, called forth unto him the   Mw10, 20; Mk3, 6; L6

12 baskets filled with left-overs   Mw14; Mk6; L9; J6

12 crops of fruit   Rev22

12 foundation stones of the city   Rev21

12 from among his followers, he chose   L6

12 gates of the holy city   Rev21

12 stars, a crown of   Rev12

12 tribes of Israel   Mw19; Rev21

12 years, had an issue of blood for   Mk5
    old daughter dying and revived   L8
    old, when Jesus was, made the pilgrimage   L2
    suffered from haemorrhages   L8

14 days lived in suspense and gone hungry   A27

14 generations from Abraham to David   Mw1
    from David to the carrying away into Babylon   Mw1
    from the carrying away into Babylon to Christ   Mw1

14 years ago was caught up   PCS12

14 years later I went again to Jerusalem   PG2

18 people on whom the tower fell   L13

24 elders in heaven   Rev4f, 19

24 other thrones in heaven   Rev4f

30 fold, the yield was   Mw13; Mk4

30 pieces of silver   Mw26f

30 years old, when Jesus began his work he was   L3

38 years, crippled for   J5

39 strokes, five times given men   PCS11

40 days and nights he fasted   Mw4

  appeared over a period of   A1

  in the wilderness   Mk1; L4

  led by the Spirit   L4

  tempted by Satan   Mk1; L4

40 in the conspiracy   A23

40 years, God was indignant for   LH3

  old, the healed man was over   A4

  tested in the desert   LH3

42 months, the beast reigned for   Rev13

  will trample the holy city for   Rev11

46 years to build the temple   J2

50 make them sit down in groups of   L9

60 fold, the yield was   Mw13; Mk4

60 years, widow put on the roll at   PTF5

70 cavalrymen, get ready   A23

70 the Lord appointed a further   L10

70 times seven, I say   Mw18

72 the Lord appointed a further   L10

77 times, I say   Mw18

99 sheep that never strayed   Mw18

100 fold, shall receive a   Mw19

  some seed yielded a   Mw13; Mk4; L8

100 sheep, suppose a man has a   Mw18

120 assembled brotherhood   A1

144 cubits high, wall of the holy city   Rev21

153 big fish   J21

200 infantry, get ready   A23

200 miles around, blood flowed   Rev14

200 spearmen, make ready   A23

276 of us were on board   A27

430 years later, a law made   PG3

490 times, I say, forgive your brother   Mw18

500 of our brothers, he appeared to   PCF15

666 the number of the beast   Rev13

1000 years, chained up Satan for a   Rev20

      reigned with Christ for   Rev20

1260 days, holy city trampled underfoot   Rev11

      woman sustained by God for   Rev12

3000 baptized that day   A2

4000 fed miraculously   M15f; Mk8

5000 fed miraculously   Mw, 16; Mk6; L9; J6

5000 number of believers reached   A4

7000 men who have not knelt to Baal   PR11

7000 people killed by the earthquake in John's vision   Rev11

10,000 times ten thousand angels   Rev5

10,000 words in an unknown tongue   PCF14

12,000 furlongs, the holy city measured   Rev21

12,000 of each of the twelve tribes received the seal   Rev7

23,000 died in one day   PCF10

144,000 received the seal   Rev7

200,000,000 squadrons of cavalry in John's vision   Rev9

39 *Tools and Weapons*

OLD TESTAMENT

anvil   Is40ff

armour   Ps45; E38

arrow   De32; SF20; KS9, 13, 19; Job16, 29, 41; Pro7, 25ff; 1s5, 7, 37, Is49; Je9, 50ff; La3;
    H3; Ps7, 11, 18, 38, 45, 57, Ps64, 76f, 91, Ps120, 127, 144; E5, 21, 39; Z9

  bronze-tipped   Job20; Ps18

awl   De15

axe   Ju9; SF13; KF6; KS6; Ps22, 74; Ec10; Is10; Je46; E26

  blunt   Ec10

  brushwood   Ju9

axehead flew off the handle   KS6

balance   E5

basket   Ex2; De23; KS10; Ps81; Je6, 24; Am4, 8

battleaxe   Je51; E9

battering-ram   E4, 21, 26; Na2

bellows, blacksmith   Job32; Je6

birdcage   Je5

bit, horse's   Is30

bow   SF18; SS1; KS6, 13; CS17, 26; Ne4; Job29; Ps37, 46, 78; Is5,7,13, 21, 41; Je6, 49ff;
    E39; Ho1ff, 7; Am2; H3; Z9ff

  steel   Job20

  strings   Ju16; Ps7, 11, 21

  strung   Ps37

breastplate   KF22; CS18; Is59

bridle   Is30, 37

bucket   Is40

buckler   KF10; CS23; Ps35; Je46; E23, 26, 38ff

  gold   KF10

cage, bird   Je5

callipers   Is44

catapult, siege   CS26

censer   E8

chain   Is40; D5

chisel   Je10

lance   Je46,50; E39

lancets   KF18

latchet, shoe   Is5

machine, siege   CS26

mattock   SF13; Is2, 7; Joe3; Mi4

maul   Pro25

millstone   De24; Ju9

nail   Ju4; CS3; Is22, 40; J10

  iron   CF22

net   Job18; Pro1, 29; Ec9; Is19, 51; Je5; E12, 26, 32, 47; Ho7; Mi7; H1

pen   Je8

  iron   Je17

pick   Ps74

plane, carpenter's   Is44

plough, plow, with my heifer   Ju14

ploughshare, plowshare   SF13; Is2; Joe3; Mi4

pruning hook   Is2, 18; Joe3; Mi4

  knife   Is2; Mi4

quiver   SS8; Job39; Ps127; Is22, 49; Je5, 51; La3; H3

  gold   CF18

razor   Ju13; As7; E5

  sharp as a   Ps52

reins   Is11; Je17

ring, iron tethering   D4

rope   Is3, 5; Je10

sabre   Job39, 41; Je6, 50

saw   SS12; CF20; Is10

  stone   KF7

scabbard   Ju47; E21

scales   Is40; Je32; E5, 45

scriber, carpenter's   Is44

shaft   H3

sheath   Je47; E21

shield   SS1; KF10; KS11; CF5; CS9, 11ff, 17, 23, 25ff, 32; Pro30; Is21ff, 37; Je46, 51; Am4; E23, 26ff, 32, 38ff; Na2; Z9

  bossed   Job15

  bronze   CS12

  gold   CS9, 12

shovel   CS4; Is30; Je52

shuttle   Job7

sickle   SF13; Je50; Joe3

siege machine   CS26

sling   SF17; CS26; Job41; Pro26; Z9

spear   Nu25; SF13, 17ff, 26; SS1ff, 21; KF18; KS11; CF11; CS11ff, 23, CS25ff; Ne4;
    Job39, 41; Ps35, 46, 57; Is2; Je6, 46; E39; Joe3; Mi4; Na2ff; H3

  fish   Job41

spike, iron   Am1

spiked weapons   CS33

sundial   KS20; Is38

sword   Nu31; De13, 20, 28; Jos5ff, 19; Ju7; SF13, 17ff, 25; SS20; KF3, 18ff; KS6, 19;
    CF5, 10; Ne4; Job33, 39; Ps7, 22, 31, 34,   Ps37, 41, 49,37, 44ff, 55, 57, 63ff,
    Ps76, 78, 89, 144, 149; Pro5, 25, Pro30; D11; Is1ff, 13ff, 21ff, 27, 51, 65ff;
    La1f, 4ff;Na2f; Zp2; Hg2; Z9, 11, Z13; E5ff, 11ff, 14, 16ff, 21, 23ff, 28ff, 35,
    38ff; Ho1ff, 7,11, 13; Joe2ff; Am1, 4, 7, 9; Mi4ff; Je2, 5ff, 9, 11ff, Je14ff, 18ff,
    Je24ff, 29, 31ff, 38ff, 44, 46ff

target, buckler, gold   KF10

tent-peg   Ju4

thong, sandal   Is5

threshing instruments, iron   Am1

throwing-stick   E39

tongs, smith's   Is44

tools, iron   KF6

traces, harness   Je2, 5

traps, metal toothed   Job18, 41

weapons, discarded   E39

wheel   E1ff, 10ff; D7

  potter's   Je18

whip   Is10

yoke   De22, 28; SF6; KF19; Is10, 14, 30, 47; Je2, 5, 27, 30, 51; La1,3,5; Ho10ff; Mi2; Na1
  cords and bars of a   Je27

NEW TESTAMENT

anchor   A27; LH6

armour   L11

axe   Mw3; L3

40 *Trades, Professions and Industry*

accountant   Ne13
adjutant-general   CS34; Is36; Je36, 52
administrators, appointed Shedrach, Meshach and Abednego   D2
ambassador   CS35; Is18; Je49; Ob1
  Pharaoh's   Is30
apothecary   CS16; Ne3; Ec10
archer, bowman   Gen21; SS11; CF10; CS14, 35; Ps55, 78; Is21; Je4, 51; Am2
armourer   KS24
army officer   De1; SF14, 17, 26; SS2ff, 8, 17f; KF1f, 9, 11, 14f, 22; KS1, 4f, 8f, 11, 15, 18,
        22, 25; CF13, 18ff, 27ff; CS16f,21,CS25, 32; Is3, 20, 22, 36, 59; Je36f, 39f, 43,
        Je52ff; E17, 23
artificer   Is3
  Egyptian   Is19
assayer   Je6
astrologer   Is47; D2, 4ff
baker   Je37; Ho7
  Pharaoh's   Gen40
barber   E5
beggar   Ps109
blacksmith   Gen4; SF13; Job32; Is44
  master   Gen4
  none to be found   SF13
brick-kiln   SS12; Je43; Na3
bricks   Gen11
bronze worker   KF7
builder   KF5; KS12, 22; CS34; Ne4; Ps81, 127; E27
burnishing   Is21
captain, army   SS4; KF9, 22; KS1, 11, 25; CS23; Is3, 59; Je39ff, 43, 51ff; D3, 11
  ship's   Jon1
carder   Is19
carding, weaving and spinning   Is19
carding, weaving and spinning   Is19

carpenter   SS5; KS12, 22; CF14, 22; CS24, 34; Ez3; Is41, 44; Je24, 29; Z1
carving, wood   KF6
caulker, calker   E27
cavalryman   Ex14; SF8; KF9, 20; Ne2; D11; H1
chamberlain   KS23; Est1ff
chancellor   Ez4
charmer, diviner   Is19
  snake   Ps58
chief constable, Babylonian   D3
  governor in the house of the Lord   Je20
  minister   CS28
  officer in the house of the Lord   Je20
chiefs of the province   Ne11
churn   Pro30
cisterns hewn from rock   De6; Ne9
clay ground for metal casting   KF7
  potter's   Is29, 41, 45, 64; Je18
clerk   CF26; CS26, 34
commander, army   De1; SF14, 26; SS2ff, 8, 17, 19;KF1f, 4, 9, 11, 15, 19; KS4ff;
      CF18ff, 25, 27; CS16, 26, 32; Is20; Je51ff; E17, 23; Na3; Z10
commissioners to bring young virgins to the king   Est2
comptroller of the household   KF4, 16, 18; KS10, 15, 18; CS26, 28; Is22, 36
confectioners   SF8
constable, chief   D3
cook,   SF8
coppersmith, master   Gen4
counsellor   CF27; D3
courier   CS30
  with the king's writ   Est3ff
courtiers of King Darius   D6
  of King Solomon   CS9
craftsmen   Ex31ff; Nu31; KF7; KS24; CS2, 24; Is44; Je10, 24, 29; Ho8, 13
  metal   KF7; CS2, 24
  skilled   Ex31
  who work in gold   Nu31
crucible, metal refining   Os12; Pro17, 27; E22
cupbearer   KF10; CS9
customs officer   KF10
dancer   So6

furnace, smelting   De4; Pro17, 27; Is48, 54; Je6; La5; E1, 22; Ma4
gaoler, jailer   Is10
gate-keeper   SS18; Ne3, 7, 11ff
gilder   Is40
glazed earthenware   Pro26
goldsmith   Ne3; Is40f, 46; Je10, 51
governor   Ez2, 5, 8; Ne3, 8; Je30, 41, 51; E23; Z9, 12
  assassination of the   Je41
  chief temple   Je20
  city   CS34
  for Israel, out of Bethlehem shall come a   Mi5
  Gedaliah appointed   KS25
  of Judah   Ne5; Hg1
  of the citadel   Ne7
  of the city   KF22; KS10, 23
  provincial Babylonian   D3
    Persian   Est1, 3ff, 9
  regional   KF4
  selected from their own number   Je30
grape-gatherer   Je6, 49; Ob1
grinding corn   La5
guard   SS8, 13, 25, 20; KF1; KS10; CF9, 18; D1
guild of doorkeepers   Ez2
    linen workers   CF4
handmill   Je25
haulier   KF5; CS2ff
helmsman   E27
herald   D3; Is52; Je49; Ob1; Na1; H2
  Nebuchadnezzar's   D3
herdsman   Gen4; SF21; Am1, 7
hewer of wood   Is10; Je46
high commissioner   Ez4
hired labourer   Is16; Ma3
hireling   Is21
horse-leach   Pro30
horseman   CS16; E38ff
hunter   Gen10, 25; Job15; Ps22, 91; Pro6, 12; Is13, 24; Je16, 48; La1; Ho12; Mi7
husbandman, farmer   Gen4; Je14, 31, 51ff; Joe1; Am5; Z13
ivory, working in   KF22; CS9; Ps45; So5; E27; Am3, 6
judge   Ju4, 10, 12, 15; CS19; Ez7; D3; Mi4

secretary   CF2; CS34; Ez4
  of state   KF4; KS18; CF18; CS34; Is36
shambles, slaughter-house   Is14; Je12
shearer   Is53
sheep breeder, sheep master   KS3
  farmer, shepherd   Gen4, 29; KS3; Job24; Ps23, 28, 49, Ps78ff, 95, 100; So1; E34; Ho12;
          Am1, 3; Is13, 31, 38, 40, Is44, 56, 61, 63; Je2, 6, 10, 12, 14, 25, 31, 33, 43, 49ff;
          Mi5, 7; Na3; Zp2; Z10f, 13
sheriff, Babylonian   D3
shield-bearer   CS14
shipmaster   Jon1
silversmith   Ju17; Pro25
singer   KF10; CF9; CS5, 29; Ez2,7,10; Ne7, 10ff; Ec2
sledge threshing   Is28
smelting furnace   De4; Je11
smith   KS24; Is44, 54; Je24, 29; Z1
snake-charmer   Ps58; Ec10
soldering   Is40
soldier   Ex14; SF13; SS10; KF1; KS3, 13; CS16, 25; Is31, 36; Je4, 46; E38ff; D11; Ho1;
          Am2; Na3; Z10
spinner   Is19
staff officer   E23
steward   Is22
stone cutter   KS12
  cutting craft   Ex31
stone squarer   KF5
  worker   CS2
stonemason   SS5
straw for bricks   Ex5
superintendent of the enforced levy   KF4
  of the regional governors   KF4
tablet engraving   Je17
teacher   Ps119; Is50
temple-servitor   Ez2, 7, 8; Ne3, 7, 10ff
tiller of the soil   Z13
timber feller   KF5; CS2; Is14
trader   CS9
treasurer   Ez1, 7; Is22
  Babylonian   D3
treasury   KS20

tutor   KS10; CF27
vagabond   Ps109
viceroy   Je51; E23
  of Babylon   D3, 6
  of Jehoshaphat   KF22
vine and fig dresser   KS25; CF27; CS26; Ls61; Je39, 52; Joe1; Am7
vintager   Am9; Ob1
wardrobe, keeper of the   CS34
watchman   SS18; KS9; So3, 5; Ps127, 130; Is1, 21, 24, 52, 56, 62; Je6, 31; E3, 33; Ho9
weaver   Job7; Is19, 38
wheel, potter's   Je18
winepress   Is5, 16, 63; Je48; La1; Ho9; Joe3
  hewn out of rock   Is5
wine-vats, the king's   Z14
woodcutter   Ec10; Je46
woodman   CS2; Ps74
woodworker   CS2; Ps74
worker in stone   CS2
  in wood   CS2
work-gangs in Egypt   Ex1
wreathenwork, metal   KS25
wrought iron   E27

NEW TESTAMENT

advocate   A24
ambassador   PE6
ambassage, envoy   L14
architect   LH11
assayer   LPF1
athlete   PTS2
attendant, court   Mw14
baker   Mw16
beloved physician, Luke   PC04
bishop   PTF3
bleacher   Mk9
boxer   PCF9
builder   A4; PCF3; LH11; LPF2
  master   PCF3

captain, army   J18
  of the temple   L22; A4f
  ship's   A27; Mk6
carpenter   Mw13; Mk6
centurion   Mw8
chamberlain   A12; PR16
clerk, town   A19
collector of taxes   Mw17
constable   Mw5
controller of the temple   A4f
coppersmith   PTS4
counsellor   L23
craftsmanship and design, an image shaped by   A17
craftsmen of any trade   Rev18
  provided a great deal of employment for   A19
deacon, deaconess   PTF3
deputy governor   A18; LPF2
doctor   Mk2; L8; PCo4
  of law   Mw5, 8f, 12, 16, 20f, 23; Mk1ff, 10ff, 14; L2, 5, 9, 15, 20, 22; J8; A4ff, 23
doorkeeper   J10
employment, engage in honest   Tt3
envoy   L14
executioner   Mk6
farmer   PTS2
fellow-worker   ThF3
fisherman   Mw4; Mk1; L5
flute player   Mw9; Rev18
fuller   Mk9
gardener   J15, 20
governor   Mw10; PCS11; PG4; LPF2
harpist   Rev14, 18
herald   Mw11; Mk1; PTS1
husbandman   Mw21; Mk12; L20; J15; PTS2; LJ5
innkeeper   K10
jailer   A16
judge   Mw5; L18; A13
keeper, prison   A5, 12
labourer   Mw20; PTF5; PTS2; LJ5
  is worthy of his hire   L10
land owner   L15

sergeant, magistrate's   A16
shambles, meat-market   PCF10
shepherd   Mw9, 25f; Mk6, 14; L2; J10; A8, 20; LPF2, 5; LJu1
ship-master   Rev18
shipmen   A27f
silversmith   A19
soldier   Mw8; L3, 7; J18f; A12, 21, 27f; PTS2
steward   Mw20; L8, 12, 16; J2; PCF4; PTS2
superintendent of taxes   L19
swineherd   Mk6
tanner   A9f
tax-gatherer   Mw5, 9ff, 18, 21; Mk2; L3, 5, 7, 15, 18
teacher   Mw23; Mk9; L2; PR12, 16; PE4; PTF1; PTS1f; LH5; LPS2;   LJF2
  of the law   Mw13; L5
tent-maker   A18
town clerk   A19
tutor   PG3
vine dresser   L13
  grower   Mw21; Mk12; L20
wages you never paid   LJ5
warder, prison   A5, 12, 16
work, he who will not, shall not eat   ThS3
  quietly for a living   ThS3
worked for a living night and day   ThF2
worker earns his pay   PTF5

41 *Trading, Import and Export*

OLD TESTAMENT

agents, trading Is23
baggage-train Is10, 29; D11
borrowing Pro22
business Ps107
  timidity in Pro11
buyer Pro20; E7
  and seller Is24
camels laden with spice Is60
caravan, trading Gen37; Is21; E27
cargo E27
commerce in goats E27
  in precious stones E27
  in sheep E27
  in spice E27
  in wine E27
  in wool E27
  land of E16ff
  Tarshish a source of your E27
convoy, traders' Is60
custom tax E24
customs officer KF10
dealer in animals Z11
  in cloth E27
  in silver wiped out Zp1
discount Pro28
export KF10
fair, trading E27
goods taken in pledge H2
harbour of Tarshish, trading Us23
import from Ophir KF10
  of almug wood KF10
  of balm E27
  of balsam E27
  of bronze E27

NEW TESTAMENT

buy or sell, no one allowed to   Rev13
buying and selling in the temple   Mw21; Mk11; L19; J2
cargoes, no longer buys their   Rev18
  of flour   Rev18
  of gold and silver   Rev18
  of horses and chariots   Rev18
  of marble   Rev18
  of oil   Rev18
  of perfume   Rev18
  of sheep and cattle   Rev18
  of slaves   Rev18
  of spice   Rev18
  of wheat   Rev18
  of wine   Rev18
cash, turned his share into   L15
corn dumped in the sea   A27
creditor, there was a certain   L7
custom-house   Mk2; L5
dealers in cattle, sheep and pigeons   J2
  in pigeons   Mw21; Mk11; J2
  in purple fabric   A16
  in the temple   Mw21; Mk11; L19; J2
debtors, creditor who had two   L7
  one by one, summoned his master's   L16
deposit, put money on   L19
goods, rich in the world's   PTF6
interest, on deposit for   L19
market place, standing idle in the   Mw20
    turn my father's house into a   J2
merchandise, brass   Rev18
  house of   J2
  no man buyeth their   Rev18
merchant   Mw13
  princes of the world   Rev18
merchants grown rich on her bloated wealth   Rev18
  of the earth   Rev18
money changer   Mw21; Mk11; J2
  lender   L7
partners in payments and receipts   PPs4
pence, why was this not sold for three hundred   Mk14; J12

profit each had made, to see what   L19
profits distributed to all in need   A4
property in land or houses, all who had   A4
rich, he was very successful, for he was very   L18
sale, you thought God's gift was for   A8
sell everything you have and distribute to the poor   L18
sellers of doves   Mk11
selling and buying in the temple, drove out all who were   Mw21
sold and bought in the temple   Mw21; Mk11; L19
tables of the money-changers   Mw21
trade with this, gave them a pound, saying   L19
traded by sea, those who   Rev18
  with five talents   Mw25
traders in all these wares   Rev18
  temple   L19
  were once the merchant princes   Rev18
trading and making money   LJ4
usury, I should have received mine own with   Mw25; L19
wares, traders in all these   Rev18
wheat, lost cargo of   A28

42 *Transport, Vehicles and Vessels*

OLD TESTAMENT

ark, Noah's   Gen6ff
  of acacia, shittim wood   De10
  of bulrushes   Ex2
  of the Covenant   De10, 31
ass   Gen49; Nu22; Jos6, 15; Ju10, 12, 19; SF9, 16, 25, 27; SS16ff; KF13; KS4, 7; CF5, 12,
       27; CS28; Ez2; Ne7; Job1, 24, 42; Pro26; Is21, 30; E23; Z9, 14
  laden   Ju19
axle, axle-tree, bronze   KF7
baggage train   Is110, 29; D11
beasts of burden   Is46
bier,   SS3; CS16
bit, horse's   Is30
bridle   Ps32; Pro26; Is30, 37
camel   Gen 24, 31, 37; Ex9; Le11; De14; Ju8ff; SF27, 30; KF4, 10; KS8; CF5, 12, 27;
       CS9; Ez2; Ne7; Est8; Job1, 42; Is21, 30, 60, Is66; Je2, 49; E25; Z14
canal, Chebar, Kebar   E1, 43
canvas sail   E27
captain, ship's   Jon1
caravan, camel   Gen37
  trading   Is21; E27
carriage   Is10, 46
cart for the Ark of God   SS6; CF13
  ox   SF6
  rope   Is5
cartwheel   Is28
caulking, ship's seams   E27
chariot   Ex14; Jos11, 17; Ju1, 4; SF8f; SS1, 15; KF1, 4, 9f, 20, 22; KS5ff, 13; CF18; CS1,
       14, 16; Ps20, 68, 104; So6; Is2, 5, 21, 31, 36f, 43, 66; Je4, 17, 22, 46, 50ff; E23,
       26ff, 39; D11; Ho10; Joe2; Mi1, 5; Na2f; H3, 10; Hg2; Z6, 9
  lining for a   E27
  of cedar wood   So3
  two-horsed   Is21

chariot wheel   Ps77
  wheels like the whirlwind   Is5
chariots   countless   Is37
  like a whirlwind   Is66
  no end to their   Is2
  of fire   KS6
convoy, traders'   Is60
crown, bronze trolley   KF7
deck, ship's   E27
dhows of Arabia   Is2
dromedary   KF4; Est8; Is60, 66; Je2
felloes, wheel   KF7
flanges, bronze trolley   KF7
fleet, Solomon's   KF9
galley   Is33
goad, ox   Ju3; SF13
handles, bronze trolley   KF7
harness   Je46; Mi1
  chariot   KF18
  ox   SS24
haulier   KF5; CS2ff
helmsman   E27
horse   Ex9; Jos11; SS15; KF4, 9ff, 20; KS5ff; Ez2; Est6, 8; Job39; Ps20, 32ff, 76, 147;
        Pro21, 26; Is2, 5, 21, 30ff, 43, 63, 66; Je4, 6, 8, 11ff, 17, 22, 46, 50f; E23, 26ff,
        38ff; Ho1,14; Joe2; Am6; Mi5; Na2f; H1, 3; Hg2; Z1, 6, 9, 12, 14
hub, wheel   E1
Jehu drives furiously   KS9
jetty, offshore piles   E27
litter   Is66
  of Solomon   So3
mariner   E27; Jon1
mast   Pro23; Is33
  of cedar   E27
mule   SS13, 18; KF1, 10; CF12; Ez2; Ne7; Est8; Ps32; Is66; E27; Z14
naves, wheel   KF7
oars, galley   Is33
  of oak   E27
oarsman   E27
outrunner   KF1

overboard, thrown, to lighten the ship   Jon1
  oxen, draught   KF1, 4, 8, 19; Ne5; Job1; Ps8, 66; Is7, 22, 30; E1; Am6
pack animals   KS3
palanquin head-rest, gold   So3
  lining, leather   So3
  of King Solomon   So3
  poles, silver   So3
  seat of purple stuff
pilot, ship's   E27
raft of logs   KF5; CS2
reins   Is11; Je17; Ho11
rigging, ship's   Pro23; Is33
rim, wheel   E1
rope, cart   SF19; Is3, 5; Je10
rowers   E27
saddle, ass   KF2, 13
saddlecloth   Ju5; E27
  woollen   E27
sail, blue and purple   E27
  canvas   Is33; E27
  patterned linen   E27
sailor   E27; Jon1
seaman   KF9
seams, caulking ship's   E27
shipmaster   Jon1
ships   Ps104; Pro30; Is60; E27
  company   E27
  from Tarshish, trading   E27
  go to sea in   Ps107
  laden with merchandise   Pro31
  merchantmen   KF10; CS8f, 20
  of Chittim   D11
  of Solomon's fleet   KF9
  of Tarshish   Is2, 23
  of Tyre   Z9
  of war   D11
  stately   Is60
  swift   Job9
  trading   CS8f, 20; Is2, 23; E27
  wrecked by the east wind   Ps48

shipwreck   KF22
skiff, reed-built   Job9
sledge, threshing   Job9
spacecraft of Ezekiel's vision   E1, 10
spokes, wheel   KF7
stables   KF4, 10; Est7; E25
swivel-pins, metal trolley   KF6
tacklings, ship's rigging   Is33
trolley, bronze   KF7; KS16, 25; CS4; Je27, 52
tyres, tires, round like the moon   Is3
undersetters, base   KF7
vessels, Arab   Je49
  of bulrushes   Is18
  of reeds   Is18
wagon   Nu7; SF6; Is66; E23; Am2
  covered   Nu7
wheel   E1ff, 10ff; D7; Na3
  within a wheel   E1, 10
wheel-forks, bronze trolley   KF7
wheels, bronze trolley   KF7
  by the four living creatures   E1, 10
  of the cherubim   E10
  with eyes   E1, 10
whip   Pro26; Na3
yoke, draught   De22, 28; SF6; KF19; Is10, 14, 30, 47; Je2, 5, 27, 30f, 51; La1, 3, 5; Ho10f; Mi2; Na1

NEW TESTAMENT

abandon ship, the sailors tried to   A27
adrift on the open sea   PCS11
anchor   A27
  safe and sure   LH6
  weighing   A27
anchors dropped from the stern   A27
  from the bows, lay out   A27
anchors slipped the   A27
ark, Noah's   Mw24; L17; LH11; LPF3

ass   Mw21; L13f; J12; LPS2

boat   Mw13, 15; J6

  battling with a head-wind in a rough sea   Mw14

  beside them, he climbed into the   Mk6

  cut the ropes of the   A27

  fishing   Mw4

  he sat in the   Mk4

  Jesus got into the   Mw8; J21

    withdrew quietly by   Mw14

  lowered the ship's   A27

  ran into a heavy squall   L8

  set off privately by   Mk6

  ship's, dropped away   A27

  to save Jesus from being crushed by the crowd   Mk3

boats, he got into one of the   L5

bow, lay out anchors from the   A27

  stuck fast   A27

captain, ship's   A27; Rev18

cargo ship to unload at Tyre   A21

carriage   A21

  sitting in his   A8

cast ashore on a rugged coast   A27

Castor and Pollux, ship of Alexandria   A28

chariot, sitting in his   A8

chariots and horses, cargoes of   Rev18

donkey   Mw21; L13f; J12

  Jesus found a   J12

dropped four anchors from the stern   A27

foresail set to the wind   A27

gear, the ship's   A27

harbour, Cretan   A27

  exposed to south-west and north-west   A27

  unsuitable for wintering   A27

head to wind, impossible to keep the   A27

helm, large ship turned by a small   LJ3

hoisted aboard the ship's boat   A27

jettisoned the ship's gear   A27

lashings of the steering paddles   A27

lightened the ship by dumping the corn at sea   A27

mainsail, lowered the   A27
on board, two hundred and seventy six of us   A27
overboard, those who can swim should jump   A27
rope   A27
rowing, toiling in   Mk6
rudder   LJ3
  bands   A27
run before the wind   A27
sail-cloth, sheet of   A10f
sailed under the lee of Clauda, Crete and Cyprus   A27
sailing with you, the lives of all who are   A27
sailor   A27; Rev18
sea-captain   Rev18
set sail for Syria   A18
ship aground, ran the   A27
  and cargo, loss of the   A27
  and sat on the sea, he entered the   Mk4
  ashore, planned to run the   A27
  bound for Phoenicia   A21
  cast the net on the right hand side of the   J21
  covered with the waves   Mw8
  departed privately by   Mk6
  embarked in a   A27
  found in Patara   A21
  had wintered in the island   A28
  he entered into a   Mw9; L8; J6
  in the midst of the sea   Mw14
  Jesus went into a   Mw13
  master   Rev18
  named Castor and Pollux   A28
  owner   A27
  running before the wind   A27
  sailed for Assos   A20
  set sail in a   A28
  should wait on him, a small   Mk3
  to unload at Tyre   A21
  turned about by a small helm   LJ3
  undergirded the   A27
  waves beat on the   Mk4
shipmen   A27

ships at sea, all who had   Rev18
  boat, lowered the   A27
  fishing   Mw4
  foundered, a third of the   Rev8
  gear, jettisoned the   A27
  standing by the lake   L5
shipwreck   A27; PCS11
sounded and found twenty fathoms   A27
steering-paddles, lashings of the   A27
stern, dropped anchors from the   A27
  pounded by the breakers   A27
tackle, tackling, ship's   A27
tempest, tossed in the   A27
undergirded the ship   A27
vessel bound for Italy, an Alexandrian   A27
voyage, risky to continue with the   A27
  will be disastrous   A27
weighing anchor   A27

43 *Treachery and Trickery*

OLD TESTAMENT

abandoned camp, the Aramaeans   KS7
accused the Jews, Chaldaeans   D3
adversaries for Solomon, Hadad and Rezon   KF11
affections, stifling their natural   Am1
allies, former, march you to the frontier   Ob1
ambush   Ps10, 17, 59
  by Jeroboam   CS13
anger of Moses for dissidents   Nu16
apostate Israel   Je3
armed bands roaming the countryside   Je40, 42
arrogance of Jacob, I loathe the   Am6
bait, let her be   SF18
bandits   KF11
beards, shaved off half their   SS10
beast, do not behave like a   SS13
betray the survivors, do not   Ob1
betrayal of Samson by Delilah   Ju16
blood on your robe   Je2
blood-guilt rests on Saul   SS21
booty of asses, camels and sheep   CF5
  of Jericho   Jos6
bribe for the king of Assyria   KS16
  her priests give direction in return for a   Mi3
  they take a   Am5
bribed to utter a prophecy   Ne6
bribery of officials   Ez4
brigands will defile Israel   E7
brutish, pastors are become   Je10
bullies and robbers, the common people are   E22
burnt goodly castles   Nu31
cage, drew him into a   E19
captured from Jerusalem, the royal treasures   KS14
cave, robbers'   Je1

false accusation   KF21
  evidence   De19
  tongue   Pro6
  witness   Pro6
    by Jezebel   KF21
faults, secret   Ps19
fled the country, Hadad   KF11
flight, put to, by the men of Ai   Jos7
    for taking forbidden things   Jos7
flotsam on the water, swept away like   Ho10
fools and blockheads one and all   Je10
forbidden plunder   Jos7
forgery of Ahab's name by Jezebel   KF21
forgetting the ties of kinship   Am1
foul play, victim of   D11
fraud, fill their master's house with violence and   Zp1
freebooters   KF11
gall, judgement turned into   Am6
garments, cut off half their   SS10
gazing-stock, make thee as a   Na3
gossip   Pro11ff, 18, 20, 26
grain, he will take a tenth of your   SF8
harbourer of forbidden things   Jos7
hid among rocks, the people   SF13
  among the baggage, Saul   SF10
  in a pit, covered and strewn   SS17
  in a well   SS17
  in pits and cisterns   SF13
  in the fields, David   SF20
hidden beneath a mantle   Ju4
  beneath a rug, Sisera lay   Ju4
  Joash, the one surviving prince   KS11
honesty twisted like briars   Mi7
humiliated, David's envoys were   SS10
hunt their kinsmen down   Am1
intimidation of Nehemiah   Ne2ff
intrigue, he will seize the kingdom by   D11
judgement for rewards, the judge who gives   Mi7
  turned into gall   Am6
  turned to wormwood   Am5

justice, hateful, you who make   Mi3
  her rulers sell   Mi3
  you have turned into poison   Am6
lay in wait for Samson, the people of Gaza   Ju16
lie in wait in the vineyards   Ju21
    on the hill-top   Ju9
  upon lie, they invent   Ps35
lies, Ephraim compasseth me about with   Ho11
looted, Aramaean gold   KS7
lot, her nobles were shared out by   Na3
lunatic, David acted like a   SF21
lured to their death, the prophets of Baal   KS10
mad, feigned himself   SF21
mislead you, confederates   Ob1
mock a hunchback, brutes who would   Ps35
net   Ps9ff, 35, 57, 66, 140
  cast over him, caught in its meshes   E17
  drives his kinsmen like a hunter into the   Mi7
  spread out, you have been a   Ho5
  to catch my feet   La1
panic of Aramaeans at Samaria   KS7
pastors are become brutish   Je10
persecute the guiltless, you   Am5
perverse and crooked generation   De32
pit they have dug to catch me   Je18
  trap   Ps7, 9, 35; Ec10
    dug in my path   Ps57
    muddy   Ps40
pledge, garments seized in   Am2
plunder, men that lust for   Ps76
  of Egypt   Ex3
  of Jericho forbidden   Jos7
  taken from you, shared out   Z14
plundered, house of the Lord to supply bribes   KS16
  houses of Jerusalem   Z14
plunderers, gave them over to   KS17
  the Lord made them prey to   Ju2
poison, you have turned justice into   Am6
prayer of Vengeance   La3
pretence to be a mourner   SS14

pretence to be ill   SS13
pricks in your eyes   Nu33
provoke me to anger, Jews   E8
pulled down, the walls of Jerusalem   Je52
raiders, the Lord made them prey to   Je52
ransom, hold men to   Am5
realm of wickedness, Edom   Ma1
rebellion against Assyria   KS18
  against the house of David   KF12
    Israel   KS3
    king of Assyria   KS18
    Nebuchadnezzar   KS24
  of Reheboam   KF11
rebels, a race of   Is30
  must live in the desert   Ps68
relapse into deeper corruption, they would   Ju2
renegades   Ps78
revenge plotted on Shimei   KF2
revolt against Joash   KS24
    Nebuchadnezzar   KS24
reward, judgement given for   Mi7
rifled, house of Jerusalem   Z14
robbed all who passed that way   Ju9
robbers' cave   Je1
  do you think that this house is a   Je7
  is this house become a den of   Je7
  lying in wait   Ho6
  shall enter my secret place and defile it   E7
  who gave Israel to the   Is42
robe, blood on the corner of your   Je2
ruffians, a band of   Ps22
rug rolled up in a bed   SF19
ruin, their feats lure them to   Ps69
rumour, alive with   Ps55
  upon rumour   E7
rumours, carrying false   Ex23
ruse, Zebel resorted to   Ju9
scandal, alive with   Ps55
scoundrel, Sheba   SS20
scoundrels, Eli's sons were   SF1ff

scoundrels surrounded the house   Ju19
secret agents like Locusts   Na3
sell justices, her rulers   Mi3
slander   Ec7
slanders, neighbours walk with   Je9
slippery as oil, their words are   Ps55
smoke from a chimney, they shall disappear like   Ho13
snare   Ps18, 64, 69, 91
   for your feet, your own kith and kin lay a   Ob1
   in the very temple of God   Ho9
   to entrap you   Jos23
   you have been a   Ho5
snares they have hidden for my feet   Je18
sow the wind and reap the whirlwind   Ho8
spies, Absalom sent throughout Israel   SS15
   as numerous as stars   Na3
   on the roof   Jos2
   sent to Bethel   Ju1
spite, the public square is never free from   Ps55
spoil, enjoy the use of   De20
   treasures of Judah carried to Babylon as   Je20
sport, enjoy the use of   De20
spy out the country of Laish   Ju18
   the land, five fighting men of Dan   Ju18
staff of reed to the house of Israel   E29
steal, shall not   De5
stumbling block   Is57; E14
   blocks I will lay before this people   Je6
tax levied on the poor   Am5
test Solomon, the Queen of Sheba came to   KF10
thickets, the people hid in   SF13
thief as your friend   Ps50
thieves or robbers come by night   Ob1
   they break into houses, they are   Ho7
thirty pieces of silver   Z11
threat to Ahab by Ben-hadad   KF20
ties of kinship, forgetting   Am1
tithe, bring within three days   Am4
traitor, friends turned   La1

traitor in his over-confidence   H2
  of Bethel let free   Ju1
traitors   Ps59, 78
  no mercy on   Ps59
  will lay their plots   D11
transgressors, clan chosen as   Jos7
trap, David has walked into a   Sf23
trap, deadly, to catch men   Je5
  for him while speaking amicably, plans a   Je9
  they will shut you fast in the   Ju2
traps for the righteous   Is29
  hidden   Ps140
treachery committed against the God of Israel   Jos22
  of Achan, remember the   Jos22
  of Jehu to Ahaziah and Jehoram   KS9
  of Jezebel   KF21
  of Joab against Amasa   SS20
  Sisera's death through   Ju4
treason! Athalia cried   KS11; CS23
tribute of grain extorted from the poor   Am5
trickery by the citizens of Ai   Jos8
  by the inhabitants of Gibeon   Jos9
  of Benjamites by feigned retreat of the Israelites   Ju20
  of Darius into condemning Daniel   D6
  of David by Joab   SS14
  of Eglon by Ehud   Ju3
  of Isaac by Jacob   Gen27
  of Isaac by Rebecca   Gen27
  of Jacob by Laban   Gen29
  of Joshua by the Gibeonites   Jos9
  of Naaman by Gahazi   KS5
  of Shechem by Jacob's sons   Gen34
  of Sisera by Jael   Ju4
  of the king of Israel by a prophet   KF20
tricks, Midianites with their crafty   Nu25
tyrants brought low   Ps107
vengeance, Jeremiah's prayer of   La3
  on Jezebel, I will take   KS9
  on their enemies, a day of   Est7
  this is the day of   Je46

violence and fraud, who fill their master's house with   Zp1

warning against Joab   KF2

well, hid in the   SS17

whip for your backs, they will be a   Jos23

whirlwind, reap the   Ho8

wicked counsellor, from you has come forth a   Na1

  generation, this   De1

  go down to Sheol in peace   Job21 wicked men move boundary stones   Job24

    reap what is not theirs   Job24

wickedness, realm of   Ma1

  rid Israel of   De17

wormwood, judgement turned to   Am5

NEW TESTAMENT

abuse and persecution, I had met him with   PTF1

  with abuse, do not repay   LPF3

ambush, the son of Paul's sister heard of the   A23

  to kill Paul, planned an   A25

anger against his brother, anyone who nurses   Mw5

arrested, John the Baptist   Mw4

arrogant, boastful and abusive, men will be   PTS3

bad men all hate the light   J3

bandit, Barabbas was a   J18

  do you take me for a   Mk14

betray brother to death, brother shall   Mk13

  Jesus, Judas went to the chief priests to   Mk14

  you, even your parents and brothers will   L21

betrayed, alas for him by whom the Son of Man is   L22

  into the hands of men, Son of Man shall be   Mw17

blaspheme, compelled them to   A26

blasphemous fellow, who is this   L5

blasphemy, put off all   PCo3

blood-money   Mw27

burst open so that his entrails poured out   A1

busybodies, we hear there are   ThS3

charlatans will make progress   PTS3

common cause against the Messiah, rulers made   A4
condemn yourself as unworthy of eternal life   A13
conflicts and quarrels, what causes   LJ4
crafty rogues, dupes of   PE4
crucified, handed Jesus over to be   J19
  the Lord of glory, powers that ruled the world   PCF2
damnation, in danger of eternal   Mk3
day of the Lord will come   LPS3
deadly sin, there is such a thing as   LJF5
defraud his brother, let no man   ThF4
den of thieves, made my house a   Mw21; Mk11; L19
denied the Holy One, ye   A3
deny me thrice, thou shalt   Mw26; Mk14; L22
destruction, they are heading for   PPS3
dregs of humanity, we are treated as   PCF4
  of the populace, recruited from   A17
enemy, he is the   ThS2
envy, rivalry, and malevolence, they are one mass of   PR1
evil doer, root out the   PCF5
  for evil, never render   PR12; ThF5; LPF3
  love of money is the root of all   PTF6
  men shall wax worse and worse   PTS3
extortioners   PCF5
faith, lopped off for lack of   PR11
false apostles   PCS11
  witness against Jesus   Mw26
fight against the Holy Spirit, you always   A7
frame a charge against him, they wanted to   Mw12
Gentiles, Herod and Pilate conspired with the   A4
get thee behind me Satan   Mw16
godless and wicked age   Mk8
gossips and busybodies   PTF5
greed, ruthlessness, defiles the man   Mk7
ground their teeth with fury   A7
hate your enemy, they were told   Mw5
hated me without reason   J15
heathen men to crucify him, you used   A2
hypocrites love to pray where all can see them   Mw6
idle, they learn to be   PTF5
idling their time away   ThS3

impious and sinful, law is aimed at the   PTF1
infuriated, the whole congregation were   L4
injustice, filled with every kind of   PR1
jeered at him, 'Hail, king of the Jews!'   Mw27
Judas said to Jesus, 'Rabbi', and kissed him   Mk14
  would you betray the Son of Man with a kiss?   L22
judgement, terrifying expectation of   LH10
justice is mine, I will repay   LH10
kidnappers, liars, perjurers, law is aimed at   PTF1
kill himself, the jailer intended to   A16
killed with the sword, he that killeth with the sword   Rev13
kiss, betrayed with a   Mw26; Mk14; L22
law of sin, a slave to the   PR7
liars and perjurers, law is made for   PTF1
libellously report me, as some   PR3
lied to the Holy Spirit   A5
lying in wait, a party more than forty strong are   A23
malice and deceit, away with all   LPF2
  and envy, our days were passed in   Tt3
   defiles the man   Mk7
   filled with every kind of rapacity and   PR1
misdeeds, responsible for other people's   PTF5
mocked him, the men surrounding Jesus   L22
    the soldiers   L23
   maltreated and spat upon, the Son of Man will be   L18
murderer, everyone who hates his brother is a   LJF3
oath not to eat or drink until they had killed Paul   A23
offence, the Pharisees have taken great   Mw15
perdition, an evident token of   PPs1
  going to   Rev17
persecuted the church of God, I   PCF15; PG1
persecution was started against Paul and Barnabas   A13
persecutor of the church in pious zeal   PPs3
perverse generation, what an unbelieving and   L9
pestilent fellow, Paul   A24
pilfer from the common purse, Judas used to   J12
plot laid against Paul   A20
poisoned their minds against Christians   A14
pretence and jealousy, away with all   LPF2
pretext of a closer investigation to do away with him   A23

property of widows, men who eat up the   Mk12

quarrels, a contentious temper, belong to the lower nature   PG5

  and conflicts, what causes   LJ4

rabble rousers   A17

railing with railing, not rendering   LPF3

rascal, swindler, son of the devil   A13

rebellion against God, the final   ThS2

  as in those days of   LH3

renounce their faith, tried to make them   A26

retribution, day of   PR2

retribution, God's agents of   PR13

  has come, thy day of   Rev11

  has overtaken them   ThF2

  the fury of   PR2

  who warned you to escape from the coming   Mw3

riot in the daytime, count it pleasure to   LPS2

  run the risk of being charged with   A19

robber, Barabbas was a   J18

robber's cave, making my house a   Mw21; Mk11; L19

  fell into the hands of   L10

  have met dangers from   PCS11

root out the evil-doer from your community   PCF5

ruin and perdition, plunge men into   PTF6

ruthless greed nothing less than idolatry   PCo3

scandal, bishop may not be exposed to   PTF3

  deaconesses who will not talk   PTF3

  monger   PR1; PTS3; Tt2

scum of the earth, we are treated as   PCF4

sham apostles   PCS1

  Christians   PG2

shipwreck of their faith   PTF1

sin, anything which does not arise from conviction is   PR14

  entered the world through Adam   PR5

  is death, the wages of   PR6

  it was the woman who fell into   PTF2

  Jews and Greeks alike are all under the power of   PR3

  lust conceives   LJ1

  not all sin is deadly   LJF5

  the sting of death is   PCF15

  wages of   PR6

sinfulness, deception of   ThS2

   their deliberate choice, make   ThS2

sinners, Jesus came into the world to save   PTF1

sins, elders who commit   PTF5

     you being dead in your   PCo2

slander, base suspicions, quibbles which give rise to   PTF6

slandered by those who claim to be Jews   Rev2

slanderer, any Christian who is a   PCF5

  or swindler, no   PCF6

slaughter, the day has come for   LJ5

Son of God, he has claimed to be   J19

    throw yourself down, if you are the   L4

spitefully, pray for those who treat you   L6

strife or vainglory, let nothing be done through   PPs2

stumbling block and retribution   PP11

   be placed in a brother's way, that no   PR14

   before the children, Balaam cast   Rev2

   to me, you are a   Mw16

   to the Jews and folly to the Greeks   PCF1

   to them that are weak   PCF8

  stone, I lay in Sion a   PR9

swindler, any Christian who is a   PCF5

  you rascal   A13

swindlers, no slanderers or   PCF6

  pagans who are   PCF5

terrorists   A21

test, conspired to put the Spirit to the   A5

  you are not to put the Lord your God to the   Mw4

thief, at what hour would come   Mw24

  come as a   LPs3

  come upon you like a   Rev3

  in the night   ThF5

  Judas was a   J12

  must give up stealing   PE4

  or robber climbs in some other way   J10

thieves, a den of   Mw21; Mk11; L19

  break in   Mw6

  fell among   L10

  or grabbers, no   PCF6

threatenings, Saul breathing out   A9

trespasses and sins, who were dead in   PE2
tricked him, saw the astrologers had   Mw2
unbelief, acted ignorantly in   PTF1
vengeance, cup of God's   Rev14
  fierce wine of his   Rev16
  has come, the great day of   Rev6
  is mine, I will repay, saith the Lord   PR12; LH10
venom, the tongue is charged with deadly   LJ3
viper's brood, you   Mw3
whisperers and scandal-mongers   PR1
wicked and godless age   Mk8
  Christ died for the   PR5
  fiery darts of the   PE6
  men and charlatans will make progress   PTS3
wickedness of men, retribution falling on   PR1
  the secret power of   ThS2
  this present age of   PG1
  will be revealed in human form   ThS2
widows, men who eat up the property of   Mk12; L20
wrath of God, seven golden bowls full of the   Rev15
  winepress of   Rev19
wrong for wrong, see that no one pays back   ThF5; LPF3
wrongs you, do not set yourself against the man who   Mw5
Zion, a stone to trip over, here I lay in   PR9

OLD TESTAMENT

alive, in the nations of patrimony leave no creature   De20

    neither man nor woman did David bring back   SF27

assassinated, the governor of Judah   Je41

behead Elisha, the king sent to   KS10

beheaded, seventy sons of Ahab   KS10

blind and lame killed by David   SS5

blood, marked with   Le8, 14

  Nile turned to   Ex7

  of the Covenant   Ex24

  waters turned to   Ex4, 7

body flung into a pit, Absalom's   SS18

bound with new ropes, Samson   Ju15ff

branding   Is3

breath, did not leave alive any that drew   Jos11

burning as a penalty   Le20ff; Jos7; D3

  torches tied to jackals' tails   Ju15

burnt after stoning   Jos7; Nu15

  by Pharaoh, Gezer   KF9

  city of Jericho   Jos6

  every town within reach of the Israelites   Ju20

  Gibeah in revenge   Ju20

  harbourers of forbidden things   Jos7

  house of the Lord   KS25

  Jerusalem   KS25

  occupants of the castle of Shechem   Ju9

  Samson's wife and her father   Ju15

  thousand men and women   Ju15

butchered on a stone, sons of Gideon   Ju9

cannibalism under siege   KS6

children burnt as sacrifice to Baalim   Le20; KS17; CS28; Is57; E16, 23

  eaten under siege   KS6

  given in pledge for food   Ne5

children, keep alive for yourselves   De20
  punished for their father's crime   Nu14, 31; Je31; E18; D6
  put to death   Ex1, 31; Nu21, 31; De2ff, 20ff, 23; Jos6ff; Ju1, 9, 11, 18, 20ff; SF7, 15, 22,
        SF27; KF11; KS8, 10, 15, 25; D6, 20; Am1
  thrown to the lions   D6
corpses, the ground was strewn with   Ju9
cracked, the skull of Abimelech   Ju9
crime after crime of Gaza and Tyre   Am1
     of Israel   Am2
crushed by the city wall, 27,000 men   KF20
cut off, great toes and thumbs of Adoni-bezek   Ju1
           of seventy kings   Ju1
    head of Goliath   SF17
      of Ishbosheth   SS4
      of Saul   SF31; CF10
    heads of the Midianite princes   Ju7
    his hands and feet   SS4
   out your right eyes as a covenant   SF11
   the oxen to pieces, Saul in his anger   SF11
   up limb by limb, the concubine   Ju19
dash to the ground their children   KS8; Is13; Ho13; Na3
death penalty   Ex21ff; Le20, 24; Nu1, 15, 25, 35; De13ff, 17, 21f, 24; Jos7f, 10; KF2; D2;
        Est2, 4ff; Je26;
  for mercy killing   SS1
  put to, any who had not gone up at Mizpah   Ju21
  the scoundrels of Gibeah   Ju20
despoiled, Solomon's temple   KS16
destroy those you have taken prisoner   KS6
destroyed by the Chaldaeans, Jerusalem was   CS36
  every male in the country   KF11
destruction, let an order be made for their   Est3
died, 20,000 men in the forest of Ephron   SS18
ear, blood on the   Le8, 14
eaten by dogs, Jezebel shall be   KF21
exterminate all Jews, orders sent out to   Est3ff
  inhabitants of the whole country   Jos9
  you, the Lord's delight to   De28
eyes, gouge out your own   SF11
  gouged out, Samson's   Ju16
  put out, Zedekiah's   KS25; Je39, 52

fell in battle, 500,000 Israelites   CS13
  through the window, Ahaziah   KS1
     Jezebel   KS9
fire consumed the officer and fifty men   KS1
    thousand men and women in the castle   Ju9
  set over his head   KF16
    to Jericho   Jos6
    to Jerusalem   KS25
    to their fortresses   KS8
  the city destroyed with   SF30
flogged and put to death, those remaining at Jerusalem   KS25; Je52
flogging   De25; Je20, 37; E26
food for birds and dogs, Baasha's family   KF16
      House of Ahab   KF21
      The people   KF14
foreskins, Philistine, taken by way of vengeance   SF18; SS3
furnace, thrown into the blazing   D3
Goliath's head, David took   SF17
gouge out your eyes as a condition of surrender   SF11
    Zedekiah's eyes   KS25
hamstrung the chariot horses, David   SS8; CF18
hand cut off   De25
hanged, bodies of the five kings   Jos10
  king of Ai   Jos8
  the seven sons of Saul   SS21
head caught in an oak tree, Absalom's   SS18
humiliation of David's envoys   CF19
hung up by the hands   La5
hurl them to death   SS21
killed, 10 sons of Haman   Est9
  20 men by Jonathan   SF14
  30 men for their clothes, by Samson   Ju14
  85 priests by Doeg   SF22
  200 Philistines for their foreskins, by David   SF18
  360 followers of Abner   SS2
  600 Philistines with an ox-goad   Ju3
  700 Aramaeans in chariots   SS10
  800 men by the Jews in Susa   Est9
  4,000 Israelites on the field   SF4
  7,000 charioteers   CF19

killed, 10,000 men of Seir   CS25

  10,000 Moabites   Ju3

  18,000 Benjamites   Ju20

  18,000 in the Valley of Salt   CF18

  18,000 Israelites   Ju20

  22,000 Aramaeans   SS8; CF18

  22,000 Israelites   Ju20

  25,000 Benjamites   Ju20

  30,000 Israelite foot-soldiers   SF4

  40,000 horsemen   SS10

  40,000 infantry   CF19

  42,000 at the fords of Jordan   Ju12

  75,000 enemies of the Jews   Est9

  100,000 infantry in one day   CS28

  120,000 troops in one day   CS28

  Agag by Samuel   SF15

  Ahab in battle   KF22

  Ahaziah by Jehu   CS22

  all oxen, asses and sheep of Nob   SF22

  Amaziah at Lachish   CS25

  Amnon, when Absalom said 'strike'   SS13

  blind and lame by David   SS5

  by a lion, the man of God   KF13

  by the flames, men carrying Shadrach, Meshach and Abednego   D3

  children and babes in arms of Nob   SF22

  Elah by Zimri   KF16

  Ephraimites unable to pronounce 'Shibboleth'   Ju12

  every creature, by Benjamites   Ju20

  every Midianite boy, by Moses   Nu31

  family of Jeroboam, by Baasha   KF15

  governor of the Philistines   SF13

  herdsmen by the army   CS14

  Joab at the altar   KF2

  Joash by his servants   CS24

  Joram's brothers by Joram   CS21

  Jehoram by Jehu   KS9

  kings of Midian by Gideon   Ju8

  Mattan at the altar   CS23

  men and women of Nob   SF22

  Nadab by Baasha   KF15

slaughter by Joshua of all at Bethel   Jos8
  Debir   Jos10
  Eglon   Jos10
  Hazor   Jos11
  Hebron   Jos10
  Jericho   Jos6
  Lachish   Jos10
  Libnah   Jos10
  Makkedah   Jos10
  Shephelah   Jos10
 from Kadesh-barnea to Gaza   Jos10
 in the land of Goshen   Jos10
 in the Negeb   Jos10
 in the villages   Jos10
of Amorites   Jos10
 beasts of Jericho   Jos6
 every living soul   Jos11
 every living thing   Jos10
 the population of the whole region   Jos10
 women and children   Jos8
commanded by Moses: indiscriminate   Ex32
 of all in the cities   De2, 3
  Amorites   Nu21
  Bashanites   Nu21
  Canaanites   Nu21
  children   De2, 3
   except girl virgins to keep   Nu31
  friends and neighbours   Ex32
  Midianites   Nu31
  women   Nu31; De2, 3
of two out of every three prisoners, by David   SS8
 42 kinsmen of Ahaziah by Jehu   KS10
of 1,000 men by Samson with an ass's jawbone,   Ju15
 10,000 at Bezek, by the Israelites   Ju1
 18,000 Edomites by David   SS8
 Agag, by Samuel   SF15
 all inhabitants, except the virgins to keep   Ju21
 Ammonites by the Israelites   Ju11
 children and babes in arms, by Saul at Samuel's instigation   SF15

slaughter of herds and flocks, by Samuel
   men and women of Jabesh-gilead, by the Israelites Ju21
   ministers of Baal, by Jehu KS10
   newborn boys, ordered by Pharaoh Ex1
   people of Jerusalem, by Judahites Ju1
   Philistines, the Israelites kept up the SF7
   prophets of Baal, by Elijah KF18
spare no one SF15
spoil their good land KS3
sticks drove against Absalom's body, three stout SS18
stoned to death, Achan, his family, and animals Jos7
    Adoram KF12
    disobedient sons De21
    Hadoram CS10
    Naboth KF21
    Zechariah CS24
stoning Le20, 24; Nu15; De13f, 17, 21ff; Jos7; KF12, 21; CS24; E16
  David threatened with SF30
strewn with their dead, the road was SF17
struck down, 185,000 Assyrian soldiers KS19
  in the face, Micaiah by Zedekiah KF22; CS18
suffocated, Ben-hadad by Hazael KS8
suicide, Saul fell on his sword CF10
sword, driven into Eglon's belly Ju3
  put to the, all the men, women and children SF15
    enemies of the Jews Est9
    every living thing in the city of priests SF22
    infants and sucklings SF15
    inhabitants of Bethel Ju1
     of Gibeah Ju20
     of Laish Ju18
    the whole army of Sisera Ju4
    their young men KS8
  Saul fell on his SF31
tear your bodies with briars Ju8
terror, threat of sudden Le26
thresh your bodies with thorns Ju8
thrown bound into the furnace, Shadrach, Meshach and Abednego D3
  down from the window, Jezebel was KS9

thrown into the Nile, every newborn baby to be   Ex1

    over a cliff, 10,000 men were   CS25

    to the lions, Daniel   D6

      Daniel's accusers, their wives and children   D6

thumbs and toes, blood on   Le8, 14

      cut off, of Adoni-bezek and 70 kings   Ju1

trampled to death, the lieutenant   KS7

vengeance, foreskins of the Philistines taken in   SF18

victims of fire and sword, captivity and pillage   D11

wounded in the belly, Saul was   SF31

NEW TESTAMENT

bandit, do you take me for a   L22

beat him, they   L22

beaten with many stripes   L12

beheaded for the sake of God's word   Rev20

    James by Herod   A12

    John the Baptist by Herod   Mw14; Mk6; L9

blindfolded him, they   L22

bound, Jesus was sent   J18

broke their legs, the soldiers   J19

cane, beat him about the head with a   Mk15

chains, Herod put John in   Mw14

    Jesus was put in   Mw27; Mk15

    men and women put in   A22

    Peter was secured by two   A12

    shackled with two   A21

condemned to death, my vote cast against them   A26

cross and save yourself, come down from the   Mk15

crucified, handed him over to be   Mk15

    him at the place called The Skull, Golgotha   L23

    Jesus   Mw27; Mk15f; L23; J19

    with Jesus, two thieves   Mw27

crucifixion   Mw23, 26f; Mk15f; L2f; A2

crucify and kill him, you used heathen men to   A2

    him, they shouted all the louder   Mw27

    some of them you will kill and   Mw23

cut off the ear of the high priest's servant   Mk14; L22; J18

dart, thrust through with a   LH12

deadly fume that kills   PCS2

death, clamouring for Paul's   A21

  Jesus put to   Mw27; Mk15; L23; J19

  should be put to   Mk14

  they shall put him to   L18

done to death, blood of all who had been   Rev18

drunk with the blood of God's people   Rev17

execution, Herod interrogated the guards and ordered their   A12

eye for eye, tooth for tooth, they were told   Mw5

flog a Roman citizen? can you legally   A22

  him and kill him, they will   L18

  some of them you will   Mw23

flogged, had the apostles   A5

  imprisoned, mobbed   PCS6

  ordered to be   A16

  Pilate had Jesus   Mw27; Mk15; J19

flogging, examine him by   A22

furnace, thrown into the blazing   Mw13

gibbet, hanging on a   A5

  put to death on a   A10

head in a charger, John the Baptist's   Mw14

irons, had him put in   A22

kill one another, to make men   Rev6

  Paul, conspired to   A23

  the heir, let us   L20

  the prisoners for fear that any should escape   A27

lash, tied him up for the   A22

maltreat them and stone them, a move to   A14

martyr Stephen, the blood of thy   A22

massacre of all children in Bethlehem, Herod ordered   Mw2

mocked, flogged and crucified, hand him over to be   Mw20

murder and treachery, they are one mass of   PR1

  defiles the man   Mk7

  of Stephen   A7

murderer, begged the release of a   A3

murderers, law aimed at   PTF1

  outside are   Rev22

murders, work of the flesh   PG5

persecute this movement to the death   A22
  you, they will   J15
persecution, beginning of violent   A8
pierced his side with a spear   J19
prison, beheaded John the Baptist in   Mw4; Mk1, 6; L3
  cast in, Paul and Silas   A16
  Herod shut John the Baptist in   Mw4; Mk1, 6; L3
  Peter kept in   A12
  Saul sending men and women to   A8
prisoners for punishment, Christians were   A22
public flogging, though we are Roman citizens, they gave us   A16
put to death on the evidence of two or three   LH10
    the Son of Man to be   Mk8
    without pity   LH10
rods, beaten with   PCS11
sawn in two, they were   LH11
scourge a Roman citizen? is it legal to   A22
  and to crucify, deliver him to   Mw20
  him, they shall   L18
scourged, Paul   A22
  took Jesus to be   Mw27; Mk15; J19
scourging, examined by   A22
shackled, Paul was   A21
  Peter was   A12
slaughtered for God's word   Rev6
stabbed his side with a lance   J19
stocks, secured their feet in   A16
stone him, the Jews picked up stones to   J10
  us, the people will   L20
  you for your blasphemy   J10
stoned by the people, fear of being   A5
  even an animal must be   LH12
  I was   PCS11
  Paul, the crowds   A14
  Stephen, they   A7
  such women are to be   J8
  they were   LH11
stones to cast at him, they took up   J8
strike him on the mouth, ordered his attendant to   A23
strokes, given thirty nine   PCS11

struck at the high priest's servant and cut off his ear   Mw26
  him on the face, one of the police   J18
sword, all who take the, die by the   Mw26
  death by the   LH11
  fall by the   L21
  put to the   LH11
thongs, tied him up with   A22
torture, condemned the man to   Mw18

45 *Wars, Battles and Armies*

adjutant-general   KF4; KS18, 22, 25; CF18; Is36; Je36, 52
    Seraiah   SS8
    Sheva   SS20
advance, beckon with arm upraised to the   Is13
ambush, for the citizens of Ai   Jos8
  set all round Gibeah   Ju20
    for the Benjamites   Ju20
archer   CF10; CS14, 35; Ps55; Je4, 51; Am2
  Ishmael was a skilled   Gen21
archers shot down from the walls   SS11
armour   SF14, 17, 31; KF10, 22; CS18; Ps45; E38
  washed of blood   KF22
armour-bearers   CF10ff
    Joab's   SS18
armoury   KS20; CS11; Ne3; Is39
  Hezekiah's   Is39
arms, call your troops to   Joe3
  capable of bearing, 470,000 in Judah   CF21
      1,100,000 in Israel   CF21
army, 232 young men of Ahab   KF20
  600 men mustered by Saul   SF13
  600 men under Hittai   SS15
  1,000 men from Maacah   SS10
  1,000 men to be with Jonathan   SF13
  2,000 men to be with Saul   SF13
  3,000 men of Benjamin   CF12
  3,000 men picked by Saul   SF13
  3,000 picked men to search for David   SF26
  3,700 men of Jehoiada   CF12
  4,600 men of Levi   CF12
  6,000 horses of the Philistines   SF13

army, 6,800 men of Judah   CF12

   7,000 Israelites of Ahab   KF20

   7,100 men of Simeon   CF12

   10,000 soldiers from Judah   SF15

   12,000 men from Tob   SS10

   17,200 men of Jediael   CF7

   18,000 men of Mansseh   CF12

   20,800 men of Ephraim   CF7

   26,000 men of Asher   CF7

   28,600 men of Dan   CF12

   30,000 chariots of the Philistines   SF13

   30,000 levied men under Solomon   KF5

   30,000 men from Judah   SF11

   30,000 men under David   SS6

   36,000 men of Izrahiah   CF7

   37,000 men of Naphtali   CF12

   40,000 men of Asher   CF12

   44,760 men of Reuben and Gad   CF5

   50,000 men of Zebulun   CF12

   120,000 men from east of Jordan   CF12

   180,000 chosen warriors under Reheboam   KF12; CS11

   180,000 men of Jehozabad   CS17

   200,000 foot soldiers at Telaim   SF15

   200,000 men of Amasiah   CS17

   200,000 men of Eliad   CS17

   280,000 men of Benjamin   CS14

   280,000 men of Johananan   CS17

   300,000 men from Israel   SF11

   300,000 men from Judah   CS14

   300,000 men of Adnach   CS17

   300,000 men of Amaziah   CS25

   375,500 men of Uzziah   CS26

   400,000 men of Abijah   CS13

   500,000 men capable of bearing arms   SS24

   800,000 men capable of bearing arms   SS24

   1,000,000 men of Zerah   CS14

   angel struck down the Syrian   Is37

   Babylonian   Je39; E26

   Chaldaean   Je37

   conscripted of the Israelites   Nu1ff

army, Edomite Nu20
  goest not forth with the Ps108
  greater than yours De20
  into battle, thou dost no longer lead our Ps44
  king is not saved by a great Ps33
    of the north and a vast D11
  kings have fled headlong with their Ps68
  of Gog E38
  of Nebuchadnezzar, Je52
  Pharaoh's Je37
    drowned Ex14
  Philistines mustered their SF28
  round you like a wall Is29
  units of 50 SF8
    of 100 and 1,000 SS18
    of 1,000 SF8
  victory by Gideon's Ju8
  with banners, terrible as an So6
arrow De32; SF20; KS9, 13, 19; Job16, 29, 41; Pro7, 25ff; Is5, 7, 37, 49; Je9, 50ff; La3;
        H3; Z9; Ps7, 11, 18, 38, 45, 57, 64, 76f, 91, 120, Ps127, 144; E5, 21, 39
  bronze-tipped Job20; Ps18
  drunk with blood De32
arsenal Je50
attack on Amalekites by David SF30
  Bethel by Joseph Ju1
  Bezek by Judah and Simeon Ju1
  Canaan, with Judah leading Ju1
  Debir by Judah Ju1
  Gath by Hazael KS12
  Gibeon by Amorites Jos10
  Hebron by Judah and Caleb Ju1
  Israel by Aradites Nu21
    by Ben-hadad KF20
    by eastern tribes Ju6
    by Eglon Ju3
    by Hazael KS10
  Jerusalem by Judah Ju1
  Judah by Aram KS15
    by Assyrians KS18
  Kiriath-arba by Judah Ju1

attack on Kiriath-sepher by Judah   Ju1
   Midianite camp by Gideon   Ju7
   Nadab by Maasha   KF15
   Pekahiah by Pekah   KS15
   quiet and carefree people of Laish by Danites   Ju18
   Shallum by Menahem   KS15
   Shechem by Abimelech   Ju9
   Thebez by Abimelech   Ju9
   Zephath by Judah and Simeon   Ju1
  through the wilderness of Edom   KS3
avenge the outrage of Gibeah   Ju20
bait, let her be   SF18
banners, an army with   So6
barracks   Ne3
bastions, battering-rams against your   Na2
battering on a leaning wall   Ps62
battering-ram   E4, 21, 26; Na2
battle array, countless host in   Joe2
  between Abner and Joab   SS2
   David and Isgobosheth   SS2
   Israel and Amorites   Nu21
    and Aradites   Nu21
    and Bashanites   Nu21
    and Benjamites   Ju20
    and Edomites   Nu20; Ob1
    and Judah   KS14
    and Midianites   Nu31
    and Sihon   De2
   Joshua and Amalek   Ex17
   Judah and Canaanites   Ju1ff
  did not die in   Is22
  in the forest of Ephron   SS18
  Lord brought disaster in every   Ju2
   mighty in   Ps24
  Lord's prowess on the field of   Z14
  Moabites, do not provoke to   De2
  no longer lead our armies into   Ps44
  of Ephraim, David fought the Israelites in the   SS18
  of Jericho, Joshua's army in the   Jos6
  Philistines advancing to   SF7

battle, Philistines mustered for   SF4
  roused the frenzy of   Is42
  tramp the muddy ways in   Z10
  war-cries on the day of   Am1
  will not save them by   Ho1
battleaxe   Je51; E9
battle-cry   Je4; E21; Ho5; Zp1
  he will raise   Is42
  signal for the   Nu31
battlefield with shouting, Saul made for the   SF14
battlements   Ps84; E27
  laid in ruins   Zp3
battle-quarters   Ps76
beacon, fire the   Je6
  for the nations   Is42
  upon the top of a mountain   Is30
bell, war-horse   Z14
besieged, Jabesh-gilead by Nahash the Ammonite   SF11
  Jerusalem by Nebuchadnezzar   KS24ff
  Thebez by Abimelech   Ju9
bodyguard, captain of the king's   KS25; Je39ff
  scattered   E12
bow   SF18; SS1; KS6, 13; CS17, 26; Ne4; Job29; Ps37, 46, 78; Is5, 7, 13, 21, 41; Je6, 49ff;
      La1ff; E39; Am2; H3; Z9ff
  steel   Job20
  strings   Ju16; Ps7, 11, 21
  strung   Ps37
bowman   Ps78
breached, the wall of Jerusalem by Jehoash   KS14
breastplate   KF22; CS18; Is59
brigandine   Je46, 51
buckler   KF10; CS23; Ps35; So4; Je46; E23, 26, 38ff
  gold   Ec9
burnt by the Israelites, every town within reach   Ju20
  in revenge, the city of Gibeah   Ju20
  the standing corn of the Philistines   Ju15
camp, army   Joe2
captain   KF9; KS1, 11, 25; Je51
  of bodyguard   KS25; Je39ff
  of chariots   KF22

captain of companies   Is59
  of fifty   KS1; Is3
  of guard   Je43, 52
  of hundred   KS11; CS23
  of raiding parties   SS4
captured, 1,700 horses   SS8
  20,000 foot soldiers   SS8
  Amaziah by Jehoash   KS14
catapult, siege   CS26
cavalier   E23
cavalry   KF9, 20; Ne2; D11; H1
  escort of   Ne2
  he will make them serve in   SF8
  horses   KF4
  Pharaoh's   Ex14
champion, the Philistine Goliath   SF17
chariot, chariots   Is31, 36, 43; Je4, 17, 22, 46, 50ff; E23, 26ff, 39; Ho10; Joe2; Na3; Z6, 9
  burn their   Jos11
  captured by David, 1,000   CF1
  commanders   KF9; KS8; CS21
  countless   Is37
  horses of Pharaoh   So1
    of Solomon, 40,000   KF4
  like a whirlwind   Is66
  no end to their   Is2
  of Ammi-nadib   So6
  of iron, Canaanite   Jos17; Ju1, 4
  of Pharaoh   Ex14
  of Solomon   KF1, 4, 10; CS1
  of Zerah, 300   CS14
  ten left to Jehoahaz   KS13
  towns   KF10; CS1, 9
  two-horsed   Is21
  washed of blood   KF22
cheer when the trumpets sound   Nu10
club   CF11; Job41; Pro25; E21
coat of mail   CS26; Ne4; Is59; Je46, 51
commander, Aramis   KS5
  Banaiah   KF2, 4
  Hananiah   CS26

munition, keep the   Na2
muster, sound of the   Je4
mustered, 32 kings with their chariots   KF20
nail, hammered through Sisera's head   Ju4
navy   KF10
night attack on the Philistines   SF14
officer in charge of 100   CF28; CS25
     of 1,000   CF13, 28; CS17, 25
  of the guard   Je37
officers dressed in blue or purple   E23
  over units of 100 and 1,000   SS18
outrunners   KF1
ox-goad as a weapon   Ju3
panic I spread before you   Jos24
  fled in, Midianites   Ju7
    Philistines   SF7
  that drove them out, not your sword   Jos24
  threat of   Le26
  will throw nations into   De7
panic-stricken, the whole country was   Jos2
plunder by Jehoshaphat and his men   Cs20
  Chaldaeans raided the camels for   Job1
  of camels and sheep   CS14
  of cities of Bashan   De3
  of city of Heshbon   De2
  of everything in the city   De20
  of houses in Jerusalem   Z14
  of Midianites   Nu31
  of Shechem's city   Gen34
  of treasures of Jerusalem taken to Egypt   CS12
  taken from you, shared out   Z14
  they turned to   SF14
post, I will stand at my   H2
quartermaster   SF17; Je51
quiver   SS8; Job39; Ps127; Is22, 49; Je5, 51; La3; H3
  gold   CF18
raided, Jerusalem by Jehoash   KS14
  the country, David   SF27
raiding parties from the Philistine camp   SF13
rampart   KF21; Ps91

ram's horn trumpet   Ex19
    at Jericho   Jos6
rebellion of Absalom   SS13ff
recaptured, cities taken by Ben-hadad   KS13
red, shields gleaming   Na2
reinforcements, Pharaoh sent to help Assyria   KS23
rescued all the Amalekite prisoners   SF30
revenge by Gideon   Ju8
  on Abner   SS3
  on the Amalekites   SF15
revolt, the Hebrews were in   SF13
rifled, the houses of Jerusalem   Z14
roll, Saul's men called the   SF14
routed by the men of Israel at Gilboa   SF31
  by the Philistines   SF4
ruffians, a band of   Ps22
ruin, leave as a mound   De13
sabre   Job39, 41; Je6, 50
scabbard   SF17; Je47; E21
scarlet, their soldiers are all in   Na2
sentry   SS13
sentry-duty   Ne7
shaft, spear   H3
sheath   Je47; E21
shield   SS1; KF10; KS11; CF5; CS9, 11ff, 17, 23, 25ff, 32; Pro30; Is21ff, 37; Je46, 51;
    Am4; E23, 26ff, 32, 38ff; Na2; Z9
  bossed   Job15
  bronze   CS12
  gold   CS9, 12
shield-bearer   SF17; CS14
shields, burnish your   Is21
  of mighty men   SO4
  of their warriors are gleaming red   Na2
  screen of   E26
shout, the whole army at Jericho   Jos6
  when the trumpets sound   Nu10
siege, Chaldaeans raised the   Je37
  closing in   Na2
  dire straits during the   Je19
  draw water for the   Na3

siege laid to Tirzah   KF16
  machine   CS26
  mount   D11
  Nebuchadnezzar laid to Jerusalem   Je37, 52; D1
  of Jerusalem by Assyrians   CS32
  of Rabbah   SS11
  of Samaria   KS6, 17ff
  raise against Jerusalem   Je6
  ramp   SS20; KS19; Is37; Je6, 32ff; E4, 17, 21, 26; D11
  towers   Is23
  works   Ec9; Is29; H1
signal post on a hill   Is30
single combat   SS2
sling   SF12; CS26; Job41; Pro26; Z9
slingers   KS3
spear   Nu25; SF13, 17ff, 26; SS1ff, 21; KF18; KS11; CF11; CS11ff, 23, 25ff; Ne4; Job39, Job41; Ps35, 46, 57; Is2; Je6, 4; E39; Joe3; Mi4; Na2ff; H3
  of Phinehas, transfixed by the   Nu25
spies sent out from Shittim   Jos1
spiked weapons   CS33
spoil from your enemies, share with your kinsmen   Jos22
  of Midian cities   Nu31
  of silver and gold   Na2
spy out all the land   De1
squadrons of Gomer and Beth-togarmah   E38ff
  of horse   Joe2; Na2
  of Moab   Nu24
  of the king of Jerusalem scattered   E12, 17
standard bearer   Is10
  march under the   Nu2
  planted as a token of vistory   Ps74
  raise the   Is13; Je51
  raised, how long must I see the   Je4
stronghold   Ps31
surrender of Jehoiachin   KS24
  of the Hagarites   CF5
surrounded, Dothan by the Aramaeans   KS6
survey the country   Jos18
sword   Nu31; De13, 20, 28; Jos5ff, 19; Ju7; SF13, 17ff, 25; SS20; KF3, 18ff; KS6, 19; CF5, 10; Ne4; Job33, 39; Ps7, 22, 37, 44ff, Ps55, 57, 63ff, 76, 78, 89, 144, 149;

sword   Pro5, 25, 30; La1f, 4ff; Is1ff, 13ff, 21ff, 27, 31, 34, 37, 41, Is49, 51, 65ff; E5ff,
             E11ff, 14, E16ff, 21, 23ff, 28ff, 35, 38ff; Je2, 5ff, 9, 11ff, 14ff, 18ff, 24ff, 29,31ff,
             Je38ff, 44, 46ff; D11; Joe2ff; Am1, 4, 7, 9; Mi4ff; Na2ff; Zp2; Hg2; Z9,11,13

  Balaam slain with the   Nu31

  curse of the   De28

  devoured with the   Is1

  drawn in front of Joshua   Jos5

  of Ehud   Ju3

  of Gideon   Ju7

  people of Leshem put to the   Jos19

  put all males to the   De13

  put inhabitants to the   De13

  ready at his side, each with his   So3

  young and old put to the   Jos6

swords, 400,000 Israelites with   Ju20

swordsmen, king of Moab took 700   Ks3

  Solomon's escort were skilled   So3

target, buckler, of gold   KF10

tent peg hammered through Sisera's head   Ju4

throwing-stick   E39

tower of strength   Ps9, 18, 20

trench, front line   SF17

troops of horses   Am4

trumpet and battle-cry, a day of   Zp1

  call   Je4, 6, 42, 52

  signal for battle-cry   Nu31

undefended city of Ai burnt   Jos8

undermining the city walls   SS20

vengeance, day of   Is61

  exacted on the Midianites   Nu31

  granted me   Ps18

  on killers of Ishbosheth   SS4

victory assured   Le26

  his right hand and holy arm have won him   Ps98

  is the fruit of long planning   Pro11

  of Gideon over the Midianites   Ju8

  praise of your   Ps20

  standards as a token of   Ps74

war any more, neither shall they learn   Is2

  book of the Lord   Nu21

45 WARS, BATTLES AND ARMIES

war broke out, none had spear or sword   SF13
    once again   SS21
  declare a holy   Joe3
  fit for, at eighty-five   Jos14
  houses of David and Saul at   SS2ff
  Israel with Judah   KF15
  let us solemnly declare   Je6
  never again be trained for   Mi4
  on Israel, the king of Aram making   KS6
  Philistines collected their forces for   SF17
  revel in   Ps68
  stamps out   Ps46
  teach each succeeding generation how to make   Ju3
  time for peace, a time for   Ec3
  trains my hands for   Ps144
  waged by David's men at Keilah against the Philistines   SF23
war-cry, war-cries, men of Israel and Judah raised   SF17
  on the day of battle, amid   Am1ff
  the Philistines raised   SF17
war-horse   E23; Joe2; Z9ff, 14
  inscribed bells on the   Z14
  plunges into battle   Je8
warrior and soldier, every   Is3
  bull-calf of all nations   Ps68
  chieftain   E32
  endowed with princely qualities, David   Ps89
  shall not save himself   Am2
  to keep you safe   Zp3
warriors, confidence of returning   Mi2
  flung into the sea   E27
  ruthless   E32
  served as   E27
  sharp arrows in store for you   Ps120
  trusted in the number of your   Ho10
watchman   So3, 5; E3, 33; Ho9
watch-tower   KS9, 17ff, 25; Is5, 21, 32; Je52; E4, 17, 21, 26
  erected on every side   KS25
  take position on the   H2
weapons, discarded   E39

NEW TESTAMENT

46 *Water, Wells and Rivers*

OLD TESTAMENT

brook, Kidron   KF15; KS23; CS15, 29ff
  of Cherith   KF17
  of Gaash   SS23
  of the willows   Is15
  The, land boundary   E48
canal, Chebar, Kebar   E1, 43
cataract   Ps42
cistern at Secu, the great   SF19
  cracked   Je2
  drink water from your own   Pro5
  each drink water from his own   KS18; Is36
  for the waters of the Old Pool   Is22
  hewn out for themselves   Je2
  rock-hewn   De6; Ne9; Je2
  Uzziah dug many   CS26
  wheel broken at the   Ec12
conduit Hezekiah built, to carry water to Jerusalem   KS20
  of the Upper Pool   KS18; Is7, 36
damned its rivers   E31
deep waters   Ps104
dew   De32, 33; Job38; Ps133; Pro3, 19; So5; Is18; D4ff; Ho6, 13ff
ditch for the water at the Old Pool   Is22
  irrigation   Ps65
flood   Ps24, 29, 69, 88
  land swept by   Is28
  Noah's   Gen6ff; Ps104; Is54
  overwhelming   Is28
  used to rise from the ground   Gen2
fords of the Arnon   Is16
  of the Jordan   Jos; Ju3, 12
  of the wilderness   SS15ff
fountain of life   Ps36

465

rivers among the sand-dunes   Is41
  dammed   E31
  dries up   Ps74
  in the barren desert   Is43
  of Babylon   Ps137
  of Cush   Is18
  of Ethiopia   Is18
  run into the sea   Ec1
saltpans, swamps and pools   E47
sea   Ps65ff, 68, 72, 78, 80, 89, 96, 98, 135; Pro8, 23
  and its waves roared   Je31
  Chinneroth   Jos12ff
  churned up by the four winds   D7
  closed over them   Ps106
  Dead   Nu34; De3; Jos3, 12, 15, 18; CS20; E39
  divided   Ps78
  Egyptian   Is11
  Great   Nu34; Jos1, 9, 15; E47ff
  he gathered the   Ps33
  Kinnereth   Jos12ff
  Mediterranean   Jos1, 9, 15; E47ff
  of Arabah   De3ff; Jos3, 12; KS14
  of Joppa   Ez3
  of Reeds   KF9; Ne9; Ps106; Je49
  of the Plain   KS14
  Red   Nu33; De1; Jos24; KF9; Ne9; Ps106, 136; Je49
    by way of the   Nu14, 21
    divided   Ex14
    locusts blown into the   Ex10
    towards the, by way of the wilderness   Ex13
  suck the abundance of the   De33
  the surging   Ps89
  Western   De34; Ps139
sea-bed   Ps18
sluices and ponds for fish   Is19
  of the rivers opened   Na2
spring at Jericho   KS2
  channels for the   Ps74
  Dragon   Ne2
  drink from your own   Pro5

spring, muddied   Pro25
  pitcher shattered at the   Ec12
  of Fright   Ju7
  of Lehi   Ju15
  of living water   Je2
  of Meribah   Nu20
  of Nephtoah   Jos15
springs, blocked by Hezekiah   CS32
  bubbling   Is35, 49
    in a thirsty land   Is35
  from parched land   Ps107
  land of   De8
  of Jordan   Ps42
  stop up their   KS3
  turn dry land into   Is41
  twelve, of Elim   Ex15; Nu33
streams blocked by Hezekiah   CS32
  from Lebanon   So4
  from the rock   Ps78
  land of   De8
  of Egypt   Is27, 37
    dried up all the   Is37
  of Judah   Joe3
  of the Euphrates   Is27
  of thy delights   Ps36
  of Ulai   D8
  out of the cliff   Ps78
  place of rivers and broad   Is33
  run into the sea   Ec1
  running   Ps42
  turbulent in flood   Je46
swamp of Libnath   Jos19
swamps, pools and saltpans   E47
torrent beside the path   Ps110
  channels for the   Ps74
  of Egypt   Nu34; Jos14; KF8; KS24; Is27
  of Kishon   Ju4; Ps83
  swept over us   Ps124
torrents, cool rain streaming in   Je18
  in dry land   Is35

torrents pour down the hill-side   Mi1
water, bitter, that causes the curse   Nu5
  from the rock   Ne9; Nu20; Is48
  from the temple in Ezekiel's vision   E47
  I purify this   KS2
  lustral   Nu8
  of contention   Nu5
  of Jordan cut off   Jos9
  of Meribah   Nu20
  piled up like a bank   Jos3
  polluted   KS2
  poured out before the Lord   SF7
  purifying   Nu8
  spring of living   Je2
  undrinkable   Ps78
water-channels dried up   Joe1
watercourse, planted beside the   Ps1
water-hole of Vaheb   Nu21
waters above the mountains   Gen6; Ps104
  deep   Ps104
  dividing the   Is63
  gathered   Gen1
  I am come into deep   Ps69
  land of   De8
  made sweet   Ex15
  of Babylon   Ps137
  of comfort   Ps23
  of Dimon   Is15
  of Meribah   Ps81, 106; E47
  of Meribah-by-Kadesh   De32
  of Nimrim   Is15
  risen   Ps69
  roar of mighty   Is17
  teem, let the   Gen1
  turned to blood   Ex7
water-spouts   Ps148
watery depths   Ps71
well by the gate of Bethlehem   CF11
  drink out of thine own   Pro5
  in Hagar's vision   Gen16

well, jump into, to escape arrest   Pro28
  keeps its water fresh   Je6
  of Abimelech   Gen21
  of Abraham   Gen21, 26
  of Beersheba   Gen21
  of Esek   Gen26
  of Hagar   Gen21
  of Horeb   Ex17
  of Isaac   Gen26
  of living water   So4
  of Massah   Ex17
  of Meribah   Ex17; Nu20
  of Moses   Ex17
  of Reheboth   Gen26
  of Secu, the great   SF19
  of Shibah   Gen26
  of Sitnah   Gen26
  of the Living One of Vision   Gen16, 25
  of wisdom   Pro18
  tainted   Pro25
  wheel broken at the   Ec12
wells, I have dug   Is37
  in the valleys   Is41
  of salvation   Is12
  stop all their   KS3

NEW TESTAMENT

brook, Kedron, Cedron   J18
cross-currents, caught between   A27
deluge upon the world of godless men   LPS2f
flood, Noah's   Mw24; L17; LPS2f
fountain   LJ3
fountains, star fell upon   Rev8
lake, a heavy squall struck the   L8
  casting a net into the   Mw4
  of Gennesaret   L5
  walking on the   Mw14; Mk6; J6
lake-side, began to teach by the   Mk4

spring called Jacob's Well   J4
springs, a third of rivers and   Rev8, 16
  of the water of life   Rev7, 21
  that give no water   LPS2
tempest, tossed in the   A27
water, does a fountain gush with both fresh and brackish   LJ3
  Jesus walking on the   Mw14; Mk6; J6
  of life   J4; Rev7
  of the Euphrates dried up   Rev16
  poisoned   Rev8
  Samaritan woman came to draw   J4
  springs of life   Rev21
  streams of living   J7
  turned into wine   J2
  walked on the   Mw14; Mk6; J6
waters, voice like rushing   Rev1
waves, tossed by the, whirled about   PE4
well, donkey or ox falls into a   L14
  Jacob's   J4
  Jesus sat down by the   J4
wells without water   LPS2

47   *Weather*

cloud   Ps18, 147; Pro8, 16
  and dense fog   Joe2; Zp1
  and wind without rain   Pro25
  darkens the dawn with thick   Am4
  dispersed like   Is44
  drop dew   Pro3
  heavy with rain   Ec11
  no bigger than a man's hand   KF18
  out of the sea, ariseth a little   KF18
  poured water   Ps77
  with flashes of fire   E1
cloud-banks   Is14
cloudburst   Is30
cloud-masses   Job26
dew   Job38; Ps133; Pro3; Ho6, 13ff
  drenched with   So5; D4ff
  heavens withhold their   Hg1
  heavy at harvest time   Is18
  nor rain, neither   KF17
  skies drip with   De33
  upon the grass   Pro19
  words distil like   De32
drought, scorching   Is25
dust, curse of   De28
dust-storm   Ps78
earth shakes, the heavens shudder   Joe2
earthquake   KF19; Is29; E38; Am1
east wind, cruel blast   Is27
  locusts carried by   Ex10
  rolled back the Red Sea   Ex14
fire and hail   Ex9
fog   Ps105; Joe2; Zp1

474

frost   Job38; Ps147
  at night   Je36
frozen, the water stands   PS147
gale   Ps148
hail   Job38; Ps78, 105, 148; Is32; Hg2
  sweeping storm of   Is28
hailstones   E38
  as hard as rock   E13
  the Lord hurled great   Jos10
hailstorm   Ex9
hoar-frost   Ps147
hurricane   Pro1; E38; Jon1
ice   Job6, 38
  crystals of   Ps148
  sheet of   E1
lightning   Ps18, 77, 97, 144; D10
  out of the fire   E1
  with rain   Je10, 51
mist, a dissolving   Is44
  from the ends of the earth   Ps135; Je10, 51
  morning   Ho6, 13
murk and gloom, a day of   Zp1
rain and tempest   Is4
  at the proper time   Le26
  both autumn and spring   De11
  cloud   Pro16
  clouds full of   Ec11ff
  falling on crops   Ps72
  forty days   Gen7
  gives or holds back   Pro25ff
  I hear the sound of coming   KF18
  in the autumn   Z10
  in the spring   Z10
  killed vines and figs with torrential   Ps78
  makes the earth blossom   Is55
  nor dew, neither   KF17
  of autumn and spring, showers in their turn   Je5
  of heaven   De11
  opens rifts for the   Ps135
  refresh the land with   Ps68

whirlwind, sows the wind and reaps the   Ho8
wild and stormy, the weather grew   Ju19
wind, cruel blast of the east   Is27
  east   Ps48
    bringing locusts   Ex10
    rolled back the Red Sea   Ex14
  fine as dust before the   Ps18
  from his storehouses   Je10
  from the Lord   Nu11
  let loose   Ps78
  mighty   Gen1
  north   Pro25
  out of his storehouses   Ps135
  smoke in the   Ps68
  south, he drove   Ps78
  sows the, and reaps the whirlwind   Ho8
  voice of the Lord   Ps29
  west, dispersing locusts   Ex10
winds of heaven, the four   Z2

NEW TESTAMENT

battling with a head-wind and a rough sea   Mw14
breeze sprang up, a southerly   A27
cloud appeared, casting its shadow over them   Mk9
  banking up in the west   L12
  cast a shadow over them   L9
  pillar of   PCF10
  removed him from their sight   A1
  white, in John's vision   Rev14
clouds carried away by the wind   LJu1
  he is coming with the   Rev1
  of heaven   Mw24
  that are carried with a tempest   LPS2
earthquake   Mw27f; Mk13; L21, 23
eclipse of the sun   Mw27; Mk15; L23
Euroclydon: the fierce north-east wind   A27
fair weather   Mw16

fierce wind, the north-eastern   A27
gales, ships driven by strong   LJ3
hail, a storm of   Rev11
   fire and blood   Rev8
hailstones weighing perhaps a hundredweight   Rev16
head-wind and a rough sea, battling with a   Mw14
    labouring against a   Mk6
head-winds at sea   A27
heat wave when the wind is from the south   L12
heavy weather, making   A27
ice, a sheet of   Rev4
lightning   Mw24; Rev8
  and thunder   Rev16
  fell from heaven   L10
  flash that lights up the earth   L17
  from the throne   Rev4
mist driven by a storm   LPS2
  seen for a while and then dispersing   LJ4
rain, a sign of   L12
  down came the   LJ5
  from heaven, he sends you   A14
  it was cold and had started to   A28
  may fall, shut up the sky so that no   Rev11
  none for three years and six months   L4
  on the honest and the dishonest   Mw5
  prayed that there should be no   LJ5
  when earth drinks in the   LH6
  when you see cloud banking up in the west   L12
rainbow round the angel's head   Rev10
  round the throne   Rev4
rains, autumn and spring   LJ5
red sky in the evening   Mw16
   in the morning   Mw16
shower, there cometh a   L12
sign of rain in the west   L12
signs of the times, can ye not discern   Mw16
sky turned black   Rev6
snow, white as   Mk9
southerly breeze sprang up   A27
squall, a heavy   Mk4; L8

storm arose on the lake, a great   Mw8
  mists driven by a   LPS2
storm of wind on the lake   L8
  subsided and all was calm   L8
  was raging, a great   A27
strong wind was blowing and the sea was rough   J6
tempest, clouds that are carried with a   LPS2
  exceedingly tossed with a   A27
thunder, peals of   Rev4, 8
  some said it was   J12
thunders spoke, seven   Rev10
whirlwind   LH12
wind, a noise like that of a strong driving   A2
  a rushing mighty   A2
  and the sea obey him, even the   Mk4
  and waves, he gives his orders to the   L8
  bloweth where it listeth   J3
  in the south forecasting a heat-wave   L12
  set the foresail to the   A27
  south, sprang up   A27f
winds, angels holding back the four   Rev7
winter, pray that it may not be   Mw24
  try to get here before   PTS4

48 *Weights, Measures and Coins*

OLD TESTAMENT

NEW TESTAMENT

measures of wheat, a hundred   L16

measuring-rod   Rev11, 21

mile, go with him two   Mw5

miles, seven from Emmaus to Jerusalem   L24

   two from Bethany to Jerusalem   J11

mite, until thou hast paid the very last   L12

   widow's   Mk12; L21

money changers   Mw21

   take no   L9

pence, fifty   L7

   five hundred   L7

   three hundred   Mk14; J12

   two   L10

penny a day agreed with the labourers   Mw20

   bring me a   Mw22; Mk12; L20

   measure of wheat for a   Rev6

   three measures of barley for a   Rev6

pennyworth, two hundred   Mk6; J6

pound, gave them each a   L19

   weight, a hundred   J19

   thirty, perfume worth   Mk14; J12

   twenty, are we to spend   Mk6

     would not buy enough bread   J6

quart of flour   Rev6

quarts of barley-meal, three   Rev6

silver coin in a fish's mouth   Mw17

   piece, show me a   Mw22; Mk12; L20

   pieces, fifty   L7

     fifty thousand   A19

     five hundred   L7

     ten   L15

     thirty   Mw26f

     two   L10

scales, a pair of   Rev6

tables of the money changers   Mw21

talent   Mw25

   every hailstone about the weight of a   Rev16

thirty pieces of silver   Mw26f

toll, tax or   Mw17

two pence, sparrows sold five for   L12

Aaron (brother of Moses)
>   Ex4ff; Le1ff; Nu1ff, 12, 20; De9f; Jos24; Ju20; SF12; CF6, 12, 15; CS31,35; Ez7; Ps77, 99, 105f, 115, 118, 133, 135; Mi6

(Levite) CF23ff

Abagtha Est1

Abda KF4; Ne11

Abdeel Je36

Abdi CF6; CS29; Ez10

Adiel CF5

Abdon (a judge) Ju12
  (son of Jehiel) CF8ff
  (son of Micah) CS34
  (son of Shimei) CF8

Abednego D1ff

Abel Gen4

Abi KS18

Abia CF3

Abiah SF8; CF6f, 24; Ne10,12

Abi-albon SS23

Abiasaph Ex6

Abiathar SS8, 15; SF22, 29ff; KF1; CF15ff, 27

Abida Gen25; CF1

Abidan Nu1, 7ff

Abiel SF9, 14; CF11

Abiezer Jos17; Ju8; SS23; CF7, 11, 27

Abigail SS2ff, 17; SF25, 27, 30; CF2

AbihailNu3ff;CF2, 5; CS11; Est2

Abihu Ex6, 24ff; Le10; Nu26; CF6, 24

Abijah KF14; CS11, 13, 29

Abijam KF14

Abimael Gen10; CF1

Abimelech (a judge) Ju8ff; SS11
  (king of Gerar)   Gen20f, 26

Abinadab SF7, 16ff; SS6; CF2, 8f, 13

Abinoam Ju4

Abiram Nu6, 26; De11; KF16; Ps106

Abishag KF1f

Abishai SF26; SS2, 10, 21ff; CF2, 11, 18

Abishalom KF15

Abishua CF6, 8; Ez7

Abishur CF2

APPENDIX A PERSONAL NAMES

Abital SS3; CF3

Abitub CF8

Abner SF14, 17, 20, 26; SS2ff; KF2; CF26ff

Abraham (Abram) Gen12ff, 17ff; DE1, 6, 34;Jos24; Ks13; CF1;Ne9; Ps47, 105; Is29, 41, 51, 63; Je33;
        E33; Mi7

Absalom SF3, 13ff; KF1ff; CF3; CS11

Achan Jos7

Achar CF2

Achbor (Akbor) Gen36; KS22; CF1; Je26, 36

Achish SF21, 27ff; KF2

Achsah Jos15; Ju1; CF2

Achzib Mi1

Adah Gen4, 36

Adaiah KS22; CF6, 8ff; CS23; Ez10; Ne11

Adalia Est9

Adam Gen2; CF1

Abdeel Gen25; CF1

Addar CF8

Ader CF8

Adiel CF4, 9, 27

Adin Ez2, 8; Ne7, 10

Adina CF11

Adlai CF27

Admatha Est1

Adna Ez10; Ne12

Adnah CS17

Adoni-bezek Ju1

Adonijah SS3; KF1ff; CF3; CS17; Ne10

Adonikam Ez2, 8; Ne7

Adoniram KF4ff

Adoni-zedek Jos10

Adoram SS20; KF12

Adrammelech KS19; Is37

Adriel SF15; SS21

Agag Nu24; SF15

Agee SS23

Agur Pro30

Ahab (king of Israel) KF16ff; KS3, 8ff, 21; CS18, 21ff; Mi6
  (prophet reviled by Jeremiah) Je29

Aharah CF8

Aharhel CF4

Ahasbai SS23

Ahasuerus Ez4; Est1ff; D9

Ahaz KS15ff; CF3, 8ff; CS27f; Is1, 7, 14, 38; Ho1; Mi1

Ahaziah (king of Israel) KF22
  (King of Judah) KS1, 8ff; CF3; CS20ff

487

APPENDIX **A** PERSONAL NAMES

Ahban CF2
Aher CF7
Ahi CF5, 7
Ahiah CF8; Ne10
Ahiam SS23; CF11
Ahian CF7
Ahiezer Nu1, 7fff; CF12
Ahihud Nu34; CF8
Ahijah SF14; KF4, 11, 14ff, 21; KS9; CF2, 11; CS9ff
Ahikam KS22; CS34; Je26, 39f, 43
Ahilud SS8, 20; KF4
Ahimaaz SF14; SS15ff; KF4; CF6
Ahiman Nu13; Jos15; Ju1; CF9
Ahimelech SF21f, 26, 30; SS8; CF18, 24
Ahimoth CF6
Ahinadab KF4
Ahinoam SF14, 25, 27, 30; SS2ff; CF3
Ahio SS6; CF8f, 13
Ahira Nu1, 7ff
Ahiram Nu26
Ahisamach Ex31ff
Ahishahar CF7
Ahishar KF4
Ahithophel CF27
Ahitophel SS15ff, 23
Ahitub SF14, 22; SS8; CF6, 9, 18; Ez7; Ne11
Ahlai CF2, 11
Ahoah CF8
Aholiab Ex31ff
Ahumai CF4
Ahuzam CF4
Ahuzath Gen26
Ahzai Ne11
Aiah Gen36; SS3, 21; CF1
Akan Gen 36; CF1
Akbor (Achbor) Gen36; KS22; CF1; Je26, 36
Akkub CF3, 9; Ez2; Ne7f,11ff
Alemeth CF7ff
Aliah CF1
Allon CF4
Almodad Gen10; CF1
Alvah Gen36
Amal CF7
Amalek Gen36; Ex17; SS8; CF1
Amariah CS19, 31; CF6, 23ff; Ez7, 10; Ne10ff; Zp1
Amasa SS17ff; KF2; CF2; CS28

488

APPENDIX A PERSONAL NAMES

Amasai (Amashai, Amashsai) (son of Azarel) Ne11
  (son of Gershom) CF6, 15; CS29
Amasiah CS17
Amaziah (king of Judah) KS12ff; CF3ff; CS24ff
  (priest of Bethel) Am7
  (son of Hilkiah) CF6
Ami Ez2
Amittai Jon1
Ammi (Lo-ammi) Ho2
Ammiel Nu13; SS9, 17; CF3,26
Ammihud Nu1, 7ff, 34; CF7, 9
Ammihur SS13
Amminadab Ex6; Nu1, 7ff; CF2, 6, 15; Ru4
Aminadib SO6
Ammishaddai Nu1, 7ff
Ammizabad CF27
Amnon SF3, 13; CF3ff
Amok Ne12
Amon KF22; KS21; CF3; CS18,33; Ne7; Je1, 25; Zp1
Amos Am1ff, 7
Amoz KS19; CS26, 32; Is1ff, 13, 21, 37ff
Amram Ex6; Nu3ff; CF1, 6, 23ff; Ez10
Amraphel Gen14
Amzi CF6; Ne11
Anah Gen36; CF1
Anaiah Ne8, 10
Anak Nu13; De9; Jos15; Ju1
Anan Ne10
Anani CF3
Ananiah Ne3
Ananthoth Ne10; SS23; CF7
Anath Ju4
Aner Gen14
Aniam CF7
Antothiah CF8
Anub CF4
Aphiah SF9
Aphses CF24
Ara CF7
Arad CF8
Arah CF7; Ez2; Ne6ff
Aram Gen10, 22; KS13;CF1f,7
Aran Gen36; CF1
Araunah SS24
Arba Jos14
Ard Gen46; Nu26

APPENDIX A PERSONAL NAMES

Ardon CF2
Areli Gen46; Nu26
Aridai Est9
Aridatha Est9
Ariel Ez8
Arioch (captain of royal bodyguard) D2
  (king of Ellasar) Gen14
Arisai Est9
Armoni SS21
Arnan CF3
Arod Nu26
Arodi Gen46
Arphaxad Gen10f; CF1
Artaxerxes Ez4ff; Ne2, 5, 13
Arza KF16
Asa KF15; CF3, 9; CS14, 20ff; Je41
Asahel SS2ff, 23; CF2, 11, 27; CS17, 31
Asaiah KS22; CF4, 6, 9, 15; CS34
Asaph (father of Joah, secretary of state) KS18; Is36
  (keeper of the royal forests) Ne2
  (Levite musician) CF6, 9, 15ff, 25; CS5, 20, 29, 35; Ez2ff; Ne7, 11ff
Asareel CF4
Asarelah CF25
Asenath Gen41, 46
Ashbel Gen46; Nu26; CF8
Asher Gen30, 35; Ex1; Nu1, 7ff; De27, 33; Ju1, 6ff; CF2, 7
Ashkenaz Gen10; CF1
Ashpenaz D1
Ashvath CF7
Asiel CF4
Asnah Ez2
Asnappar (Osnappar) Ez4
Aspatha Est9
Asshur CF1ff
Asriel Nu26; Jos17
Asshar Gen41
Asshurim Gen25
Assir Ex6; CF6
Atarah CF2
Ater Ez2; Ne7, 10
Athiah Ne11
Athaliah KS8, 11; CF8; CS22ff
Athlai Ez10
Attai CF2, 12; CS11
Azaliah KS22; CS34
Azaniah Ne10

Azareel CF12, 25, 27; Ez10
Azarel Ne11ff
Azariah (Abed-nego) D1ff
  (Jezaniah, son of Hoshaiah) Je42ff
  (Levite priest) CS26, 29, 31; Ne3, 7f, 10, 12
  (son of Ahimaaz) CF6
  (son of Jehalelel) CS29
  (son of Jehoshaphat) CS21
  (son of Jehu) Ez7
  (son of Jeroham) CS23
  (son of Johanan) CF6
  (son of Kilkiah) CF6
  (son of Nathan) KF4
  (son of Obed) CS15, 23
  (son of Zadok) KF4
  (son of Zephaniah) CF6
  (Uzziah,king of Judah) KS14
Azaz CF5
Azaziah CF27; CS31
Azbuk Ne3
Azel CF8ff
Azgad Ez2, 8; Ne7, 10
Aziza Ez10
Azmoth SS23; CF8ff, 11, 27
Azriel CF5, 27; Je36
Azrikam CF3, 8ff; CS28; Ne11
Azubah KF22; CF2; CS20
Azzan Nu34
Baal CF5 8ff
Baal-hanan Gen36; CF1, 27
Baalis Je40
Baana KF4; Ne3
Baanah SS4, 23; KF4; CF11; Ez2; Ne7, 10
Baara CF8
Baaseia CF6
Baasha KF15, 21; KS9; CS16; Je41
Bakbakkar CF9
Bakbuk Ez2; Ne7
Bakbukiah Ne11f
Balaam Nu22; De23; Jos13, 24; Ne13; Mi6
Baladan KS20; Is39
Balak Nu22; Jos24; Ju11; Mi6
Bani SS23; CF6, 9; Ez2, 8, 10; Ne3, 8ff
Barak Ju4; SF9
Barakel (Barachel) Job32
Bariah CF3

Barkos Ez2; Ne7
Baruch Ne3, 10f; Je32, 36, 43, 45
Barzillai SS17f; KF2; Ne7
Basemath Gen26, 36, 38
Basmath KF4
Bathsheba SS11; KF1ff; CF3
Bathshua CF2
Bavai Ne3
Bazluth (Bazlith) Ez2; Ne7
Bealiah CF12
Bebai Ez2, 8, 10; Ne7, 10
Becher Gen46; Nu26; CF7
Bechorath SF9
Bedad Gen36; CF1
Bedan CF7
Beeliada CF14
Beera CF7
Beerah CF5
Beeri Gen26; Ho1
Beeroth CF11
Bela Gen14, 36, 46; Nu26; CF1, 5, 7f
Belshazzar D5, 7
Belteshazzar (Daniel) D1ff
Ben-abinadab KF4
Benaiah SS8, 20f; KF1ff; CF4, 11, 15, 18, 27; CS20, 31; Ez10; E11
Ben-ammi Gen19
Ben-dekar KF4
Ben-geber KF4
Ben-gershom Ju17
Ben-hadad KF15, 20; KS6, 8, 13; CS16; Am1
Ben-hana CF4
Ben-hayil CS17
Ben-hesed KF4
Ben-hur KF4
Beninu Ne10
Benjamin (a priest) Ez10; Ne3, 12
  (Ben-oni) (son of Jacob) Gen35, 42ff;Ex1; Nu1, 7ff; De27, 33; SF10ff; CF2, 7f, 11; Ez1; Je6; Ho5; Ob1
  (son of Bilhan) CF7
Beno CF24
Benob SS21
Ben-oni (Benjamin) Gen35
Ben-zoheth CF4
Beor Gen36; Nu22; De23; Jos13, 24; CF1; Mi6
Bera Gen14
Berachah CF12

APPENDIX A PERSONAL NAMES

Berachiah CF6
Bered CF7
Beri CF7
Beriah Gen46; Nu26; CF7f,23ff
Besai Ez2; Ne7
Besodiah Ne3
Beth-rapha CF4
Bethuel Gen22, 24, 28
Bezai Ez2; Ne7, 10
Bezalel Ex31f; CF2;CS1; Ez10
Bezer CF7
Bichri SS20
Bidkar KS9
Bigtha Est1
Bigthan (Bigthana) Est2
Bigvai Ez2, 8; Ne7, 10
Bildad Job2, 8, 18, 25, 42
Bilgai Ne10
Bilgah CF24; Ne12
Bilhah Gen29, 35, 46
Bilhan CF1, 7
Bilshan Ne7
Bimhal CF7
Binea CF8f
Binnui Ez3, 8,10; Ne3,7,10, 12
Birsha Gen14
Birzavith CF7
Bithiah CF4
Biztha Est1
Boaz CF2; Ru2ff
Bocheru CF8f
Bohan Jos15
Bukki Nu34; CF6; Ez7
Bukkiah CF25
Bunah CF2
Bunni Ne9f
Buz Gen22; CF5
Buzi Ez1
Cain Gen4
Calcol CF2
Caleb Nu13, 26, 32f; De1; Jos14f, 21; Ju1, 3; CF2, 4, 6
Canaan Gen9f; CF1
Caphtor De2
Carcas Est1
Careah (Kareah) KS25
Carmi Gen46; Ex6; Nu26; Jos7; CF2f, 5

APPENDIX A PERSONAL NAMES

Carshena Est1
Chenaanah KF22
Cheran Gen36; CF1
Chileab SS3
Chilion Ru1f
Chimham (Kimham) SS19; Je41
Col-hozeh Ne3, 11
Conaniah CS31, 35
Coniah Je22
Coz CF4
Cozbi Nu25
Cush Gen10; KS19; CF1
Cushan-rishathaim (Chushan-rishathaim) Ju3
Cushi Je36; Zp1
Cyrus CS36; Ez1, 3; Is44; D1, 6, 10
Dalaiah CF3
Daliah CF4
Dalphon Est9
Dan Gen30, 35, 46; Ex1; Nu1, 7ff; De27, 33; Jos19; CF2, 7
Daniel (a priest) Ne10
   (Danel) (Belteshazzar) E14, 28; D1ff
   (family of Ithamar) Ez8
   (son of David) CF3
Darda KF4; CF2
Darius Ez4ff; Ne12; D5f, 9, 11; Hg1ff; Z1, 7
Darkon Ne7
Darlon Ez2
Dathan Nu16, 26;De11; Ps106
David Ru4; SF16ff, 29; SS1ff; KF1ff, 8, 11, 14, 17ff; CF2f, 6, 9f, 12; Cs1ff;Ez3, 8; Ne12; Pro1; Ec1;
      So4; Is7,9, 16, 22, 29, 37ff, 55; Je13, 17, 21ff, 33, 33, 36; E34, 37; Ho3; Am6, 9; Z12ff
Debir Jos10, 15
Deborah Gen35; Ju4
Dedan Gen10, 25; CF1
Delaiah CF24; Ez2; Ne6ff;Je36
Delilah Ju16
Diblaim Ho1
Dibri Le24
Diklah Gen10; CF1
Dinah Gen30, 34, 46
Diphath CF1
Dishan Gen36; CF1
Dishon Gen36; CF1
Dodai CF27
Dodavahu CS20
Dodo Ju10; SS23; CF11

494

APPENDIX A PERSONAL NAMES

Doeg SF21
Dumah Gen25; CF1; Is21
Ebal Gen36; CF1
Ebed Ez8
Ebed-melech Je38ff
Eber Gen10; CF1, 8; Ne12
Ebiasah CF6, 9, 26
Eden CS29, 31
Eder CF23
Edom (Esau) Gen36
Edrei De1
Eglah SS3; CF3
Eglon Ju3
Ehi Gen46
Ehud Ju3; CF7ff
Eker CF2
Ekron SF5ff
Eladah CF7
Elah (an Edomite) Gen36
   (chief in Edom) CF1
   (father of Shimei) KF4
   (king of Israel) KF16; KS15, 17ff
   (son of Caleb) CF4
   (son of Uzzi) CF9
Elam Gen10; CF1, 8, 26; Ez2, 8, 10; Ne7, 10, 12; Is22
Elasah CF2, 8f; Ez10; Je29
Eldaah Gen25; CF1
Eldad Nu11
Elead CF7
Eleazar (family of Parosh) Ez10; Ne12
   (son of Aaron) Ex6, 27; Le10; Nu20, 25; De10; Jos14, 17, 21, 24; Ju20; CF6, 9; Ez7, 8
   (son of Abinadab) SF7
   (son of Dodai) CF27
   (son of Dodo) SS23
   (son of Mahli) CF23ff
Elhanan SS21f; CF11, 20
Eli SF1ff; CF11, 20
Eliab Nu1, 7ff, 16, 26; De1; SF16ff; CF2, 6, 12ff; CS11
Eliad CS17
Eliada SS5; KF11; CF3
Eliah CF8
Eliahba SS23; CF11
Eliakim KS18, 23; CS36; Ne12; Is22, 36
Eliam SS11, 23
Eliasaph Nu1, 3, 7ff

APPENDIX A PERSONAL NAMES

Eliashib CF3, 24; Ez10; Ne3, 12ff
Eliathan CF25
Elidad Nu34
Eliel CF5f, 8, 11f, 15; CS31
Elienai CF8
Eliezer (a Levite) Ez8
  (a priest) CF15; Ez10
  (of Damascus) Gen15
  (son of Becher) CF7
  (son of Dodavahu) CS20
  (son of Moses) Ex18; CF23, 26ff
Elihoenai Ez8
Elihu (son of Barakel) Job32ff
  (son of Shemaiah) CF26ff
  (son of Tohu) SF1
Elijah (family of Elam) Ez10
  (family of Immer) Ez10
  (the prophet) KF17ff; KS1ff,9; CS21; Ma4
Elika SS23
Elimelech Ru1ff
Elionai CF3f, 7, 26; Ez10;Ne12
Eliphal CF11
Eliphaz (son of Esau) Gen36; CF1
  (Job's friend) Job2, 4, 15, 22, 42
Eliphelehu CF15
Eliphelet CF3, 8, 14; Ez8, 10
Elisha KF19; KS2ff, 13
Elishah Gen10; CF1
Elishama (a priest) CS17
  (adjutant-general) Je36
  (son of Ammihud)Nu1,7f;CF7
  (son of David) SS5; KS5;
  (son of Jekamiah) CF2ff
Elishaphat CS23
Elisheba Ex6
Elishua SS5; CF14
Elizaphan Nu3ff, 34; CF15; CS29
Elizur Nu1. 7ff
Elkanah Ex6; SF1; CF6, 9, 12; CS28
Elnaam CF11
Elnathan KS24; Ez8; Je26, 36
Elon (a Hittite) Gen26, 30, 46
  (a Zebulunite) Nu26
  (one of the judges) Ju12
Elpaal CF8

Elpelet CF14
Elphelet SS5, 23
Eluzai CF12
Elzabad CF12, 26
Elzaphan Ex6
Elzaphon Le10
Emim Gen14
Enan Ni1, 7f
Enoch (son of Cain) Gen4
  (son of Jared) Gen5; CF1, 5
  (son of Midian) Gen25
  (son of Reuben) Gen46;Ex6; Nu26
Enosh (Enos) Gen4; CF1
Ephah Gen25; CF1ff
Ephai (Ophai) Je40
Epher Gen25; CF1, 4ff
Ephlal CF2
Ephod Nu34
Ephraim Gen41, 46; Nu1, 7ff, 26; De33; Jos16; Ju1ff; CF2,7; Is9; Je7, 31; E37; Ho4, 11, 13
Ephrath CF2
Ephrathah CF2, 4
Ephron Gen23
Er Gen38, 46; Nu26; CF2, 4
Eran Nu26
Eri Gen46; Nu26
Esarhaddon KS19; Ez4; Is37
Esau Gen25f, 33, 36; Jos24; CF1; Je49; Ob1; Mal
Eshbaal CF8ff
Eshban Gen36
Eshbani CF1
Eshcol Gen14
Eshek CF8
Eshtemoa CF4
Eshton CF4
Esther (Hadassah) Est2ff
Etam CF4
Etha KF4
Ethan CF2, 6, 15
Ethbaal KF16ff
Ethan CF4
Ethni CF6
Eve Gen3
Evi Nu31
Evil-merodach (Ewil-marduk) KS25; Je52
Ezbai CF11

Ezbon Gen46; CF7
Ezekiel E1, 24
Ezer Gen36; CF1, 4, 7, 12; Ne3, 12
Ezra CF4; Ez7; Ne8, 12
Ezrai Ne12
Ezri CF27
Gabbai Ne11
Gad (son of Jacob) Gen30, 35, 46; Ex1; Nu1; De27. 33; CF2, 5
    (the prophet) SF22, 24; CF21, 29; CS29
Gaddi Nu13
Gaddiel Nu13
Gadi KS15
Gaham Gen32
Gahar Ez2; Ne7
Galal CF9; Ne11
Gamaliel Nu1, 7ff
Gamul CF24
Gareb SS23; CF11
Gashmu (Geshem) Ne6
Gatam Gen36; CF1
Gaza De2
Gazez CF2
Gazzam Ez2; Ne7
Geber KF4
Gedaliah ('a great man') KS25; Je52
    (a priest) Ez10
    (son of Ahikam) Je39ff
    (son of Amariah) Zp1
    (son of Jeduthun) CF25
    (son of Pashhur) Je38
Gedor CF8f
Gehazi KS4, 8
Gemalli Nu13
Gemariah Je29, 36
Genubath KF11
Gera (a Benjamite) SS16f; KF2; CF8
    (grandson of Benjamin) Gen46; Ju3
Gershom Ex2, 18; Ju18; CF6, 15, 23, 26; Ez8
Gershon Gen46; Ex6; Nu33ff; CF6, 23; CS29
Gesham CF2
Geshem (Cashmu) Ne2, 6
Geshur CF2
Gether Gen10; CF1
Geuel Nu13
Gibbar Ez2
Gibeon Ne7

498

APPENDIX A PERSONAL NAMES

Giddalti CF25
Giddel Ez2; Ne7
Gideon Ju6ff
Gilalai Ne12
Gilead Nu26,36,Jos17;CF2,5ff
Ginath KF16
Ginnethon Ne10, 12
Gishpa Ne11
Gog CF5; E38ff
Goliath SF17, 21; SS21; CF20
Gomer (son of Japheth) Gen10; CF1
  (wife of Hosea) Ho1
Guni Gen46; Nu26; CF5, 7
Haahashtari CF4
Habakkuk H1
Habaziniah Je35
Hacaliah (Hachaliah) Ne1, 10
Hadad Gen25, 36; KF11; CF1
Hadadezer SS8, 10; KF11; CF18f
Hadar Gen36
Hadassah (Esther) Est2ff
Hadlai CS28
Hadoram Gen10; CF1, 18; CS10
Hagab Ez2
Hagabah Ez2; Ne7
Hagar Gen16, 21, 25
Haggai Ez5; Hg1f
Haggedolim Ne11
Haggeri CF11
Haggi Gen46; Nu26
Haggiah CF6
Haggith SS3; KF1ff; CF3
Hakkatan Ez8
Hakkoz (Koz) CF24; Ne3, 7
Hakupha Ez2; Ne7
Hallohesh Be3, 10
Ham Gen5ff; CF1
Haman Est3ff, 9
Hammedatha Est3,9
Hammoleketh CF7
Hamor Gen33f; Jos29; Ju9
Hamuel CF4
Hamul Gen46; Nu26; CF2
Hamutal KS23ff; Je52
Hanamel Je32
Hanan (son of Igdaliah) Je35

499

APPENDIX A PERSONAL NAMES

Hanan (son of Shashak) CF8f, 11; Ez2; Ne7f, 10, 13
Hananel (Hananeel) Je31
Hanani (a priest) Ne12
  (brother of Nehemiah) Ne1,7
  (family of Immer) Ez10
  (father of Jehu) CS16, 19; KF16
  (son of Heman) CF25
Hananiah (a chief) Ne10
  (a priest) Ne12
  (a prophet) Je28, 36ff
  (family of Bebai) Ez10
  (governor of the citadel) Ne7
  (king's commander) CS26
  (Shadrach) D1ff
  (son of Heman) CF25
  (son of Shashak) CF8
  (son of Shelemiah) Ne3
  (son of Zerubbabel) CF3
Haniel CF7
Hannah SF1ff
Hanniel Nu34
Hanun SS10; CF19; Ne3
Haran Gen11; CF2
Harbona Est1, 7
Hareph CF2
Harhaiah Ne3
Harhas KS22
Harhur Ez2; Ne7
Harif Ne7
Harim CF24; Ez10; Ne3, 7, 10, 12
Hariph Ne10
Harnepher CF7
Harosheth Ju4
Harsha Ez2; Ne7
Harum CF4
Harumaph Ne3
Haruz KS21
Hasadiah CF3
Hashabiah CF6, 9, 25ff; CS35; Ez8; Ne3, 10ff
Hashabnah Ne10
Hashabniah Ne3, 9
Hashbaddanah Ne8
Hashem SS23; CF11
Hashhub Ne11
Hashum Ez2, 10; Ne7f, 10
Hasrah CS34

APPENDIX A PERSONAL NAMES

Hassenaah Ne3
Hassenuah CF9
Hasshub CF9; Ne3, 10
Hassophereth Ez2
Hasupha Ez2; Ne7
Hathach Est4
Hathath CF4
Hatipha Ez2; Ne7
Hatita Ez2; Ne7
Hattil Ez2; Ne7
Hattush CF3; Ez8; Ne3, 10, 12
Havilah Gen10; CF1
Hazael KF19; KS8ff; CS22; Am1
Hazaiah Ne11
Hazarmoth Gen10; CF1
Hazelelponi CF4
Hazo Gen22
Heber Gen46; Nu26; Ju4; CF4f
Hebron Ex6; Nu3ff; CF6, 15, 23ff
Hegai (Hege) Est2
Helah CF4
Heldai CF27; Z6
Heled SS23; CF11
Helek Nu26; Jos17
Helem Z6
Helez SS23; CF2, 11, 27
Helkai Ne12
Helon Nu1, 7ff
Hemam Gen36
Heman KF4; CF2, 6, 15, 25; CS5, 29, 35
Hemdan Gen36
Hen Z6
Henadad Ez3; Ne3, 10
Hepher Nu26; Jos17; CF4, 11
Hephzi-bah KS21
Heresh CF9
Heth Gen10; CF1
Hezeki CF8
Hezekiah (Hizkiah) (family of Ater) Ez2; Ne7, 10
    (king of Judah) KS16ff; CF3ff; CS28ff; Pro25; Is1, 36f, 39; Je15, 26;Ho1; Mi1; Zp1
Hezion KF15
Hezir CF24; Ne10
Hezrai SS23
Hezro CF11
Hezron Gen46; Ex6; Nu26; Ru4; CF2f, 5

APPENDIX **A** PERSONAL NAMES

Hiddai SS23
Hiel KF16
Hilkiah (comptroller) KS18; Is22, 36
  (father of Gemariah) Je29
  (father of Jeremiah) Je1
  (high priest) KS22; CF9; CS34f; Ne11
  (son of Hosah) CF26
  (son of Shallum) CF6; Ez7; Ne8
Hillel Ju12
Hirah Gen38
Hiram (craftsman) KF7; CS2ff
  (king of Tyre) SS5; KF5, 9ff; CF14; CS2f, 8
Hizkiah (Hezekiah) Zp1
Hobab Ju4
Hobaiah Ne7
Hod CF7
Hodaiah CF3
Hodaviah (Hodiah) CF4f, 9; Ez2f; Ne8ff
Hodesh CF8
Hodiah (Hodaviah) CF4f, 9; Ez2f; Ne8ff
Hodvah Ne7
Hoglah Nu26ff, 36; Jos17
Hoham Jos10
Homam CF1
Hophni SF1ff
Hophra (Pharaoh) Je44
Horam Jos10
Hori Gen36; Nu13; CF1
Horonaim SS13
Hosah CF16, 26
Hosea Ho1ff
Hoshaiah Ne12; Je42ff
Hoshama CF3
Hoshea (a chief) Ne10
  (king of Israel) KS15ff
  (son of Azaziah) CF27
  (son of Elah) KS15ff
Hotham CF7, 11
Hothir CF25
Hul Gen14; CF1
Huldah KS22; CS34
Hupham Nu26
Huppah CF24
Huppim Gen46
Hur Ex17, 31; Nu31; CF2ff; CS1; Ne3
Hurai CF11

Huram CF8
  (Hiram) (craftsman) KF7; CS2ff
  (king of Tyre) SS5; KF5, 9ff;CF14;CS2f, 8
Huri CF5
Hushai SS15ff; KF4; CF27
Husham Gen36; CF1
Hushim Gen46; CF7
Huzzab Na2
Ibhar SS5; CF3, 14
Ibneiah CF9
Ibri CF24
Ibzan Ju12
Ichabod SF4, 14
Idbash CF4
Iddo (a chief) Ez8
  (father of Aminadab) KF4
  (father of Berechaiah) Z1
  (seer) CS9, 12
  (son of Joah) CF6
  (son of Zechariah) CF27; Ez5; Ne12
Igal Nu13; SS23
Igdaliah Je35
Igeal CF3
Ikkesh SS23; CF11
Imla CS18
Imlah KF22
Immer CF9, 24; Ez2, 10; Ne3, 7, 11; Je20
Imna Nu26; CF7
Imnah Gen46; CF7; CS31
Imrah CF7
Imri CF9; Ne3
Iob Gen46
Iphedeiah CF8
Ira SS20ff; CF11, 27
Irad Gen4
Iram Gen36; CF1
Iri CF7
Irijah Je37
Ir-nahash CF4
Iru CF4
Isaac Gen17, 21f, 27; De1, 6, 4; Jos24; KS13; CF1; Ps105; Je33; Am7
Isaiah (a Benjamite) Ne11
  (family of Merari) Ez8
  (the prophet) KS19; CS26, 32; Is1ff, 13, 20, 37ff
  (son of Athalia) Ez8
  (son of Hananiah) CF3

APPENDIX A PERSONAL NAMES

Isaiah (son of Rehabiah) CF26
Iscah Gen11
Ishbah CF4
Ishbak Gen25; CF1
Ishbosheth SS2ff, 23
Ishhod CF7
Ishi CF2, 4ff
Ishma CF4
Ishmael (son of Abraham) Gen16ff, 25; CF1; Ps55
  (son of Azel) CF8ff
  (son of Jehohanan) CS23
  (son of Nethaniah) KS25; Je40ff
  (son of Pashhur) Ez10
Ishmaiah CF12, 27
Ishmerai CF8
Ishpan CF8
Ishuah Gen46
Ishui Gen46
Ishvah CF7
Ishvi Nu26; CF7
Ishyo SF14
Ismachiah CS31
Ispah CF8
Israel (Jacob) Gen32, 46; Ex32; F1, 5; Ez8
Issachar Gen30, 35, 46; Ex1; Nu1ff; De27; CF2, 26
Isshiah CF7, 12, 23ff
Isshijah Ez10
Ithali CF11
Ithamar Ex6, 27ff; Le10; CF6, 24; Ez8
Ithiel Ne11; Pro30
Ithmah CF11
Ithra SS17
Ithran Gen36; CF1, 7
Ithream SS3; CF3
Ittai SS15ff
Izhar Ex6; Nu3ff, 16; CF6, 23ff
Izrahiah CF7; Ne12
Izri Cf25
Izziah Ez10
Jaalah Ez2; Ne7
Jaanai CF5
Jaare-oregim SS21
Jaasiel CF27
Jaasau Ez10
Jaazaniah (army captain) KS25

504

APPENDIX A PERSONAL NAMES

Jaazaniah (son of Azzur) E11
  (son of Jeremiah) Je35
  (son of Shaphan) E8
Jaaziah CF24
Jaaziel CF15ff
Jabal Gen4
Jabesh KS15
Jabez CF4
Jabin Jos11; Ju4; SF12; Ps83
Jachin Gen46; Ex6; Nu26; CF9, 24
Jacob Gen25, 29ff, 37, 42ff; Ex1; De1, 6, 32, 34; Jos24; SF12; KS13; CF1; Ps20, 22, 44, 46f, 53, 59, 75f,
        Ps81, 84f, 94, 99, 105, 132, 135, 146ff; Is2, 8f, 14, 17, 27, 29, 40ff, 48ff, 58ff,65; Je2, 5, 10,
        Je30f, 33, 46, 51; La1ff; E20, 28, 37, 39; Ho12; Am3, 6ff; Ob1; Mi1ff, 7; Ma1f
Jada CF2
Jaddai Ez10
Jaddua Ne10, 12
Jadon Ne3
Jael Ju4
Jahath CF4, 6, 23ff; CS34
Jahaziel CF12, 16, 23ff; CS20; Ez8
Jahdai CF2
Jahdiel CF5
Jahdo CF5
Jahleel Gen46; Nu26
Jahmai CF7
Jahzeel Gen46; Nu26
Jahzerah CF9
Jahziel CF7
Jair (a judge) Ju10; CF2
  (father of Elhanan) SS21; CF20
  (son of Manasseh) De3;KF4
  (son of Shimei) Est2
Jakeh Pro30
Jakim CF8, 24
Jakobah CF4
Jalam Gen36; CF1
Jalon CF4
Jamin (a Levite) Ne8
  (son of Ram) CF2
  (son of Simeon) Gen46; Ex6; Nu26; CF4
Jamlech CF4
Japheth Gen5ff; CF1
Jaffia Jos10; SS5; CF3, 14
Japhlet CF7
Jarah CF9
Jareb Ho5, 10

Jared Gen5; CF1
Jaresiah CF8
Jarha CF2
Jarib CF4; Ez8, 10
Jaroah CF5
Jashen SS23
Jashobeam CF12, 27
Jashoboam CF11
Jashub Nu26; CF7; Ez10
Jasiel CF11
Jathniel CF26
Javan Gen10; CF1
Jaziz CF27
Jeaterai CF6
Jecoliah KS15; CS26
Jeconiah ('a prisoner') CF3
  ('king of Judah') Est2
  (son of Jehoiakim) Je24, 27
Jedaiah (a priest) Ez2
  (returned exile) Z6
  (son of Harumaph) Ne3,7,11ff
  (son of Shimri) CF4, 9, 24
Jediael CF7, 11, 26
Jedidah KS22
Jedidiah SS12
Jeduthun CF9, 16, 25; CS5, 29, 35; Ne11
Jeezer Nu26
Jehaleel CF4
Jehdeiah CF24
Jehezekel CF24
Jehiah CF15
Jehiel (a tutor) CF27
  (father of Abdon) CF8ff, 23
  (father of Obadiah) Ez8
  (father of Shecaniah) Ez10
  (Levite musician) CF15ff
  (Levite storeman) CF26, 29
Jehoaddah CF8
Jehoaddan CS25
Jehoaddin KS14
Jehoahaz CS21, 25, 36
Jehoash KS13ff; CS25; Ho1; Am1
Jehohanan (a priest) Ne12
  (father of Azariah) CS28
  (family of Bebai) Ez10

APPENDIX A PERSONAL NAMES

Jehohanan (son of Meshelemiah) CF26
Jehoahaz (king of Israel) KS13ff; CS25
   (king of Judah) KS23; CS21, 36
Jehoiachin KS24ff; CS36; Je52; E1
Jehoiada (a priest) KS11f; CS22ff; Je29
   (father of Benaiah) SS8, 20ff; KF1ff; CF11f, 18, 27
Jehoiakim (Eliakim) KS23; CF3; CS36; Je1, 22, 24, 26, 35ff, 45ff, 52; D1
Jehoiarib CF9, 24
Jehonadab KS10
Jehonathan CS17; Ne12
Jehoram (a priest) CS17
   (king of Israel) KS1, 3, 8; CS22
   (Joram) (king of Judah) KF15, 22
Jehoshaphat (a priest) CF15
   (father of Jehu) KS9
   (king of Judah) KF15, 22; KS1, 3, 8; CF3; CS17, 19ff
   (secretary of state) SS8, 20; KF4; CF18
Jehosheba KS11; CS22
Jehozabad KS12; CF26; CS17, 24
Jehozadak (Josedech) CF6; Hg1ff; Z6
Jehu (charioteer king of Israel) KS9ff, 13ff; CF2; CS22, 25; Ho1
   (son of Anathoth) CF12
   (son of Hanani) KF16, 19; CS19ff
   (son of Josibiah) CF4
Jehubbah CF7
Jehucal Je37
Jehudi Je36
Jeiel CF5, 15f; CS20, 26, 29, 35; Ez8, 10
Jekameam CF23ff
Jekamiah CF2ff
Jekuthiel CF4
Jeleth Gen36
Jemimah Job42
Jemuel Gen46; Ex6
Jephthah Ju11; SF12
Jephunneh Nu26, 34; De1; Jos14ff, 21; CF4, 6ff
Jerah Gen10; CF1
Jerahmeel CF2, 24; Je36
Jerai CF26
Jered CF4
Jeremai Ez10
Jeremiah (a Gadite) CF12
   (father of Hamutal) KS23ff; Je52
   (father of Jaazaniah) Je35
   (of Gederah) CF12
   (of Manasseh) CF5

Jeremiah (the prophet) CS35f; Ez1; Ne10, 12; Je1, 7, 11, 14, 18ff, 26ff, 36ff, 40, 42ff, 49, 51; D9

Jeremoth CF7ff, 23, 25; Ez10

Jeriah CF23ff

Jeribai CF11

Jeriel CF7

Jerimoth CF7, 12, 25, 27; CS11, 31

Jerioth CF2

Jeroboam I (king of Israel) KF11f, 21; KS3, 9f, 23; CS10

  II (king of Israel) KS14f; CF5; Ho1; Am1, 7

Jeroham (a Benjamite) CF8f, 12

  (father of Adaiah Ne11

  (father of Azareel) CF27

  (father of Azariah CS23

  (father of Elkanah) SF1;CF6

Jerubbaal (Gideon) Ju6ff;SF12

Jerubbesheth SS11

Jeshebeab CF24

Jesher CF2

Jeshishai CF5

Jeshohaiah CF4

Jeshua (Joshua) (son of Azania) Ne9f

  (son of Jozadak) Ez10

  (Levite official) CF24; CS31; Ez2ff; Ne7f, 12

Jeshurun (Jesurun) De32f; Is44

Jesimiel CF4

Jesse Ru4; SF16ff; CF2, 10; CS11; Ps72; Is11

Jether Ju8; KF2; CF2, 4

Jetheth CF11

Jethro Ex3, 18Jetur Gen25; CF1

Jeuel CF9

Jeush Gen36; CF1, 7ff, 23; CS11

Jeuz CF8

Jezaniah (Azariah) Je40, 42

Jezebel KF16ff, 21; KS9

Jezer Gen46; Nu26; CF7

Jeziel CF12

Jezliah CF8

Jezoar CF4

Jezreel CF4; Ho1ff

Jibsam CF7

Jidalph Gen22

Jieil CF11

Joab (commander) SF26; SS2ff; KF1ff, 11, 18ff, 26ff; CF2, 11

  (craftsman) CF4; Ez2,8; Ne7

Joah KS18; CF6, 26; CS29, 34; Is36

Joahaz CS34

Joash (king of Judah) KF22; KS11ff; CF3ff, 25; CS18
  (of Ophrah) Ju6ff
  (son of Becher) CF7
  (son of Shemaah) CF12
  (storeman) CF27

Job Job1ff; E14

Jobab Gen10, 36; Jos11; CF1, 8

Jochebed Ex6; Nu26

Joed Ne11

Joel (a priest) Ez10
  (son of Azariah) CF15;CS29
  (son of Laddan) CF23, 26ff
  (son of Pethuel) Joe1
  (son of Samuel) SF8; CF4ff
  (son of Zichri) Ne11
  (warrior of David) CF11

Johohanan Ne6

Joiada Ne3, 12ff

Joiakim Ne12

Joiarib Ez8; Ne11ff

Jokim CF4

Jokshan Gen25; CF1

Joktan Gen10; CF1

Jonadab SS13; Je35

Jonah KS14; Jon1ff

Jonathan (a scribe) Je37
  (son of Abiathar) SS15; KF1
  (son of Adin) Ez8
  (son of Gershom) Ju18
  (son of Jada) CF2
  (son of Joiada) Ne12
  (son of Kareah) KS25; Je40
  (son of Saul) SF13f, 19; SS1ff; CF8ff
  (son of Shage) CF11
  (son of Shammah) SS23
  (son of Shimeai) SS21
  (son of Uzziah) CF27

Jorah Ez2

Jorai CF5

Joram (king of Judah) KF15,22
  (son of Isaiah) CF26
  (son of Toi) SS8

Jorkoam CF2

APPENDIX **A** PERSONAL NAMES

Josabad CF12
Josedech (Jehozadak) Hg1f;Z6
Joseph (a priest) Ne12
  (family of Binnui) Ez10
  (son of Asaph) CF25
  (son of Israel) Gen30ff; Ez1; Nu1ff, 13; De27, 33; CF2, 5, 7; Ps77, 81, Ps105; E37; Am5ff
Joshah CF4
Joshaphat CF11
Joshaviah CF11
Joshbekashah CF25
Joshua (Hoshea) (son of Nun) Ex17, 24; Nu13, 26, 32; De1, 3, 31; Ju2; Jos1ff; KF16; KS23; CF7; Ne8
  (Jeshua, a Levite) Ne7, 12
  (son of Jehozadak) Z3, 6; Hg1f
Josiah (king of Judah) KF13; KS21, 23; CS33ff; Je1, 3, 22, 25ff, 35ff, 46;   Zp1
  (son of Amon) CF3
  (son of Zephaniah) Z6
Josibiah CF4
Josiphiah Ez8
Jotham (king of Judah) KS15; CF3, 5; CS26ff; Is1, 7; Ho1; Mi1
  (son of Jahdai) CF2
  (son of Jerubbaal) Ju9
Jozabad CS31, 35; Ez8, 10; Ne8, 11
Jozachar KS12
Jozadak Ez3, 5, 10
Jubal Gen4
Jucal Je38
Judah (a Levite) Ne12
  (son of Hassenuah) Ne11
  (son of Jacob) Gen29ff; Ex1; Nu1, 7ff; De27; Ju1; Ru4; CF2, 5, 10; Ez1,10; Is48, 65; E37; Ob1
Judith Gen26
Juphunneh Nu13
Jushab-hesed CF3
Kabzeel SS23
Kadmiel Ez2ff; Ne7, 9f, 12
Kalcol KF4
Kallai Ne12
Kareah (Careah) KS25; Je40ff
Kedar Geb25; CF1
Kedemah Gen25; CF1
Kedorlaomer Gen14
Kehaniah CF26
Keilah CF4
Kelaiah (Kelita) Ez10
Kelub CF4, 27
Kemuel Gen22; Nu34; CS18
Kenaanah CF15

Kenan Gen5; CF1
Kenani Ne9
Kenaniah CF15
Kenaz Gen36; Jos15; Ju3; CF1, 4
Keren-happuch Job42
Keros Ez2; Ne7
Kesed Gen22
Keturah Gen25; CF1
Keziah Job42
Kimham (Chimham) SS19; Je41
Kir Is22
Kir-hareseth KS3
Kish (father of Saul) SF9f, 14; SS21; CF12
  (father of Shimei) Est2
  (son of Abdi) CS29
  (son of Jehiel) CF8ff
  (son of Mahli) CF23
  (son of Ner) CF8
Kishi CF6
Kislon Nu34
Kittim Gen10; CF1
Kohath Gen46; Ex6; Nu3ff; CF6, 15, 23; CS29,34
Kolaiah Ne11; Je29
Korah Gen36; Ex6; Nu16; CF1ff, 6, 9
Kore CF9, 26; CS31
Koz (Hakkoz) Ne3, 7
Kushaiah CF15
Laadah CF4
Laadan CF7, 23, 26
Laban Gen24ff
Lael Nu3ff
Lahad CF4
Lahmi CF20
Laish SF25; SS21
Lamech Gen4ff; CF1
Lappidoth Ju4
Leah Gen29ff; Ru4
Lebanah Ez2; Ne7
Lebo-hamath KF8
Lemuel Pro31
Letushim Gen25
Leummim Gen25
Levi Gen29ff; Ex1; De2; CF2, 6, 23; Ez8; Ps135; Z12; Ma2
Libni Ex6; Nu3ff; CF6
Likhi CF7

Lo-ammi (Ammi) Ho1
Lo-ruhama (Ru-hamah) Ho1
Lot Gen11ff; De2; Ps83
Lotan CF1
Lud Gen10; CF1
Luz Gen48
Maabarah Is10
Maacah (concubine of Caleb) CF2
  (father of Shephatiah) CF27
  (grandmother of Asa) KF15; CS15
  (king of Gath) KF2
  (mother of Abijah) CS13
  (mother of Absolom) SS3; CF3
  (son of Reumah) Gen22
  (wife of Jehiel) CF8
  (wife of Machir) CF7
  (wife of Reheboam) CS11
Maadai Ez10
Maadiah Ne12
Maai Ne12
Maasai CF9
Maaseiah (Mahseiah) (a chief) Ne10
  (a clerk) CS26
  (a governor) CS34
  (a priest) Ez10; Ne8, 12; Je21, 37
  (father of Neriah) Je32, 51
  (son of Ahaz) CS28
  (son of Adaiah) CS23
  (son of Baruch) Ne11
  (son of Shallum) Je35
  (temple musician) CF15
Maaz CF2
Maaziah CF24; Ne10
Machbanai CF12
Machi Nu13
Machie Jos13, 17
Machir (son of Amiel) SS9, 17
  (son of Manasseh) Nu26f, 36; De3; CF2, 7
Madai Gen10; CF1
Magdiel Gen36; CF1
Magog Gen10; CF1
Magor-missabib (Pashhur) Je20
Magpiash Ne10
Mahalah CF7
Mahalaleel Ne11

APPENDIX A PERSONAL NAMES

Mahalalel Gen5; CF1
Mahalath Gen28; CS11
Maharai CF27
Mahasham CF8
Mahath CF6; CS29, 31
Mahazioth CF25
Mahlah Nu26ff, 36; Jos17
Mahli Ex6; Nu3ff; CF6, 23; Ez8
Mahlon Ru1ff
Mahol KF4
Maknadebai Ez10
Malachi Ma1
Malcham CF8
Malchiah (district ruler) Ne3
  (father of Pashhur) Je21, 38
  (Melichu, a priest) CF9; Ez10; Ne8, 10ff
  (temple musician) CF6
  (temple official) CF24
Malchiel Gen46; Nu26; CF7
Malchiram CF3
Malluch (a priest) Ez; Ne10, 12
  (son of Hashabiah) CF6
Mamre Gen14
Manahath Gen36; CF1
Manasseh (family of Hashum) Ez10
  (king of Judah) KS20f; CF3; CS32ff; Je15
  (son of Joseph and Asenath) Gen41, 46, 48, 50; Nu1, 7ff, 26; De3, 29, 33; Jos1ff, 12f, 16ff; Ju1f; KF4
Manoah Ju13
Maoch SF27
Maon CF2
Mara (Naomi) Ru1
Mareshah CF2
Marsena Est1
Mash Gen10; CF1
Massa Gen25; CF1
Matred Gen36; CF1
Matri SF10
Mattan KS11; CS23; Je38
Mattaniah (a Levite) CF9; CS20, 29; Ne11f
Mattaniah (family of Pahath-moab) Ez10
  (Zedekiah, king of Judah) KS24
  (son of Heman) CF25
Mattenai Ez10; Ne12
Mattithiah CF9, 15ff, 25; Ez10; Ne8
Medad Nu11

Medan Gen25; CF1
Mehetabel Gen36; CF1; Ne6
Mehida Ez2; Ne7
Mehir CF4
Mehujael Gen4
Mehuman Est1
Meinim Ez2
Melatiah Ne3
Melchizedek Gen14; Ps110
Melech CF8ff
Melichu (Malluch) Ne10, 12
Melzar D1
Memucan Est1
Manahem KS15
Meonothai CF4
Mephibosheph (son of Jonathan) SS21
   (son of Saul) SS4, 9,16,19, 21
Merab SF14, 18; SS21
Meraiah Ne12
Meraioth CF6, 9; Ez7; Ne11ff
Merari Gen46; Ex6; Nu3ff; CF6, 9, 15, 23ff;
Mered CF4
Meremoth Ez8; Ne3, 10, 12
Meres Est1
Meribaal CF8ff
Merodach-baladan KS20; Is39
Mesh CF2, 8
Mesha KS3
Meshach (Mishael) (exile) D1ff
   (son of Japheth) Gen10;CF1
Meshelemiah CF9, 26
Meshezabek (Meshezabeel) Ne3, 10ff
Meshillemith CF9
Meshillemoth CS28; Ne11
Meshobab CF4
Meshullam (a Gadite) CF5
   (adjutant-general) KS22
   (family of Kodath) CS34
   (gatekeeper) Ne12
   (priest) Ne10
   (prominent citizen) Ez8, 10; Ne12
   (son of Berechiah) Ne3, 6, 8
   (son of Elpaal CF8
   (son of Hodaviah) CF9
   (son of Joed) Ne11

514

APPENDIX **A** PERSONAL NAMES

Meshullam (son of Meshillemith) CF9
  (son of Zadok) Ne11
  (son of Zerubbabel) CF3
Meshullemeth KS21
Methuselah Gen5; CF1
Methushael Gen4
Meunim Ez12; Ne7
Mibhar CF11
Mibsam Gen25; CF1, 4
Mibzar Gen36; CF1
Mica SS9; CF9; Ne10ff
Micah (father of Abdon) CS34
  (from Ephraim) Ju17ff
  (of Moresheth) Je26; Mi1
  (son of Meribbaal) CF8ff
  (son of Shimei) CF5
  (son of Uzziel) CF23ff
  (son of Zabdi) Ne11
Michael (a Gadite) CF5
  (father of Omri) CF27
  (father of Sethur) Nu13
  (father of Zebadiah) Ez8
  (son of Baaseiah) CF6
  (son of Beriah) CF8
  (son of David) CS21
  (son of Izrahiah) CF7
Michaiah (father of Akbor)KS22
  (officer) CS17
  (son of Gemariah) Je36
  (son of Imla) KF22; CS18
  (son of Zaccur) Ne12
Michal SF14, 18; SS3; CF15
Micri CF9
Midian Gen25ff; Ju6ff; CF1; Ps83; Is10
Mijamin CF24;Ez10; Ne10, 12
Mikloth CF8ff
Mikneiah CF15
Milalai Ne12
Milcah Gen11ff; Nu26ff, 36; Jos17
Miniamin CS31; Ne12
Miriam (daughter of Bithia) CF4
  (sister of Moses) Ex15; Nu12; CF6; Mi6
Mirmah CF8
Mishael (a priest) Ne8
  (Meshach) (exile) D1ff
  (son of Uzziel) Ex6; Le10

Misham CF8
Mishma Gen25; CF1, 4
Mishmannah CF12
Mispar Ez2
Mispereth Ne7
Mithredath Ez1, 4
Mizraim Gen10
Mizram CF1
Mizzah Gen36; CF1
Moab Gen19; CF4
Moadiah Ne12
Molid CF2
Mordecai (a chief) Ez2; Ne7
  (son of Jair) Est2ff
Moses Ex2ff; Le1ff; Nu1ff; De1ff; Jos1ff, 13, 24; Ju18; SF12; KF8; KS14, 18, 23; CF6, 23, 26; CS23, 25,
      33ff; Ez3, 6ff; Ne1,8ff;   Ps77, 99, 103, 106; Is63; Je15; D9; Mi6; Ma4
Moza CF2, 8ff
Muppim Gen46
Mushi Ex6; CF6, 23
Naam CF4
Naamah Gen4; KF14; CS12
Naaman Gen46; Nu26; KS5; CF8
Naarah CF4
Naarai CF11
Nabal SF25, 27, 30; SS2ff
Naboth KF21; KS9
Nadab Ex6, 24ff; Le10; Nu26; KF15; CF2, 6, 8ff, 24
Naham CF4
Nahamani Ne7
Naharai SS23; CF11
Nahash SF11; SF10,17; CF19
Nahath CF1, 6; CS31
Nahbi Nu13
Naheth Gen36
Nahor Gen11ff; Jos24
Nahori CF1
Nahshon Ex6; Nu1, 7ff; Ru4; CF2
Nahum Na1
Naomi Ru1ff
Naphish Gen25; CF1
Naphtali Gen30ff; Ex1; Nu1,7ff; De27, 33; Ju1ff; KF7
Nathan SS5, 7, 12, 23; KF1,4; CF2ff, 11, 14, 17, 29; CS9, 29; Ez8, 10; Z12
Nathan-melek KS23
Neariah CF3ff
Nebai (Nobai) Ne10

APPENDIX A PERSONAL NAMES

Nebaioth Gen25ff; CF1

Nebat KF11, 16ff, 21ff; KS3, 9f, 13, 17, 23; CS9f, 13

Nebo Ez10

Nebuchadnezzar (Nebuchadrezzar) KS24; CF6; CS36; Ez1, 5; Ne7; Est2; Je21f, 24, 27ff, 32, 34, 37, 39, Je43ff, 46, 49, 51ff; E26, 29ff; D1ff

Nebusarsekim Je39

Nebushazban Je39

Nebuzaradan KS25; Je39f, 41, 43, 52

Necho KS23; CS35ff; Je46

Nebadiah CF3

Nehemiah Ez2; Ne1, 3, 7f, 10, 12

Nehum Ne7

Nehushta KS24

Nekoda Ez2; Ne7

Nemuel Nu26; CF4

Nepheg Ex6; SS5; CF3, 14

Nephishesim (Nephushesim) Ne7

Ner SF14, 26; SS2ff; KF2; CF8ff

Nergalsarezer (Nergal-sharezer) Je39

Neriah Je32, 36, 43, 45, 51

Nethaneel NU1ff, 7ff; CF2, 15, 24, 26; CS17, 35; Ez10; Ne12

Nethaniah KS25; CF25; CS17; Je36, 40ff

Netophah CF11

Neziah Ez2; Ne7

Nimrod Gen10; CF1; Mi5

Nimshi KF19; KS9; CS22

Noadiah Ez8; Ne6

Noah (daughter of Zelophehad) Nu26ff, 36; Jos17

  (the patriarch) Gen5ff; CF1; Is54; E14

Nobai (Nebai) Ne10

Nogah CF3, 14

Nohah CF8

Nun Nu13, 26; De1; Jos1; Ju2; KF16; CF7; Ne8

Obadiah (a Gadite) CF12, 27

  (a Levite) CS34

  (a priest) Ne10, 12

  (a prophet) Ob1

  (comptroller) KF18ff; CS17

  (son of Arnan) CF3

  (son of Azel) CF8ff

  (son of Izrahiah) CF7

  (son of Jehiel) Ez8

  (son of Shemaiah) CF9

Obal Gen10

Obed Ru4; CF2, 11, 26; CS23

Obed-edom SS6; CF13, 15ff, 26; CS25

Obil CF27
Ocran Nu1, 7ff
Oded CS15, 28
Og Nu21; De3, 29ff; Jos2, 9, 12ff; KF4; Ne9; Ps135f
Ohad Gen46; Ex6
Ohel CF3
Oholibamah Gen36; CF1
Omar Gen36; CF1
Omri KF16; KS8; CF7 9, 27; CS22; Mi6
On Nu16
Onam Gen36; CF1ff
Onan Gen38; Nu26; CF2
Ophai (Ephai) Je40
Ophir Gen10; CF1
Ophrah CF4
Oreb Ju7; Ps83
Oren CF2
Ornan CF21; CS3
Orpah Ru1
Osnappar (Asnappar) Ez4
Othni CF26
Othniel Jos15; Ju1, 3; CF4, 27
Ozem CF2
Ozni Nu26
Paarai SS23
Padon Ez2; Ne7
Pagiel Nu1, 7ff
Pahath-moab Ez2, 8, 10; Ne3, 7, 10
Palal Ne3
Pallu Gen46; Ex6; Nu26; CF5
Palti Nu13; SF25
Paltiel Nu34; SS3
Parmashta Est9
Parnach Nu34
Parosh Ez2, 8, 10; Ne3, 7, 10
Parshandatha Est9
Paruah KF4
Pasach CF7
Paseah (Phaseah) CF4; Ez2; Ne3, 7
Pashhur (Pashur) (a priest) Ez2, 10; Ne7, 10
  (chief officer) Je20
  (son of Malchiah) CF9; Je21,38
Pedahel Nu34
Pedahzur Nu, 7ff
Pedaiah KS23; CF27; Ne3, 8, 11, 13
Pekah KS15ff; CS28; Is7

Pekahiah KS15

Pelaiah CF3; Ne8, 10

Pelaliah Ne11

Pelatiah CF3ff; Ne10; E11

Peleg Gen10ff; CF1

Pelet CF2, 12

Peleth Nu16; CF2

Peninnah SF1

Penuel CF4, 8

Peresh CF7

Perez Gen38; Nu26; Ru4; CF2ff, 9, 27; Ne11

Perida Ne7

Peruda Ez2

Pethahiah CF24; Ez10; Ne9, 11

Pethuel Joel

Peulthai CF26

Pharaoh (title) Gen12ff; De11; KF3, 9, 11; KS17ff, 23; CF4; Ps135ff; So1; Is19, 30, 36; Je25, 27, 43f, 47

Phaseah (paseah) Ne3, 7

Phicol Gen21ff

Phinehas (son of Eleazar) Ex6; Nu25, 31; Jos22, 24; Ju20; CF6, 9; Ez7ff; Ps106
  (son of Eli) SF1ff, 14

Pildash Gen22

Pilha Ne10

Piltai Ne12

Pinon Gen36; CF1

Piram Jos10

Pispah CF7

Pithon CF8ff

Pochereth-hazzebaim Ez2; Ne7

Poratha Est9

Potiphar Gen37

Potiphera Gen41ff

Puah Ex1

Pue Gen46; Nu26;Ju10; CF7

Pul KS15; CF5

Purah Ju7

Put Gen10; CF1

Putiel Ex6

Queen of Sheba KF10; CS9

Raama CF1

Raamah Gen10

Rab-mag Je39

Rab-saris KS18; Je39

Rab-shakeh KS18; Is36

Rachel (Rahel) Gen29ff; Ru4; SF10; Je31

APPENDIX A PERSONAL NAMES

Raddai CF2
Rahab Jos2
Raham CF2
Rakem CF7
Ram Ru4; CF2; Job32
Ramiah Ez10
Rapha CF8
Raphah CF8
Raphu Nu13
Reaia CF5
Reaiah CF2, 4; Ez2; Ne7
Reba Nu31
Rebecca Gen22ff
Rechab SS4; KS10; Ne3; Je35
Reelaiah Ez2
Regem CF2
Regem-melech Z7
Rehabiah CF23f, 26
Rehob Ne10
Rehoboam KF11; CF3; CS9ff
Rehum Ez2, 4; Ne3, 10, 12
Rei KF1
Rekem Nu31; CF2
Remaliah KS15ff; CS28; Is7ff
Rephael CF26
Rephah CF7
Rephaiah CF3ff, 7, 9; Ne3
Reshaph CF7
Reu Gen11; CF1
Reuben Gen29ff; Ez1; Nu1, 7ff, 26; De11, 27, 33; Jos14; CF2, 5
Reuel Gen36; Nu1, 7ff; CF1, 9
Reumah Gen22
Rezia CF7
Rezin KS15ff; Ez2; Ne7; Is7ff
Rezon KF11
Ribai SS23; CF11
Rimmon SS4
Rinnah CF4
Riphath Gen10
Rizpah SS3, 21
Rodanim Gen10; CF1
Rohgah CF7
Romamti-ezer CF25
Rosh Gen46
Ru-hamah (Lo-ruhamah) Ho2
Ruth Ru1ff

APPENDIX A PERSONAL NAMES

Sabta CF1
Sabtah Gen10
Sabtecha Gen10; CF1
Sacar CF11, 26
Sallai (Sallu) CF9; Ne11ff
Salma CF2
Salmon Ru4
Salu Nu25
Samgar-nebo Je39
Samlah Gen36; CF1
Samson Ju13ff; SF12
Samuel (son of Ammihud) Nu34
 (son of Elkanah) SF1ff, 19, 28; CF6, 9, 26, 29; CS35; Ps99; Je15
 (his ghost) SF28
 (son of Tolah) CF7
Sanballat Ne2, 4ff, 13
Saph SS21
Sarah Gen17ff; Is51
Sarai Gen11ff
Saraph CF4
Sargon Is20
Sarsechim Je39
Saul (first king of Israel) SF9ff; SS1ff, 16; CF5,8f, 12, 26; Is10
 (king of Edom) Gen36; CF1
 (son of Simeon) Ex6; Nu26; CF4
 (son of Uzziah) CF6
Seba Gen10; CF1
Segub KF16; CF2
Seir Gen36; CF1
Seled CF2
Semachiah CF26
Sennacherib KS18ff; CS32; Is36ff
Seorim CF24
Serah Gen46; Nu26; CF7
Seraiah (adjutant general) SS8
 (chief priest) KS25; Ne12; Je52
 (quarter master) Je51
 (son of Azariah) CF6; Ez7
 (son of Azriel) Je36
 (son of Hilkiah) Ne11
 (son of Kenaz) CF4
 (son of Tamhumeth) Je40
 (tribal leader) Ez2; Ne10
Sered Gen46; Nu26
Serug Gen11; CF1
Seth (Sheth) Gen4; CF1

Sethur Nu13
Shaaph CF2
Shaashgaz Est2
Shabbethai Ne8, 11
Shachia CF8
Shadrach Diff
Shaharaim CF8
Shallum (doorkeeper) CF9; Ez2; Ne7
  (king of Israel) KS15; Je22
  (father of Hezekiah) CS28
  (son of Hallohesh) Ne3
  (son of Josiah) CF3
  (son of Naphtali CF7
  (son of Tikvah) KS22; CS34
  (son of Sisamai) CF2
  (son of Zadok) CF6; Ez7
  (uncle of Jeremiah) Je32, 35
Shallun Ne3
Shalmai Ez2; Ne7
Shalman Ho10
Shalmaneser KS17ff
Shama CF11
Shamed CF8
Shamer CF6
Shamgar Ju3
Shamhuth CF27
Shamir CF24
Shamlai Ez2
Shamma CF7
Shammah Gen36; SF16ff; SS23; CF1
Shammai CF2, 4
Shammoth CF11
Shammua (son of David)CF14
  (son of Galal) Ne11ff
  (son of Zaccur) Nu13
Shamsherai CF8
Shapham CF5
Shaphan (adjutant-general) KS22, 25; Je36
  (father of Ahikam) Je26, 39f, 43
  (father of Elasah) Je29
  (father of Jaazaniah) E8
  (son of Azaliah) CS34
Shaphat Nu13; KF19; KS3; CF3, 5, 27
Sharai Ex10
Sharar SS23

522

Sharezer (Sherezer) KS19; Is37; Z7

Shashak CF8

Shashal Ez10

Shavsha CF12

Sheal Ez10

Shealtiel (father of Zerubbabel) Ez3ff; Ne12; Hg1f

  (son of Jeconiah) CF3

Sheariah CF8

Sheba Gen10ff; SS20; CF1, 5

Shebaniah CF15; Ne9f, 12

Sheber CF2

Shebna KS18; Is22, 36

Shecaniah (a priest) Ne12

  (father of Hattush) Ez8

  (father of Jahaziel) Ez8

  (father of Shemaiah) CF3; Ne3

  (son of Arah) Ne6

  (son of Obadiah) CF3, 24; CS31

Shechem Gen33ff; Nu26; Jos17ff; CF7

Shedeur Nu1, 7ff

Shehariah CF8

Shelah Gen10ff; Nu26; CF1f, 4

Shelemiah (doorkeeper) CF26; Ne3

  (father of Jehucal) Je37f

  (father of Nethaniah) Je36

  (a priest) Ne13

Sheleph Gen10; CF1

Shelesh CF7

Shelomi Nu34

Shelomith (daughter of Dibri) Le24

  (daughter of Reheboam) CS11

  (daughter of Zerubbabel) CF3

  (son of Josiphiah) Ez8

Shelomoth CF23f, 26

Shelumiel Nu1, 7ff

Shem Gen5ff; CF1

Shema CF2, 5, 8; Ne8

Shemaah CF12

Shemaiah (a clerk) CF24

  (a Levite) CS17, 29, 31, 35

  (a 'man of God') KF12

  (a priest) Ez10; Ne10, 12

  (a 'prominent man') Ez8

  (a prophet) CS12; Je29

  (father of Delaiah) Je36

Shemaiah (father of Shimri) CF4
  (father of Uriah) Je26
  (son of Delaiah) Ne6
  (son of Elizaphan) CF15
  (son of Hasshub) CF9; Ne11
  (son of Joel) CF5
  (son of Mattanaiah) Ne12
  (son of Meshelemaiah)CF26
  (son of Shecaniah) CF3;Ne3
Shemariah CF12; CS11; Ez10
Shemeber Gen14
Shemer KF16
Shemida Nu26; Jos17; CF7
Shemiramoth CF15ff; CS17
Shenazzar CF3
Shephatiah (a Haruphite)CF12
  (a tribal leader) Ez2, 8; Ne7
  (son of David) SS3; CF3
  (son of Jehoshaphat) CS21
  (son of Maacah) CF27
  (son of Mahalalel) Ne11
  (son of Mattan) Je38
  (son of Reuel) CF9
Shephi CF1
Shepho Gen36
Shephuphan CF8
Sherah CF7
Sherebiah Ez8; Ne8f, 12
Sheresh CF7
Sheshai Nu13; Jos15; Ju1
Sheshan CF2
Sheshbazzar Ez1
Sheth (Seth) CF1
Shethar Est1
Shethar-bozenai Ez5
Sheva CF2
Shilhi KF22; CS20
Shillem Gen46; Nu26
Shiloh SF14
Shilshah CF7
Shimea CF2ff, 6, 8
Shimeah SS13
Shimeai SS21
Shimeam CF9
Shimeath KS12; CS24

Shimei (a Levite) CS29, 32; Ez10
  (a tribal leader) CF8
  (of Ramah) CF27
  (opponent of Adonijah) KF1
  (son of Gerah) SS16; KF2
  (son of Gershon) Ex6; Nu3; CF6, 23; Z12
  (son of Gog) CF5
  (son of Jahath) CF6
  (son of Jeduthun) CF25
  (son of Kish) Est2
  (son of Libni) CF6
  (son of Pedaiah) CF3
  (son of Zaccur) CF4
Shimon CF4
Shimpath CF8
Shimri CF4, 11, 26; CS29
Shimrith CS24
Shimron Gen46; Nu27; CF7
Shimshai Ez4
Shinab Gen14
Shinar Gen14
Shiphi CF4
Shiphtan Nu34
Shiprah Ex1
Shisha KF4
Shishak KF11, 14; CS12
Shitrai CF27
Shiza CF11
Shobab SS5; CF2ff, 14
Shobach SS5
Shobai Ez2; Ne7
Shobal Gen36; CF1, 4
Shobek NE10
Shobi SS17
Shoham CF24
Shomer KS12; CF7
Shophach CF19
Shua CF7
Shuah Gen25; CF1, 4
Shual CF7
Shubael CF23ff
Shuham Nu26
Shuni Gen46; Nu26
Shupham Nu26
Shethelah Nu26; CF7

APPENDIX A PERSONAL NAMES

Sia Ne7
Siaha Ez2
Sibbecai CF27
Sibbechai SS21; CF20
Sidon Gen10; CF1
Simeon (family of Harim) Ez10
  (son of Jacob) Gen29ff; Ex1; Nu1; De27; Jos19; Ju1; CF2, 4
Sippai CF20
Sisamai CF2
Sisera (army commander) Ju4f; SF12; Ps83
  (temple servitor) Ez2; Ne7
Sithri Ex6
Sodi Nu13
Solomon SS5, 12; KF1ff; KS21, 23; CF3, 6, 14, 18, 22, 28ff; CS1ff, 10f, CS13, 30, 33ff; Ez2; Ne7, 12ff;
          Pro1; So1, 3, 8; Je52
Sophereth Ne7
Sotai Ez2; Ne7
Suah CF7
Susi Nu13
Tabbaoth Ez2; Ne7
Tabeal Is7
Tabeel Ez4
Tabrimmon KF15
Tahan Nu26; CF7
Tahash Gen22
Tahath CF6ff
Tahpenes KF11
Tahrea CF9
Talmai Nu13; Jos15; Ju1; SS3, 13; CF3
Talmon CF9; Ez2; Ne7, 11ff
Tamar (daughter of Absalom) SS14
  (daughter-in-law of Judah) Gen38; Ru4; CF2ff
  (sister of Absalom) SS13
Tanhumeth KS25; Je40
Taphath KF4
Tappuah CF2
Tarea CF8
Tarshish Gen10; CF1, 7; Est1
Tartan KS18; Is20
Tattenai Ez5
Tebah Gen22
Tebaliah CF26
Tehinnah CF4
Tekoa CF11
Telah CF7

526

Telem Ez10
Temah Ez2; Ne7
Teman Gen25ff; CF1
Temeni CF4
Terah Gen11; Jos24; CF1
Teresh Est2
Tibni KF16
Tidal Gen14
Tiglath-pileser (Tilgat-pilneser) Ks15ff; CF5; CS28
Tikvah KS22; CS34
Tilon CF4
Timna Gen36; CF1
Tiras Gen10; CF1
Tirhakah KS19; Is37
Tirhanah CF2
Tiria CF4
Tirzah Nu26ff, 36; Jos17
Toah CF6
Tob-adonijah CS17
Togarmah Gen10; CF1
Tohu SF1
Toi SS8
Tola (son of Issachar) Gen46; Nu26
  (a judge) J10; CF7
Tou CF18
Tubal CF1
Tubal-cain Gen4
Ucal Pro30 Uel Ez10
Ulam CF7ff
Ulla CF7
Unni CF15; Ne12
Ur CF11
Uri Ex31ff; KF4; CF2; CS1; Ez10
Uriah (Urijah) (a Hittite) SS1, 23; KF15; CF11
  (a priest) Ks16; Ez8; Ne3, 8; Is8
  (a prophet) Je26
Uriel CF6, 15; CS13
Uthai CF9; Ez8
Uz Gen10ff; CF1
Uzai Ne3
Uzal Gen10; CF1
Uzza CF6, 8, 13; Ez2; Ne11ff
Uzzah SS6
Uzzi CF6f 9; Ez7; Ne11ff
Uzzia CF11

527

APPENDIX A PERSONAL NAMES

Uzziah (family of Immer) Ez10
  (Azariah) (king of Judah) KS15; CS26ff; Is1,6ff; Ho1; Am1; Z14
  (son of Uriel) CF6
  (son of Zechariah) Ne11
Uzziel Ex6; Le10; Nu3ff; CF4, 6ff, 15, 23ff; CS29; Ne3
Vaizatha (Vajezatha) Est9
Vashti Est1ff
Vophsi Nu13
Zabad CF2, 7,11; CS24; Ez10
Zabbai Ez10; Ne3
Zabbud KF4
Zabdi Jos7; CF8, 27; Ne11
Zabdiel CF27; Ne11
Zabud KF4
Zaccai Ez2; Ne7
Zaccur Nu13; CF4, 24ff; Ne10, 12ff
Zacher CF8
Zadok (accountant) Ne13
  (chief at Jerusalem) Ne3,10
  (officer of tribes) CF27
  (the priest) SS8, 15ff; KF1ff; CF6.9.15f, 18; Ez7; Ne11; E40, 48
  (warrior of David) CF12
Zaham CS11
Zalaph Ne3
Zalmunna Ju8; Ps83
Zaphenath-paneah (Joseph) Gen14
Zaphon Ju12
Zattu Ez2, 8, 10; Ne7, 10
Zavan Gen36; CF1
Zaza CF2
Zebadiah CF8, 12; CS17; Ez8, 10
Zebah Ju8; Ps83
Zebediah CF26ff; CS19
Zebidah KS23
Zebina Ez10
Zeboyim Gen14
Zebul Ju9
Zebulun Gen30ff; Ex1; Nu1, 7ff; De27, 33; Jos19; Ju1, 4, 6; CF2
Zechariah (a Merarite) CF15
  (a priest) CF15ff; CS35; Ne8, 12
  (a Reubenite) CF5
  (family of Elam) Ez10
  (family of Kohath) CS34
  (family of Parosh) Ez8
  (father of Abijah) CS29
  (king of Israel) KS14f, 18

Zechariah (king's officer) CS17
  (of Manasseh) CF27
  (official at Jerusalem) Ne11
  (son of Bebai) Ez8
  (son of Benauah) CS20
  (son of Hosah) CF26
  (son of Isshiah) CF24
  (son of Jeberechiah) Is8
  (son of Jehiel) CF9
  (son of Jehoiada) CS24
  (son of Jehoshaphat) CS21
  (son of Meshalemia) CF
  (the prophet) CS26; Ez5; Z1, 7
Zedekiah (a priest) Ne10
  (Mattaniah) (king of Judah) KS24; CS36; Je1, 21, 24, 27, 29, 32, 34, Je37ff, 44, 49, 51ff
  (son of Hananiah) Je36
  (son of Josiah) CF3
  (son of Kenaanah) KF22; CS18
  (son of Maaseiah) Je29
Zeeb Ju7; Ps83
Zelek SS23; CF11
Zelophedad Nu36
Zelophehad Jos17; CF1
Zemira CF7
Zephaniah KS25; Je21, 29, 7, 52; Zp1; Z6
Zephi CF1
Zepho Gen36
Zephon Nu26
Zerah Gen36ff; Nu26; Jos7; CF1, 4, 6, 9, 27; CS14; Ne11
Zerahiah CF6; Ez7ff
Zeresh Est5ff
Zereth CF4
Zeruah KF11
Zerubbabel CF3; Ez2ff; Ne7, 12; Hg1ff; Z4
Zeruiah SF26; SS2, 8, 14ff; KF2; CF2, 11, 18, 27
Zetham CF23, 26
Zethan CF7
Zethar Est1
Zia CF5
Ziba SS9, 16, 19
Zibeon Gen36; CF1
Zibia CF8
Zibiah KS12; CS24
Zichri Ex6; CF8ff, 26ff; CS23, 28; Ne11ff
Ziha Ex2; Ne7, 11
Zillah Gen4

APPENDIX A PERSONAL NAMES

Zilpah Gen29ff
Zilthai CF8
Zimmah CF6
Zimran Gen25; CF1
Zimri (king of Israel) KF16; KS9
  (son of Jarah) CF9
  (son of Jehoaddah) CF8
  (son of Salu) Nu25
  (son of Zerah) CF2
Ziph CF4
Ziphah CF4
Ziphion Gen46
Zippor Nu22; Jos24; Ju11
Zipporah Ex2ff, 18
Ziza CF4, 23; Cs11
Zobebah CF4
Zohar Gen23ff; Ex6
Zoheth CF4
Zophah CF7
Zophai CF6
Zophar Job2, 11, 20, 42
Zuar Nu1, 7ff
Zuph SF1; CF6
Zur Nu25, 31; CF8ff
Zuriel Nu3ff
Zurishaddae Nu1, 7ff
Zuzim Gen14

NEW TESTAMENT

Aaron L1; A7; LH, 9
Abel Mw23; L11; LH11, 12
Abiathar Mk2
Abijah (Abia) Mw1; L1
Abiud Mw1
Abraham Mw1, 8, 22; Mk12; L1, 3, 13, 16, 19f; J8; A3, 7, 13; PR9, 11; PCS11; PG3f; LH2, 6f, 11;
          LJ2; LPF3
Achaicus PCF16
Achaz (Ahaz) Mw1
Achim Mw1
Adam L3; PR5; PCF15; PTF2; LJu1
Addi L3

APPENDIX A PERSONAL NAMES

Aeneas A9

Agabus A11, 21

Agar (Hagar) PG4

Agrippa A25f

Ahaz (Achaz) Mw1

Alexander (a coppersmith) A19; PTS4
  (a disciple) PTF1
  (a priest) A4
  (son of Simon) Mk15

Alphaeus (father of James) Mw10; Mk3; L6; A1
  (father of Levi) Mk2

Aminadab (Amminadab) Mw1; L3

Amon Mw1

Amos L3

Ampliatus (Amplias) PR16

Ananias (who cured Saul) A9, 22
  (who dropped dead) A5
  (high priest) A23f

Andrew Mw4, 10; Mk1, 3, 12; L6; J1, 6, 12; A1

Andronicus PR16

Anna L2

Annas L3; J18; A4

Antipas Rev2

Apelles PR16

Apollos A18f; PCF1, 3f,16; Tt3

Apphia Ph1

Aquila A18; PR16; PCF16; PTS4

Aram (Arni) L3
  (Ram) Mw1

Archelaus Mw2

Archippus PC04; Ph1

Aretas PCS11

Aristarchus A19f, 27; PCo4; Ph1

Aristobolus PR16

Arni (Aram) L3

Arphaxad (Arpachsad) L3

Artemas Tt3

Asa (Asher) Mw1; L2

Asyncritus PR16

Augustus Caesar L2; A25

Azariah (Ozias) Mw1

Azor Mw1

Balaam LPS2; LJu1; Rev2

Balak Rev2

Barabbas (Bar-Abbas) Mw27; Mk15; L23; J18

Barak LH11

Bar-Jesus (Elymas) A13

Bar-Jona (Simon Peter) Mw16

Barnabas A9,11ff; PCF9; PG2

Barsabbas (Joseph Justus) A1

Bartholomew Mw10; Mk3; L6; A1

Bartimaeus Mk10

Beor (Bosor) LPS2

Berachiah (Barachias) Mw23

Bernice A25f

Blastus A12

Boanerges (James and John) Mk3

Boaz (Booz) Mw1; L3; LPS2

Caesar (title) Mw22; L2f, 20; J19; A11, 17, 25, 27; PPs4

Caiaphas Mw26; L3; J11, 18; A4

Cain LH11; LJF3; LJu1

Cainan (son of Arphaxad) L3

  (son of Enosh) L3

Candace (Kandake) A8

Carpus PTS4

Cephas (Simon Peter) J1; PCF1, 3, 9, 15; PG1f

Chloe PCF1

Chuza L8

Cis (Kish) A13

Claudia PTS4

Claudius Caesar A11

  Lysias (commandant) A23

Clement PPS4

Cleopas L24

Cleophas (Clopas) J19

Cornelius A10

Cosam L3

Crescens PTS4

Crispus A18; PCF1

Cyrinius (Quirinius) L2

Damaris A17

Daniel Mw24; Mk13

David Mw1, 9, 12, 15, 20ff; Mk2, 10ff; L1ff, 6, 18, 20; A1f, 4, 7, 15; PR1, 4, 11; PTS2; LH4, 11; Rev3, 5, 22

Demas PCO4; PTS4; Ph1

Demetrius A19; LJT1

Didymus (Thomas the twin) J11, 20f

Dionysius A17

Diotrephes LJT1

Dorcas (Tabitha) A9

Drusilla A24

Eber (Heber) L3
Eleazar Mw1
Eliakim Mw1; L3
Elias (Elijah) Mw11, 16f, 27; Mk6, 8f, 15; L1, 4, 9; J1; PR11
Eliezer L3
Elijah (Elias) Mw11.16f, 27;Mk6, 8f, 15; L1, 4, 9; J1; PR11
Elisha (Eliseus) L4
Eliud Mw1
Elizabeth (Elisabeth) L1
Elmadam (Elmodam) L3
Elymus (Bar-Jesus) A13
Enoch L3; LH11; LJu1
Enosh (Enos) L3
Epaenetus PR16
Epaphras PCo1, 4; Ph1
Epaphroditus PPs2, 4
Er L3
Erastus A19; PR116; PTS4
Esaias (Isaiah) Mw3f, 8, 12f, 15; Mk7; L3f; J1,12; A8; PR9f
Esau PR9; LH11f
Esli L3
Esrom (Hezron) Mw1; L3
Eubulus PTS4
Eunice PTS1
Euodia (Euodias) PPS4
Eutychus A20
Eve PCS11; PTF2
Ezekias (Hezekiah) Mw1
Felix A23ff
Festus (Porcius) A25
Fortunatus PCF16
Gaius A19f; PR16; PCF1; LJT1
Gallio A18
Gamaliel A5, 22
Gideon (Gedeon) LH11
Gog Rev20
Hagar PG4
Heber (Eber) L3
Heli L3
Hermas PR16
Hermes PR16
Hermogenes PTS1
Herod (Agrippa) A12f, 23, 25f
  (Antipas the Tetrarch) Mw14, 22; Mk3, 6, 8, 12; L3, 8f, 13, 23; A4
  (the Great) Mw2; L1

Herodias Mw14; Mk6; L3
Herodion PR16
Hezekiah (Ezekias) Mw1
Hezron (Esrom) Mw1; L3
Hosea (Osee) PR9
Hymenaeus PTF1; PTS2
Isaac Mw1, 8, 12; Mk12; L3, 13, 20; A3, 7; PR9; PG4; LH11; LJ2
Isaiah (Esais) Mw3f, 8, 12f, 15, 26; Mk1, 7; L3f; J1, 12; A8, 28; PR9f, 15
Jacob (grandfather of Jesus) Mw1
  (son of Isaac) Mw8, 22; Mk12; L1, 3, 13, 20; J4; A3, 7; PR9, 11; LH11
Jairus L8
Jambres PTS3
James (brother of Jesus) Mw13; Mk6; PG1
  (brother of John) Mw4, 10, 17; Mk1, 3, 5, 9f, 13f; L5f, 8f; A1, 12, 15, 21; PCF15; PG2; LJ1
  (brother of Joseph) Mk15f
  (brother of Jude) LJu1
  (son of Alphaeus) Mw10; Mk3; L6; A1
Jannai (Janna) L3
Jannes PTS3
Jared L3
Jason A17; PR16
Jeconiah (Jechonias) Mw1
Jehosphaphat (Josaphat)Mw1
Jephthah (Jephthae) LH11
Jeremiah (Jeremias) (Jeremy) Mw2, 16, 27
Jesse Mw1; L3; A13; PR15
Jesus Bar-Abbas Mw27
  Christ Mw1ff; Mk1ff; L1ff; J1ff; A1ff; PR1ff; PCF1ff PCS1ff; PG1ff; PE1ff; PPs1ff; PCol1ff; ThF1ff;
    ThS1f; PTF1ff; PTS1ff; Ttl1ff; Ph1;LH2ff; LJ1ff; LPF1ff; LPS1ff; LJF1ff; LJS1; LJT1;
    LJu1; Rev1, 11, 14, 17, 19f, 22
  Justus PCo4
Jezebel Rev2
Joanna (Johanan) (father of Joda) L3
  (wife of Chuza) L8, 24
Job LJ5
Joda (Juda) L3
Joel A2
Johanan (Joanna) L3
John (Jon, Jonah, Jonas) (father of Simon Peter) Mw16; J1, 21
  (the Baptist) Mw2ff, 9, 11, 14, 16f; Mk1, 6, 8, 11; L1, 3, 5, 7, 9, 11, 16, 20, Mk22; J1, 3, 5, 10; A1, 11,
    A13, 18, 19
  (the Evangelist) Mw4, 10,17; Mk1, 3ff, 9f, 13f; L5f, 8f; A1, 3f, 8, 12f; PG2; LJF1; LJS1; Rev1, 22
John (the Evangelist)
  Mark A12, 15
Jonah (Jonas) Mw12, 16; L11

APPENDIX A PERSONAL NAMES

Jonam L3
Jonathan A4
Joram Mw1
Jorim L3
Josaphat (Jehoshaphat) Mw1
Jose (Joshua) L3
Josech (Joseph) L3
Joseph (Joses) (brother of Jesus) Mw13; Mk6
  (father of Jesus) Mw1; L1ff; J1, 6
  (of Arimathaea) Mw27; Mk15; L23; J19
  (son of Jacob) J4; A7; LH11
  (son of Jonam) L3
  (Josech) (son of Juda) L3
  (Joses) (son of Mary) Mk15
  (son of Mattathiah) L3
  Barnabas (Joses) A4
  Barsabbas (Justus) A1
Joses (Joseph) (Barnabas) A4
   (brother of Jesus) Mw13; Mk6
   (son of Mary) Mk15
Joshua (Jose) (Father of Er)L3
  (son of Nun) A7; LH4
Josiah (Josias) Mw1
Jotham (Joatham) Mw1
Juda (Joda) L3
Judah (Juda) (son of Joseph) L3
  (Judas) (son of Jacob) Mw1; L3
Judas (Juda) (brother of Jesus) Mw13; Mk6
  (resident of Damascus) A5
  (revolutionary) A5
  (Judah) (son of Jacob) Mw1; L3
  (son of James) L6; J14; A1
  Barsabbas A15
  Iscariot Mw10, 26f; Mk3, 14; L6, 22; J6, 12f, 18;A1
Jude LJu1
Julia (Julias) (Junias) PR16
Julius (centurion) A27
Junias (Julia) Julias) PR16
Justus (Jesus Justus) PCo4
  (Joseph Barsabbas) A1
  (Titius) A18
Kandake (Candace) A8
Kish (Cis) A13
Korah (Core) LJu1
Lamech L3

Lazarus J11f; L16
Lebbaeus (Thaddaeus) Mw10
Levi (son of Alphaeus) Mk2
  (son of Jacob) LH7
  (son of Melchi) L3
  (son of Symeon) L3
  (tax gatherer) L5
Linus PTS4
Lois PTS1
Lot L17; LPS2
Lucas (Luke) PCS13; PCo4; PTS4; Ph1
Lucius A13; PR16
Luke (Lucas) PCS13; PCo4; PTS4; Ph1
Lydia A16
Lysianus L3
Lysias A24
Maath L3
Magog Rev20
Mahalaleel (Maleleel) L3
Malchus J18
Manaen A13
Manasseh (Manasses) Mw1
Mark (Marcus) PCo4; PTS4; LPF5; Ph1
Martha L10; J11f
Mary (convert in Asia) PR16
  (mother of James) Mw27f; Mk15f
  (mother of Jesus) Mw1f, 13; Mk6; L1f, 24; J2; A1
  (mother of John Mark) A12
  (of Magdala) Mw27f; Mk15f; L8, 24; J19f
  (sister of Martha and Lazarus) L10 J11f
  (wife of Clopas) J19
Mathusala (Methuselah) L3
Matthan Mw1
Matthat (father of Heli) L3
  (father of Jorim) L3
Mattathia L3
Mattathiah (Mattathias) (father of Joseph) L3
  (father of Maath) L3
Matthew Mw9f; Mk3; L6; A1
Matthias A1
Melchi (father of Levi) L3
  (father of Neri) L3
Melchizedeck (Melchisedec) LH5ff
Melea L3
Menan (Menna) L3
Methuselah (Mathusala) L3

APPENDIX **A** PERSONAL NAMES

Michael (archangel) LJu1; Rev12

Mnason A21

Moses Mw8, 17, 19, 22f; Mk1, 7, 9, 12; L2, 5, 9, 16, 20, 24; J1, 3, 5ff; A3, 6f, 13, 15, 21, 26; PR5, 9f; PCF9f; PCS3; PTS3; LH3, 7, 10ff;

Naaman L4

Naasson (Nahshon) Mw1; L3

Naggai (Nagge) L3

Nahor (Nachor) L3

Nahshon (Naasson) Mw1; L3

Nahum (Naum) L3

Narcussus PR16

Nathan L3

Nathanael J1, 21

Naum (Nahum) L3

Nereus PR16

Neri L3

Nicanor A6

Nicodemus J3, 7, 19

Nicolas A6

Noah (Noe) Mw24; L3, 17; LH11; LPF3; LPS2

Nympha (Nymphas) PCo4

Obed Mw1; L3

Olympas PR16

Onesimus PCo4; Ph1

Onesiphorus PTS1

Osee (Hosea) PR9

Ozias (Azariah) Mw1

Parmenias A6

Patrobas PR16

Paul (formerly Saul) A13ff; PR1; PCF1, 3, 16; PCS1, 10; PG1; PE1, 3; PPs1; PCo1, 4; ThF1f; ThS1, 3; PTF1; PTS1; Ph1; LPS3

Peleg (Phalec) L3

Perez (Phares) (Pharez) Mw1; L3

Persis PR16; LJu1; Rev15

Peter (Simon) (Cephas) Mw4, 8, 10, 14ff, 26; Mk3, 5, 8ff, 13f, 16; L5f, 8f, 12, 22; J18, 20f; A1ff, 8f, 11f, A15; PG1f; LPF1; LPS1

Phalec (Peleg) L3

Phanuel L2

Pharaoh (title) A7; PR9; LH11

Phares (Perez) (Pharez) Mw1; L3

Philemon Ph1

Philetus PTS2

Philip (apostle) Mw10; Mk3; L6; J1, 6, 12, 14; A1
  (brother of Herod) Mw14; Mk6; L3
  (the Evangelist) A6, 8, 21

APPENDIX A PERSONAL NAMES

Philologus PR16
Phlegon PR16
Phoebe (Phebe) PR16
Phygelus PTS1
Pilate (Pontius) Mw27; Mk15; L3, 13, 23; J18f; A3f, 13; PTF6
Porcius Festus A24f
Priscilla (Prisca) A18;
Prochorus A6
Publius A28
Pudens PTS4
Pyrrhus A20
Quartus L2
Quirinius (Cyrinius) L2
Rachel Mw2
Ragau (Reu) L3
Rahab (Rachab) (mother of Salma) Mw1
   (prostitute at Jericho) LH11; LJ2
Ram (Aram) Mw1
Rebecca (Rebekah) PR9
Reheboam (Roboam) Mw1
Reu (Ragau) L3
Rhesa L3
Rhoda A12
Roboam (Reheboam) Mw1
Rufus Mk15; PR16
Ruth Mw1
Sadoc (Zadok) Mw1
Sala (Shelah) L3
Salathiel (Shealtiel) Mw1; L3
Salma (Salmon) Mw1
Salome (daughter of Mary) Mk15f
   (daughter of Herodias) Mw14; Mk6
Samson LH11
Samuel A3, 13; LH11
Sapphira A5
Sarah (sara) PR4, 9; LH11; LPF3
Saruch (Serug) L3
Saul (king of Israel) A13
   (Paul) A7ff
Sceva A19
Secundus A20
Sem (Shem) L3
Semein (Semei) L3
Sergius Paulus A13
Serug (Saruch) L3

APPENDIX A PERSONAL NAMES

Seth L3

Shealtiel (Salathiel) Mw1; L3

Shem (SeM) L3

Shelah (Sala) L3

Silas A15, 17f

Silvanus PCS1; ThF1; ThS1; LPF5

Simeon (Symeon) (father of Levi) L3

  (Niger) A13, 15

  (of 'Nunc Dimittis') L2

Simon (a leper) Mw26; Mk14

  (a magician) A8

  (a Pharisee) L7

  (a tanner) A9f

  (a Zealot) Mw10; Mk3; L6;A1

  (brother of Jesus) Mw13; Mk6

  (carried the cross) Mw27; Mk15; L23

  Iscariot (father of Judas) J6, 13

  Peter (Cephas) (Bar-jona) Mw4, 10, 16f; Mk1,3, 14; L4ff, 22, 24; J1, 6; J13, 18, 20f; A10f; LPS1

Solomon Mw1, 6, 12; L11f; J10; A7

Sopater A20

Sosipater PR16

Sosthenes A18; PVF1

Stachys PR16

Stephanas PCF1, 16

Stephen A6, 8, 11, 22

Susanna L8

Symeon (Simeon) L3

Syntyche PPs4

Tabitha (Dorcas) A9

Tamar (Thamar) Mw1

Terah (Thara) L3

Tertius PR16

Tertullus A24

Thaddaeus (Lebbaeus) Mw10; Mk3

Thara (Terah) L3

Theophilus L1; A1

Theudas A5

Thomas (Didymus the Twin) Mw10; Mk3; L6; J11, 4, 20f; A1

Tiberius L3

Timaeus Mk10

Timon A6

Timothy (Timotheus) A16ff; PR16; PCF4, 16; PCS1; PPs1f; PCo1; ThF1, 3; ThS1; PTF1, 6; Ph1; Ttl, 3

Theophilus A1

Titius Justus A18

Titus PCS2, 7f, 12f; PG2; PTS4; Ttl, 3

Trophimus A20f; PTS4

Tryphaena PR16

Tryphosa PR16

Tychicus A20; PE6; PCo4; PTS4; Tt3

Tyrannus A19

Urban (Urbane) PR16

Uriah (Urias) Mw1

Zacchaeus L19

Zacharias (Zechariah) (father of Berachiah) Mw23
   (father of John the Baptist) L1, 3, 11

 Zadok (Sadoc) Mw1

Zarah (Zara) Mw1

Zebedee Mw4, 10, 20 26f; Mk1, 3, 10; L5; J21

Zechariah (Zacharias) (father of Berachiah) Mw23
   (father of John the Baptist) L1, 3, 11

 Zelotes (Simon called) L6

Zenas Tt3

Zerubbabel (Zorobabel) (Father of Abiud) Mw1
   (father of Rhesa) L3

APPENDIX B   *Place Names*

OLD TESTAMENT

Aabah De1
Abarim Nu33; Je22
  Mount Nu27; De32
  Valley of E39
Abdon Jos19, 21; CF6
Abel-beth-maacah SS20; KF15; KS15
  -keramim Ju11
  -mayim CS16
  -meholag KF4, 19
  -meholah Ju7
  -mizraim Gen50
  -shittim Nu33
Accad Gen10
Acco Jos19; Ju1
Achor, Vale of Jos7, 15; Is65; Ho2
Achzib Jos15, 19; Ju1
Adadah Jos15
Adam Jos3
Adamah Jos19
Adami-nekeb Jos19
Addan Ez2
Addar Jos15
Addon Ne7
Adithaim Jos15
Admah Gen10, 14; De29; Is15; Ho6, 11
Adoraim CS11
Adullam Jos12, 15; CS11; Ne11
  Cave of SF22; SS23; CF11; Mi1
Adummim Jos15, 18
Ahava Ez8
  River Ez8
Ahlab Ju1
Ai Gen12f; Jos7ff, 12; Ez2; Ne7; Je49
Aiah Ne11
Aijalon Jos19, 21; Ju1, 12; SF14; CF6, 8; CS11, 28
  Vale of Jos10
Ain Nu34; Jos15, 19, 21; CF4
Akrabbim Ju1; Jos15
Akshaph Jos11ff, 19
Alamellech Jos19
Alemeth CF6

Almon Jos21

Almon-diblathaim Nu33

Aloth KF4

Alush Nu33

Amad Jos19

Amalek Nu24; CF18; Ps83

Amalekite land Gen14

Amam Jos15

Amana, Mount So4

Ammah, Hill of SS2

Ammon SS11; KF14; CS12; Ne13; Ps83; Is11; Je9, 27, 41, 49; E25; Am1; Zp2

Amonite land Gen 11

Anab Jos11, 15

Anaharath Jos19

Ananiah Ne11

Anath Ju3

Anathoth Jos21; KF26; CF6, 11ff, 27; Ez2; Ne7, 11; Is10; Je1, 11, 32

Anem CF6

Aner CF6

Anim Jos15

Aphak Jos19

Aphek Jos12f,15;SF4,29;KF20
  -in-Sharon Jos12

Aphekah Jos15

Aphik Ju1

Aphrah Mi1

Ar Nu21ff; De2; Is15

Arab Jos15

Arabah Jos11f, 18; SF23, 30; SS4; KS25;Je39, 52; E47; Z14
  Gorge of the Am6
  Sea of De4; Jos3, 12; KS14

Arabia KF10; Job39; Is2, 21; Je25; E27

Arabim, Gorge of Is15

Arad Nu21, 33; Jos12; Ju1

Aram SS15; KF10ff; KS3f, 6ff, 12ff; CS16, 22, 28; Is7, 17, 22; E16; Ho12; Am1; Z9
  -naharaim De23; Ju3; CF19
  -zobah CF19

Ararah Jos15

Ararat Gen8; KS19;Is37; Je51

Argob De3; KF4; KS15

Arieh KS15

Ariel Is29

Arnon, Fords of Is16
  Gorge of Nu22ff; De22ff; Jos12ff; KS10

Arnon, River Ju11; KS10; Je48

APPENDIX **B** PLACE NAMES

Aroer Nu32; De2, 3; Jos12, 13; Ju11; SF30; SS24; KS10; CF5, 11; Is17; Je48
Arpad KS18; Is10, 36ff; Je49
Aruboth KF4
Arvad E27
Asal (Azal) Z14
Ashan Jos15, 19, 21; CF4, 6
Ashbea CF4
Ashdod Jos11, 13, 15; SF5ff; CS26; Ne13; Is20; Je25; Am1, 3; Zp2; Z9
 -pisgah Jos12
Asher Jos17, 19; KF4; E48
Ashkelon Jos13; Ju1, 14; Je25, 47; Am1; Zp2; Z9
Ashkenaz (Ashchenaz) Je51
Ashnah Jos15
Ashtaroth De1; Jos9, 12ff; CF6, 11
Ashterothikarnaim Gen14
Ashtoreth SF31
Asshur Gen2, 10, 25; Nu24; Ps83; E27
Assyria Nu24; KS15ff; CF5ff; CS28,30ff; Ez4ff;Is8,10ff, 19ff, 27ff, 30ff,Is36ff; Je2, 50; E31f; Ho5, 7ff,
     14; Mi5, 7; Na3; Zp2; Z10
Ataroth Nu32; Jos16; CF2
 -addar Jos16, 18
Athak SF30
Atharim Nu21
Atroth-shopham Nu32
Ava (Avva) KS17
Aven E30; Ho10
 Vale of Am1
Avith Gen36; CF1
Avvim Jos18
Azal (asal) Z14
Azekah Jos10, 15; SF17; CS11; Ne11; Je34
Azmon Nu34; Jos15
Aznoth-tabor Jos19
Baal CF4
 Heights of Nu22
 of Break-through (Baal-perazim) SS5; CF14
Baalah Jos15; CF13
 Mount Jos15
Baalath Jos19; KF9; CS8
 -beer Jos19
 -judah SS6
Baal-gad Jos12ff
 -hamon So8
 -hazor SS13
Baal-hermon CF5
 Mount Ju3

Baal-meon Nu32; E25
 -peor De4
 -perazim SS5; CF14
 -shalisha KS4
 -zephon Ex14; Nu33
Babel Gen10f
Babylon KS17, 20 24ff; CS32f, 36; Ez1ff; Ne7, 13; Est2; Ps87, 137; Is13ff, 21, 39, 43, 47ff, 52;Je20f, 24,
        Je27, 29, 32, 34, 36ff, 46, 49ff; E12, 17, 19, 21, 24, 26, 29ff, 32; D1ff; Mi4; Z2, 6
Bahurim SS3, 16, 19, 23; KF2; CF11
Baither Jos15
Bajith Is15
Balah Jos19
Bamoth Nu21
 -baal Jos13
Barhum SS23
Bashan Nu21; De1, 3, 29; Jos9, 12ff, 17, 20; KF4; KS10; CF5ff; Ne9; Ps22, 68; Is2, 33; Je22, 50; E27;
        Am4; Na1; Mi7
Bath-gallim Is10
 -rabbim
Bealoth Jos15
Be-ashtarah Jos21
Be-ashtaroth Jos21
Beer Ju9
 -elim Is15
 -lahai-roi Gen16
 Waterhole of Nu21
Beeroth Jos9,18; SS4,23; Ne7
 -bene-jaakan De10
Beersheba Gen21, 26; Jos15, 19; Ju20; SF8; SF24; KF19; KS12, 23; CF4; CS19, 24, 30; Ne11; Am5, 8
Ben-hadad Je49
Bene-barak Jos19
 -jaakan Nu33
Benjamin, land of SF7; SS2, 21ff; KF4; CF27; Ps80; Je1, 6, 17, 32ff; E48
Ben-hinnom, Valley of Jos15, 18; KS23; CS28, 33; Je7, 19, 32
Beon Nu32
Berakah, Valley of CS20
Bered Gen16
Berothai SS8
Berutha (Berothah) E47
Besor, Ravine of SF30
 -barah Ju7
 -beel-meon Jos13
 -birei CF4
 -car SF7
 -dagon Jos15, 19

Besor-diblathaim Je48
 -eden KS19; Is37; Am1
Bethel Gen12f, 28, 35; Jos7, 12, 16, 18; Ju1ff, 20ff; SF10; KF12, 16; KS2, 10, 17, 23; CF7; CS13, 25;
   Ez2; Ne7,11; Je48; Ho10, 12; Am3f, 7
 hill country of SF13
 -sharezer Z7
Beth-emek Jos19
Bether, Mountains of So2
Beth-ezel Mi1
 -gader CF2
 -gamul Je48
 -gilgal Ne12
 -haggan KS9
 -hakkarem (haccarem) Ne3; Je6
 -hanan KF4
 -haram Jos13
 -hoglah Jos15, 18
 -horon Jos18,21; SF13; CF6
  Lower Jos16, 18; KF9; CF7; CS8
  Pass of Jos10
  Upper Jos16; CF7; CS8
 -jeshimoth Nu33; Jos12ff; E25
 -joab CF2
 -lebaoth Jos19
Bethlehem Gen35; Jos15, 19; Ju12, 17ff; Ru1; SF16f, 20; SS2, 21ff; CF2, 4, 11; Ez2; Ne7; Je41; Mi5
Beth-maacah KS25; Je40
 -marcaboth Jos19; CF4
 -meon Je48
 -millo Ju9
 -nimrah Nu32; Jos13
 -pazzez Jos19
 -pelet Jos15; SS23; Ne11
 -peor De3, 34; Jos13
 -rehob Ju18; SS10
 -shan SF31
 -shean os17; Ju1; KF4; CF7
 -shemesh Jos15, 19, 21; Ju1; SF6; KF4; KS14; CF6; CS25, 28; Je43
 -shittah Ju7
 -taoouah Jos15
 -togarmah E38
Bethuel SF30; CF4
Bethul Jos19
Beth-zur Jos15; CF2; CS11; Ne3
Betonim Jos13
Beulah (Israel) Is62
Beyond-Euphrates Ez4f, 7; Ne2ff

Bezek Ju1; SF11

Bezer-in-the-wilderness De4; Jos20ff; CF6

Bileam CF6

Bilhah CF4

Bithron SS2

Bizjothjoh Jos15

Blessing (Berakah), Valley of CS20

Bohan, Stone of Jos18

Bokim Ju2

Borashan SF30

Bozez, Rock of SF14

Bozkath Jos15; KS22

Bozrah Gen36; CF1; Is34, 63; Je48ff; Am1; Mi2

Bramble-bush (Seneh) Rock SF14

Bubastis E30

Buz Je25

Cabbon Jos15

Cabul Jos19; KF9

Cain Nu24; Jos15

Calah Gen10

Calneh Am6

Calno Is10

Canaan Gen12, 15, 17, 23; Ex6, 16; Nu13ff; De1ff; Jos14ff; Ps135, 195ff; Is19, 23; E16; Ob1; Zp2

Caphtor Je47; Am9

Carchemish CS35; Is10; Je46

Carem Jos15

Carmel Jos15, 19; SF15, 25, 27, 30; SS2ff, 23; CF11; So7; Je46, 50; Am1, 9; Mi7; Na1
    Mount KF18; KS2; Am1

Casiphia Ez8

Chaldea (Chaldaea) Gen11; Je32, 50ff; E1, 11, 16

Chebar (Kebar) River E1, 3, 10, 43;

Chemosh (Kemosh) Je48

Chephar-haamonai Jos18

Cherith Brook KF17

Cherub (Kerub) Ne7

Chilmad E27

Chinneroth (Kinnereth), Sea of Jos12

Chittim (Kittim) Nu24; Is23; E27; D11

Chub E30

Cilicia E27

City of David (Zion) SS5; KF8ff, 22; KS9, 12, 24ff; CF11, 15; CS8, 16, 21, 25, CS27ff; Ne3, 12; Is22
    of the Sun (Heliopolis) Is19

Coa KF10; CS1

Crier's Spring Ju15

Culom Jos15

Cush Gen2; Is11, 18, 20, 37; E29ff, 38ff; Na3; Zp3

Cushan H3

Cuthah Ks17

Dabbesheth Jos19

Daberah Jos21

Daberath Jos19; CF6

Damascus Gen4; SS8; KF11, 15; KS8, 14, 16; CF18; CS16, 24, 28; So7; Is7f, 10, 17; Je49; E27, 47; Am1, 5; Z9

Dan Gen14; De34; Jos19; Ju18; SS24; KF12, 15; KS10; CS16, 30; Je4, 8; E27, 48; Am8
   Camp of Ju18

Dannah Jos15

David, City of (Zion) SS5; KF8ff, 22; KS9, 12, 14ff; CF11, 15; CS8, 16, 21,25, CS27ff; Ne3, 12; Is22

Dead Sea Gen14; Nu34; De3; Jos3, 12, 15,18; CS20; E39

Debir Jos11ff, 21; Ju1; CF6

Dedan Is21; Je22, 49; E25, 27, 38

Diblah (Diblath) E6

Dibon Nu21, 32; Jos13; Ne11; Is15; Je48
   -gad Nu33

Dilan Jos15

Dinhabah Gen36; CF1

Dimnah Jos21

Dimon Is15
   Waters of Is15

Dimonah Jos15

Dividing Rock SF23

Dizahab De1

Dophkah De1

Dor Jos11ff, 17; Ju1; KF4; CF7

Dothan Gen37; KS6

Dragon Spring (Well) Ne2

Dumah Jos15

Dura, Plain of D3

Ebal, Mount De11, 26, 27; Jos8

Ebed Ju9

Eben-ezer SF4, 7

Eber Nu24

Ebez Jos19

Ebronah Nu33

Ecbatana Ez6

Eden Gen2; E27, 31, 36; Is51; Am1
   garden in Gen2

Eder Jos15

Edom Nu20, 24, 33; Ju11; SS8; KF9, 11, 22; KS3, 8, 16; CF1, 18; CS8, 20f, 25; Ps60, 76, 83, 108, 137; Is11, 34, 63; Je9, 25, 27, Je40, 49; La4; E25, 27, 32, 35ff; D11; Am1ff, 9; Ob1; Joe3; Mal

Edomite land Gen32

Edrei Nu21; De3; Jos12ff, 19

Eglaim Is15

APPENDIX B PLACE NAMES

Eglath-shelishiyah Je48

Eglon Jos10f, 15

Egypt Gen12, 37, 39ff, 45ff, 50; Ex1ff, 17ff, 22f, 32ff; Jos13, 24; Ju2; SF2, 12, 15, 27; KF3ff, 9ff; KS17,
        KS23ff; CS1ff, 9ff, 26, 35ff; Ne9; Ps68, 78, 80ff, 87, 105ff, Ps114, 135; Pro7; Is11, 19ff, 23,
        Is27, 30ff, 36ff, 43, 45, 52; Je2, 9, 11, 16, 23ff, 26, 31f, 34, 37, 41f, 46; E17, 19ff, 23, 27,
        E29ff; D11; Ho2, 7ff, 11ff; Joe3; Am2ff, 8ff; Mi6ff; Na3; Hg2; Z10, 14

  Torrent of Nu34; Jos15; KF8; KS24; Is27

Ekron Jos13, 15, 19; Ju1; SF5ff, 17; KS1; Je25; Am1; Zp2; Z9

Elah, Vale of SF17, 21

Elam Gen14; Ez2; Ne7; Is11, 21; Je25, 49; E32; D8

Elaph Jos18

Elath De2; KF9; KS14, 16

El-berith Ju9

Elealeh Nu32; Is15ff; Je48

El-Elohey-Israel Gen33

Elim Ex16; Nu33

Elishah E27

Ellasar Gen14

Elon Jos19; KF4

  -bez aanannim Jos19; Ju4

Eloth KF9; CS8, 26

El-paran Gen14

Eltekeh Jos19, 21

Eltekon Jos15

Eltolad Jos15, 19

Emek-achor Ho2

  -keziz Jos18

Enam Jos15

En-dor Jos17; SF28

  -eglaim E47

  -gannim Jos15, 19, 21

  -gedi Jos15; SF23ff; CS20; So1; E47

  -haddah Jos19

  -hakkore Ju15

  -harod Ju7; SF29; Ps83

  -hazor Jos19

  -mishpat Gen14

Enoch City Gen14

Enrimmon Ne11

En-rogel Jos15,18; SS17; KF1

  -shemesh Jos15, 18

  -tappuah Jos17

Ephah Is60

Ephes-dammin SF17

Ephraim Jos19ff,24; SS2, 13, 18; CF27; CS13, 15, 17, 19, 25, 30, 34; Ps60, 78, 80, 108; Is7, 17, 28; Je31,
      50; E48; Ho5ff, 14; Ob1; Z9ff

APPENDIX **B** PLACE NAMES

APPENDIX **B** PLACE NAMES

Gebal Ps83; E27

Gebalites, land of the Jos13

Gebbim (Gebim) Is10

Geder Jos12

Gederah Jos15; CF4, 12

Gederoth Jos15; CS28

Gedor Jos15; CF4, 12

Ge-harashim CF4; Ne11

Geliloth Jos22

Gerar Gen10, 20, 26; CS14

Gerizim, Mount De11, 27; Jos8; Ju9

Geshur SS3, 13ff; CF3

Geshurite country Jos13

Gezer Jos10, 12, 16, 21; Ju1; KF9; CF6ff, 14, 20

Giah SS2

Gebbethon Jos19, 21; KF15ff

Gibea CF2

Gibeah Jos15, 18; Ju19; SF10ff, 22ff; SS23; CF11; CS13; Is10; Ho5, 9ff

Gibeath-haaraloth Jos5

Gibeon Jos9, 18, 21; SS2, 20; KF9; CF8ff, 14, 21; Ne3; Je28, 41

  Great Stone of SS20

  Vale of Is28

Gihon KF1

  River CS32ff

Gilboa SF28

  Mount SF31; SS1; CF10

Gilead Gen31; Nu32; De2, 4, 34; Jos12ff, 17, 20; Ju10, 20; SS2, 17, 24; KF2, 4, 17; KS10, 15; CF2, 5ff, CF26ff; Ps60, 108; Je8, 22, 46, 50; E47; Ho6, 12; Am1; Ob1; Mi7; Z10

  Mount So4, 6

Gilgal De11; Jos4ff, 14; Ju2; SF10ff; SS19; KS2, 4; Ho4, 9; Am4ff; Mi6

  camp of Jos9ff

Giloh Jos15; SS15

Gilron River Gen2

Gimzo CS28

Girgashite land Gen15

Gittah-hepher Jos19

Gittaim SS4; Ne11

Goath Je31

Gob SS21

Gog's Horde, Valley of E39

Golan De4; Jos20ff; CF6

Gomer E38

Gomorrah Gen10ff, 18ff; De29; Is1, 13; Je23, 49ff; Am4; Zp2

Goshen Gen45f; Jos11, 15

Goyim Gen14

Gozan KS17ff; Is37

Gozan River KS17; CF5
Great Pool in Gibeon Je41
  Sea Nu34; Jos1, 9, 15; E47ff
Greece (Grecia; Javan) Is66; D8, 10ff; Z9
Gudgodah De10
Gur KS9
 -baal CS26
Habor CF5
  River KS17ff
Hachilah, Hill of SF23ff
Hadad-rimmon Z12
Hadashah Jos15
Hadid Ez2; Ne7, 11
Hadrach Z9
Hakkephirim Ne6
Halah KS17ff; CF5
Hali Jos19
Halhul Jos15
Ham, lands of Ps78, 105ff
  villages of Nu32
Hamath SS8; KF8; KS14, 17ff, 24ff; CF18; CS8; Ps76; Is10ff, 36; Je39, 49; E47; Am6; Z9
Hammath Jos19
Hammon Jos19; CF6
 -dor Jos21
Hamonah E39
Hamon-gog, Valley of E39
Hananiah Ne3
Hanes Is30
Hannathon Jos19
Hapharaim Jos19
Hara CF5
Haradeh Nu33
Harim Ne7; Ez2
Harod SS23; CF11
Harosheth-of-the-Gentiles Ju4
Harran (Haran) Gen11f, 27; KS19; Is37; E27
Hashmonah Nu33
Hauran E47
Havilah Gen2, 25; SF1
Havvoth-jair Nu32; De3; Jos13; Ju10; CF2
Hazar-addar Nu34
Hazar-enan Nu34; E47
 -gaddah Jos15
 -hatticon E47
 -shual Jos15, 19; CF4; Ne11

APPENDIX **B** PLACE NAMES

Hazar-susah Jos19
  -susim CF4
Hazazon-tamar Gen14; CF20
Hazer Je49
Hazeroth Nu11, 33; De1
Hazor Jos11ff, 15, 19; Ju4; SF12; KF9; Ne11
  -hadattah Jos15
Hebron Gen13, 23, 37; Jos10ff, 20; Ju1, 16; SF30; SS2ff, 15; KF2; CF2ff, 11ff; CS11
Helam SS10
Helbah Ju1
Helbon E27
Heleph Jos19
Heliopolis (City of the Sun) Is19
Helkath Jos19, 21
Hena KS18ff; Is37
Hepher Jos12; KF4
Hephzi-bah (Jerusalem) Is62
Heres, Mount Ju1,8
Hermon, Mount De3; Jos11ff; CF5; Ps42, 89, 133; So4
Heshbon Nu21, 32; De1f, 29; Jos9, 12ff, 21; Ju11; CF6; Ne9; So7; Is15ff; Je48ff
Heshmon Jos15
Hethlon E47ff
Hezron Jos15
Hiddekel River (Tigris) D10
Hilen CF6
Hill of God SF10
Hinnom, Valley of Jos15; Ne11
  Valley of the Sons of CS33
Hittite country Jos1
  land Gen15
Hivite land Gen15
Hobah Gen14
Holon Jos15, 21; Je48
Hor, Mount Nu20, 23ff; De32
Horeb Ex3; CS5; Ps106; Ma4
  Mount Ex33; KF8, 19; De1, 18
Horem Jos19
Horesh SF23
Hor-haggidgad Nu33
Hormah Nu14, 21; De1; Jos12, 15, 19; Ju1; SF30; CF4
Horonaim Is15; Je48
Hosah Jos19
Hukok Jos19; CF6
Humtah Jos15
Hur Jos13
Hushah SS21; CF4, 20

552

APPENDIX B PLACE NAMES

Ibleam Jos17; Ju1; KS9, 15

Idalah Jos19

Idumea (Edom) Is34; E35

Ijon (Iyyon) SS24; KF15; KS15; CS16

Immer Ez2; Ne7

India Est1, 8

Ionia (Javan) E27

Ir-melach Jos15

Iron Jos15

Irpeel Jos18

Ir-shemesh Jos19

Israel Ex2ff, 9, 11f, 14ff, 37f, 32, 34, 39; Le4, 10, 16f, 20, 22, 25; Nu1, 3f, Nu7, 10f, 16, 18ff, 31f, 36; De1f, 4ff, 9f, 13, 17ff, 25ff, 29,31ff; Jos1, 3ff, 7ff, 13f,21ff; SF1ff; SS1ff; KF1ff; KS1ff; CF1ff; CS1ff; Ez1ff; Ne13; Ps22, 25, 41, 50, 53, 68ff, 71ff, 76, 78, 83, 89, 98, Ps105ff, 114ff, Ps118, 121ff, 125, 129ff, 135ff, 147; Pro1; Ec1; So3; Is1, 4ff, 7ff, 14, 17, 19, 21, 24, 27, 30ff, Is34, 40ff, 43ff, 52, 54, Is56ff, 60, 63; Je2ff, 5, 9ff, 12ff, 17ff, 23ff, 27ff, 34f, 37ff, 45ff, 48ff; La2; E4, 6ff, 17, 9ff, 25, 27ff, 33ff, 38ff, 43, 45, 47ff; D9;Ho1ff; Joe2ff; Am1ff; Ob1; Mi1ff, Mi5ff; Na2; Zp3; Z8ff, 12; Ma1, 4

Issachar Jos17; KF4; CS30; E48

Ithnan Jos15

Ittah-kazin Jos19

Ivvah KS18; Is37

Iye-abarim Nu21, 33

Iyim Nu33; Jos15

Iyyon (Ijon) SS24; KF15; KS15; CS16

Izalla E27

Jaar Ps132

Jabbok Nu21

  ford of the   Gen32

  Gorge De2; Jos12

  River Ju11

Jabesh SF31

  -gilead Ju21; SF11, 31; SS2; CF10

Jabez CF2

Jabneel Jos15, 19

Jabneh CS26

Jacob Mi3, 5; Na2

Jagur Jos15

Jahaz Nu21; De2; Jos13, 21; Ju11; Is15; Je48

Jahazah Je48

Jahzah CF6

Janim Jos15

Janoah Jos15; KS15

Japhia Jos19

Jarkon Jos19

Jarmuth Jos10, 12, 15, 21; Ne11

Jashub Jos17

Jattir Jos15, 21; SF30; CF6

Jaudi KS14

Javan (Ionia) Is66; E27

Jaw-bone Hill (Ramath-lehi) Ju15

Jazer Nu21, 32; Jos13, 21; SS24; CF6, 26; Is16; Je48

Jearim, Mount Jos15

Jebus (Jerusalem) Jos18; Ju19; CF11

Jebusite land Gen15

Jehoshaphat, Valley of Joe3

Jehovah-jireh Gen22

  -shalom Ju6

  -shammah E48

Jehud Jos19

Jericho Nu22, 33; Jos2, 6, 12, 16, 18, 24; SS10; KF16; KS2, 25; CF6, 19; CS28; Ez2; Ne3, 7; Je39, 52
  Valley of De34

Jeruel CS20

Jerusalem Jos10, 12, 14, 18; Ju1, 19; SS5, 10, 24; KF2ff, 9ff; KS9, 12, 18; KS22ff; CF3, 6, 8ff, 11, 19;
         CS1ff; Ez1ff; Ne1ff, 11ff; Est2; Ps51, Ps68, 79, 102, 116, 122, 125, 135, 137, 147; Ec1; So1,
         So3, 5ff, 8; Is1ff, 7, 10, 22, 14, 27ff, 30ff, 36ff, 40ff, 52, 59ff, 62ff; Je1ff, 9, 11, Je13ff, 17ff,
         23ff, 27, 29, 32ff, 39ff, 42, 44, 51ff; La1f, 4; E4ff, 8,E11ff, 21ff, 26, 33, 36; D1, 5ff, 9;
         Joe2ff; Am1ff; Ob1; Mi1, 3ff; Zp1, 3; Z1ff, 7ff, 12ff; Ma2ff

Jeshanah SF7; CS13

Jeshimon Nu23; SF23, 26

Jeshua Ne11

Jetur CF5

Jezreel Jos15, 19; SF25ff; SS2ff; KF4, 18ff; KS8ff; CF3; CS22
  Vale of Jos17; Ju6; Ho1

Jiphtah Jos15

  -el, Valley of Jos19

Jithlah Jos19

Jogbehah Nu32; Ju8

Jokdeam Jos15

Jokmeam KF4; CF6

Joknean Jos19, 21

  -in-Carmel Jos12

Joktheel Jos15; KS14

Joppa Jos19; CS2; Ez3; Jon1
  Sea of Ez3

Jordan CF6; Je12, 49; E47; Z11
  fords of the Jos2; Ju3,7,12
  mouth of the Jos15

Jordan, Plain of Gen13; De3; SS18; KF7
  River Gen50; Nu22, 32ff; De9, 27; Jos1, 13, 16, 19, 22; Ju11; SS2,16, SS19, 24; KF2, 17; KS2, 5ff, 10;
         CF12, 19; Ps114; Je12, 50
  Spring of Ps42

Jordan, Vale of SF31
Joseph, district of KF11
  land of Z10
Jotbah KS21
Jotbathah Nu33; De10
Judah De34; Ru1; SS2ff, 24; KF12, 19ff; KS1ff; CF2ff; CS10ff; Ez1ff; Ne1ff, 11; Est2; Ps60, 68ff, 76,
        97, 108, 114; Pro25; Is1ff, 5, 7ff, 19, 22, Is25, 28, 36, 40; Je1ff, 7, 9, 11, 13ff, Je17ff, 26ff,
        30ff, 36ff, 42, 44ff, Je49ff; La1ff, 5; E4, 8ff, 21, 26ff, 48; D1, 5, 9; Ho1, 4ff, 12; Joe3;
        Am1ff, 7; Ob1; Mi1, 5ff; Zp1, 2; Hg1ff; Z1ff, 8ff, 12, 14; Ma2ff
  country of Jos11, 20
  land of SF22, 30
  wilderness of Ju1, 15
Juttah Jos15, 21
Kabzeel Jos15; CF11
Kadesh Gen14; Nu20, 33; Ju11; SS24; Ps29
  -barnea Nu32, 34; De1, 9; Jos14ff
  River E47
Kadmonite land Gen15
Kambul Je51
Kamon Ju10
Kanah Jos19
  Gorge of Jos16ff
Kanneh E27
Karka Jos15
Karkor Ju8
Karnaim Am6
Kartah Jos21
Kartan Jos21
Kattah Jos19
Kebar (Chebar), River E1, 3, 10, 43
Kedar Ps120; So1; Is21, 42, 60; Je2, 49
Kedemoth De2; Jos13, 21; CF6
Kedesh Jos12, 15, 19ff; KS15; CF6
Kehelathah Nu33
Keilah Jos15; SF23; Ne3
Kekabzeel Ne11
Kemosh (Chemosh) Je48
Kenath CF2
  villages of Nu32
Kenite land Gen15; Nu24
Kenizzite land Gen15
Kephar-ammoni Jos18
Kephirah Jos9, 18; Ez2
Kereth Zp2
Kerioth Am2
  -hezron Jos15

APPENDIX **B** PLACE NAMES

Kerith, Ravine of   KF17

Kerub (Cherub)   Ez2; Ne7

Kesalon   Jos15

Kesil   Jos15

Kesulloth (Cheshulloth)   Jos19

Kibroth-hattaavah   Nu11, 33; De9

Kibzaim   Jos21

Kidon   CF13

Kidron Brook   KF15

  Gorge   SS15; KF15; KS23; CS15. 29ff

  River   KF2, 15; KS23; Je31

Kinah   Jos15

King's Pool   Ne2

  Valley   Gen14

Kinnereth (Chinneroth)   Nu34; De3; Jos11, 19; KF15

  Sea of   Jos12ff

Kir   KS16; Is15; Am1, 9

  -hareseth   Is16

  -heres   Je48

Kiriath (Kirjath-arba)   Gen23; Jos14ff, 20; Ju1; Ne11

  -baal   Jos15, 18

  -huzoth   Nu22

  -jearim   Jos9, 15, 18; Ju18; SF7; CF2, 13; CS1; Ez2; Ne7; Je26

  -sannah   Jos15

  -sepher   Jos15; Ju1

Kiriathaim (Kirjathaim)   Nu32; Jos13; CF6; Je48; E25

Kirioth (Kerioth)   Je48

Kishion   Jos19

Kishon   Jos21; KF18

  River   Ju4ff

  Torrent of   Ps83

Kisloth (Chisloth) -tabor   Jos19

Kithlish   Jos15

Kitron   Ju1

Kittim (Chittim)   Nu24; Is23; Je2; E27

Koa   E23

Kozeba   CF4

Kun (Chun)   CF18

Laban   De1

Lachish   Jos10, 12, 15; KS14, 18; CS11, 25, 32; Ne11; Is36; Mi1

Lahir   KS19; Is37

Lahmas   Jos15

Laish   Ju18; Is10

Lakkum   Jos19

Lasha   Gen10

Lebanon De1, 11; Jos1, 9; KF5, 9; KS19; CF5; CS8; Ez3; Ps29, 72, 92, Ps104; So3ff, 7; Is2, 10, 29, 33, 35, 37, 40, 60; Je18, 22; E17, 27, E31; Ho14; Na1; H2; Z10ff

Mount Ju3

Vale of Jos11f

Lebaoth Jos15

Lebo-hamath Nu13, 34; Jos13; Ju3; KS14; CF13; E47; Am6

Lebonah Ju21

Lecah CF4

Lehi Ju15; SS23

Hollow of Ju15

Leshem Jos19

Levi E48

Libnah Nu33; Jos12, 15, 21; KS8, 19, 23; CF6; Is37ff

Swamp of Jos19

Libya E30, 38; Na3

Lod CF8; Ez2; Ne7, 11

Lo-debar Jos13; SS9, 17; Am6

Lower Beth-horon KF9

Pool Is22

Lower Town of Jerusalem (Maktesh) Zp1

Lubim (Libya) Na3

Lud (Lydia) Is66; E27, 30

Luhith Is15; Je48

Luz Gen28; Jos16, 18; Ju1

Lydia (Lud) Is66; E27, 30

Maacah SS10; CF19

Maarath Jos15

Machbenah CF2

Machir Ju5

Machpelah Gen23, 25, 50

Madmannah Jos15; CF2

Madmen Je48

Madmenah Is10

Madon Jos11ff

Magbish Ez2

Magog E38ff

Mahanaim Gen32; Jos13, 21; SS2, 17, 19; KF2, 4; CF6

Mahaneh-dan Ju13, 18

Makaz KF4

Makheloth Nu33

Makkedah Jos10, 12, 15

Maktesh (Lower Town of Jerusalem) Z91

Mamre Gen13, 23

Manach Jos15

Manahath CF8

Manasseh CS15, 30, 34; Ps60, 108; E48

Manasseh, land of KS10
  territory of De34
Maon Jos15
  wilderness of SF23ff
Marah Ex15; Nu33
Maralah Jos19
Mareshah Jos15; CF4; CS11, 14, 20; Mi1
Maroth Mi1
Mashal CF6
Masrekah Gen36; CF1
Massa Pro30f
Massah De6, 9; Ps95
Mecherah CF11
Meconah Ne11
Medeba Nu21; Jos13; CF19; Is15
Medes, City of the KS17
Media KS17ff; Is21; Est1; E27; D8
  Province of Ez6
Mediterranean Jos9; Ps80, 89; E47ff
  Vale of CS35; Z12
Megiddo Jos12, 17; Ju1; KF4, 9; KS9; CF7
Mehalbeh Jos19
Meholah SS21
Meholoah SF18
Memphis Ho9
Mephaath Jos13, 21; CF6; Je48
Merathaim Je50
Meribah Nu20
  -by-kadesh De32; E47ff
  Waters of Ps81, 95, 106
Merom, Waters of Jos11
Mesha Gen10
Meshech Ps120; E27, 32, 38f
Meshek Is66
Mesopotamia Ju3
Metheg-ha-ammah SS8
Me-zahab Gen36; CF1
Michmas Ez2; N7
Michmash Ne11; Is10
  Pass of SF13ff
Michmethah Jos16ff
Middin Jos15
Midian Ex2, 4; Nu22; Jos13; KF11; Is9, 60; H3
Migdal-eder Gen35
  -el Jos19

Migdal-gad Jos15
Migdol Ex14; Nu33; Je44, 46; E29ff
Migron SF14; Is10
Millo SS5
Minni Je51
Minnith Ju11; E27
Misgab Je48
Mishal Jos19, 21
Misrephoth Jos11, 13
Mizar, Hill of Ps42f
Mizpah Jos11, 18; Ju10, 21; SF4, 7; KF15; CS16; Ne3; Je40ff; Ho5
  Vale of Jos11
Mizpeh Jos15; Ju11; SF22
Moab Nu21ff, 33; De1ff, 34; Jos24; Ju11; SF12, 22; SS8, 23; KS3; CF11, 18; Ne13; Ps60, 108; Is11,
        15ff, 25; Je9, 25, 27, 40, 48; E25; D11; Am2; Mi6; Zp2
Moabite country CF1, 8; Ru1
Moithcah Nu33
Moladah Jos15,19; CF4; Ne11
Moreh Gen12, 22
Moreh, Hill of Ju7
Moresheth Je26; Mi1
 -gath Mi1
Moriah, Mount CS3
Moseroth Nu33; De10
Mount of Olives (Mount Olivet) SS15; KS23
Mozah Jos18
Naamah Jos15; Job2
Naaran CF7
Naarath Jos16
Nahalal Jos19, 21; Nu21
Nahalol Ju1
Naioth SF19
Naphtali De34; Jos20; Ju4; KF4,15; KS15;CS16, 34; Ps68; Is9; E48
Neah Jos19
Nebaioth Is60
Neballat Ne11
Nebo Nu32ff; CF5; Ez2; Ne7; Is15; Je48
  Mount De32, 34
Negeb Gen12f, 20; Nu13, 33; De1, 34; Jos11, 15; Ju1; SF27ff; SS24; CS28; Je13, 17, 32ff; E20ff, 47f;
        Ob1; Z7
Neiel Jos19
Nephish CF5
Nephtoah River Jos15
 springs of Jos18
Netaim CF4

Netophah SS23; KS25; Ez2; Ne7; Je40

Nezib Jos15

Nibshan Jos15

Nile River Ex1ff; Is18ff, 63; Je46; E29ff, 32; Am8ff; Na3; Z10

Nimrah Nu32

Nimrim Je48

  Waters of Is15

Nineveh Gen10; KS19; Is37; Jon1, 3f; Na1ff; Zp2

No Je46; E30; Na3

 -ammon Na3

Nob SF21ff; Ne11; Is10

Nobah Nu32; Ju8

Nod Gen4

Nodab CF5

Nohah Ju20

Noph Is19; Je2, 44, 46; E30

Nubia Job31; Ps68; Pro20; Is43

Oboth Nu21, 33

Og, Kingdom of Nu32; De1

Old Pool Is22

Olives (Olivet) Mount of SS15; Z14

On E30

Ono CF8; Ez2; Ne6ff,11

  Plain of Ne6

Ophel CS27, 33; Ne3, 11

  Wall of Ne3

Ophir (Uphaz) KF9, 22; CF29; CS8; Job28; Ps45; Is13; Je10; D10

Ophni Jos18

Ophrah Jos18; Ju8ff; SF13

  of the Abiezrites Ju6

Oreb, Rock of Ju7; Is10

Outbreak-on-Uzza (Perez-uzza) SS6; CF13

Paddan-aram Gen25, 28

Pai CF1

Palestina (Palestine) Is14; Joe3

Pannag E27

Parah Jos18

Paran Gen21; De1; KF11

  Mount De33; H3

  wilderness of Nu10, 12; SF25

Parvaim CS3

Pas-dammin SS23; CF11

Pathros Ps68; Is11; Je44; E29ff

Pau Gen36

Pekod Je50; E23

Peniel Gen32

Penuel Ju8; KF12
Peor Jos15; Ps106
  Mount Nu23
Perath Je13
Perazim, Mount Is28
Perez-uzzah (uzza) Gen15
Perizzite land Gen15
Persia (Pharas) CS36; Ez1, 3ff; Ne12; Est1; E27; D8, 10
Pethah-tikvah (Gate of Hope) Ho2
Pethor Nu22; De23
Pharas (Persia) E27, 38ff
Philistia KF4; Ps60, 83, 108; Is14; Je47; Joe3
Philistine country KS8, 18
Pi-beseth E30
  -hahiroth Ex14; Nu33
Pirathon Ju12; SS23; CF11
Pisgah, Mount Nu21ff; De34
  springs of De3, 4
  watershed De3, 4; Jos12ff
Pishon River Gen2
Pithom Ex1
Plain, Sea of the KS14
Pool, Lower Is22
  Upper Is36
Punon Nu33
Put (Pul) Is66; Je46; E27, 30, 38f; Na3
Raamah E27
Rabbah (Rabbath) De3; Jos13, 15; SS11, 17; CF20; E21, 25; Am1
Rabbath Ammon Je49
Rabbith Jos19
Rachal SF30
Rakkah Jos19
Ramah Jos18ff; Ju4, 19; SF1, 7, 15ff, 25; KF15; CF27; CS16; Ez2; Ne7, 11; Is10; Je31, 40; Ho5
Ramathaim SF1
Ramath-lehi Ju15
  -negeb Jos19
Rameses Ex1, 13; Nu33
  land Gen47
Ramoth De4; Jos20ff; CF6
  -gilead KF4, 22; KS8ff; CS18, 22
  -mizpeh Jos13
  -negeb SF30
Reba Jos13
Rechah CF4
Red Sea (Sea of Reeds) Nu33; De1; Jos2, 24; KF9; Ne9; Ps106, 136; Je49
Reheboth Gen26, 36

APPENDIX **B** PLACE NAMES

Rekem Jos13, 18
Remeth Jos19
Rephaim Gen15; SS5, 23
  Vale of Jos15, 18; CF11, 14; Is17
Rephidim Ex17; Nu33
Reuben, land of KS10; E48
Rezeph KS19; Is37
Rhodes E27
Riblah Nu34; KS24ff; Je39, 52; E6
Rimmon Jos15, 19, 21; CF4, 6; Is10; Z14
  -Parez Nu33
  Rock of Ju20
Rissah Nu33
Rithmah Nu33
Rogelim SS17, 19
Rosen Gen10
Rosh Is66; E38ff
Sahmir Jos15
Salcah De3; Jos12; CF5
Salem Ps76
Salt, Valley of CS25
Samaria KF13, 16, 20ff; KS1ff; CS18, 25, 28; Is7ff, 36ff; Je23, 31, 41; E16; Ho7f, 10, 13; Am3ff, 6, 8;
       Ob1; Mi1
  Hill of KF16
Sansannah Jos15
Saphir Mi1
Sarid Jos19
Sea, The (Dead Sea) E39
Seba Ps72; Is43
Sebam Nu32
Secacah Jos15
Secu SF19
Seir Gen14, 32f, 36; Nu24; De1, 33; Jos11, 24; CS20ff, 25; Is21; E25, 35
  hill country of CF4
  Mount Jos15
Seirah Ju3
Sela Ju1; KS14; Is16, 42
  -hammalekoth SF23
Senaah Ez2; Ne7
Seneh, Rock of SF14
Senir CF5; E27
Senir, Mount De3; So4
Sephar Gen10
Sepharad Ob1
Sepharvaim KS17ff; Is36ff
Shaalabin Jos19

APPENDIX **B** PLACE NAMES

Shaalbim Ju1; KF4
Shaalbon SS23; CF11
Shaalim SF9
Shaaraim Jos15; CF4
Shaarim SF17
Shadud Jos19
Shahazumah Jos19
Shalisha SF9
Shamir Ju10
Shapher, Mount Nu33
Sharon CF5, 27; So2; Is33,35
Sharuhen Jos19
Shaveh Gen14
 -kiriathaim Gen14
Shear-jashub Is7
Sheba KF10; Jos19; Job6; Ps72; Is60; Je6; E27, 38
Shebarim Jos7
Shechem Gen12, 33; Jos17, 20, 24; Ju9, 21; KF12; CF6ff; CS10; Ps60, 108; Je41; Ho6
Shelah, Pool of Ne3
Shema Jos15
Shemaiah CS11
Shepham Nu34
Shephelah De1; Jos9, 11f, 15; Ju1; KF10; CF27; CS1, 9, 26, 28; Je17, 32ff; Ob1; Z7
Shephem CF27
Sheshak (Babylon) Je25, 51
Shigionoth H3
Shihor (Sihor) Jos13; CF13; Is23; Je2
Shikkeron Jos15
Shilhim Jos15
Shiloah River Is8
Shiloh Jos18ff; Ju21; SF1ff; KF2, 11, 14; CS7, 10; Ps78; Je7, 26, 41
Shimron Jos11, 19
 -meron Jos12
Shinar Gen10f; Jos7; Is11; D1; Z5
Shining Rock (Bozez) SF14
Shion Jos19
Shittim Nu25; Jos2ff; Mi6
 Gorge of Joe3
Shoa E23
Shochoh SF17
Shuah Job2
Shual SF13
Shunem Jos19; SF28; KS4
Shur Gen16, 25; Ex15; SF15, 27
Shushan (Susa) Ez4; Ne1; Est1ff; D8
Sibmah Nu32; Jos13; Is16; Je48

Sibraim E47
Siddim Gen14
Sidon (Zidon) Ju1, 18; SS24; KF16ff; CF22; Is23; Je25, 27, 47; E27ff; Joe3; Z9
  Greater Jos11, 19
Sihon Ne9; Je48
  kingdom of Nu32; Jos13
Sihor (Shihor) Jos13; CF13; Is23; Je2
Silla KS12
Simeon CS15, 34; E48
Simmagir Je39
Sin Ex16; Ne9; Ps68
Sinai Ex16, 19; De33
  Mount Ex19; Ne9; Ps68
  wilderness of N1ff, 9, 33
Sinim Is49
Siphmoth SF30
Sirah SS3
Sirion, Mount De3
Sitnah Gen26
So KS17
Soco CF4; CS4, 11, 28
Socoh Jos15; SF17; KF4
Sodom Gen13f, 18f; De29; Is1ff, 13; Je23, 49ff; La4; E16; Am4; Zp2
Sorek, Valley of Ju16
Sores Jos15
Succoth Gen33; Ex13; Nu33; Jos13; Ju8; KF7, 20
  Valley of Ps60, 108
Suhar E27
Suph De1
Suphah Nu21
Susa (Shushan) Ez4; Ne1; Est1ff; D8
Syene Is49; E29ff
Syria Job39; Is7, 17; Ho12; Am1
Syrtes Ho9
Taanach Jos12, 17, 21; Ju1; KF4; CF7
Taanath-shiloh Jos16
Tabbath Ju7
Taberah Nu11; De9
Tabor Jos19; SF10; CF6; Ps89; Je46
  Mount Ju4; Ho5
Tadmor CS8
Tahath Nu33
Tahpanhes (Tahapanes) (Tehaphnehes) Je2, 43f, 46; E30
Tamar KF9; E47ff
Tappuah Jos12, 15, 17; KS15
Tarah Nu33

APPENDIX B PLACE NAMES

Taralah Jos18
Tarshish CS20; Ps48, 72; Is2, 23, 60, 66; Je10; E27, 38; Jon1, 4
Tatam Jos15
Tehaphnehes (Tahapanes) (Tahpanhes) Je2, 43f, 46; E30
Tekoa Jos15; SS23; CF2, 4, 27; CS11, 20; Ne3; Je6; Am1
Tekoah SS14
Tel-abib E3
Telaim SF15, 27
Telassar KS19; Is37
Telem Jos15
Tel-harsha Ez2; Ne7
 -melah Ez2; Ne7
Tema Job6; Is21; Je25
Teman Gen36; Jos12; CF1; Job2; Je49; E25; Am1; Ob1; H3
Tharshish KF22
Thebez Ju9
Tibhath CF18
Tigris, River Gen2; D10
Timnah Jos15, 19; CS28
Timnath Gen38; Ju14
 -serah Jos19, 24
Tiphsah KF4
Tirza KF16
Tirzah Jos12; KF14; KS15; So6
Tishbe KF17
Tob Ju11; SS10
Tochen CF4
Togarmah E27, 38
Tolad CF4
Tophel De1
Topheth (Tophet) KS23; Je7, 19
Torrent of Egypt Nu34; Jos15; KF8; KS24; Is27
Transjordan De1, 4
Tubal Is66; E27, 32, 38ff
Tyre (Tyrus) Jos19; SS5, 24; KF5, 7, 9; CF22; CS2ff; Ps45, 83; Is23;Je25,27,47; E26ff; Ho9; Joe3;
         Am1; Z9
Ulai, Stream of D8
Ummah Jos19
Uphaz (Ophir) Je10; D10
Upper Pool Is36
Ur Gen11; Ne9
Uz Job1; Je25; La4
Uzza KS21
Uzzah SS6
  Outbreak on SS6; CF13
Uzzen-sherah CF7

Vaheb, Waterhole of Nu21
Vale of Achor Jos7,15;Is65; Ho2
  Aijalon Jos10
  Aven Am1
  Elah SF17, 21
  Gibeon Is28
  Jezreel Jos17; Ju6; Ho1
  Jordan SF31
  Lebanon Jos11f
  Megiddo CS35; Z12
  Mizpah Jos11
  Palm Trees De34; Ju1, 3; CS28
  Rephaim Jos15,18; CF11, 14; Is17
  Trouble (Emek-chor) Ho2
Valley of Abarim E39
  Ben-hinnom Jos15, 18; KS23; CS28, 33; Je7, 19, 32
Valley of Berakah CS20
  Craftsmen (Ge-harashim) CF4
  Blessing (Berakah) CS20
  Ge-harashim CF4
  Gog's Horde (Hamon-gog) E39
  Hinnom Jos15; Ne11
  Jehoshaphat Joe3
  Jericho De34
  Jiphtah-el Jos19
  Salt SS8; KS14; CF18; CS25
  Sorek Ju16
  Succoth Ps60, 108
  the King's Pool Gen14
  the Sons of Hinnom CS33
  Zeboim SF13
Watchers, Field of the Nu23
Waterhole of Beer Nu21
 of Vaheb Nu21
Western Sea De34; Ps139
Yaan SS24
Zaanaim Ju4
Zaanan Mi1
Zair KS8
Zalmon Ps68
  Mount Ju9
Zalmonah Nu33
Zamri Je25
Zanoah Jos15; CF4; Ne3, 11
Zaphon Jos13
Zared, Gorge of Nu21; De2

Zarephath KF17; Ob1
Zarethan KF4
Zartanah KF4
Zeboim Ne11
  Valley of SF13
Zeboyim Gen14; De29
Zebulon Jos19
Zebulun Jos19; CS30; Ps68; Is9; E48
  land of Ju12
Zedad Nu34; E47
Zela Jos18; SS21
Zelzah SF10
Zemaraim Jos18
Zenan Jos15
Zephath Ju1
Zephathah CS14
Zer Jos19
Zered, Brook of De2
Zeredah KF11; CS4
Zererah Ju7
Zereth-shahar Jos13
Ziddim Jos19
Zidon (Sidon) Ez3; Is23; Je25, 27, 47; E27ff; Joe3; Z9
Ziklag Jos15, 19; SF27ff; SS1ff; CF4, 12; Ne11
Zin Nu13, 27, 33ff; Jos15
  wilderness of De32
Zion SS5; KF8; CF11; CS5; Ps2, 9, 14, 20, 50f, Ps53, 65, 69, 84, 87, 97, 99, 102, 110, 132ss, 137, 146f,
        149; So3; Is1ff, 10, 12, 14, 16, 28, 30, 33, 35, 40, 46, 49, 51ff, 59ff, 64, Is66; Je3f, 6, 8ff, 14,
        Je25, 30ff, 50ff; La1f, 4ff; Joe2ff; Am1, 6; Mi1, 3ff; Zp3; Z1ff, 8f
  Mount Ps48, 74, 76, 78, 125f, 128ff; Is8, 10, 18, 24, 29, 31, 37; La5; Ob1; Mi4
Zior Jos15
Ziph Jos15; CF2; CS11
  wilderness of SF23, 26
Ziphron Nu34
Ziz CS20
Zoan Nu13; Ps78; E30
Zoar Gen13f, 19; De34; Is15, 19, 30; Je48
Zobah SF14; SS8, 10, 23; KF11; CF11, 18
Zobath-hamath CF18
Zoheleth, Stone of KF1
Zorah Jos15, 19; Ju13, 18; CS11; Ne11
Zuph SF9
Zur Jos13

NEW TESTAMENT

Abilene L3Achaia A18f; PR15f; PCF16; PCS1, 11; ThF1

Adramyttium A27

Adria, Sea of A27

Aenon J3

Akeldama (Blood Acre) (Potter's Field) Mw27; A1

Alexandria A18, 28

Amphipolis A17

Antioch A6, 11, 13f, 18, 23; PG2; PTS3

Apollonia A17

Appii Forum A28

Arabia PG1, 4

Arimathaea Mw27; Mk15; L23; J19

Armageddon Rev16

Asia, Province of A2, 6, 16, 19ff, 24, 27; PR16; PCF16; PCS1; PTS1; LPF1

Assos A20

Athens A17f; ThF3, 5; ThS3

Attalia A14

Azotus A8

Babylon Mw1; A7; LPF5; Rev14, 16ff

Beroea (Berea) A17, 20

Bethabara (Bethany) J1

Bethany Mw21, 26; Mk11, 14; L19, 24; J1, 11f

Bethesda J5

Bethlehem Mw2; L2; J7

Bethphage Mw21; Mk11; L19

Bethsaida Mw11; Mk6, 8; L9f; J1, 12

Bithynia A16; LPF1

Blood Acre (Akeldema) (Potter's Field) Mw27; A1

Caesarea A8ff, 18, 21, 23, 25

  Philippi Mw16; Mk8

Calvary L23

Cana-in-Galilee J2, 21

Canaan (Chanaan) Mw15; A7, 13

Capernaum Mw4, 8, 11, 17; Mk1f, 9; L4, 7, 10; J2, 4, 6

Cappadocia A2; LPF1

Cauda (Clauda) A27

Cedron (Kedron) J18

Cenchreae (Cenchrea) PR16

Chanaan (Canaan) Mw15; A7, 13

Charran (Harran) A7

Chios A20

Chorazin Mw11; L10

Cilicia A6, 15, 21, 27; PG1

City of David (Bethlehem) L2

Clauda (Cauda) A27

Cnidus A27

Colossae (Colesse) PCo1

Corinth A18f; PCF1, 4, 16; PCS1, 6, 9f; PTS4

Cos (Coos) A21

Crete A27; TF1

Cyprus A4, 11, 13, 15, 21, 27

Cyrene Mw27; Mk15; L23; A2, 11, 13

Dalmanutha Mk8

Dalmatia PTS4

Damascus A9, 22, 26; PCS11; PG1

Decapolis (Ten Towns) Mw4; Mk5, 7

Derbe A14, 16, 20

Egypt Mw2; A2, 7, 13; Rev11; LH3, 11; LJu1

Emmaus L24

Ephesus A18ff; PCF15f; PE1; PTF1; PTS1, 4; Rev1f

Ephraim J11

Ethiopia A8

Euphrates, River Rev9, 16

Fair Havens A27

Field of Blood A1

Gabbatha (The Pavement) J19

Gadarenes, country of Mw8

Galatia (Gallia) (Gaul) A16, 18; PCF16; PG1; PTS4; LPF1

Galilee Mw2ff, 17, 19, 21, 26ff; Mk1, 3, 6, 9, 14ff; L1ff, 8, 13, 17, 23ff; J1, 4, 6f, 12; A1, 9f, 13

Gallia (Galatia) (Gaul) A16, 18; PCF16; PG1; PTS4; LPF1

Gaza A8

Gennesaret Mw14; Mk6; L5

Gergesenes, country of Mw8

Gethsemane Mw26; Mk14

Golgotha (Place of the Skull) Mw27; Mk15; A23; J19

Gomorrah (Gomorrha) Mw10; Mk6; PR9; LPS2; LJu1

Greece A20

Harran (Charran) A7

Hierapolis PCo4

Iconium A13f, 16; PTS3

Idumaea Mk3

Illyrium PR15

Israel Mw2, 8ff, 15, 19; L1f, 4, 7, 22, 24; J1, 3; A1ff, 9, 13, 26, 28; PR9ff; PG6; PE2; PPs3; LH8; LPS2; Rev7, 21

Italy A18, 27

Ituraea L3

Jairus Mk5

APPENDIX **B** PLACE NAMES

Jericho Mw20; Mk10, 18f; LH11

Jerusalem Mw2ff, 15f, 20f, 23; Mk1, 3, 7, 10f, 15; L2, 4ff, 9f, 13, 17ff, 21, L23f; J1ff, 10ff;A1f, 4ff, 8ff, 15f, 18ff, 25f, 28; PR15; PG1f, 4; PCF16; LH12; Rev3, 21

Joppa A9f

Jordan Mw3, 19; Mk1; Ls7; J1, 3, 10

Judaea (Judea) (land of Judah) (Juda) Mw2ff, 19, 24; Mk1, 3, 10, 13;L1ff, 21, 23; J3f, 7, 11; A1f, 8f, A11f,15, 21, 26, 28; PR15; PCS1; PG1; ThF2; LH8

Kedron (Cedron), Ravine of J18

Laodicea PC02, 4; PTF6; Rev1, 3

Lasea A27

Libya A2

Lycaonia A14

Lycia A27

Lydda A9

Lystra A14, 16; PTS3

Macedonia A16, 18ff; PR15; PCF16; PCS1f, 7ff, 11; PPs4; ThF1, 4; PTF1;

Madian (land of Midian) A7

Magadan (Magdala) (Magedan) Mw15, 27f; Mk8, 15; L8; J19f

Malta (Melita) A28

Mesopotamia A2, 7

Miletus (Miletum) A20; PTS4

Mitylene A20

Mount of Olives (Olivet) Mw21, 24, 26; Mk11, 13f; L19, 21f; J8; A1

Myra A21, 27

Mysia A16

Nain L7

Naphtali (Nephthalim) Mw4

Nazareth Mw2, 4, 21; Mk1, 10, 14, 16; L1f, 4, 18, 24; J1, 18f;A2ff, 6, 10, 22, 26

Neapolis A16

Nephthalim (Naphtali) Mw4

Nicopolis Tt3

Nineveh Mw12; L11

Olives (Olivet), Mount of Mw21, 24, 26; Mk11, 13f; L19, 21f; J8; A1

Onesiphorus PTS4

Pamphylia A2, 13ff, 27

Paphos A13

Patara A21

Patmos Rev1

Pavement, The (Gabbatha) J19

Perga A13f

Pergamum (Pergamos) Rev1f

Phenice (Phoenicia) (Phoenix) A11, 15, 21, 27

Philadelphia Rev1, 3

Philippi A16, 20; PCS13; PPs1; ThF2

Phoenicia (Phenice) (Phoenix) A11, 15, 21, 27

Phrygia A2, 16, 18; PTF6

APPENDIX **B** PLACE NAMES

Pisidia A13f

Place of the Skull (Golgotha) Mw27;Mk15; L23; J19

Pontus A2, 18; LPF1

Potter's Field (Blood Acre) (Alkeldama) Mw27;A1

Ptolemais A21

Puteoli A28

Rama Mw2

Red Sea A7; PCF10; LH11

Rhegium A28

Rhodes A21

Rome A2, 18f, 23, 28; PR1; PE6; PPs4; PTS1, 4

Salamis A13

Salem LH7

Salim J3

Salmone A27

Samaria A1, 8f, 15; L17; J4

Samos A20

Samothrace (Samothracia) A16

Sardis Rev, 3

Sarepta L4

Seleucia A13

Sharon A9

Shechem (Sychem) A7

Sheep-pool (Bethesda) J5

Sidon Mw11, 15; Mk3, 7; L4, 6, 10; A12, 27

Siloam L13; J9

Sinai (Sina), Mount A7; PG4; LH12

Sion (Zion), Mount PR9, 11; LH12; LPF2; Rev14

Skull, Place of the (Golgotha) Mw27;Mk15; L23; J19

Smyrna Rev1f

Sodom (Sodoma) Mw10f; Mk6; L10, 17; PR9; LPS2; LJu1; Rev11

Spain PR15

Sychar J4

Sychem (Shechem) A7

Syracuse A28

Syria Mw4; Mk7; L2; A15, 18, 20f; PG1

Syrtis A27

Tarsus A9, 11, 22

Ten Towns (Decapolis) Mw4; Mk5, 7

Thessalonica A17, 27; PPs4; ThF1ff; PTS4

Three Taverns (Tres Tabernae) A28

Thyatira A16; Rev1f

Tiberius, Sea of J6, 21

Trachonitis L3

Transjordan Mw4; Mk3, 10

OLD TESTAMENT

Aaronite Ne10, 12; CF27; CS13, 26

Abiezrite Ju6

Adullamite Gen38

Agagite Est3

Ahohite SS23; CF27

Amalekite Ex17; Nu13; De25;
    Ju1, 3, 6ff, 10; SF14f, 27ff; SS1; CF4

Ammonite Nu21; De2, 23; Ju3, 10; SF11ff; SS8ff, 17, 23; KF11; KS24; CF11, 18ff; CS20ff, 24, 26ff;
    Ez9; Ne2, 4, 13; Je25, 40ff, 49; E21, 25; D11; Am1

Amorite Gen10; Ex3; Nu13, 22; De1ff, 7, 20; Jos3, 5ff, 9, 12, 24; Ju1, 3, 6; SF7; SS21; KF4, 9, 21;
    KS21; CF1; CS8; Ez9; Ne9; Is17; E16; Am2

Anakim Jos11, 14ff

Anamite Gen10; CF1

Apharsathchite Ex4

Apharsite Ez4

Arab (Arabian) CS17, 21, 26; Ne2ff, 6; Is13, 21; Je3, 49; E30

Aramaean Ju18;SS8,10;KF20, 22; KS5ff, 24; CF7, 18; CS1, 18, 22, 24,28; Is7, 9; Je35; Am9

Aramite Ju10

Arbathite SS23

Arbite SS23

Archevite Ez4

Archite Jos16; SS15ff; CF27

Arkite Gen10; CF1

Arvadite Gen10; CF1

Ashdodite Ne4

Asherite Nu7; Jos19, 21; SS2; CF6; CS30

Ashurite E27

Assyrian Is10, 14, 43, 52; E16, 23, 31; La5; Ho11;Mi5

Avvim De2; Joe13

Avite KS17; CF17

Babylonian Ez4; Je32; E23

Barhumite SS23

Bashanite Nu21

Beerothite SS4, 23

Benjamite Nu7; Jos18, 21; Ju3, 10, 19ff; SF9, 13, 22; SS2ff,16, 19ff; KF2, 12, 15; CF6, 9, 12, 21, 27;
    CS11, 15, 17, 25; Ne11; Est2; Ps68, Je37

Buzite Job32

Calebite SF25, 30

Canaanite Gen12f; Ex3; Nu13, 21; De7, 20; Jos3, 5ff, 9, 12ff; Ju1, 3; SS24; Ez9; Ne9; Ob1; Z14

APPENDIX **C** RACES AND TRIBES

Caphtorite Gen10; De2; CF1

Carite KS11

Carmelite SS23

Casluhite Gen10; CF1

Chaldean (Chaldee) Gen11; KS24ff; CS36; Ez5; Ne9; Job1; Is13, 23, 43, 47ff; Je21f, 24, 32, 35, 37ff, 43, Je50ff; E1,12,23; D1ff, 9; H1

Chemarim Zp1

Cherethite (Cherethim) (Kerethite) SF30; SS15; KF1; E25; Zp2

Cushite SS18; CS12, 14, 16, 21; Je38ff, 46; D11; Am9; Zp2

Cuthite KS17

Danite Nu7; Jos19, 21; Ju1, 13, 18; CF27; CS2

Dedanim Is21

Dehavite Ez4

Dinaite Ez4

Edomite De23; SF14, 21; SS8; KF11; KS8, 14, 16; CF18; CS21, 25, 28; Is43

Egyptian Ex2; Ju10; SF4, 30; SS23; CF11; Ez9; Is10, 19ff; Je46; E16, 29; La5

Elamite Ez4

Elkoshite Na1

Ephraimite Nu7; Jos16f, 21; Ju8, 10ff; SF1; CF9, 27; CS28; Ps78; Is7;Ho13

Ephrathite SF17; KF11; Ru1

Esau, descendants of De21

Eshtaulite CF

Ethiopian CS12; Ps72; Is20; Je13, 38ff, 46; E30; D11; Zp2

Ezrahite KF4

Gabalite KF5

Gadite Nu7; De4, 29; Jos1ff, 12ff, 21ff; SS23; CF5ff, 12, 26

Garmite CF4

Gebalite Jos13

Gederite CF27

Gentile (non-Israelite) Je46

Gershonite Nu7; Jos21; CF26, 29

Geshurite Jos12ff; SF27

giants, race of Gen6; Nu13; De3; Jos12; SS21; CF20; Ez2

Gibeathite CF12

Gibeonite SS21; CF12; Ne3

Gileadite Ju10, 12; SS17ff; KS15; Ne7

Gilonite SS15, 23

Girgashite Gen10; De7; Jos3; CF1; Ne9

Gittite SS6, 15ff; CF7

Gizonite SS23; CF11

Gizrite SF27

Grecian (Greek) D8; Joe3

Gushurite De3

Hachmonite SS23; CF11, 27

Hagarene Ps83

Hagarite CF5

Hagerite CF27

Hamathite Gen10; CF1

Hamite CF4

Hararite SS23; CF11

Haruphite CF12

Hermonite Ps43

Hittite Gen23; Ex3; Nu13; De7, 20; Jos3, 9, 12; Ju3; SF26; SS11, 23ff; KF9ff; CF1, 11; CS1, 8; Ez9; Ne9; E16

Hivite Gen10, 34; Ex3; De7, 20; Jos3, 9, 12; Ju3; SS24; KF9; CF1; CS8; Is17

Horite Gen14; De2

Horonite Ne2, 13

Hushathite CF27

Ishmael, descendants of Gen25

Ishmaelite Ju8; SS17; CF2, 27; Ps83

Israelite Gen46; Ex1ff; Le1ff; Nu1ff; De1ff; Jos3ff; Ju1ff, 6f, 13, 19ff; SF2, 4, 7, 9ff, 17, 28f, 31; SS3, 10f, 16ff, 21, 24; KF6, 8f, 11f, 16, KF18, 20, 22; KS3, 7ff, 16ff, 21; CF9ff; CS5, 7f, 10f, 13, 24f, 28, CS31, 33;Ez2f, 6ff, 10; Ne2, 10f, 13; Ps103; Je16, 23; E2ff, 8, E11ff, 18, 22, 24, E28ff, 33, 35, 37ff, 48; D1, 9; Am3, 9; Ho1, 3

Issacharite CF6, 21, 27

Ithrite SS23; CF2, 11

Jacob, descendants of Gen 37

Jahite CS11

Jairite SS20

Japheth, descendants of Gen10

Japhletite Jos16

Jebusite Gen10; Ex3; Nu13; De7, 20; Jos3, 9, 12, 15, 18; Ju3, 19; SS5, 24; KF9; CF1, 11, 21; CS3, 8; Ez9; Ne9; Z9

Jeconiah, descendants of SF6

Jerahmeelite SF27, 30

Jew (reference to Israelites as) Ez2ff; Ne1ff, 13; Est2ff; Je41; Z8

Jewry (reference to Israelites as) D5

Joseph, descendants of Jos16; Ju1; Ps78

Judaean Je32, 34, 38, 40f, 43ff

Judah, descendants of Jos7, 15, 21; Ju10; KF1ff; SF27ff

Judahite Nu7; CF6, 9; CS15, 25; Ne4ff, 11; Ps78

Kedarite Is42

Kenite Ju1, 4; SF15, 27, 30; CF2

Kenizzite Jos14

Kerethite (Cherethim) (Cherethite) SF30; SS8, 15, 20; KF1; CF18; E25; Zp2

Kittian CF1

Kohathite Nu7; Jos21; CS6, 9; 20

Korahite Nu26; CF9, 12, 26; CS20

Lehabite Gen10; CF1

Leummin Is43

Levite Nu3ff; Ju17; SS15; KF8; CF6, 9, 13ff, 27; CS5, 8, 11ff, 17, 19, 23, CS29, 34ff; Ez1ff; Ne3, 7ff, Ne13; Is66; Je33; E40, 45, 48; Ma3

APPENDIX C RACES AND TRIBES

Libyan CS12, 16; Je46; E30; D11; Na3
Lydian Gen10; CF1; Je46
Lubim CS12, 16
Maacathite De3; Jos12; CF4; SS23; Je40
Machirite Jos13
Mahavite CF11
Manahethite CF2
Manasseh Ju6ff; CF5ff, 9, 26ff; CS30ff
Manassite Nu7; De4; Jos13, 21ff
Mede (Median) Est1ff; Is13,21; Je25, 51; D5ff, 9, 11
Merarite Nu7; Jos21; CF15, 26
Meronothite CF27; Ne3
Meunite CF4; CS20, 26
Midianite Nu21; Ju6ff, 10
Mishraite CF2
Mithrite CF11
Moabite Nu21ff; De2ff, 23; Ju10; Ru4ff; SF14; SS8; KF11; KS3, 13, 24; CF11, 18; CS20ff, 24; Ez9;
     Ne13; Ps83
Morasthite Je26; Mi1
Naamathite Job2, 11, 20, 42
Naphtali, descendants of Jos19, 21; Ju6ff
Naphtalite Nu7; CF2, 6ff, 27
Naphtuhite Gen10; CF1
Nazarite (Nazirite) Nu6; Ju13; SF1; La4; Am2
Nephelamite Je29
Nephilim Gen6; Nu13
Nephisim (Nephusim) Ez2
Nethinim Ne3; Ez8
Netophathite SS23; CF2, 9, 27; Ne12; Je40
Nubian CS12; Ps87; Is45; Je13
Paltite SS23
Pathrusite Gen10; CF1
Pekethite KF1
Pelethite SS8, 15, 20; CF18
Persian CS36; Est1ff; D6
Perizzite Gen13; Ex3; De7, 20; Jos3, 9, 12, 17; Ju3; KF9; CS8; Ne9
Philistine Gen10; Ex13; Jos13; Ju3, 10; SF4, 12, 17, 27ff; SS3; KF15ff; KS8,18; CF1,10ff, 14, 18;
     CS9, 17, 21, 26, 28; Ps87; Is2, 9, 11, Is14; Je25, 47; E16, 25; Am1, 6, 9; Ob1; Zp2; Z9
Pirathonite Ju12; SS23; CF27
Puhite CF2
Rechabite CF2; Je35
Rehobite SS8
Rephaim De3; Jos12; SS21; CF20
Reuben, descendants of Ex6
Reubenite Nu7; De3ff, 29; Jos1ff, 12ff, 21ff; CF5ff, 11, 26ff

Rhodian E27
Sabaean Is45; E23; Joe3
Sepharvite KS17
Shaalbonite SS23
Shelanite CF9; Ne11
Shem, descendants of Gen10
Shilonite KF15; CS9
Shimeathite CF2
Shuhite Job2, 8, 18, 25, 42
Shulamite So6
Shumathite CF2
Shunammite KF1ff; KS4
Sidonian (Zidonian) De3; Jos13; Ju3, 10, 18; KF5, 11; KS23; Ez3; E32
Simeon, descendants of Ex6
Simeonite Nu17; Jos19, 21; CF4, 6, 27
Simite Gen10
Sinite CF1
Sophrite CF2
Suchathite CF2
Sukkiim CS12
Sukkite CS12
Susanchite Ez4
Syrian (Aramaean) KS7, 9ff; Is9; Je35
Tachmonite SS23
Tarpelite Ez4
Tekoite SS23; Ne3
Temanite Job2, 4, 15, 22, 42
Timnite Ju15
Tirathite CF2
Tishbite KF17; KS1, 9
Tizite CF11
Tyrian CS2; Ez3; Ne13; Ps87
Zareathite CF2
Zeboyim (Zeboim) Ho11
Zebulunite Nu7; Jos19, 21; Ju12; CF6, 27; CS30
Zemarite Gen10ff; CF1
Zerahite CF27
Zidonian (Sidonian) Ju3, 10, 18; KF11, 16; KS23; E32
Ziphite SF23, 26
Zorathite CF4
Zorite CF2
Zuphite SF1

NEW TESTAMENT

Alexandrian A6, 18, 27
Arab (Arabian) A2
Asherite L2
Asian A20
Athenian A17
Benjamite A13; PR11; PPs3
Canaanite Mw10, 15; Mk3; A13
Chaldaean A7
Colossian PCol
Corinthian A18; PCF1; PCS1, 6
Cretan (Cretian) A2; TF1
Cypriot A4
Cyrenian Mk15; L23; A6
Damascene PCS11
Derbaean A20
Doberian A20
Egyptian A7, 21; LH11
Elamite A2
Emmorite A7
Ephesian A19, 21; PE1
Ethiopian A8
Gadarene Mw8; Mk5; L8
Galatian A18; PG1, 3
Galilean Mk14; L13, 22f; J4, 7, 12
Gerasene Mk5; L8
Gergesene Mw8; L8
Grecian (Greek) Mk7; J12; A6, 9, 14, 16ff, 20; PR1f; PCF10; PG2f; PCo3
Israelite Mw27; L1; J1; A7, 10; PR9, 11; PCS3,11; PPs3; LH11; LJu1; Rev2, 7
Italian LH13
Hebrew A6; LH1
Judah (Juda), tribe of LH7; Rev5
Laodicean PCo2; Rev3
Levite L10; J1; A4
Lycaonian A14
Macedonian A16, 19, 27
Magdalene Mw27f; Mk15f; L8, 24; J19f
Mede (Median) A2
Mesopotamian A2
Midianite A7
Nazarene Mw2; A24
Nephthalim Mw4

APPENDIX C RACES AND TRIBES

Ninevite L11
Parthian A2
Philippian PPs1, 4
Phoenician Mk7
Roman Mw22, 27; J11; A16, 25; PR1
Samaritan Mw10, L9f, 17; J4, 8; A8
Scythian PCo3
Syrian L4
Syrophenician Mk7
Tarsian A21
Thessalonian A20; ThF1, 5; ThS1, 3

THE BIBLICAL MALE LINE OF DESCENT

FROM ADAM TO JESUS

Adam and Eve

Seth: Enosh: Kenan: Mahalalel: Jared: Enoch: Methuselah:
Lamech: Noah: Shem: Arphaxad: Shelah: Eber: Peleg: Reu: Serug:
Nahor: Terah: Abraham: Isaac: Jacob: Judah: Perez: Hezron: Ram:
Amminadab: Nahshon: Salma: Boaz: Obed: Jesse: David:
Solomon: Reheboam: Abia: Asa: Jehoshaphat: Joram: Ahaziah:
Joash: Amaziah: Azariah: Jotham: Hezekiah: Manasseh: Amon:
Josiah: Jehoiakim: Jeconiah: Shealtiel: Zerubbabel: Abiud:
Eliakim: Azor: Zadok: Achim: Eliud: Eleazar: Matthan: Jacob:
Joseph and Mary
Jesus

A Brief Biblical Chronology

c. 1900 BC Abraham left Ur and travelled to Canaan

BRONZE AGE IN THE MIDDLE EAST

c. 1750 BC Joseph sold into slavery by his brothers, and eventually becomes the official in charge of grain distribution in Egypt.

c. 1700 BC Joseph invites Hebrews to Egypt to escape famine.

c. 1700—1290 BC Hebrews (Israelites) remain in Egypt

c. 1290 BC Moses leads the Israelites from Egypt

c. 1290—1250 BC Israelites living as nomads

c. 1260 BC Moses receives the ten commandments

c. 1255 BC Moses attacks Palestinian towns and rulers

c. 1250 BC Moses dies and his successor Joshua conquers Canaan

IRON AGE COMMENCES IN THE MIDDLE EAST

c. 1200—1080 BC Israelites ruled by tribal leaders: the Judges

c. 1100 BC Samson pulls down the Philistine temple

c. 1080 BC Samuel, the last of the Judges and the first of the Prophets

580

A BRIEF BIBLICAL CHRONOLOGY

c. 1020 BC Saul appointed first king of the Israelites

c. 1010 BC Saul's son-in-law David slays the Philistine Goliath

c. 1000 BC David anointed king of the Israelites by Samuel

c. 940 BC Solomon, David's second son, becomes king of Israel

c. 930 BC Solomon builds his Great Temple

922 BC Israel is divided into two kingdoms: Israel and Judah

922 BC Reheboam becomes king of Judah

922 BC Jereboam I becomes king of Israel

917 BC the Pharaoh Shishak raids Jerusalem

915 BC Abijam becomes king of Judah

913 BC Asa becomes king of Judah

901 BC Nadab becomes king of Israel

900 BC Baasha kills Nadab and becomes king of Israel

877 BC Elah becomes king of Israel

876 BC Zimri kills Elah and becomes king of Israel

876 BC Zimri dies in a skirmish with Omri the army commander

876 BC Omri becomes king of Israel

874 BC Samaria becomes the capital of Israel

873 BC Jehoshaphat becomes king of Judah

870 BC Ahab marries Jezebel of Tyre

869 BC Ahab becomes king of Israel

868 BC Ahab and Jezebel restore pagan worship of Baal

860 BC The prophet Elijah opposes Ahab and Jezebel

850 BC Ahab killed in battle with the Syrians

850 BC Ahaziah becomes king of Israel

849 BC Jezebel's son Jehoram becomes king of Judah

849 BC Jehoram becomes king of Israel

845 BC The prophet Elijah dies and passes his mantle to Elisha

842 BC Ahaziah becomes king of Judah

842 BC Jezebel thrown to her death

842 BC Jehu becomes king of Israel

842 BC Athaliah becomes queen of Judah

837 BC Athaliah killed by her priests in favour of Jehoash

837 BC Jehoash becomes king of Judah at the age of seven

815 BC Jehoahaz becomes king of Israel

801 BC Joash becomes king of Israel

800 BC Amaziah becomes king of Judah

790 BC Amaziah declares war on Joash of Israel and is defeated

786 BC Jeroboam II becomes king of Israel

783 BC Amaziah killed by plotters against him

783 BC Uzziah becomes king of Judah

c. 760 BC Isaiah preaches

750 BC Jotham becomes king of Judah

746 BC Zechariah becomes king of Israel

745 BC Zechariah murdered by Shallum

745 BC Shallum briefly becomes king of Israel

745 BC Shallum murdered by Menahem

745 BC Menahem becomes king of Israel

A BRIEF BIBLICAL CHRONOLOGY

742 BC King Pul or Tiglath-Pileser of Assyria subjects Israel to tribute

740 BC Israel and Judah both submit to Tiglath-Pileser of Assyria

738 BC Pekahiah becomes king of Israel

737 BC Assyrian Tribute taxes cause riots in Israel, led by Pekah

737 BC Pekah kills Pekahiah and becomes king of Israel

735 BC Ahaz becomes king of Judah

734 BC War between Israel and Judah, backed by Assyria

732 BC Hoshea becomes Assyrian puppet king of Israel

722 BC Samaria as the capital of Israel finally taken over by the
       Assyrian king Tiglath-Pileser

715 BC Hezekiah becomes king of Judah

687 BC Manasseh becomes king of Judah and reintroduces Baal worship

642 BC Amon becomes king of Judah

640 BC Amon murdered by his own servants

640 BC Josiah becomes king of Judah at the age of eight

c. 638 BC Judah strongly influenced by High Priest Hilkiah

A BRIEF BIBLICAL CHRONOLOGY

635 BC Josiah commences repairs to the Temple of Solomon

c. 620 BC The prophet Jeremiah preaches

612 BC With the destruction of Nineveh, the end of the Assyrian empire
and birth of the new Babylonian empire under king Nabopolassar

609 BC Josiah killed by Egyptians at the battle of Megiddo

609 BC Jehoahaz briefly becomes king of Judah

609 BC Jehoiakim becomes king of Judah

605 BC Nebuchadnezzar II becomes king of Babylonia

598 BC Jehoiachin becomes king of Judah

597 BC Zedekiah becomes king of Judah

587 BC Jerusalem as the capital of Judah captured by the Babylonians

587—538 BC the Hebrews exiled in Babylon

539 BC Cyrus the Great conquers Babylon

538 BC Release of the Jews by edict of Cyrus

520 BC Rebuilding Solomon's Temple commenced

c. 500—50 BC The Jews in Palestine are ruled successively by Syrians,
Persians, Greeks, Egyptians and finally Romans

A BRIEF BIBLICAL CHRONOLOGY

37 BC Herod the Great rules Palestine under the Romans

20 BC Herod builds his Temple

c. 5 BC Jesus Christ is born

4 BC Herod Antipas takes the throne

25 AD Jesus teaching

27 AD Pontius Pilate rules Palestine

30 AD Jesus is crucified

41 AD Herod Agrippa rules Palestine

45 AD As Saul, Paul sees the light on the road to Damascus

47 AD Paul begins his journeys

58 AD Paul is imprisoned

66 AD Jewish uprisings commence against the Romans

70 AD Destruction of Jerusalem

116 AD Further Jewish uprisings

135 AD Jews finally expelled from Jerusalem

Editor's Note

I consider myself to be what is known as a Broad Church Anglican; someone who loves the principle of Christianity, who has always ardently accepted the teaching of Jesus Christ, but who equally wholeheartedly rejects any dogmatic type of religious materialism. Even today, the Church has its Pharisees, those who prefer a solid moralistic foundation of belief and reject the whisper of the captive soul. Passion has several meanings: the suffering of Jesus, the agony of the inevitable consequence of his acceptance of his Father's will; then there is the passion of physical indulgence in a wholly non-religious sense; but there is also the type of passion that involves powerful emotional expression of religious sentiment. This last type of passion, valued by many highly religious people, seems to me to form a barrier between the human and the spiritual, between man and God.

This barrier is nowhere more apparent than in one's approach to the Bible – or indeed to any holy book in any religion. To accept every word in the Bible as representing ultimate truth is one thing; to pick out words and phrases, verses and sentences here and there in order to make a point is quite another. Both may be errors, but the first is an emotional error, the second an intellectual one. We could say that the intellectual approach to such matters, by looking for what seems to be evidence to clinch an argument, seems to be an attempt to fit the "mind of God" into the human mind. The emotional approach involving blind belief creates clouds of passion and removes the necessity to feel responsible for one's own actions. Both these extremes of attitude have always been at the root of dogma and bigotry, the true spirit of the Inquisition!

I make no apology for including the section titled *Divinity* among all the other sections of a work many see as encompassing nothing but "divinity". My categorisation is to a large extent subjective; I suppose this is inevitable. "Divinity" in the sense in which I have used the word, could perhaps be better described as "mysticism", that is, direct communion with the presence of God through submission of the self and the desires of the self – the very opposite of "passion" or religious vehemence. The trappings and proclamations of religion, from the laws of Moses to the finest detail of sacrificial accoutrement, from the judgments of Solomon to the directives of Paul, these are not "divine" in this sense, though they may certainly have been "inspired".

Inspiration, indeed, is the quality that has given the various and varied books of the Bible their authority: an intangible quality of inspiration that conveys itself to the reader, and which led to these books having been selected as authoritative sources of guidance. But because thoughts, ideas, statements or writings are "inspired" does not necessarily mean that they are unassailably true for all time. An idea or pronouncement that is *just what is needed* at the time, that has come, as it were "out of the blue" – this is inspiration. Times and places are of course constantly changing, and so are the needs of the moment. I believe this obvious but easily overlooked factor needs to be borne in mind when weighing up the truth of such matters.

"Be still," say the words of Psalm 46, "and know that I am God". This is one mention of the possibility of true divinity in the Old Testament. Another mention of true divinity that I consider to be of the greatest importance, and so rarely to be found in the OT, is the experience of Elijah, who, having been *inspired* to seek refuge in a cave on Mount Horeb, is guided to discover that the true path to divinity lay, not in passionate denouncement and indignation, not in the violence of gales and earthquakes or the burning ardour of wildfire, but in the still small voice that may be heard only when all those passions hold their peace, and the soul is laid open to receive the word of God in stillness, while both thoughts and emotions are at rest.

This brings me to what I consider to be the crux of all matters religious and spiritual: True spirituality is to be found only where materiality is absent, and if you equate spirituality with "holiness" or "divinity", these qualities cannot exist within a material state. Our brain and with it our thoughts and emotions, like our physical bodies, are wholly based within materiality, and cannot by themselves receive holiness. But, from personal experience, I know that we have non-material souls. A soul is not a scientific fact, not a material entity, not something that can be demonstrated, proved or analysed. It can only be experienced. The soul includes every part and facet of ourselves in its makeup, but it is far more than a mere sum of these parts. Attempts to analyse soul are doomed to failure.

Almighty God is a name which, for me, covers the all and everything, both material and spiritual, the basic life force or source of energy that has its origin where there is nothing tangible, beyond the known universe, but yet permeating every part of it. And so Almighty God is, by definition, impersonal, and because of this, our personal selves, our thoughts and emotions, cannot get to know God or communicate with him. Divine communication can only be done by way of our souls, and this is the gap which religion attempts to bridge. Unfortunately, however, the reality of "soul" is usually completely overlooked or misunderstood, or mistaken for devoutly emotional feelings, by religious people, teachers and priests alike. The reality is, the soul may receive directly from the divine source by way of that which is known as the Holy Spirit, and this "reaching-out" quality of Almighty God, this Spirit, may enter the soul that is receptive and open to receive it. This is the point where "inspiration" becomes "divinity". This is the only way by which God the Impersonal may become God the Personal.

This, of course, is the foundation of the Trinity, the principle of the three. The life of Jesus was indeed a living symbol of this soul communication as representing the straight and narrow path leading to the kingdom of heaven. As he pointed out to the Pharisees who questioned his doing good works on the sabbath day, he is the door of the sheepfold – he symbolises the way in to a spiritually secure situation where rules and regulations and archaic laws are of no relevance – and that no one could gain access to the Father except through him. That is, by way of the soul that is open to receive from the divine source.

Many have wondered how and why the "character" of God seems to range through the books of the Bible from a ruthless, vengeful being who visits death and destruction on even the most innocent of people, to the loving, readily forgiving Father acknowledged by Jesus. The reason lies, not in the nature of God, but in the nature of the channel that receives what may be called divine inspiration. In other words, our souls are coloured through and through with our own characteristics, our own faults and peculiarities. Thus I have to say that those who are fortunate enough to receive a revelation from the divine source, tend to receive and transmit the nature of God as being in some way a giant, supernatural version of their own selves. Look at the Old Testament stories in the light of this piece of knowledge, and all those ancient contradictions which have baffled so many over the years, will be explained.

Forget about the fairy tale aspects of Christianity that were thought necessary to turn the life of an obscure preacher into the greatest religion the world has known. Forget about the virgin birth in any material sense: accept it in its symbolic sense as referring to one who had escaped being influenced by any of the faults most of us inherit at birth. He, apparently alone among men at that time, was able to receive the true nature of the divine source.

Forget also about the story of physical resurrection: common sense insists that there can be no accommodation for physical bodies in any non-material state. These and other similar stories represent attempts to explain the spiritual in terms of the material. But in rejecting such things as unworthy of serious belief, please do not make the mistake of rejecting the truly divine truths at the core of it all. The human soul – the Son of Man, being open to receive the Holy Spirit, may become the Son of God. This is the true reality.

Dominic Breeze
June 2010